VAN 1915

THE GREAT EVENTS OF VASBOURAGAN

by

A-Do

Translated from Armenian and prepared for publication by

Ara Sarafian

Gomidas Institute
London

FUNDAÇÃO
CALOUSTE
GULBENKIAN

The publication of this book was made possible with the support of the Calouste Gulbenkian Foundation

ISBN 978-1-909382-37-4

For more information and updates concerning this work please visit our website

Gomidas Institute
42 Blythe Rd.
London W14 0HA
United Kingdom
www.gomidas.org
info@gomidas.org

CONTENTS

ILLUSTRATIONS

Contents

[*] Appended to A-Do's work
[**] Redrawn original map

Editor's Note

A-Do's *Metz Depkeru Vaspourakanoum 1914-15 Tvakannerin* (hereafter *Van, 1915*) was originally published in 1917 and remains the most important report on what happened to Armenians in Van and its environs in 1915.[*] As his work attests, A-Do's report was based on a solid body of data the author collected from eye-witnesses, private papers of individuals, contemporary newspapers (most notably *Ashkhadank* in Van) and captured Ottoman records.[†] His report is also remarkable for its lucid and popular style of writing.

A-Do gives a clear narrative of events concerning the victimisation of Armenians in the Ottoman Empire, especially during World War I. He distinguishes between different types of violence suffered by Armenians, from the everyday abuses of a corrupt and autocratic state to systematic massacres and genocide. His report discusses how Armenians were aware of developments around them, their attempts to placate the authorities, and their desperate efforts to defend themselves. As one reads *Van 1915*, one can see how the authorities co-opted Kurds against Armenians in massive blood-letting, and prepared the ground-work for the eventual Turkification of that region.[‡]

Undoubtedly, the major turning point in these developments was April 16, 1915, when the authorities started the systematic murder of Armenian men and the destruction of Armenian communities. A-Do gives detailed first person accounts of such mass killings

---

[*] A-Do, *Metz Depkeru Vaspourakanoum 1914-15 Touakannerin*, Yerevan, 1917. For French translation see A-Do, *Van 1915: Les grands événements du Vaspourakan*, (Présenté par Jean-Pierre Kibarian), Paris: Société Bibliophilique Ani, 2015.

[†] For contemporary English language accounts of the events in question, see Onnig Mkhitarian "An Account of the Glorious Struggle of Van-Vasbouragan" and Haig Gossoyan "The Epic Story of the Self-Defense of Armenians in the Historic City of Van" (both translated by Samuels Tarpinian) in *The Defence of Van* (Vasbouragan Compatriotic Society, Michigan, 1967 and a new edition by Gomidas Institute, London, 2017). Also Clarence Ussher, *An American Physician in Turkey: a Narrative of Adventures in Peace and War*, Houghton Mifflin Company, Boston and New York, 1917 (Sterndale Classics, London, 2002); Gracey Higley Knapp, *The Mission at Van: In Turkey in Wartime*, Privately Printed, 1916. The most critical sources concerning the events in question can be found in several hundred survivor-statements that were collected in the south Caucasus in 1915–16 and recently published in Yerevan for the scrutiny of scholars. See Amatouni Virapyan (ed.), *Hayots Tseghaspanoutyounu Osmanyan Tourkiayoum*, Volume 1, Van Province, Armenian National Archives, Yerevan, 2012. There are also the private papers of American missionaries in the ABCFM archives in Houghton Library (Cambridge, Mass.). Such archival records allow a critical evaluation of the substance of the above-mentioned published primary accounts. Other critical accounts in Armenian include Vasbouragan Compatriotic Society (Tabriz), *Vasbouragan: Van-Vasbouragani Abrilian Herosamardi Dasnyevhinkamyagin Artiv*, 1915-1930, Mkhitarian Press, Venice, 1930.

[‡] Regarding the broader Young Turk Turkification programme, see Fuat Dündar, *Modern Türkiye'nin Şifresi İttihat Ve Terakki'nin Etnisite Mühendisliği (1913-1918)*, İletişim Yayınları, Istanbul, 2015.

with examples from Hirj (Hayots Tsor), Agants and Panon (Arjesh), and Pergri Ghala (Pergri). These were among the 449 Armenian inhabited villages he lists at the outset of his work.[*] According to the information he gathered, about half of all Armenians living in 51 villages in Arjesh were massacred, abducted, died of diseases or simply vanished in the wake of the April 16th massacres. He notes that those communities that completely submitted to the authorities, as those in the region of Arjesh, were not spared. This pattern was also repeated elsewhere. The orders to massacre Armenian men were comprehensive and did not seem to spare anyone.[†] The subsequent pillage of villages and the abuse of women and children, including murder and rape, was prevalent but less organised.

However, there were cases of successful resistance to the massacres, the most noteworthy cases being in the city of Van, where Armenians barricaded themselves in two defensive zones, and the district of Shadakh, which mobilised for defence early on.[‡] Despite the superior forces of their opponents, Armenians at these two locations overcame their difficulties through their grit, organisation, and morale, especially after their initial – unexpected – successes. A-Do's description of the Armenian resistance in Van and Shadakh is compelling because of its detail, and his account goes on to cover the deliverance of these regions with the advance of Russian armies, the establishment of a provisional Armenian government in Van, and the mass exodus of Armenians when the Russian army retreated. His report, which was printed before the October Revolution in 1917, ends with the expectation that Armenian refugees would soon return to their lands in Vasbouragan.

Transliteration

We have transliterated Armenian proper nouns into English according to western and eastern Armenian standards, i.e. western Armenian for the Ottoman Empire and eastern Armenian for the Russian Empire and Persia. Practically all geographical references have remained in their original Armenian form (e.g. Alchavaz, Arjag, Kharpert) though some

---

[*]   A-Do made an earlier study of Armenian communities in the Ottoman provinces of Van, Bitlis and Erzeroum between June and August 1909. This study was based on a short trip and his data was derived from different Armenian sources which he cited in great detail. See A-Do, *Vani, Pitlisi yev Erzroumi Vilayetneru. Ousoumnasiroutyan Mi Pords Ayt Yerkri Ashkharhagrakan, Vichakagrakan, Iravakan Yev Tntesakan Droutyan*, Yerevan, 1912. Also see his journal covering his trip in "Housher Tachkahayastani Chanaparhordoutiunidz," *Nor Hosank*, Tiflis, 1913-14. A-Do's information in *Van 1915* is more comprehensive but does not discuss sources – which means that his work still need to be critically appraised. Both of his datasets (1912 and 1916) are ground-breaking, if only for the names of Armenian inhabited settlements they provide. To date, there is no comparable data available in Turkish archives concerning the ethnic profile of this region. This is probably due to the partisan management of Turkish archives and the fact that Armenians, Kurds, and Assyrians made up well over 90 percent of the population of these areas of the Ottoman Empire. This historical fact is still anathema in the Turkish Republic.

[†]   There were very few exceptions to these massacres and abuse, as in the case of Lezk (Van-Dosp), which was part of a military cordon.

[‡]   See Chapters XV–XIX

exceptions were made for conventional English usage (e. g. Constantinople, Smyrna). We also used conventional English spellings for most Ottoman terms (e.g. kaimakam, sanjak or pasha). Finally, we have included a glossary of Armenian, Turkish and Russian terms at the end of this work.

Maps and Illustrations

We have reproduced all of A-Do's original illustrations, though all of the maps in the report have been redrawn for clarity. Only the maps of the Aykesdan and the old city were simplified by leaving out some names and symbols. However, the missing information remains in A-Do's narrative. We have also posted these two maps, complete with all information in place, on our website at *www.gomidas.org*. We have also appended some new maps and photographs into this work to better reflect A-Do's narrative. These additional materials and redrawn maps appear with our logo and they are clearly identified in this book's table of contents.

Dates and Times

Since A-Do presented all dates in the old Julian calendar, we have converted them into the new Gregorian calendar – i.e. by adding 13 days to his use of the old calendar. Thus, for example, April 11, 1915 in the old calendar has become April 24, 1915 in the new calendar. When years have been mentioned in the Ottoman Hijri calendar, their corresponding Gregorian year has been inserted in brackets. Thus, 1331 appears as 1331 [1915].

Where entire months have been indicated in A-Do's original work, we have left them unchanged. Where part of a month has been indicated, we have modified the reference: "beginning of" to middle of, "middle of" to end of, and "end of" to beginning of the following month.

Time references have been left as in the original work, i.e. conventional time, sometimes followed by Ottoman times in brackets.

Acknowledgements

I'd like to thank Ara Stepan Melkonian, Garabet Moumdjian and Vincent Lima for their support in the translation of this work. Special thanks go to Pietro Shakarian, Barlow Der Mugrdechian, Raymond Kevorkian and Kayane Nalbandian for their unstinting support. I'd also like to thank the History Museum of Armenia (Yerevan), the AGBU Nubarian Library (Paris), the Armenian National Archives (Yerevan), the Armenian Studies Program (CSU-Fresno) and the American University of Armenia for providing vital materials on-line and in print. Finally, I'd like to say a big thank you to the Armenian Communities Department of the Calouste Gulbenkian Foundation (Lisbon) for making this project possible. Needless to say, all shortcomings are my own.

Ara Sarafian
Gomidas Institute, London
September, 2017

Hovhannes Ter Martirosian (A-Do)
A Biographical Note

A-Do was an Armenian intellectual and social scientist who was born in Nor Bayazed on January 4th, 1867 and died in Yerevan on February 7th, 1954. He was one of the notable personalities of the Armenian world at the end of the 19th and early 20th centuries. He was a rare individual who dedicated his intellectual life to the study of key episodes in the history of Armenians.

A-Do came from a trading family. His father and two brothers were involved in commerce and animal husbandry. He was the second child in a large family of five boys and three girls.

Despite his father's many activities, he was able to educate his children well. He sent his eldest son, Siragan, to study at a secondary school in Yerevan. When A-Do finished primary school, he was sent to a private school in Nor Bayazed. He studied there for close to three months, then went to a state school which, with its better amenities, left a deep impression on the young student during his four years there.

In 1880, A-Do's father decided to also send his son to study at a secondary school in Yerevan, but he died that year and his family fell on hard times. A-Do's brother, Siragan, returned to Nor Bayazed and took on the burdens of the large family. He was not very successful in Nor Bayazed and decided to open a shop in Yerevan and move the family there.

On 2 September 1881, the 15 year old A-Do left Nor Bayazed for Yerevan to work with his brother. Yerevan impressed the boy from Bayazed "coming from, as they say, a dry, parched and poor Bayazed, devoid of greenery, and then seeing Yerevan with its vineyards and greenery, especially in September, when it is a sea of fruits and plenty."[*]

His brother's shop was on a square called Meydan and A-Do spent two and a half years there as a salesman. Siragan was rarely at the shop because he was involved in social activities and worked as a correspondent for *Mshag*, which was printed in Tiflis.[†] The burden of running the shop fell mainly on the shoulders of the young A-Do.

In September 1882, the Ter Martirosian family moved from Nor Bayazed to Yerevan, and this had a positive effect on A-Do, as he related, "I received the care of my mother and was free of the muddled life I was leading. I found comfort in the company of my mother and siblings after the boredom of the shop."[‡]

---

[*]   A-Do, *Im Hishoghoutiunneru,* [My Memoirs), pp. 11-12, Ter Martirosian family archives.

[†]   Armenian National Archive (ANA), fond 314, file 21, c. 1, p. 34.

[‡]   *Hishoghoutiunner,* p. 15

Siragan's work as the correspondent of *Mshag* newspaper gave A-Do the opportunity to read this newspaper. By his own admission, *Mshag* "became my reading and school and led to everything else with which I was involved in the future."[*]

A-Do looked for opportunities to improve his education and such opportunities arose, especially in the summer, when students from different Russian universities and the Kevorkian Seminary came to Yerevan for their vacations. He learned about Russian and world literature and political developments from them.

A-Do found another source to improve his education. Levon Dikranian, a native of Yerevan and a medical doctor by profession – also the mayor of Yerevan between January 1894 and June 1895 – happily allowed his personal library to be used by his fellow residents.

At the beginning of 1884, Siragan sold his shop and began working with his friends. A-Do, in turn, was forced to accept employment at the Aghstafa's office of the "Nadezhda" company. He worked there until the end of July and returned to Yerevan.

In September 1885, A-Do started to work at the Afrikian merchant house as a salesman. The Afrikians were not only well known businessmen but also philanthropists. Dikran Afrikian, who was a well-educated man, opened village schools through his own personal means. He assumed the burden of furnishing such schools and paying their teachers. As A-Do noticed, the payments were made by Afrikian personally and not the merchant house. He carried out these activities so that "The peasant class gets used to self-reliance and not become beggars by getting used to receiving everything for free."[†]

A-Do praised the Catholicos Magar A. Teghoudsi, whose first feat was reopening the Armenian schools which had been closed down by the Russian authorities. This took place in 1886.

Yerevan province was well known for the cultivation of cotton and A-Do studied, in great detail, the cultivation of the crop and its purchase and sale. He did not fail to see a major development in the owners of Moscow and Lodz cotton factories gradually buying more and more of the cotton in Yerervan province and pushing out the local merchants. This development and other key issues were the subject of A-Do's first study, "The Cotton Trade in Yerevan," published in *Mshag* (23 Jan. 1888, no. 9).

Between 1889 and 1891, A-Do attended and graduated from Yerevan secondary school.

In 1890, he became one of the founders of an Armenian Revolutionary Federation (ARF) chapter in Yerevan. He and his fellow activists, Gedeon Aharonian, Galoust Aloian (Toros Davrish) and others, also helped to establish chapters in Echmiadzin, Masdara and other places.[‡] His youngest brother, Mikayel, also became a member of the ARF.

---

[*]   *Ibid*, p. 16
[†]   *Hishoghoutiunner*, pp. 36-37.
[‡]   Khoudinyan, G., *HH Dashnaktsoutyan Knnagan Patmoutyoun (agounknerits minchev 1895 tvagani vercheru)*, Yerevan, 2006, p. 270.

A-Do continued his activities. When Catholicos Magar Teghoudtsi died in 1891 and a new Catholicos had to be elected, he and other progressive intellectuals wanted to see the much loved and trusted Mgrdich Khrimian on the throne. There was a contest and finally, on 5 May 1892, Khrimian was consecrated as the Catholicos of All Armenians. It is clear that A-Do actively participated in promoting Khrimian for the position.

In 1892, A-Do finished an interesting study, which was dedicated to the 40-year history of the Armenian parish school of Nor Bayazed (1852-92).[*] The study demonstrated his abilities in carrying out serious research. He signed his study "Former student, Hovhannes Ter Martirosyants."[†]

In his memoirs, A-Do tried to avoid discussing his and his brother Mikayel's involvement with the ARF. This was understandable. During the Soviet era, membership — even former membership — in a national political organisation could lead to not only arrest but also execution by firing squad. Family members and acquaintances would also suffer. Consequently, A-Do made no comments or references to his former political activities. For this reason, he remains silent about any involvement in smuggling guns and materials to western Armenia. However, we know about such activities because of Russian police reports on A-Do. On 15 and 26 January 1896 the police in Aghstafa seized 13,000 rounds of small-arms ammunition shipped by someone called Mardirosoff. These bullets were sent through a company called "Nadezhda," where A-Do had worked. According to the historian G. Khoudinyan, "Those ammunition rounds were sent by a member of the ARF Central Committee, Hovhannes Ter Martirosian (A-Do)."[‡] The mention of "Nadezhda" company suggests that in all probability the ammunition was actually sent by A-Do, given that he had worked in the Aghstafa office of that company and probably kept contacts there.

For whatever reason, A-Do left the ARF but maintained his relations with his friends who remained in the party. Yeprem Sarkisian comments that A-Do "never stood against his mother political party [the ARF] and only made well-intentioned criticism."[**]

A-Do worked at the "Khanzadian Magazin" shop until 1905. According to his own admission, he was never attracted by business, which was simply an occupation for him for his daily needs and education. While working for "Khanzadian Magazin," he had the opportunity to go to Moscow, where he visited museums and galleries. He was greatly impressed by the Bolshoi Theatre, where he saw a concert by the world-renown singer, Feodor Chaliapin.

---

[*]   Nahabedian, S., "Pasdatghter Nor-Bayazed Kaghaki Himnatrman yev Hayots Dzkhagan Yergdasyan Ousoumnarani Patmoutyan Masin," *Banber Hayasdani Arkhivneri*, Yerevan, 2011, N 2, p. 4-20.

[†]   *Idem*, p. 20.

[‡]   Khoudinyan, ibid, p. 338.

[**] Sargsian, Ye., "A-Do (Hovhannes Ter Martirosian)," *Hayrenik*, Boston, 1952, no 4, p. 91.

In 1903 A-Do published his work, "Makedonia." This interesting study concerned Ottoman rule in Macedonia, anti-Turkish movements, and the May Reforms Project for the Armenian provinces in the Ottoman Empire.[*]

A-Do also penned a booklet related to the 1890s Hamidian massacres – the story of Murad of Aghsraf village in the Arjesh district of Van province. He described the plight of refugees at the border.[†]

By the 1900s, A-Do was a well-known and respected figure in social and political circles in Yerevan. His contemporary Yeprem Sarkisian described him as a tall, thin, and strong-featured man who had dark and restless eyes and an intense personality. He was serious to the point of being gloomy, as well as self-sufficient. He always appeared in deep thought as if he had to remember something important and could not do so.[‡]

On 3 November 1905, A-Do's life took a decisive turn when he was admitted as an independent student to the law faculty of Kharkov University. There were major developments at that time throughout the Russian Empire, including in Kharkov, leading to the Russian Revolution of 1905. The governor of Kharkov in those years was General Nikolay Peshkov, a man A-Do would meet in 1916, when Peshkov was appointed as the Governor-General of Western Armenia.

The 1905 revolution allowed Russian citizens, including Armenians, to publish books that had been previously forbidden by the censors. A-Do used the opportunity to publish a booklet dedicated to Mikayel Nalbandian.[**]

The revolutionary movements forced A-Do to leave his education and return to Yerevan, where there were serious clashes between Armenians and Tatars. Those clashes were encouraged by the Russian authorities to undermine the revolutionary currents against the regime. The young A-Do began collecting a large volume of material about these clashes. For example, in July 1905 he was in Sharour-Nakhichevan districts and in October 1906 in Kantsag province. As a result, he prepared a new work in which he analysed the developments of those years on the basis of his invaluable documents, newspaper accounts, and personal observations.

His contemporary Yeprem Sarkisian relates how, while people were fearful of renewed Armenian-Tatar clashes, "A cold blooded A-Do would go around, like a doctor examining a patient, and take notes – When was the first shot fired? At what time? By whom? From where? Then he would ask how others joined in or in what direction they moved? How long were the battles? Who was where? Where were Armenians? What did the Turks do? etc."[††]

---

[*]   A-Do, *Makedonia*, St. Petersburg, 1903, pp. 12-13.

[†]   *Ibid*, "Hayreniki Garodu," St. Petersburg, 1905, p. 7.

[‡]   Sarkisian, Ye., "A-Do (Hovhannes Ter Martirosian)," *Hayrenik*, Boston, 1952, no 4, p. 91.

[**]   A-Do, *Mikayel Nalbandiani Gyanki Hedakrkir Mi Edj Yev Bakunini Nran Kratz Namakneru*, Yerevan, 1908.

[††]   Sargsian, Ye., "A-Do (Hovhannes Ter Martirosian)," *Hayrenik*, Boston, 1952, no 4, p. 91.

Having finished his study on the Armenian-Tatar clashes, A-Do gave his work to the publishers, surrendering all rights to them "because he did not have the means to have the work published himself."[*]

We should note that A-Do's work on the Armenian-Tatar clashes remains, even today, an unequalled account because the author personally visited the locations where the clashes took place – and collected information from witnesses and participants in the fighting.

In 1908, A-Do wrote *Azatagrakan Sharzhoumu Rousastanoum* [The Liberation Movement in Russia].[†] In the introduction to the volume, he noted: "Thanks to the freedom of the press achieved in Russia, we are able to present Armenian readers with the present publication, dedicated to the two centuries-long movement for the freedom of the people of Russia."[‡]

This publication irked the Russian authorities and its author was accused of a criminal act. The Tiflis censor's office ordered the confiscation of the entire print run of the book, but A-Do managed to save a significant number of them from confiscation. While the investigation against him was still continuing, he decided to go to St. Petersburg to study at the Therapeutic Diseases Institute. However, A-Do also wished to realise his long-held dream of visiting western Armenia and collect information about Armenians there. In 1908 he had the opportunity to go to western Armenia following the 1908 Ottoman constitutional revolution and the fall of Sultan Abdul Hamid II.

On 23 June 1909, A-Do crossed the Russo-Turkish frontier into Bayazed. He stayed there for two days and found the Armenians in that region 40 to 50 years behind Russian Armenians in terms of education.[**] These were the negative and disastrous consequences of Ottoman rule on western Armenian social and economic life.

He went on to visits Van, Moush, Sasoun, Erzurum (Garin), Khnous and other places to collect demographic and other information about Armenians.[††]

A-Do's contemporary, Ashot Atanasian, who was a native of Yerevan, as well as an agronomist, writer, public speaker and community activist, makes the following remark in his unpublished memoirs about his years in Seminary. "At the end of the [18]80s we first noticed *Mshag*'s new correspondent in Yerevan, Siragan Ter Martirosian. His younger brother, the well-known economist and Armenian writer, A-Do, who both in his training and education (as a graduate of a parish school) was more accomplished than his brother."

---

[*]   A-Do, *Hay-Tourkagan Undharoumu Kovkasoum (1905-06), Pastakan, Vijakagrakan, Deghagrakan Lousabanoutiunnerov*, Yerevan, 1907, pp. 1, 88.

[†]   A-Do, *Azatagrakan Sharzhoumu Rousastanoum ir Tsagman Aradjin Orerits*, Yerevan, 1908.

[‡]   *Ibid*, p. 1.

[**]   *Hishoghoutiunner*, p. 102.

[††]   A-Do, *Vani, Pitlisi yev Erzroumi Vilayetneru. Ousoumnasiroutyan Mi Pords Ayt Yerkri Ashkharhagrakan, Vichakagrakan, Iravakan Yev Tntesakan Droutyan*, Yerevan, 1912. Also see "Housher Tachkahayastani Chanaparhordoutiunidz," *Nor Hosank*, Tiflis, 1913-14.

As Ashot Atanasian noted, A-Do carried out his main studies between the 1890s and 1920 and was truly a noted literary and political figure with his "series of studies."[*]

On 17 March 1909, at a court hearing in Yerevan, A-Do was given a one-year prison sentence and the 987 confiscated copies of his book were ordered to be destroyed. A-Do appealed against the decision of the court by writing to St. Petersburg – and since the response was expected in two or three months, he decided to go to western Armenia, to finish up his studies there. His work mostly required information on tax collection. He once more crossed the Russo-Turkish border and went to Bayazed and a few surrounding villages. His journey took eight days.

The Russian court eventually condemned him to one-year imprisonment, which he served in Lower Aghta (currently the town of Hrazdan in the Kotayk region of Armenia).

When World War I broke out on 1 August 1914, the Young Turkish government used the opportunity to carry out the genocide of western Armenians. A large number of Armenians on the border regions abandoned everything and sought refuge in the Caucasus – mainly in Yerevan province, other Armenian areas, as well as Baku, Tiflis and the north Caucasus. Under these circumstances, A-Do could not remain inactive and started his investigations in refugee stations for information and the possibilities of helping them.

In 1915, some Armenians were able to resist Turkish and Kurdish attacks and a large number were thus able to save themselves. One such area where there was successful resistance was Van-Vasbouragan. The Armenian population of Van, after withstanding a siege of one month against superior Turkish and Kurdish forces, saved itself by 17 May 1915. Their victory was possible with the advance of Armenian volunteer forces in the Russian army. A temporary provincial administration was appointed under the direction of Aram Manougian, a well-known activist in the Armenian liberation movement. Many Armenian social, religious and political activists rushed to Van to help that Armenian administration. Amongst them was also A-Do.

A-Do set out on 4 June 1915 and returned on 25 July 1915. While in Van, he collected detailed information about the successful defence of Armenians in the province and the activities of the Armenian administration.

A-Do gave the following impression of the Armenian administration reigning in Van: "Everyone [in the governor's building], the workers, as busy as they were, wrote down, calculated, listened, answered, and responded to people's needs – and everything was done willingly and without grumble – because of the knowledge that they were realising a great ideal."[†]

A-Do's work was so well known that the correspondent of *Hovid* was reluctant to give a great deal of information to his readers because, as he explained, "The A-Do is making a

---

[*]   ANA, Fond. 314, file 21, p. 34.
[†]   *Hishoghoutiunner*, p. 190.

detailed description of all the developments in the region for publication and I think it is unnecessary for me to give piecemeal information."[*]

By 14 July 1915 information was circulating that the different units of the Caucasian IVth Corps had started to retreat. The Armenian administration of Van called on Armenians to form military units. However, the unexpected retreat of the Russian army spread terror in the population. Perhaps worse, the Russian commanders did not agree to arm the Armenian defenders of the city. Consequently, Armenians were forced to retreat and the terrible retreat of Van-Vasbouragan began.

During this period A-Do was asked to transport some invaluable hand-written manuscripts to Echmiadzin. On 24 July, he and two friends delivered close to 200 such manuscripts to the Catholicosate.

After his return from Van, A-Do turned to organising and studying the materials he had collected. True to form, this is how he described his work: "The keen awareness that the writer has to note everything most carefully, that he has to be objective and precise, took time and effort, and I carefully went over what people said they had seen and heard, checked and re-checked their description of events with many additional questions and probes."[†]

In mid-January 1917, Siragan Dikranian of the Caucasian Refugee Stations of the Red Cross in St. Petersburg approached A-Do with the proposal that the latter should go to Salmast (Persia), where there was a refugee station and to examine the conditions there.[‡]

A-Do went to Salmast shortly afterwards, where he collected data on the refugees. On April 13th, 1917, he passed through Tabriz and reached Salmast on the 16th. Here, he not only examined the condition of Armenians but also Assyrians.[**]

He collected interesting data on the Assyrians of Choulamerg. According to his calculations, there were 13,260 Assyrians in that region and most came from the villages of Ghalasar and Payachoug.[††]

A-Do was greatly touched by the terrible plight of the Armenians from the Aghpag district. As he related, he had been in many different places, written down many accounts of atrocities by Turks and Kurds, but "there was nothing comparable to what had taken place against the small number of Armenians in Aghpag. There were terrible massacres, mass conversions, and assimilation into Kurdish families in a manner and scale not seen elsewhere."[‡‡] Furthermore, when the Russian army occupied northern Persia, a large number of such "Kurdified" Armenians reasserted their identities. Their numbers included Armenians who had been forcibly converted at the time of the Hamidian massacres.[***]

---

[*]   *Hoviv*, Tiflis, No. 39, 11 November 1915, p. 609.
[†]   *Hishoghoutiunner,* pp. 222-23.
[‡]   *Ibid,* p. 224.
[**] *Ibid,* pp. 241-43.
[††] *Ibid,* p. 241.
[‡‡] *Ibid,* p. 252.
[***] *Ibid,* pp. 253-58.

On 6 June 1917, A-Do went to Khoy and on to Van in the company of the prelate of Adrbadagan-Van, Bishop Nerses Melik-Tankian. A-Do collected information in several districts of Van, including on Kurdish tribes living there. When he finished, he returned to Yerevan on 17 June, 1917.

Towards the end of that year and the beginning of 1918, the situation in Armenia became critical. The Bolsheviks had struck against the Russian government and called on Russian soldiers to stop fighting. Many Russian soldiers in the Caucasian army started to desert the Russo-Turkish frontier in vast numbers.

Armenia and the Armenian people now faced a near impossible future. The Armenian National Council and its military union tried to form an Armenian national army. A-Do mentions the gathering of the Armenian military union in Yerevan on 30 November 1917, "This meeting was comforting for Armenians who were worried by their poor prospects and an uncertain future. The meeting promised hope and was of general interest."[*]

Taking advantage of the fact that most of the Russian army had left, the Ottoman army went on a general offensive along the whole Russo-Ottoman front in February 1918. Armenians faced a grave, almost hopeless situation, but there were still people willing to resist.

The Turkish army made rapid progress and was on the Ararat plain in 1918, threatening to finally exterminate all Armenians. Despite the dangers, A-Do continued to record and document what was happening. He explains the 1918 battles of Sardarabad and Bash-Abaran in great detail. He makes a special study of these decisive battles in the history of Armenians, citing not only the contemporary press and the archives of the Armenian army corps, but also his own observations. He gives unique insights into the activities of important participants: General Movses Silikian (Moisey Silikov), Dro (Drastamat Kanaian), Major (later General) Daniel Beg Piroumian, whom he named the "holy trinity."

When the Armenian republic was declared on 28 May 1918, A-Do presented a report on the republic's plans to improve the condition of refugees, rebuild the economy, and oppose Turkish-Tatar attacks.

World War I came to an end on 11 November 1918 with the victory of the Entente powers – and the Ottoman army began to withdraw from Armenia.

Soon, the Armenian government decided to examine the atrocities committed by the Turks and compile a report on the Armenian participation in the war including the defence put up by western Armenians. The initiative came from the central body of the Armenian Compatriotic Unions and its head, the well-known writer and activist Hovhannes Toumanian. The latter also headed an organisation that was created in Tiflis at the end of 1918, the Commission for the Examination of the Losses Suffered by Armenians in the Great War. This commission also had a historical section headed by General Al. B. Koulebiakin, who had participated in the Russo-Turkish war of 1914-18.

---

[*] *Ibid*, p. 286.

At the beginning of December, A-Do received a formal request from the Armenian Foreign Minister Sirakan Tigranian to work with the special commission in Tiflis and to compile information on the Armenian human and material losses during the war. A-Do went to Tiflis in early January 1919, but soon concluded that he could not work with the commission.

In 1919, A-Do started working in the newly established union of cooperatives in Armenia (HayCo-op). He worked in this organisation as the director of its demographic section until 1949.[*]

He also continued his research and studies and drew up some important works: *Hayoutyan Yergounku* [The Birthpangs of Armenians], which focused on one of the most important periods in the history of Armenians – from the beginning of World War I to 1919. However, this work was never printed, probably because of the May Events of 1920, the Turkish onslaught in September, and the Sovietisation of Armenia on December 2nd.

The Sovietisation of Armenia was initially weak as Garegin Nzhdeh continued to struggle in Zangezour. However, after the suppression of this uprising against Bolshevik rule in April 1921, the new authorities attempted to calm matters down by negotiation and dissuading Armenians from armed opposition. Towards such ends, they sent a delegation to Zangezour, including Davit Ananoun (Davit Ter Danielian), Hovhannes Melikian and A-Do.[†] The meetings took place in Sisian.

As Ye. Sargsyan notes, the aforementioned individuals, as opposed to the other officials on the delegation, warned their interlocutors that no credit should be given to the promises of the Bolshevik Melnikov (Artashes Karinian). A-Do warned his friends on the opposite side: "They are telling lies, do not believe them, they are lying!"[‡] Sargisian also adds that "A-Do was broken-hearted and repeated the words of an old and honourable revolutionary, 'You know what you are doing, be careful!' He then made sure that the aid they had left for the families of our comrades reached their proper beneficiaries."[**]

During the Soviet era, A-Do worked tirelessly at HayCo-op, though the co-operative proved to be less than what it had been originally envisaged. A-Do worked with different tasks as the true professional he was.

Drs. Rouben Gasparyan and
Rouben Sahakyan
Yerevan, Armenia

---

[*]   In a questionnaire dated 30 May 1922, A-Do states that HayCo-op came into existence in 1918. This was probably wrong because he also says that that organisation was in its third year of existence. See ANA, 41/1/1, p. 4.

[†]   Simonyan, A. H., *Khorhrtayin Hayastani yev Lernahayastani Karavaroutiunneri Nergaya-tsoutsichneri Sisiani Banaktsoutiounneru* (1921 Mayis), Yerevan: Armenian Academy of Sciences (Lrapen hasarakakan gitoutyounneri), 1998, No. 2, p. 69.

[‡]   Sarkissian, Ye., *op. cit.*, p. 93

[**]   *Ibid.*

VAN 1915

THE GREAT EVENTS OF VASBOURAGAN

THE GREAT EVENTS OF VASBOURAGAN, 1914 –1915

Foreword

The events that took place in the Armenian inhabited regions of the Ottoman Empire during the present world war constitute some of the most glorious pages of Armenian history. Although Armenians have experienced many catastrophes and endured much suffering during countless massacres and exile, the present disaster may be considered to be a singular event. Armenians have taken up the sword on many occasions and shown great tenacity to ensure their survival, but the heroism and determination they have recently exhibited in many places has been unequalled even in their own annals of history. These instances of supreme suffering and heroic battles represent a new chapter in Armenian history, as shown by hundreds of testimonies and written statements.

I am one of the chroniclers of these events and have chosen to focus on Vasbouragan, one of the cradles of Armenian civilisation, where great events have taken place. I've visited several of Vasbouragan's centres, after the region was captured by the Russians, and seen where massacres and heroic deeds have taken place. I have heard from witnesses and participants, and observed the immense skill and strength of Armenians during their short-lived administration of this region. I have also witnessed the great exodus from this area, as I joined the refugees and tasted the bitterness of their fate.

I am now recording the events that took place in this region, and occasionally in other areas, dedicating my work to the Armenian nation that continues to struggle against every catastrophe.

It has been my wish to write exactly what has happened, as best as I could, leaving it to others to judge the success of my endeavours.

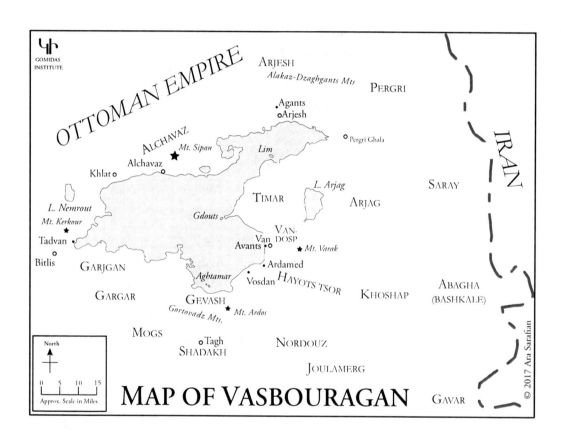

MAP OF VASBOURAGAN

Chapter I

A Brief Introduction to Vasbouragan

Before we discuss the great events of Vasbouragan, it is important that we provide information about the geography of the region and the demographic profile of Armenians.

The six *vilayet*s (provinces) of Van, Bitlis, Erzeroum, Kharpert, Sivas and Diyarbekir have been inhabited by Armenians since antiquity. These provinces, which became bloody theatres of war each time the Russian and Ottoman Empires clashed, were also the objects of special reforms just before World War I.

Thanks to its topography and history, Van was the most important among these six provinces. While it is true that the others boasted the plentiful production of grain, tobacco, grapes and even cotton, Van boasted its mountains and rivers, small orchards, a beautiful blue lake and mild climate, as well as historical monuments and outstanding natural beauty.

To the east of Van were the Dilman and Ourmiye regions of the Persian khanate of Maku; to the north was the province of Erzeroum; to the west, Bitlis and, to the south, Diyarbekir and Mosul.

According to Ottoman administrative divisions, the province of Van comprised two *sanjak*s (sub-provinces): Van and Hakkiari. The latter was originally a separate province but was later attached to Van for political reasons. Hakkiari was in the south and Van in the north.

Hakkiari's administrative centre was Bashkale, the seat of the *mutasarif* (sub-governor). There were very few Armenians in Hakkiari. Almost the entire region was inhabited by Kurds. The only area where Armenians lived in this sub-province was Aghpag, with its monastery of Sourp Partoghimeos (St. Bartholomew). At one time, this whole area was densely populated by Armenians. Around 80,000 Assyrians lived in Choulamerig under their spiritual leader, Mar-Shimon.

The sanjak of Van or Vasbouragan presented a very different picture. A large number of Armenians lived in this region and had a national consciousness and great capacity for progress. It was for this reason that Vasbouragan occupied such an important place in the Armenian world.

This sanjak was also an ornament of nature, the like of which was not found anywhere else. Lake Van and its basin spread out to form an incredible view.

The Gortvats mountains, with their many peaks, rose on the southern shores of the lake. The most important peaks were Ardos and Yegher. The two summits of Varak, (the patriarch of the mountains of Vasbouragan) and the Timar mountains were at the eastern end of the lake. The stalwart Mount Sipan and the region's sacred mountain Masis [Mount Ararat] were to the north. The unbelievably beautiful Aladagh or Dzaghgants

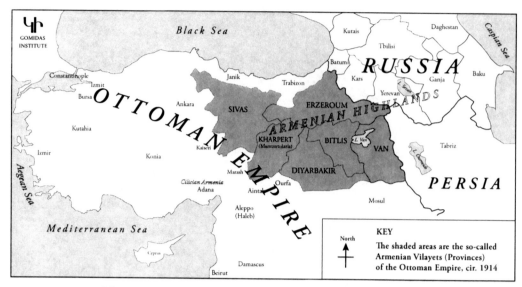

The Armenian Provinces of the Ottoman Empire, cir. 1914

mountains were a short distance away. The massive Nemrud and its unruly hatchling, the historic Kerkour, spread along the lake's western shore. These beautiful mountain ranges and their sharp-pointed peaks formed a wonderful basin for Lake Van. Many rivers, both large and small, emerged in these mountains and irrigated innumerable valleys and mountain-sides.

Vasbouragan's climate was also distinct. Winters were not as harsh as, for example, in Erzeroum; nor were the summers the scorching fields of Diyarbekir. Van had a mild climate, even in flat areas, where vineyards and orchards flourished, such as those around the towns of Van and Arjesh. The climate was mild and Lake Van and its mountainous surroundings were most pleasing.

Lake Van, because of its size, was also a very important means of communication. The lakeside roads were fraught with indescribable difficulties and travellers lost many days traversing them. For example, the journey from Van to Tadvan – in other words from the eastern to the western shores of the lake – took three days to traverse overland, while the same journey took 12 hours by boat. Communications were eased in the same proportion in all directions thanks to the use of boats. Both passenger and freight movement were facilitated by the lake.

Vasbouragan's physical appearance and beauty were beyond any comparison, comprising a spectacular basin with a magnificent lake and four islands. One could feel boundless serenity in this unmatched landscape, as one breathed and became enthused by the surroundings. People living in the embrace of its nature were healthy, energetic and very creative.

These factors were responsible for Vasbouragan's unique place in recorded history from ancient to modern times. Indeed, Van drew the attention of many conquerors, including those who chiselled the cuneiform script in rocks in some places.

Over the centuries, a number of cities flourished and castles were built on the lake's shores. These were the cities of Arjesh, Alchavaz, Khlat, Tadvan and Vosdan. The most famous was the city of Van, built at the top of sheer cliffs by the beautiful Semiramis, who marvelled at the wonderful views over the lake. Vasbouragan and its environs were thus settled by people along the lake shore and surrounding mountains.

The city of Van and its suburbs were located on a flat plain to the south-east of the lake, in an area called Van-Dosp. There were four districts (*kazas*) to the north of the lake, delineating the easternmost reaches of Van-Dosp. These were Timar, Pergri, Arjesh and Alchavaz. Three additional district, from east to west, were Hayots Tsor, Gevash and Garjgan, all located on the lake's south-eastern shores. There were thus eight districts, including Van-Dosp itself, forming the first group of districts on the lake shore.

The second group began at Pergi and extended, first southwards, then westwards, adding seven more districts to the vilayet of Van: these were Arjag, Saray, Khoshab, Nordouz, Shadakh, Mogs and Gargar.

Van-Dosp was well known for its abundant produce thanks to Semiramis' irrigation system. Aykesdan, Van citadel, and its twin-peaked Mount Varak were to the east. The monasteries of Varak and Sourp Krikor (St. Gregory) were on the foothills of this mountain. The large village of Avants, which was the town's port, was in Van-Dosp, as was the historic village of Ardamed, famed for its apples.

Timar was renowned for its mountainous topography. The Sev or Marmed river flowed across Timar to the lake. The two historic islands in the lake, Lim and Gdouts, were just off the shores of Lake Van, near the mouth of the Timar. In addition to being places of worship, these famous monasteries also provided sanctuary for people during times of massacre. Janig, Marmed and Aliur were famous among the villages of this region, the latter being the most populous one and noted for its vineyards.

Pergri was well known for its two plains: Pergri-Ova on the lake-side and the beautiful Abagha. Bordering the khanate of Maku, Pergri was once densely populated by Armenians who abandoned the region over time. The Tandourek and Tapariz mountains formed a long valley to the north of Abagha. A large, roaring river, the Bandi Mahou with an abundance of fish, flowed through this valley and into Lake Van. Pergri Ghala was the administrative centre of the district, with Kordzout and Bsdig being the best known villages.

Arjesh was famous for its fruit harvest and vineyards. The Tali Chai, Irishad and Ororan rivers, which were renowned for their fish, flowed through this region. Agants, which was a small town surrounded by vineyards, was its centre. The Zilan valley, inhabited by Kurdish bandits, was located here. The district's northern border was formed by the beautiful Alakaz mountain range.

The Alchavaz region was renowned for its cereals, although there were also vineyards in some places. Ardzge was the local administrative centre, with the remains of an ancient castle rising on the shores of the lake. The beautiful and majestic Mount Sipan – solitary and symmetrical with a sharp peak – rose in the centre of the district.

Hayots Tsor was famous for its long, golden valley, through which flowed the Khoshab River. Semiramis' irrigation system began in this area. The best known villages were Gem, Ankgh, Kerdz and Vosdan.

Gevash was famous for many things. It was rich in vegetation and included fine villages, among which were Nareg, Mokhrapert, Nor Kiugh and Pelou. It was also abundant in rivers and streams, among which were the Vosdan, Dshogh, Pshavants and Mokhrapert.

Historic Mount Ardos was at Vosdan, its green foothills extending to the lake. There were no Armenians living there, though the palace of the Rshdouni princes was located there.

The islands of Aghtamar and Arder, each with their monasteries, were off the shore of lake Van near Gevash. Both of the monasteries of Nareg and Chaghar Sourp Nshan were in this area, the former containing the tomb of Sourp Krikor of Nareg and the latter that of Yeghishe, famed for his angelic voice.

Garjgan was well known for its verdant mountains with their steep forested slopes often lurching to the edge of the lake and creating beautiful scenes – although the forest were being mercilessly felled. Other noteworthy places in the district were Sorp with its port, and the villages of Ourants and Yeghekis.

Arjag, located among the second ring of districts around Lake Van, was renowned for its lake by the same name, although its water was extremely salty. This district cultivated grain and its prominent villages were Arjag and Kharagonis.

Shadakh was famous for its spectacular topography. It was mostly mountainous and was rich in meadows. It was also poor in grains, with only two small areas at Peasantasht and Khorzank providing adequate supplies. The main occupations in this region were raising sheep and shawl-making. This region was criss-crossed by a number of deep valleys through which flowed the Sivdgin river and the upper reaches of the eastern Tigris. The spot where these two rivers met created an enchanting view. This was also where Tagh, the district's centre, was located. The people of Shadakh were well known for their bravery and hardiness.

Mogs (or Moks) was also well known for its mountainous terrain. It was furrowed by many deep valleys and there were no plains. Mount Yegherov formed the district's northern border. Many streams flowed off its slopes and formed the Mogs river, which flowed into the eastern Tigris. The main occupations in this area were sheep-raising and shawl-making. The centre of this district was composed of 100 houses which were divided into four quarters.

The district of Gargar presented a beautiful picture like Mogs. It was composed of two parts – Upper and Lower Gargar. Lower Gargar was within the administrative boundaries of Bitlis province.

This was the general picture of the sanjak of Van or Vasbouragan, which is the main focus of this study.

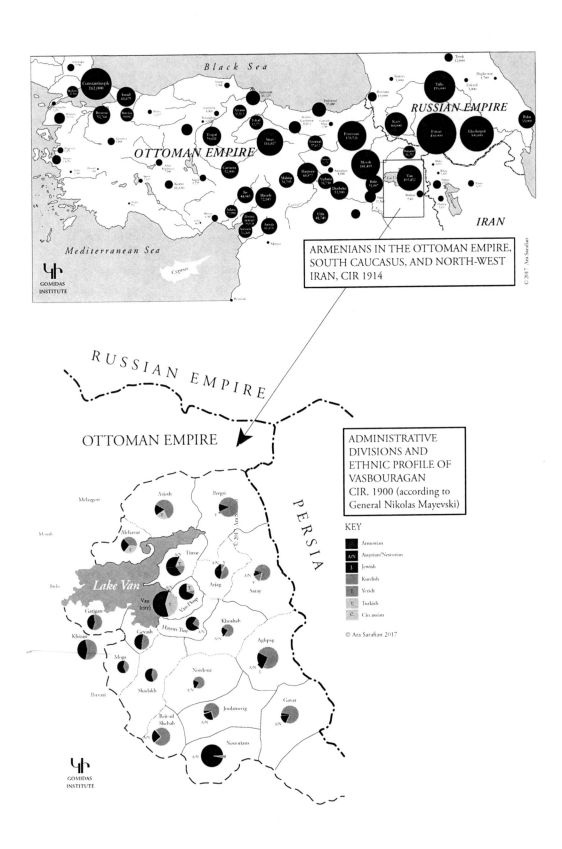

ARMENIANS IN THE OTTOMAN EMPIRE, SOUTH CAUCASUS, AND NORTH-WEST IRAN, CIR 1914

ADMINISTRATIVE DIVISIONS AND ETHNIC PROFILE OF VASBOURAGAN CIR. 1900 (according to General Nikolas Mayevski)

KEY

Armenian
A/N Assyrian/Nestorian
J. Jewish
Kurdish
Y. Yezidi
T. Turkish
C. Circassian

© Ara Sarafian 2017

Chapter II

Population Statistics for Armenians in the Province of Van [1914]

VAN-DOSP

	Settlement	Households	Inhabitants
	Van City	4,230	22,470
	City Outskirts		
1	Avants	339	1,592
2	Lezk	192	1,178
3	Shahbaghi	167	895
4	Sghka	104	660
5	Tsorovants	14	100
6	Goghbants	32	218
7	Shoushants	80	559
8	Kouroubash	108	698
9	Gentanants	49	285
10	Pertag	56	581
11	Dzvsdan	80	530
12	Ardamed	130	720
13	Lamzgerd	35	206
14	Tarman	68	482
15	Farough	35	210
16	Vosgepag	45	270
17	Ermants	3	24
18	Sevakrag	2	16
19	Toni	25	198
20	Aregh	28	192
		1,592	**9,614**

TIMAR DISTRICT

	Settlement	Households	Population
1	Ardavez	15	118
2	Koch	26	137
3	Adigeozal	31	226
4	Giusnents	138	825
5	Bayrak	28	195

6	Drlashen	95	657
7	Adnagants	31	247
8	Dzagdar	38	231
9	Amenashad	40	204
10	Annavank	50	254
11	Marmed	153	811
12	Trkashen	5	35
13	Panz	8	69
14	Janig	100	714
15	Norshen	45	270
16	Keopriukeoy	3	21
17	Ader	71	444
18	Pirgarip	57	373
19	Koms	53	340
20	Aghjaveran	32	147
21	Meydanjouk	8	56
22	Darabeg	37	243
23	Sosrat	42	251
24	Shahgyaldi	22	156
25	Norovants	37	215
26	Khzhishg	132	775
27	Amoug	40	212
28	Ererin	151	938
29	Keochani	111	705
30	Geolou	15	91
31	Khavents	106	633
32	Aliur	343	1,955
33	Yekmal	31	226
34	Asdvadzadzin (Diramer)	63	462
35	Poghants	71	451
36	Averagi	187	1,061
37	Jigrashen	76	475
38	Pert or Nor Kiugh	30	210
39	Shvakar	3	22
40	Tashoghli	1	7
		2,525	**15,411**

PERGRI DISTRICT

	Settlement	Households	Population
1	Kortakn [Kortkan]	8	80
2	Salakhane	8	56

3	Teron	22	150
4	Snt [Sind]	20	140
5	Ashekeran	10	70
6	Avasor	13	91
7	Khan	15	105
8	Ghaymaz	30	210
9	Khachan	60	600
10	Nazarava	28	196
11	Alikalen	2	14
12	Yekmal	18	110
13	Chibkhlou	13	91
14	Bazid Agha	2	11
15	Gondourma	1	19
16	Kanegavan	4	28
17	Tikma	20	140
18	Kyababig	51	379
19	Sourp Tatos	25	211
20	Angiuzag	59	311
21	Kordzout	128	790
22	Keoshk	10	70
23	Antsav	17	108
24	Aregh	15	105
25	Bsdig Kegh	74	447
26	Pergri	25	187
27	Kizil Kilise	5	58
28	Pshikmpet	5	47
29	Kharashig	1	8
30	Koms	3	20
31	Mouja	3	21
32	Davzar	1	10
33	Pedants	1	10
34	Pert	6	42
35	Metghoul	7	49
36	Dirakli	6	42
37	Sharafkhana	1	7
38	Sheykh Haydar	2	14
39	Khachan	2	14
40	Khaji Khatoun	9	63
41	Bishi	4	28
		734	**5,152**

ARJESH DISTRICT

	Settlement	Households	Population
1	Agants	304	2,078
2	Plourmag	90	645
3	Khargen	35	285
4	Irishad	29	304
5	Ororan	36	410
6	Papshgen	8	85
7	Majars	24	160
8	Chrashen	5	61
9	Haspisinag	31	254
10	Haroutiun	22	180
11	Sosgoun	84	615
12	Khojalou	12	84
13	Aghs	3	31
14	Ardzvaperi Vank	20	120
15	Pay	5	46
16	Geoz Inner	15	145
17	Geoz Upper	11	105
18	Kalakav	2	18
19	Gdradz Kar	32	250
20	Aghsraf	56	491
21	Kantsag	26	206
22	Joudgyah	38	390
23	Dzaydzag	28	211
24	Panon	22	180
25	Paykhner	34	273
26	Moy	7	78
27	Pertagh	44	318
28	Chakh Beg	5	49
29	Antsav	5	37
30	Piromar	5	46
31	Hakrag	7	85
32	Haghi	4	31
33	Kokn	3	16
34	Kyartis	7	110
35	Sinamesh	3	19
36	Inchasou	4	55
37	Khacherov	12	110
38	Medzopavank	34	305

39	Tatalou	4	23
40	Zeve	3	25
41	Karachalou	5	29
42	Kozer	60	360
43	Shgavdian	3	25
44	Gelkan	2	14
45	Komeshavan	10	67
46	Grakom	50	411
47	Madghavank	9	68
48	Dilan	9	67
49	Armizonk	26	241
50	Arjronits Vank	5	61
51	Kenapori Vank	5	37
		1,303	**10,313**

ALCHAVAZ DISTRICT

	Settlement	Households	Population
1	Ardzge	80	535
2	Aren [Arin]	117	698
3	Norshen	34	211
4	Eketsor	17	143
5	Ziraklou	45	330
6	Karoz	17	118
7	Sipanner	100	675
8	Beshnakomer	32	255
9	Khorants	47	433
10	Ghouzel	20	120
11	Anoush Aghpiur	10	43
12	Norshnchough	48	403
13	Vijgatsroug	16	119
14	Pargat	15	139
15	Gojer [Gojerer]	56	401
16	Karakeshish	40	489
17	Archra	33	189
18	Arnchgouys	55	421
19	Ourou	6	28
20	Kadikeoy	4	27
21	Dantsoud	8	47
22	Khorerov	3	19
23	Orangazi	7	46
		810	**5,889**

HAYOTS TSOR DISTRICT

	Settlement	Households	Population
1	Toni	13	120
2	Nor Kegh	88	513
3	Aregh	26	175
4	Hntesdan	37	209
5	Ourtoug	42	247
6	Khek	34	219
7	Asdvadzashen	48	351
8	Aradents	40	235
9	Angshdants	67	411
10	Eremerou	82	432
11	Gghzi	44	312
12	Vochkhrants	11	67
13	Pzhngerd (Upper)	7	53
14	Khosb	52	291
15	Hirj	30	205
16	Kiziltash	51	314
17	Kerdz	104	637
18	Bltents	65	386
19	Moulk	7	33
20	Kharagants	36	219
21	Trkashen	12	60
22	Marks	20	170
23	Gem	100	547
24	Ankgh	108	678
25	Mashdag	64	394
26	Ishkhani Kom	70	409
27	Keoshg	40	232
28	Sourp Vartan	18	114
29	Khorkom	65	435
30	Karvants	2	14
		1,383	**8,482**

GEVASH DISTRICT

	Settlement	Households	Population
1	Atanants	65	372
2	Sbidag Vank	18	124
3	Hili	28	28
4	Karatashd	19	130
5	Padagants	75	406

6	Dshogh	50	330
7	Hirj	41	225
8	Pshavants	60	310
9	Pakhvants	42	215
10	Harpert	42	350
11	Boghonis	18	120
12	Nareg	123	610
13	Paykhner	100	520
14	Sare	17	105
15	Mokhrapert	103	550
16	Nor Kiugh	87	413
17	Untsag	34	286
18	Pelou	77	443
19	Shadvan	20	170
20	Timar	27	174
21	Haghoun	18	134
22	Varents	31	176
23	Kantsag	60	366
24	Nanigants	35	231
		1,190	**6,913**

GARJGAN DISTRICT

	Settlement	Household	Population
1	Prkhous	31	180
2	Gandvou	17	143
3	Ganjars	27	162
4	Ourendous	15	119
5	Smbon	20	134
6	Khoums	30	230
7	Garp	25	175
8	Mrors	16	97
9	Gentrants	32	260
10	Vanig	40	313
11	Oghvants	57	403
12	Stous	17	126
13	Gout	45	350
14	Hntsan	8	80
15	Ourants	96	805
16	Sorp	40	297
17	Karvag	20	145
18	Ousounts	10	70

19	Pegants	8	60
20	Yeghekis	69	510
21	Koms	60	394
22	Arants	25	182
23	Khartsit	30	220
24	Vanki	15	110
25	Khntsorkin	50	362
26	Pashvantsk	25	185
27	Dzapor	12	84
		840	**6,178**

ARJAG DISTRICT

	Settlement	**Households**	**Population**
1	Kharagonis	230	1,525
2	Arjag	180	1,170
3	Hashpshad	18	126
4	Kizilja	65	423
5	Nabat	25	165
6	Mkhgner	48	308
7	Chobanoghlou	26	168
8	Bakhezeg	15	98
9	Ermants	5	35
10	Sevan	67	439
11	Zarants	37	240
12	Lim	22	143
13	Mandan	60	390
14	Kartalan	3	21
15	Haspsdan	22	154
16	Shamshadin	70	465
17	Hazara	45	305
18	Boghazkiasan	12	84
19	Chakhmakh	12	78
20	Daghveran	37	244
21	Aghtash	7	49
22	Yalgouzaghach	7	49
		1,013	**6,679**

SARAY DISTRICT

	Settlement	**Households**	**Population**
1	Satmants	30	210
2	Akhorig	50	350

3	Avzarig	11	77
4	Hasan Tamran	27	189
		118	**826**

KHOSHAB DISTRICT

	Settlement	Households	Population
1	Salakhana	28	130
2	Zenis	5	32
3	Kilisa	5	30
4	Phans	3	20
5	Pout	3	20
6	Krel	70	567
7	Hourtoug	52	420
8	Pakagyadouk	15	80
9	Gangvar	32	205
10	Kasrik	6	34
11	Hokots Vank	3	28
12	Kasr	30	180
		252	**1,746**

SHADAKH DISTRICT

	Settlement	Households	Population
1	Tagh	219	1095
2	Navhand	4	28
3	Shivrash	4	28
4	Makoshk	10	63
5	Kasr	1	9
6	Vakhrov	12	88
7	Akrous	2	14
8	Arikom	10	64
9	Krments	7	43
10	Babonts Mzre	12	84
11	Mardakerots	3	21
12	Bashkants Mzre	9	63
13	Shino Mzre	4	28
14	Haro Mzre	2	14
15	Sheghjants	3	24
16	Kvers	8	96
17	Shamo Mzre	12	84
18	Arosig	6	34
19	Yeritsou Mzre	4	28

20	Mousgaven	10	67
21	Georantashd	12	87
22	Nar	8	63
23	Karader	1	19
24	Darents Ver	4	29
25	Darents Var	6	34
26	Sivdgin Komer	21	151
27	Sivdgin	45	310
28	Hashgants	15	105
29	Pols	13	132
30	Keosents Mzre	10	59
31	Tsough	4	37
32	Hiki	17	97
33	Sozvants	10	85
34	Bagh	9	58
35	Martsegh	2	12
36	Tghasbar	14	102
37	Dzidzants	25	196
38	Jnoug	25	230
39	Hinents	21	205
40	Gaghbi	66	431
41	Gorovank	6	71
42	Sak	12	48
43	Kajet	92	452
44	Armshad	64	675
45	Sarget	20	104
46	Khoumar	15	75
47	Aregh	28	206
48	Kainemeran	12	107
49	Shidan	42	302
50	Kaghazis	30	214
51	Martanos	8	50
		999	6,721

MOGS DISTRICT

	Village	Households	Population
1	Kjoghs	9	35
2	Dzardants	6	33
3	Taramakh	3	21
4	Haghmghouns	3	21
5	Makni	5	25

6	Tinis	15	95
7	Komants	18	100
8	Khrer	11	123
9	Dzapants [Dzapkants]	25	175
10	Kjav	14	115
11	Havaris	12	63
12	Hatsaplour	11	66
13	Haghin	45	204
14	Her	6	41
15	Sags	5	25
16	Gitris	20	148
17	Komer	17	76
18	Sors [Sours]	26	194
19	Boulents	25	152
20	Vanig	4	30
21	Par	20	111
22	Knegants	32	188
23	Piurant	7	45
24	Ljan	7	38
25	Harnants	18	130
26	Loulents	5	39
27	Kaytants	31	222
28	Nanents	21	173
29	Shen	4	29
30	Hasknjav	19	104
31	Anabad	4	33
32	Petategh	5	39
33	Norovants	13	66
34	Kasr	7	38
35	Atjants	16	81
36	Garkjants	21	121
37	Arinch	30	217
38	Demkar	11	46
39	Khalents	5	28
40	Marakants	13	52
41	Spkants	14	85
42	Haglvan	13	96
43	Prtnout	2	9
44	Sip	16	124
45	Anjghots Tagh	19	128
46	Tashdi Tagh	44	204

47	Yebrahaments Tagh	26	127
48	Kaghaki Tagh	19	144
		721	**4,459**

GARGAR DISTRICT

	Settlement	Households	Population
1	Arghou	8	75
2	Tatsou	64	400
3	Yeghekis	56	400
4	Pergri	25	200
5	Hals	7	60
6	Khntsoroud	20	130
7	Hargents	30	282
8	Hougourtsou [Herkiurgin]	9	70
9	Tsgor	17	144
10	Voriz	27	174
11	Tsakhogh	5	30
12	Dzogou	21	86
13	Khrordents	45	350
14	Dap [Tap]	9	88
15	Mjgants	15	128
16	Miulk	3	22
17	Giji	20	121
18	Argents	13	108
19	Haght	26	170
		420	**3,038**

AGHPAG DISTRICT

	Settlement	Households	Population
1	Bashkale	200	1,645
2	Sourp Partoghimeos	40	244
3	Hasbisdan	45	260
4	Melkavan	16	70
5	Erngiani	27	205
6	Bzhngerd	15	112
7	Kharadoun	11	65
8	Sorader	4	18
9	Pis	4	24
10	Baz	5	49
11	Soran	24	163

12	Heresan [Erisan]	11	74
13	Alas	35	280
14	Alalyan	7	45
15	Beza	9	79
16	Rasoulan	8	54
17	Choukh	15	96
18	Bablhasan	5	18
19	Karaplour	1	4
		482	**3,505**

NORDOUZ DISTRICT

	Settlement	Households	Population
1	Aghsin	12	70
2	Pirbadalan	35	327
3	Koghan	20	218
4	Hekyan	5	28
5	Hostayan	27	145
6	Noraper	10	48
7	Dim	32	179
8-9	Skiuns Upper and Lower	54	340
10	Shamans	45	275
11	Makoshk	17	137
		257	**1,767**

JOULAMERIG DISTRICT

	Settlement	Households	Population
1	Pagan	39	270
2	Khalilan	22	175
3	Merman	4	30
4	Khanas	5	32
5	Piran	3	27
		73	**534**

GYAVAR DISTRICT

	Settlement	Households	Population
1	Diza	200	1,200
2	Karpel	80	480
		280	**1,680**

ALL REGIONS

	Town and District	Households	Population
1	Van	4,230	22,470
2	Van-Dosp	1,592	9,614
3	Timar	2,525	15,411
4	Pergri	734	5,152
5	Arjesh	1,303	10,313
6	Alchavaz	840	5,859
7	Hayots Tsor	1,383	8,482
8	Gevash	1,190	6,913
9	Garjgan	840	6,178
10	Arjag	1,013	6,679
11	Saray	118	826
12	Khoshab	252	1,746
13	Nordouz	257	1,767
14	Shadakh	999	6,721
15	Mogs	721	4,459
16	Gargar	420	3,038
17	Aghpag	482	3,505
18	Choulamerig	73	534
19	Gevar	280	1,680
		19,222	**121,377**

Chapter III

The New Turkey

On 24 July, 1908, a momentous event took place at the heart of the Turkish Empire with the declaration of a constitution that ended unjust autocratic rule in the country.

One day earlier, Ottoman Turkey had seemed destined to remain in a state of paralysis. The country was ruled by the autocratic will of Sultan Abdul Hamid II. There was no room for private or public action. The country was overrun by a network of spies, and the prisons were full of the best elements of the country. The state treasury had been pilfered and was empty. The bankers demanded incredible sums and governors raised taxes as they pleased. Because of the empty treasury, the army was under great stress, officials were not paid, and bribery had become the main source of income for officials. Bribery, undue office-holding, corruption and much worse meant that law-courts were subject to executive pressure. Similarly, educational institutions were in the hands of fanatics, and the press simply reflected the wishes of the autocracy and its censors.

This was the general condition of the country, where Christians fared the worst. Other than the general excesses of the autocratic regime, Christian communities were subject to exceptional mistreatment. Their churches and religion, as well as schools and languages were kept under pressure. They were not given government offices, nor were they called into the army, thus emphasising a fundamental separation between Christians and Muslims. Christians also did not have protectors in the state administration, especially in the courts, where Shariah law prevailed.

Christians were often accused of anti-state activities and persecuted, even though such activities were invariably against serious miscarriages of justice. Youngsters thus had to choose between exile, imprisonment, or going to the mountains to join opposition groups.

The only people who were not subjected to robbery and persecution were foreign nationals who enjoyed extraordinary rights. For example, the Ottoman government did not have the right to search their premises, nor to prosecute or imprison them. Court-cases and sentences against them were only valid if carried out in the presence of foreign consuls. Although they enjoyed all the freedoms of the land, such nationals were exempt from taxes.

These rights were established by foreign governments for their nationals through a number of capitulatory concessions that reflected the irregular state of affairs in the Ottoman Empire. As long as such a state of affairs prevailed, so did the extraordinary rights of foreign powers and their nationals. The European powers even had their own postal system in the Ottoman Empire – and this system was trusted more by Ottoman subjects than their own state service. These extraordinary measures were a necessity because the normal state of affairs in the Ottoman Empire was intolerable for the nationals of European powers.

These privileges were now threatened by a new Ottoman constitution.

On 24 July, 1908, Sultan Hamid announced the inviolability of private persons and their property, freedom of conscience and speech, as well as freedom of the press and assembly. These rights were thereafter to be enjoyed by all subjects irrespective of their national or religious identity. Starting from that day, in order to establish the rule of law, Sultan Hamid II convened an Ottoman Parliament based on general electoral principles.

The declaration of a new order also included a general amnesty.

Prison doors were opened and the best elements of the country, who had been imprisoned for years, were set free. The borders were opened and thousands of exiles and refugees returned to their homeland. Armenian, Macedonian and Albanian revolutionary groups descended from the mountains and former enemies were joined in a fraternity of joyful marches and festivities welcoming the constitution.

Christians especially welcomed such a constitution which bestowed equal rights on all. For example, Christians were now to serve in the army and were freed of the burden of military exemption taxes. They were to be allowed to become state and military officials. Armenians, especially, would have their confiscated lands and properties, seized during the darkest years of Hamidian injustices, returned.

So, 24 July 1908 was heralded as a new dawn for the people of the Ottoman Empire, especially Armenians.

However, Sultan Hamid, that tyrant of tyrants, whose hands were covered with the blood of Christians and whose reign had faded with the curses of many nations, did not give up his privileges nor introduce the constitution willingly. No autocrat or tyrant ever resigns willingly nor concedes an iota of power. Only force compels autocrats to bow their heads to the demands of their subjects. Such was the case with Sultan Hamid.

What was the force that brought down Sultan Hamid? Was it the masses? Unfortunately not. The Muslim masses remained in dark slumber and their understanding of the world was blinkered by the thick fog of fanaticism. They were not compassionate and had no awareness of their rights. While Christian communities had such critical awareness, they were subdued by the conservatism of the Muslim masses.

The old autocracy in Ottoman Turkey was actually replaced by the army and a circle of officers who came to govern as quickly as the constitution was introduced. They then chose repressive practices to stay in power. The masses remained indifferent to developments.

This was the awful side of the Ottoman constitutional revolution and led to terrible calamities in the future.

While Sultan Hamid was in power and confident of his autocratic rule, a group of military officers of the Third Army in Macedonia, Salonica and Monastir – many of whom had received a European education – began organising revolutionary activities. Soon, the Second Army in Adrianople was influenced by these revolutionary stirrings. Revolutionary committees were formed within military ranks and these elements established relations with the longstanding revolutionary committee in Paris. The movement in Macedonia gradually grew bigger, as more soldiers, whose loyalties were questionable, were sent there.

Monastir became the main centre of the revolution, led by two officers, Enver and Niyazi Beys. When these two officers raised the standard of revolution in Resne, the government sent its forces against them from Smyrna [Izmir]. However, instead of putting down the rebels, these forces actually joined the rebels. Meanwhile, the Grand Vezier, Ferid Pasha, who responded to the revolutionary movement by declaring the constitution, was replaced by Said Pasha.

The situation became even more threatening on July 23, when the Ottoman army at Chatalja prepared to march on Constantinople and threatened bloodshed in the streets of the capital. This was the moment Sultan Hamid, who was preparing to go on his *Selamlik* [Friday prayers] was forced to sign the constitution with his trembling hands. The new decree was announced to the population by the firing of cannons and ensuring the new order was established without bloodshed.

While the coup was accomplished and new people appeared on the scene, the levers of power still remained in the hands of the old regime. The so called "Young Turks" or the party of "Union and Progress," which came to head the revolutionary movement, was not able to govern the country after the declaration of the constitution. Perhaps it was too inexperienced to rule a whole country and chose to merely supervise the government. The honeymoon period passed peacefully.

The Young Turks, by staying away from high offices, were able to remain faithful to their high principles of universal freedoms, voting rights, a parliamentary system and responsible ministries.

However, they soon came to head the government and organised a military coup. This was because they experienced a number of difficulties: they faced a powerful coalition against them composed of public officials who had been dismissed from office, a mass of spies who had been withdrawn from their normal activities, the Ahrar political party which included Christians, as well as provincial officials of the old regime who had backed the Young Turks but could not come to terms with the new state of affairs.

The Young Turks thus faced powerful opposition during the elections to the first parliament that convened on December 17, 1908. Among the new parliamentarians were a number of different national representatives, such as 60 Arabs, 25 Albanians, 23 Armenians, 13 Bulgarians, Serbians and Jews, so that among the 275 members of the Ottoman Parliament, 133 were from different national groups. On the other hand, the Muslims' representatives, with few exceptions, supported the Committee of Union and Progress (CUP). Despite this composition of the Ottoman parliament, the Young Turks were still defeated on January 13, when they expressed their non-confidence in Grand Vizier Kamil Pasha and forced a new election. The national minorities and a number of Muslims voted against the Young Turks.

This defeat compelled the Young Turks to rally all votes behind them. When they garnered such support, they ousted Kamil Pasha, Minister of Interior Hilmi Pasha, and

Minister of Justice Tevfik Pasha. Who were the members of the Young Turks' party? The January 1909 parliamentary session showed that they depended on the army and had the power to subvert the wishes of parliament. During that session, the navy made it clear that it was not subject to the Minister for the Navy, while the representative of the army, Habib Bey, announced after a series of speeches, that the army was opposed to Kamil Pasha. He was supported by many members of the armed forces in parliament.

After this incident, there was greater resentment against the Young Turks. While the Ahrar party and national blocks accused the Committee of Union and Progress of acting autocratically within Parliament, the clergy and the *softas* accused them of betraying and undermining Islam.

These developments were followed by the fiend at Yildiz, Abdul Hamid and his circle, who were waiting to rise again. They encouraged discontented elements and used the softas to spread propaganda in the army in Constantinople, so that on April 13 1909 there was a new revolution in the capital with the support of the army. This time, the movement was under the banner of overthrowing the constitution and re-establishing the Shariat.

The Young Turk leaders, surprised by these developments, fled, while parliament held a session to the sound of gunfire and released a statement agreeing to the demands of the rebels. Sultan Abdul Hamid then pardoned the rebels and asked Tevfik Pasha to form a new government and uphold the principles of the Shariat. The Sultan thus overthrew the very people he had bowed to on 24 July 1908.

This new reactionary movement only lasted a few days because on April 26 1909, Mahmud Shevket Pasha, who headed army units in Saloniki, marched on Constantinople. The Saloniki army took over the capital following bloody clashes, and on April 27, 1909 Abdul Hamid was formally deposed at San Stefano and replaced by Mehmet Reshad. This ceremony took place in the presence of members of the Ottoman parliament and with the agreement of the Sheikh ul Islam.

During the reactionary movement in Constantinople on March April 13, many inflammatory telegrams were sent to the provinces, especially against Armenians, so that fanatics took matters into their own hands and anti-Armenian massacres broke out in Adana. For several days, Adana and its surrounding areas were the scenes of bestial atrocities, with wild mobs attacking and killing Armenians, entering the city's Armenian quarters and homes, looting and burning properties, all with the full knowledge and encouragement of officials. Thousands perished and – in order to hide the scale of the killings – cartloads of corpses were thrown into the Sihoun [Seyhan] river, so that they would be carried away to the Mediterranean Sea.

It is beyond this study to give a detailed description of the Adana massacres, though the event was a major episode in the bloody annals of Armenian history. There are some detailed reports on the incident and we could summarise them by pointing out that over 18,000 Armenians were killed, 7,000 of whom were in the city, and the rest in surrounding fields and villages. The Adana massacres, in terms of victims, opened a new page in the history of modern Turkey.

The Adana or Cilician Massacres (1909). The aftermath in Adana *(above)* and Tarsus *(below, left)*

Had Mahmoud Shevket Pasha's army been mobilised and occupied Constantinople a few days later, the terrible massacres would have spread to the Armenian provinces and we would have witnessed the complete annihilation of Armenians – on a scale not found even in Armenian history. Fortunately, the victorious army entered Constantinople in good time and the Armenian massacres were limited to the Adana atrocities.

Therefore, the Young Turks forced Sultan Abdul Hamid to declare the constitution on 24 July 1908 and then suppressed the April 13 1909 reaction, thus leading people to think that the constitutional movement would still flourish. But that was not to be the case.

After the suppression of the April 13 movement, the Young Turks, who until then, one could say, operated behind a curtain of secrecy, came into the open and took the reins of government into their own hands. The ministries passed to Talaat, Javid, Haji Adil and Khalil Beys, while Mahmoud Shevket Pasha became responsible for the army.

Important issues regarding state administration were first discussed and settled within the Committee of Union and Progress, and then passed to the executives of the state for implementation. While it was true that ministers were picked from experienced men of the old regime, they had no real role in making decisions and were expected to implement the directives of the CUP. If ministers opposed the decisions handed to them, they could be removed from office. Hilmi Pasha, for example, lost his ministerial position in such a manner.

Naturally, when the Young Turks took over government, they created a new coercive regime. Along with Sultan Abdul Hamid, they also drove away members of the former Sultan's regime and punished or exiled many officials and individuals who were suspected of being involved in the reactionary movement. The opposition to the Young Turks thus got bigger, and the new regime, in order to keep control of the reins of government, resorted to more extreme measures and paved the way to the tragedy of the Young Turks.

The pressing question was now the following: on which sections of society would the Young Turks depend?

If the new regime stuck to its principles and acted on them in the interest of the state, thereby turning the country towards the rule of law and positive economic and social development, then the discontented Arab tribes and Christian nations would have been quite satisfied and the interference of European states in the internal affairs of the Ottoman Empire would have come to an end. But the old regime and its former officials, spies and spiritual leaders could not accept such a new order. Neither did the ignorant Muslim masses, who, against their own interests, acted with blind fanaticism under the leadership of religious fanatics and the banner of the Shariat. The good of the country and reason demanded a new order, while the ignorant multitudes and the opposition demanded a return to the old order and the Shariat.

Unfortunately, the Young Turks chose the Shariat. Europe had offered them little and when they took over the reins of government they were not able to remain free of conservative pressures at home.

They therefore introduced a new element into the constitution whereby they obliged the Sultan to defend the Shariat while they promised to keep new laws within its spirit. The Sheikh-ul-Islam meanwhile declared that the new constitutional order was not against the Shariat.

Thus the Young Turks came under the protection of Islam and increasingly turned to Pan-Islamism.

* * *

Sometimes government policies can lead to disasters, especially in countries composed of different national or racial elements, when governments promote the sectarian interests of dominant groups and pave the way to inter-communal strife to the detriment of all.

The Young Turks started with the wonderful notion of the liberation of nations, fomented a revolution, and formed a popular government. Unfortunately, they then stepped backwards to the Shariat, turned to Pan-Islamism, and allowed the destruction that followed.

The Young Turks' control of government turned into a catastrophe not only for the Committee of Union and Progress, but the whole of the Ottoman Empire. The ranks of the party soon grew, the honest elements increasingly withdrew, and a few individuals took charge. The latter were soon joined by elements of the old regime, so that Abdul Hamid's policies were implemented once more under a more European-looking mask. The results are well known and could be summarised as the destruction of Christians, especially the extermination of Armenians, which the Young Turks attempted in a systematic manner.

What is the evidence?

Firstly, the Adana Massacres of 1909. That massacre, as we saw, took place during the counter-revolution of April 13 and was organised by the old regime. However, in essence, the massacre took place with the collaboration of the Young Turks. It took place with the backing of the local governor and police force, including officials who had joined the Young Turks and represented the party. Furthermore, the army sent to establish peace in the region also participated in the murder of Armenians. The Young Turks condemned themselves for those crimes when they made sure that the Adana governor, Ali Jevad and his sub-governors, were not prosecuted after the events, while Armenians who had defended themselves were condemned.

It is remarkable that the military court-martial sent to investigate the Adana Massacre were considered unfair even by the Muslims. Indeed, Ismail Fazil Pasha, who was sent to Adana to investigate the injustices, was forced to retire for writing a critical report.

The first court-martial was recalled and a second one was sent out, but this did not dispense justice either, thus leading to suspicions that it had secret instructions to follow in the footsteps of the first.

Finally, two members of parliament were sent to Adana as inspectors. One was Yusuf Kemal Bey, a Turk, and the other Hagop Babigian, an Armenian who represented Rodosto. The Turkish representative remained blind to the obvious murders that had taken place and when the two representatives returned to Constantinople they presented two contradictory reports.

In the end, the Armenians, who defended themselves by opening fire on the Turkish gangs attacking them, were held to be as guilty as the attackers. According to the decision of the courts-martial in early May, six Armenians were hanged alongside nine Muslim murderers. 18,000 Armenians had been killed: there had been 18,000 murders, and in that sea of murders, the Young Turks only punished nine Muslim murderers, while six people were given death sentences from the ranks of the few Armenian defenders.

The heartbreaking details of the Adana massacres and the unjust stance of the court-martial towards Muslim murderers and innocent Armenians had such an impact on the Armenian parliamentary inspector Babigian that he suffered greatly, became ill after his return to Constantinople, and died, leaving behind his report exposing the Adana murders.

The second occasion when the Young Turks showed their hostility to Armenians was in their reluctance to address the return of Armenian lands that had been confiscated by the state administration. During the ancient regime there were countless cases of the plunder of Armenian properties and the confiscation of Armenian lands, and it was inconceivable that the issue would not be addressed with the peaceful promises of the constitution. The new authorities announced that landless Armenians who had been robbed of their lands would receive their properties back through appropriate administrative steps. However, those promises were not fulfilled, and in many cases ignored. Armenian appeals and protests led nowhere. It would be naive to think that the lack of progress was due to the inexperience of provincial officials. The problem reflected the sentiments of Constantinople. The Young Turks wanted to appear as if they desired to resolve the problem, but in practical terms they wanted to bury it. They linked the issue to Pan-Islamism and turned against the Armenians. Consequently, the appeals sent to the Patriarchate from the provinces, and the Patriarchate's appeals to the government were ignored, until new incidents could be used to deflect them.

The new problems thus began when the Young Turks, at the head of government, gradually adopted Sultan Hamid's discriminatory policies towards Christians.

The Young Turk oppressive policies started in Macedonia and Albania by betraying their own promises. The various organisations and assemblies that had been formed during the honeymoon of the constitutional period, as well as the assemblies of the Bulgarian teachers, were shut down. The government began to disarm Christians on the pretext that there were revolutionary groups among them while it drew support from Muslims. The persecution of Christians was more serious in Albania, where most of northern Albania was devastated by Javid Pasha in 1910.

The national and cultural movement that characterised the early constitutional period in the Armenian provinces was also ended by the Young Turks. While feigning good relations with the leadership of the main Armenian political party, the Tashnaktsoutiun (Armenian Revolutionary Federation *hereafter* ARF), they also began to conspire against them. This was the same ARF with whom they had collaborated without reservation to topple the regime of Sultan Abdul Hamid and establish a legitimate and pluralist Ottoman state. The Young Turks in Constantinople sent secret instructions to spy on Armenian activists in the provinces, including the order to murder Raphael Yeritsian, the administrative head of Aghtamar diocese of Gargar, in 1911.

The attitude of the Young Turks did not change even after the conscription of Christians into the army in 1910. While it is true that that development was expected to soften anti-Christian discrimination, it now seemed as if it had the opposite effect, because Muslims could not accept seeing Christians under the flag of their former oppressors.

The situation didn't change in Serbia or Mesopotamia either. The dissatisfied Arab tribes did not see the fulfillment of promises made to them during the declaration of the constitution. Local autonomy remained mere words.

The Young Turks, while in office, gradually digressed from the promises they had made, cut their ties with communities who wished to see an egalitarian system, and followed Sultan Hamid's policies where Christians were concerned. They also failed to establish ties with the upper echelons of the ruling Muslim elites to strengthen their own power base. Worse still, there was no peace and cooperation within the ranks of the CUP. Soon, the party split, and a large number of their deputies formed a separate group with its own programme.

This group was led by a well-known revolutionary, Colonel Sadik, who headed the powerful opposition to his former comrades. The Young Turks, losing authority and comrades, reverted to force and even terror. On June 9, 1911, Colonel Sadik's close ally and journalist Zeki was treacherously murdered.

Also, the Young Turks, having lost their Parliamentary majority, reverted to the desperate step of dissolving Parliament, with the hope of returning with a new majority.

On January 18, 1912, the parliament was dissolved, following the rejection of a law proposed by the government to increase the powers of the Sultan.

The new elections took place in an atmosphere of threats and intimidation, and a newly elected parliament was convened on April 18 with a solid majority supporting the Young Turks. The opposition parties soon abandoned the field and there was further discontent. The army, which previously supported the Young Turks, turned against it. For example, some military units in Monastir took to the mountains and called on the government not to undermine the constitution. In response, the minister responsible for the army, Mahmoud Shefket Pasha, introduced a bill to forbid military personnel joining political parties.

However, the new law was counter-productive and led to the formation of the military "Protectors of the Homeland" league.

This new political party criticised the government, which it claimed was taking the country to its doom and inviting European intervention, and made the following demands:

1. Change the composition of the government to one that enjoyed the trust of Europeans.

2. Dismiss irresponsible people who intervened in the inner working of government.

3. Dissolve Parliament and prepare for new elections without the interference of the police.

The military league soon organised the armed forces around itself and sent representatives to the Sultan with their demands. The atmosphere thus became very complex, political conflict loomed on the horizon, and the Young Turk government yielded. Members of the opposition were appointed to government positions, such as Ahmed Moukhtar Pasha as premier; Kyamil and Nazim Pashas as ministers; and Noradoungian as Foreign Minister.

Moukhtar Pasha dissolved parliament and set the date for new elections, which were undermined in the same way as the earlier elections by the Young Turks.

During this period, the first Balkan War broke out. While the outbreak of hostilities was entirely due to the earlier actions of the Young Turks who had followed the policies of Abdul Hamid, all blame for the disastrous outcome for Turks was laid at the feet of the new authorities who were in power when the war broke out, despite the fact that they had been opponents of the Young Turks.

The Balkan War had already started when the energetic and quite popular Young Turk activist Enver Bey returned from Tripoli. Enver went into the new conflict with an eye of raising the standing of his political party. However, the war ended with the defeat of the Turks and the January 17, 1913 Note by the six European powers demanding the surrender of Adrianople to Bulgaria. The Prime Minister at this time was Kyamil Pasha, while the Minister of War was Nazim Pasha. On January 22, Prime Minister Kyamil Pasha's government sued for peace, and this was the moment seized by the Young Turks.

A day after the meeting of the Council of State, on January 23, two Young Turk hotheads, Enver and Talaat Beys, at the head of 200 men, stormed the Sublime Porte when the Council of Ministers was meeting and killed the Minister of War, Nazim Pasha. They then forced Kyamil Pasha to resign and appointed Mahmud Shevket Pasha as Prime Minister. The Young Turks thus took control of the government once more.

The Muslim masses remained indifferent and accepted the new developments – once again displaying a unique characteristic of the Ottoman constitutional movement.

When the Young Turks took over government, the situation in the Ottoman Empire did not improve. One could say it got worse. The murder of Nazim Pasha created problems within the army, as he had many supporters in the ranks. Moreover, in May 1913, a draft peace agreement was signed in London, and it became apparent that the Young Turk government could not manage to retain Adrianople. Gradually, the resentment led to the revenge-killing of Mahmoud Shefket in Bayazid Square on June 15, as he was driving to the Sublime Porte.

Thus began a new era in the Young Turks rule which was characterised by acts of terror and a bloody road to a European War.

The murder of Mahmud Shevket led to many arrests, trials and exile. A number of gallows were set up in the same Sultan Bayazid Square, where 12 military personnel and officials were hung on June 24, including Sultan Hamid's son-in-law and Damad Salih

Pasha, Topal Tevfik, Captain Kyazim and Munib Bey. The courts-martial also condemned to death, in absentia, such notables as Prince Sabah Eddin, Sherif Pasha and the former Minister of Interior Reshid Bey – all of whom had fled abroad. After these exiles, the government passed into the hands of three representatives of the Young Turks: Enver, Talaat and Jemal Beys. Enver Bey took Nazim Pasha's portfolio, having murdered the minister himself.

Enver's appointment as the new Minister of War meant that he was free to act, and during the wars among the Balkan states [after the First Balkan War], he marched on Adrianople and took it unopposed in July 1913. The Bulgarian army at that time was occupied against Serbia and could not resist the Turks. Adrianople passed to Ottoman Turkey once more.

After this success the Young Turks, or more accurately, the government of the Enver-Talaat-Jemal faction, got carried away and derided everyone else, though they had lost Tripoli and most of European Turkey in the Italian and Balkan wars. As they became more oppressive against their opponents, they also continued persecuting Christians.

For example, they forced the Christian population of Adrianople and surrounding areas they had reconquered to emigrate under the threat of massacre. New persecutions also started in Asia Minor, where they wanted to force out the Christian population and settle Muslims from the lost provinces in Macedonia.

Similar persecutions continued and increased with respect to Armenians.

On 21 June 1913, the Russian Ambassador in Constantinople, Giers, in consultation with the representatives of the Great Powers, presented a new Armenian Reforms project.

The Young Turk government was infuriated and turned on the Armenians in the provinces with new abuses and persecutions. The government opposed the reforms by provoking the fanaticism of the Muslim masses, while playing the Russian-British-French alliance against the German-Austrian-Italian one, as in the Hamidian days.

The main points of the Russian proposal were:

1. To form a single Armenian province from the six Armenian provinces of Van, Bitlis, Erzeroum, Kharpert, Sivas and Diyarbekir – leaving out those areas in which Armenians constituted an insignificant number.

2. To appoint a Christian Inspector General selected by the Great Powers of Europe for the proposed Armenian province.

3. All officials of the new Armenian province, including regional governors, to be appointed by the Inspector General.

4. The Armenian province to have its own assembly of an equal number of elected Christian and Muslim representatives. Equal numbers of Christian and Muslim officials should also be appointed.

These proposals were discussed by the ambassadors of the six powers between July 16 and August 6.

As expected, there were disagreements about the proposal, as the German-Austrian-Italian alliance defended its interests and opposed the Russian-British-French triple alliance. Only Russia and Germany were interested in the Armenian reforms. While

Russia insisted on its plans, Germany tried to curtail them by every means possible, encouraging the Turkish government to delay matters, broaden suggestions to the whole country, and always find an excuse to play for time.

So, as the Armenian Reforms proposal was delayed by seven or eight months, Germany cleverly managed to show itself to be a friend of the Turkish government and reinforced its influence in the Sultan's capital.

Meanwhile, the Young Turk government receiving secret instructions from Germany, delayed matters, argued on each point to gain time, and sent secret orders to the provinces to persecute Armenians. The results of these efforts were soon made clear by the voices of protests and loss of hope in the provinces.

"For eight months, this historical city of Turkish Armenia has been subject to extraordinary pressures, murders and pillage," a protester from Yerznga [Erzincan] said.

"The pillaging and murders are taking place under the noses of the authorities, and the government remains indifferent" someone wrote from Erzeroum.

"Armenians are being disarmed in the city and wider province, while Muslims are being armed. Once more, there is no more mutual trust," came cries from Van.

Meanwhile, there was an anti-Armenian boycott in Constantinople, *Azadamard* newspaper began receiving threatening letters, and there were strained discussions between the Sublime Porte and the National Assembly about giving Armenians 20 seats in the Ottoman Parliament.

Because of German perfidity, by December, the Young Turk government's oppression of Armenians reached a point when there was talk of new massacres, at the time when the reforms project was nearing its final form.

"While a week ago, Armenians had delighted at the news of the government accepting the principle of European control, the happy smiles have now been replaced by the prospect of terrible massacres."

But the Young Turk government was careful not to take this murderous step, restrained by the Russian government's announcement that it would push the question of responsibility in case of massacres. The Turkish government therefore signed the proposed Reforms project agreement on February 8, 1914.

The Armenian Reforms project was finally accepted but included Germany's own preferences and conditions:

1. Armenia should be divided into two regions. The first should be composed of Erzeroum, Sivas and Trabizon vilayets, and the second one of Van, Bitlis, Kharpert and Diyarbekir vilayets.

2. The two Inspectors General should oversee the executive and legislative bodies, appoint and dismiss all officials except for governors, head the armed forces of their areas, and solve Armenian-Kurdish land disputes.

3. Each vilayet administration should be headed by a legislative body or an elected council, which, along with the inspector general, should hear the governor's reports, oversee the vilayet income and budget, reform the system of tax collection, designate tasks

to administrative bodies, as well as direct public works, education and public health issues.

4. Elected councils should be composed of an equal number of Christians and Muslims in Van and Bitlis vilayets, as well as in Erzeroum, until a new census is undertaken. The remaining four vilayets should have councils in proportion to the Christian and Muslim populations.

5. The general councils should elect provincial committees of four, in the same proportion as their parent bodies, which are to prepare and present the general councils with reports on important issues and other materials for consideration.

6. Armenian should be used alongside Turkish in courts.

7. The male population of the Armenian vilayets are to carry out their military service in their places of origin.

8. The Hamidiye troops are to become reserve cavalry forces and be disarmed during peacetime.

As can be seen, the Russian draft proposal was detrimental to the Armenians, and in return for their acceptance, Von Sanders was appointed as the Inspector General of the Ottoman army, thereby laying a new foundation for German influence.

Indeed, the Russian proposal for Armenian reforms was changed so much that little was preserved of it in the new one, as the Young Turk government continued the destructive policies of the Hamidian era. The Young Turks, who did not wish to consider the new Reforms project, though they had formally accepted it, created new difficulties and barriers, and began new schemes.

The six Great Powers were to elect two Inspectors General and present them to the Sultan for his approval, a step that became a process for delay. The opponents to reforms could slow matters down and win time, a tactic the Young Turks had inherited from Abdul Hamid. Now it was the Germans, the international salesmen, who were whispering in the ears of the Young Turks and wrangling for weeks about the appointment of the Inspectors General, until April 27 [1914], when the Sublime Porte finally accepted two names among five candidates presented by the six powers.

On May 8 the two Inspectors General reached Constantinople to make their arrangements with the Sublime Porte. Esad Bey, the Prime Minister's translator, greeted them at the train station and the following day the Inspectors General were invited to dinner with the Minister of Interior, Talaat Bey. Thus began a session of pure oriental flattery.

Who were the Inspectors General?

1. Westenenk, the Inspector General for Van, Bitlis, Kharpert and Diyarbekir region, was a Dutchman who had served for many years in the Dutch West Indies.

2. Hoff, Inspector General for Erzeroum, Sivas, Trabizon region, was a Norwegian who had served for many years in military-administratve positions.

After a few seemingly favourable receptions, the Sublime Porte turned to the agreement that needed to be signed with the Inspectors General and new delays and quibbling started. The problems revolved around the military and administrative authority of the Inspectors Generals. After two weeks of delays and discussions, on May 19, the Inspectors General threatened to leave Constantinople.

Only after this threat, on May 23, was an agreement signed and the two inspectors returned to their countries in order to settle their private affairs and then return to their official postings.

The Inspectors General returned to Constantinople in the first half of June, where they spent a few days selecting their aides and translators, and then continued on their journeys: Westenenk going to Sivas and Hoff to Trabizon and then Van via Erzeroum.

And so the two Inspectors General of the Armenian vilayets set off to take up their new duties, carrying the respect and hopes of the Armenian people, as well as the quiet enmity and hatred of Turks. However, before reaching their destinations, all of Europe was in disarray as war erupted, and the great states of Europe, including Germany, Austria, Russia, France, Great Britain, Serbia and Belgium were drawn into a world war, while others states mobilised, including Ottoman Turkey – which saw its salvation in the upcoming storm.

Chapter IV

The European War

The Young Turk government's poor attitude towards Armenians has already been discussed. Armenians were trying to put an end to the land question, while the government did not give the matter any attention. Armenians wanted proportional representation in Parliament, but their demands were rebuffed. Despite new persecutions and disorder in the provinces, the government did not take steps to address them. Instead, the authorities disarmed Armenians. While provincial Armenians prepared to greet European inspectors General Hoff and Westenenk with great fanfare, the government sent secret instructions to provincial officials not to pay any attention to their arrival – and to disturb the reception organised by Armenians (as shall be seen later). As this tense standoff continued, a general war broke out in Europe.

At the end of July, 1914, a great conflagration started in the heart of Europe and spread like lightning across the whole continent. This was the European war that the whole world had dreaded.

It is beyond this work to consider the factors that led to this war; they were very complicated and part of the tangle of international relations, as well as intractable and insoluble historical issues.

The general explanation for the war concerned the establishment of colonies, controlling markets, ensuring favourable trade deals and ultimately imposing the belligerents' will on the world. These were the main issues on the agenda of European powers, or more correctly, nations, and the primary causes of competition. These differences led to a system of alliances and an arms race. Each state rushed to arm itself in order not to be subjugated by others. Each state tried to ally itself in order not to be isolated in a terrible conflict.

During the previous two decades, two system of alliances developed in Europe. One was between Germany, Austro-Hungary and Italy, and the other, in response to the first, between Russia, France and Great Britain.

Each alliance attempted to build up its armed forces, both on land and sea, leading to unprecedented preparations for war. Germany, in the first group, led the way by expending all of its resources and energies over the previous 40 years to accelerate its advance in military technology, and to create a well-prepared standing army, unequalled by any other state in the history of Europe.

Given the pace of armament, it was inevitable that there would be a disastrous end through war, and that the powerful would look for an excuse for war – as was the case with the most powerful player, Germany.

What was the pretext?

According to the Congress of Berlin in 1878, two provinces of Ottoman Turkey, Bosnia and Herzegovina, became part of the Austro-Hungarian Empire. The majority of the population of these provinces were Serbs, who could not accept their status under the peculiar rule of a multi-national Austria instead of an independent Serbia. As soon as Bosnia passed under Austrian rule, a secret pro-Serbia movement was initiated. While Austria suppressed it, the movement actually got more powerful by striking deep roots amongst the people – as could be seen elsewhere among oppressed people – and it organised revolutionary deeds. One such deed took place in Sarajevo, the capital of Bosnia, the seat of the representative of the Austrian government and viceroy of Bosnia.

On 28 June 1914, the crown prince of Austro-Hungary, Prince Franz Ferdinand and his wife were on a visit to Sarajevo for a reception in his honour at the town hall. As they were driven to the reception, a Serb by the name of Tsabrinovich threw a bomb into their automobile. The prince immediately caught the bomb and threw it out of their carriage, wounding two members of his guard of honour and six civilian onlookers. However, the attempted assassination did not end there. After the reception, on their return journey, the crown prince and his wife were assassinated by a Serbian student called Princip who fatally wounded both of them.

The murderers were arrested, followed by investigations and further arrests. Meanwhile, there were protests and massacres of Serbs in Sarajevo and Bosnia, as well as the destruction of their homes and shops.

After a few days, peace was re-established and it appeared the situation had calmed down. However, in less than a month, on July 23, the Austrian ambassador to Serbia presented a set of demands to the Serbian government. This Note accused Serbia of harbouring secret societies which enjoyed the support of members of the Serbian armed forces and officials. It stated that these societies were responsible for the murders in Sarajevo, and that Serbia should meet the following Austro-Hungarian demands within 48 hours. Serbia had to:

1. Condemn and suppress anti-Austrian propaganda in Serbia.
2. Close down the "Narodnaya Odprana" society.
3. Censor all anti-Austrian references in state school programmes.
4. Retire all officers and officials indicated by the Austro-Hungarian government.
5. Allow the Austro-Hungarian police to work with the Serbian police to suppress the anti-Austrian movement in Serbia.
6. Allow Austro-Hungarian representatives to be present when Serbians were interrogated for the Sarajevo atrocity.
7. Arrest the Serbian officials Voytankevic and Milan Tsiganovich.
8. Punish the officials, Shabatsi and Loznitsi, who allowed the murderers to cross the border.

The Serbian government responded to the ultimatum in a friendly tone, accepting some of the demands, but objecting to the demands for the presence of Austrian policemen and other representatives in Serbia as a violation of Serbian sovereignty.

Austro-Hungary considered the Serbian response to be inadequate and ordered mobilisation and arranged for its ambassador to immediately leave Belgrade. Serbia also mobilised. However, prior to the Serbian response being sent, the Russian ambassador to Vienna asked the Austro-Hungarian government to give Serbia more time to respond. This request was refused and Russia also ordered mobilisation.

Great Britain then asked Germany, France and Italy to attend a conference in London for matters to be resolved peacefully. Germany refused the proposal and announced that the problem was between Austria and Serbia, and if a third party intervened, it too would be drawn into the conflict. Germany also mobilised after that announcement.

Finally, France intervened, trying to resolve matters peacefully but also failed.

If it is accepted that Austro-Hungary took each of its steps in consultation with Germany, then we may understand how Germany masterminded the unacceptable demands made by Austro-Hungary and carefully refused the proposals of Russia, Great Britain and France for a peaceful resolution. In actual fact, no European power had a great interest in war, or was prepared for one, as Germany.

Germany wanted war, and it was difficult to find a better pretext for one. The Sarajevo incident was a good way to mobilise Austro-Hungary and then drag it into the conflict as Germany wished. Secondly, Germany's opponents, Russia, France and Great Britain had internal problems. For example, Russia was facing major strikes in industrial centres, such as Petersburg, Moscow, Warsaw and Baku, and many factories had stopped working. In Great Britain, public opinion was focused on Home Rule, the decades old issue of Irish autonomy, which had resurfaced after many refusals in the House of Lords. The issue had won the approval of Parliament for the third time and was due to become law. Opponents of Home Rule were creating new problems and proposing to separate Ulster from consideration. The Irish issue had polarised positions and threatened serious political conflict between different parties in Great Britain.

France was also not spared internal troubles. Prior to the severance of Austro-Serbian relations, Paris was gripped by the examination of a well-known murder case. In the middle of March that year, the wife of the Minister of Finance, Henrietta Caillaux, entered the editorial office of *Figaro* and shot dead the editor of the newspaper Gaston Calmette. That murder assumed political colouring, as *Figaro* was a fierce opponent of the republicans and had led a campaign against Minister Joseph Caillaux, publicising such matters as Caillaux's family and married life. Mrs. Caillaux, who was involved in these revelations, could not bear this state of affairs and decided to murder the editor of *Figaro* and did so.

This murder, which created much furore and even some demonstrations in Paris by the monarchists, intensified the antagonism between the republicans and their opponents.

Meanwhile, Germany, which had a network of spies across the world and carefully followed developments, considered the moment suitable to unveil its decades-long preparations. While there were effort to stop the deterioration of diplomatic relations between Austria and Serbia by any means, Russia, France and Great Britain spared no efforts to avoid a European conflagration. Austro-Hungary was the first to unsheathe her sword in the belief that no state would dare intervene in a war between her and Serbia. Royal circles were terrified of developments and agreed to negotiate in order to avoid a terrible war. At that moment, on August 1, Germany declared war on Russia and began military manoeuvres against France, overrunning the Duchy of Luxemburg and violating the neutrality and independence of Belgium.

After these developments, it was impossible to avoid a general European inferno. The conflict spread like wildfire, assuming terrible dimensions across all of Europe, pulling in Germany, Austro-Hungary, Russia, and then the Far East with Japan.

From that day, the world was nurtured by gunpowder, destruction and the loss of life.

Suddenly internal disagreements were replaced by incredible patriotic support for war, and people held hands in all countries and marched on their enemies. Calls for peace were silenced and on July 31, one of the greatest Frenchman, Jean Jaures, was murdered in Paris by a mad assassin.

Chapter V

Seferberlik or Mobilisation

Just as the general European war broke out, it drew in more states and nations. All were joining the war with the conviction that they would be victorious and benefit from their victory. This was also the situation in Ottoman Turkey, which had already drawn its sword in battle three times in six years – against Italy, Albania, and the Balkan states. Although they had lost in all three wars, they also chose to enter this conflict with the dream of reconquering the territories they had lost in the 19th century.

The Young Turk government, which did not have its own independent foreign policy, became an instrument in the hands of the Germans, a country that was used to pulling chestnuts out of the fire with the hands of others. The Young Turks believed in German promises and rushed into the war.

"A terrible war has broken out in Europe, military reservists have been called up in neighbouring countries, and our state interests and the defence of our country force us to prepare for the unexpected." It was on such a pretext that on August 3, two days after Germany declared war on Russia, Ottoman Turkey declared *seferberlik* – an Arabic word that in its current context meant mobilisation.

Every man between 20 and 45, without exception, was called up for military service. Not only were Muslims, who had been subject to military service for decades, called to arms, but also Christians, including Armenians, who had only started serving in the army after 1910 and had practically no reservists among them.

The Turkish government was imitating Europe but implementing policies in its own manner – one could even say in an upside-down fashion. It was declaring mobilisation and forcing into service men who had never served in the army and could not use weapons. Thus confusion spread in the country.

The orders were strict and threatening, and all men had to leave their occupations and gather around recruitment centres, though many ran away and hid. Not only was military service avoided by Christians, who could not understand what was going on, but also by Muslims.

Seferberlik was a pointless and foolish exercise which threatened to wreck the economy of the poor people of Ottoman Turkey. This period was the most intense time in the working season, the most important one in which to earn a living, especially in Turkish Armenia, which had an almost entirely agrarian economy. This was the time to gather fodder, but the peasants were driven to the barracks without proper regard for their age or physical condition. In the words of an observer from Erzeroum:

> Here, all 20 and 45 year olds were called to arms without exception. They did not consider family needs, nor physical infirmities or weaknesses. Among the new recruits one could meet lame, blind, sick and deranged people. They had all

been taken into the army and dug trenches outside cities on hillsides all day. Despite this work, they were barely able to provide a dry piece of bread for their families.

Similarly, an eyewitness in Boulanik gave one of many similar descriptions in newspapers at that time:

> While the Armenians of Boulanik had just started to consider themselves free of centuries of suffering and were happy in the false hopes of a promising future, they suddenly received telegraphic news from the Bosphorous announcing mobilisation. The next day the government decided to disperse units of the army and police force among the villages. Without proper registers, the men – tall and short, old and young, blind and disfigured, lame and invalid, naked and pitiable – were gathered like sheep and taken to Kop and then dispersed further. In Kop alone, 300 to 500 youngsters were taken away, and now they are registering the older men.

Such scenes were not the only evils of seferberlik that descended on Ottoman subjects during the European War. Seferberlik also brought another calamity that was particular to Ottoman Turkey and unusual elsewhere. This was called *Tekyalifi Harbiye*, also an Arabic phrase, meaning War Tax.

The Ottoman coffers were empty as usual when the government decided to raise an army of a million men. Who was going to clothe and feed such an army? Naturally, the much impoverished people. For this purpose, the authorities created the Tekyalifi Harbiye and its many stores and "commissioners."

What was the essence of this organisation? The confiscation of everything needed by the army from the people – grains, animals, other food supplies, fodder, hay etc.

Tekyalifi Harbiye, as mentioned, meant war tax. The goods they requisitioined were supposed to be bought but the authorities merely issued paper receipts which were never honoured. If Tekyalifi Harbiye was a tax, why did the authorities give special receipts? And if the receipts were to be honoured and the value paid, why was it called a tax? This was the chaos created by that body which led to organised plunder and theft.

Tekyalifi Harbiye commissioners entered shops and homes, opened stores, explored water-wells, dug up passages, and forcefully confiscated manufactured goods, sugar, fuel, grains, animals and a thousand and one other things – giving their owners a piece of paper in return.

Most of this looting was at the expense of Armenians. The following is an account of Tekyalifi Harbiye activities given by an eye-witness in the Sultans' capital, Constantinople, and it is not difficult to imagine the situation in the provincial cities.

> They have a meeting and decide who will give what. They always pick on Armenian and Greek merchants. Then a huge automobile arrives in front of the shop like an angel of death. Any merchant who sees the vehicle park in front of his shop is terrified by the prospect of bankruptcy. They enter the premises, load everything onto the huge grey automobile, and leave, after giving him a piece of paper. They also discount half of the estimated value of goods. To whom should the merchant give the paper receipt to cash it? That is Allah's business.

The Ipranossians, Aslanians, Garabedians, Topalians enjoyed several visits from the angel of death's automobile. Especially poor Topalian, he suffered three visits. And yesterday his shop was closed because there was no more stock left in it. They took 250 gold liras' worth of linen and cotton and so on.

But the theft by Tekyalifi Harbiye was worse on hard-working villagers. It was not enough that the workers in these families had been drafted into the army; now they also took the bread from their families.

Tekyalifi Harbiye was supposed to be collected from peasants as actual produce and limited to one-tenth of their stock. For example, if a peasant had 10 sheep and 10 sacks of wheat, they had to give one sheep and one sack for the needs of the army. These limits were set by the centre but were subject to change at the commissioner's whim during collection. Although the commission was formed mainly of the *kaimakam, mal mudir, kadi* and two representatives of the people, the latter often played no role in the decision making – after all, this was a time for mobilisation and it was impossible to oppose war taxes.

The commission was allowed to make demands on a village without going into details and to claim part of the crops and produce according to its own reckoning. There were no real limits set, only that decided by the commission, or more accurately, the kaimakam's disposition. Sometimes the amount was less than what was previously determined, but more often, or very often, it was more, especially in the case of Armenians.

They demanded wheat, barley, flour, fat, cheese, cracked wheat (*tsavar* or *bulgur*), grass, hay, socks, footwear, fuel and much more from the villages.

Here is a short list for an idea of how heavy the new war tax was.

Alchavaz district had 23 Armenian inhabited villages with 823 Armenian households. These households had to pay the following for the Tekyalifi Harbiye:

> 3,800 kiles of wheat
> 2,300 sheep
> 800 Liras (money)
> Large amounts of fats, cheese, socks, grass, hay and so on

A kile was equal to 1.5 poods [54 lbs.]

If this taxation was converted into cash, taking a pood of wheat at one ruble, each sheep at seven rubles, and one lira as 10 rubles, we reach the figure 80,000 rubles, without mentioning other products. Therefore, each household paid 100 rubles in wheat, sheep and cash.

One description from Shabin-Karahissar stated:

> They confiscated the poor peasant's fat, a year's store of wheat and flour, all the horses, donkeys, oxen, and sheep, and finally the shoes on his feet and socks. They even had an eye on the clothes covering his nakedness.

The behaviour of the Turkish government in this lamentable state of affairs included farcical elements. For example, in the city of Van, in an area called Akhtar-Bazg, where there were 70 Armenian households, the Tekyalifi Harbiye demanded 50 *ichligs* (*foufayga*), 50 pairs of socks, 50 pairs of undergarments, five *mezar* (towels) to dry cracked

Recruitment in Van (1914)

wheat (*tsavar* and *gorgod*). Although they also demanded horse-saddles, they accepted five pieces of felt and five carpets instead, as it was difficult to find saddles in town. Of course, such demands did not end there – they were repeated three times, and collected three times. Similar demands were made in all quarters.

But the farcical element remained. One day the government demanded yoghurt from the town quarters, as it was unable to feed the army. They placed a large cauldron in a house in the middle of a quarter, and every household, once a week, brought their yoghurt to fill the pot for the army.

To turn to the tragic once more, the state was short of pack animals because of the great need to transport supplies and war materials. Therefore, the government started to confiscate people's carts and pack animals. One newspaper in Boulanik reported:

> They registered all of the sledges belonging to Armenians in the district, as well as oxen, buffaloes, horses, mules and donkeys – all of which were prepared – so that they could transport the army supplies as needed. Now the work in the fields has stopped... The government has not left a single ox, cart, horse, mule, or donkey. Life has stopped and the alarm can be heard from the plain of Erzeroum.

Such was the seferberlik and Tekyalifi Harbiye in Ottoman Turkey.

Chapter VI

The Turkish Government's Probes

Mobilisation began and all men between 20 and 45 were called up without exception. They gathered at registration centres, though many took flight because there was no proper organisation. Furthermore, many households were left without providers and dissatisfaction set in. Both Muslims and Christians fled. Armenians found preparations for conscripts to be particularly unfair and in some places they fled in large numbers – a natural reaction following the unlawful arrangements.

However, these desertions were not planned. Armenian leaders did not support such behaviour and advised people to carry out their civic duties in full, though the notion of civic duties in the Ottoman Empire was questionable. By Armenian leaders, we do not have in mind the representative bodies in Constantinople and the provinces, nor the Patriarchate and the Prelacies which were generally loyal and supportive of the government's arrangements; we mean the leading organisation operating on the ground, the Armenian Revolutionary Federation (ARF).

When the European war broke out and the Ottoman Empire declared mobilisation, the ARF was holding its General Assembly in Erzeroum. Consequently, the General Assembly put these new developments on its agenda and proclaimed that Ottoman Armenians, as Ottoman citizens, were obliged to perform their civic duties.

An incident that took place during those months should be mentioned, as it illustrated how the ARF conducted itself during mobilisation.

A large number of youngsters in Van opposed mobilisation and did not register as required. The local state authorities noticed these infractions and resorted to force. On the 3rd or 4th day after the declaration of mobilisation, a group of gendarmes appeared in the main square in Ararouts quarter and forced all Armenians to the local government building. This naturally created a tense situation.

The ARF representative, Aram, was absent from the city at that time. He was travelling in the provinces as a diocesan inspector and returned after the incident at Ararouts quarter had taken place.

"This is not a good sign and we have to do something about it," he thought. He then invited 300 young men to meet him and led them in a procession from Aykesdan to the governor, accompanied by a fanfare of drums and pipes. The governor thanked Aram for his exemplary conduct. All of the young men were registered and the incident was forgotten.

There were still some desertions, but they remained incidental, as Armenian leaders, who were well-informed of the situation, were advising people to carry out their civic duties.

But what was the Ottoman government doing? What was it doing to win over Armenians and gain their loyalty?

After the declaration of mobilisation, the Young Turk government ended the promised Armenian Reforms with one stroke of the pen, though these reforms had been the result of several decades of work.

As mentioned earlier, the Inspectors General of the Armenian provinces, Hoff and Westenenk, had been sent from Constantinople and were still on their way when mobilization was announced. Hoff reached Van on August 17, 1914. The governor of the province, Tahsin Bey, who was an influential Young Turk, did not pay much attention to him and sent Armenag Effendi, the provincial translator, to greet him. Hoff, who expected a more fitting reception, was offended and did not stop in Van. Instead, immediately after seeing the governor, he proceeded to Ardamed and wrote a blunt note to the governor, saying that he would be coming to the city formally on August 22. This was a protest against the governor's inappropriate behaviour. The letter had its intended effect and on August 22 the governor officially welcomed Hoff with great pomp and ceremony outside his office, in the presence of high civil and military officials. After that reception, Hoff visited the foreign consulates and the Armenian prelacy, where many Armenians of Van had gathered. Encouraged by this welcome, Hoff returned to Ardamed.

The welcome shown by Armenians to Hoff did not please the governor, who let his feelings be known.

After a few days, on August 29, Hoff received a telegram from Minister of Interior Talaat Bey with the following message: "In light of the European war and the mobilisation of our country, we are ending the implementation of reforms for the time being and ask you to return to Constantinople."

On October 31, Hoff left Ardamed without passing through Van and returned to Constantinople via Garjgan. The Armenian Reforms issue was thus buried. That was how the Young Turk government conducted itself at a time when it had the support of Armenians and the ARF representative had led a procession of young men to conscription at the government office to show Armenian loyalty to the state. It is not difficult to imagine what Armenians might have thought following Hoff's departure.

The Young Turk government was passing through a strange period at that time. While it dismissed the proposed Armenian Reforms, it also asked for Armenian support by making stupid promises. The weak Ottoman government had become an instrument of Germany and dreamed of attacking the Russian Empire and occupying the Caucasus. It pinned its hopes on the support of the people of the Caucasus. It was sure of the support of Caucasian Muslims, and naive enough to believe in Georgian support, but it remained unsure of Armenian backing.

Thus, during mobilisation, when the ARF General Assembly was finishing its meeting in Erzeroum, three Young Turk representatives arrived from Constantinople for a meeting with ARF leaders.

The Turkish representatives were Naji Bey, Boukhar Eddin and Hilmi Bey. They approached the ARF representatives Vramian, Agnouni and Rosdom and asked them to spread propaganda amongst Armenians in the Caucasus and Persia, in order to organise volunteers and support Ottoman forces against Russia.

ARF General Assembly Participants, Erzeroum (Garin), 1914

"There will be war. A Caucasian rising is a certainty. The people of Daghestan, the Turks, even Georgians will rise. Let the Armenians join them, and in return, we promise to give Armenians autonomy," the Turkish representatives said. And to illustrate their words, they produced a map with new boundaries where the provinces of Tiflis and Kutais, the region of Batumi and a part of Trabizon were given to Georgia. All of Daghestan, the province of Baku and part of Kantsag province were given to the Caucasian Turks. The region of Kars, Yerevan province, and a part of Kantsag, as well as Van and a part of Bitlis were given to an autonomous Armenia.

The ARF representatives listened to these proposals and were amazed how the Turkish representatives pretended to be stupid. The Turks had been unable to accept the proposed Armenian Reforms and wrecked them, and now they were promising three Caucasian and three Ottoman provinces to Armenians. The ARF representatives responded by stating that they could not accept such a proposal, that Armenians in the two Empires should carry out their respective duties to their governments, and that the Ottoman state should not enter the war because the country would only suffer.

Naturally, the Turkish representatives were dissatisfied by such a response and left, considering the Armenian position to be treachery. There were similar proposals made to Armenians in Moush and Van with the same results. The matter was thus settled.

After the Erzeroum meeting, the Ottoman government's position towards Armenians changed. The ARF activists at the Erzeroum meeting were placed under surveillance and expelled from the city. A few Caucasian Armenian students who were undertaking studies in Moush and Sassoun were arrested and escorted to Erzeroum and then to the Caucasus.

In addition to the pressures of mobilisation and military taxation, the Armenian population in these regions was now actively hounded.

Ottoman authorities also decided not to arm Armenians. They took this step in an indirect manner, by reviving an old law, whereby people were allowed to avoid conscription by paying a 43 lira exemption tax. Although that law could have applied to everyone, the offer was only made to Armenians. This was a shrewd step to keep Armenians disarmed while enriching the coffers of the state. Many young Armenians chose to pay and be exempted from conscription, if only temporarily. They were asked to pay again and again, until, as will be seen, they were sent to their terrifying deaths.

However, the majority of Armenian conscripts could not afford the exemption tax and had to bear arms until they were eventually disarmed and massacred.

These early measures concerning Christians led to Armenian mistrust and suspicion of the government's intentions. The government gave further reasons for concern when it began harassing Armenian officials. The word "harassment" is not enough to explain what was happening because the appointment of Armenian officials not only petered out but many Armenian officials were actually dismissed from office. The number of such officials in Armenian regions was not great, a tiny proportion compared to the Armenian population, as they had only been appointed during the few years of the Constitutional era. Those Armenians had been appointed because the government had wanted to win Armenians over to its side, but these same officials were now removed from office and sent away without any satisfactory explanation.

For example, before the start of the Russo-Turkish war, the authorities removed the kaimakam of Girjanis [sic] district in the province of Erzeroum, who happened to be Krikor Zohrab's brother.* They also removed Bedros Bey, the kaimakam of Alchavaz district and appointed Naji Bey of Van.

These were Armenian kaimakams, that is, responsible local officials who might have had some significant influence on the government. But the authorities also dismissed others who had practically no influence on it, such as the three police officers in Van – Boghos Der Boghosian, Shahen Prtoian and Armenag Shadakhtsian – whom the authorities proposed to transfer to Mosul, resulting in two of the men resigning their positions.

The authorities were not satisfied with the dismissal of such Armenian officials and also showed their negative disposition in the appointment of new officials as well. For example, the governor of Van, Tahsin Bey, who was considered an educated and often fair-minded man, was appointed as the governor of Erzeroum prior to the outbreak of the Russo-Turkish war. In his stead came the mutesarrif of Bashkale, Jevdet Bey, who was Enver Bey's brother-in-law. Jevdet, who was already known as a bad character, was the son of the former governor of Van, Tahar [Tahir] Pasha.

At the beginning of 1908, a few months before the constitutional revolution, one of the ARF activists in Van, Tavit, who was upset by his comrades, betrayed the whereabouts of a cache of hidden weapons belonging to the ARF. During this period, the governor of Van was a despicable man called Ali Bey. He lost his position after the 1908 Constitution

---

* We have not been able to identify such a district of Erzeroum or the appointment of Krikor Zohrab's brother to it. — A.S.

and, during his return journey to Constantinople via the Caucasus, was shot dead by a vengeful Armenian in Batumi.

Following the searches resulting from Tavit's betrayal, an arms' cache was discovered at Sourp Krikor (St. Gregory) monastery and led to many arrests and abuses. During this period, the kaimakam of Saray achieved particular notoriety, when he accused a merchant from Van, Bedros Piroumian of Khachan village in Abaghay, of being a revolutionary. The kaimakam ordered two cats to be dropped into Bedros' undergarments and beaten with a stick so that the animals would cut up the poor man's body. Bedros only survived for a day after that ordeal.

Not content with what he had done, the brutal kaimakam gave a terrible beating to Bedros' 12 year-old son, Sarkis, and then had horse-shoes nailed to the child's feet to force a confession about the whereabouts of other weapons. The kaimakam was thereafter called the horseshoer [*nalband*] kaimakam. That kaimakam was Jevdet Bey, who was promoted from his position in Saray to that of mutesarrif at Bashkale, and then governor of Van. Could there have been any doubts that the Turkish government was not preparing to carry out the persecution of Armenians when it appointed Jevdet-the-horseshoer as the governor of Van?

However, the main cause of Armenian distrust regarding the government's intentions was the treatment of Armenian and Muslim recruits in the army. While Muslims were sent to well-ordered units, Armenians were sent to poor ones. Muslims were favoured and allowed to remain close to their home towns and villages, while Armenians were sent to far away places. Muslims were given arms, while Armenians were mostly used as labourers to dig trenches and work on roads. Such discrimination was apparent even in the early days of mobilisation.

The 1914 conscription into the Ottoman army was followed by similar conscription into the gendarmerie and its local and mobile units. The differences between local and mobile units was clear, especially the advantages given the former in terms of billeting, clothing, food, and other criteria.

The first dubious steps against Armenians were taken during the initial registration process. Very few Armenians were able to register in their local units, the exceptional cases being due to interventions made by key intermediaries. The authorities made special efforts to send Armenians far away from their homes, usually to mobile units in unfamiliar regions. Additionally, from the outset, Armenian recruits were left without the simplest training, unlike the previously trained and better clad Muslim soldiers.

One obvious case of the offensive treatment of Armenians was the manner in which they were led to believe that there were not enough arms for all recruits, followed by the advice that Armenians should simply go to their main units for all necessary military supplies. Needles to say, Muslim conscripts received arms at the outset as a matter of priority, though this was also partly because they were already trained soldiers. Afterwards, as if it were special treatment, officials often stated that instead of bearing arms, Armenians should do what they were supposedly most suited to do – working as craftsmen and labourers. This major separation in the army was demanded by the highest authorities of the state.

As one conscript, H. Kaligian, described the Turkish government's policies towards Armenians during mobilisation in Van:

> One does not need to be a psychologist to understand the heart-breaking condition of Armenian conscripts, as they were insulted and required to do belittling work on roads, trenches, or in supply stores, while Muslims – often illiterate Kurds – marched proudly past them with their rifles slung on their shoulders, as if they were the masters of the land.

Given these circumstances, Armenian soldiers subjected to such abusive conditions began to desert. Such desertions started principally amongst those working on roads and trenches, where, along with physical difficulties, they had to endure inadequate shelter, lack of food and scant clothing. Very few Armenians serving under arms deserted before the outbreak of the Russo-Turkish war.

The Ottoman authorities were planning for war with Russia and the Turkish government persecuted Armenians because the latter sympathised with the Russians. These Turkish plans were quite apparent from the first days of mobilisation.

* * *

When Great Britain declared war on Germany on August 6 [sic], 1914, it confiscated two warships that had been ordered by the Turkish government, the *Sultan Osman* and *Mehmed the Conqueror*. These warships were close to completion at the British Armstrong shipyard and were confiscated by the British government, which paid the Ottomans for them in accordance with military law.

At the same time, the Ottoman government bought two warships from Germany and these immediately sailed to the Bosphorus. These were the *Geoben* and the *Breslau*.

It is ridiculous to think that Germany at that time, when it had declared war on several countries and needed warships herself, would sell two of its best warships to the Turks. The truth was that Germany did not sell those warships but simply sent them to the Bosphorus under the Turkish flag in order to attack Russia when needed. These arrangements were early indications of the future plans of Ottoman Turkey which had declared itself a neutral power.

But Russian leaders at that time were too preoccupied to anticipate Turkish plans.

A second Ottoman plan of action against the Russians was the formation of militias and irregular forces (*chetes*). The militia or *milis* forces were composed of men between the ages of 17 and 20, and those over 45. These were people who were not conscripted during the general mobilisation and their ranks included Kurdish deserters. These militia forces were to replace the gendarmes who were to be sent to the front.

The irregular forces were given particular attention and the Turkish government pinned great hopes on them. The authorities picked the most experienced and well-known soldiers from the reserves for the new units, which were to perform the most audacious tasks.

One member of these forces was the representative of the Young Turks, Naji Bey, who had come to Erzeroum from Constantinople to meet with representatives of the ARF. He

The Central Powers, August, 1914

chose 3,000 of the best soldiers in Erzeroum and Van and led them to Persia to agitate against the Russians and start operations if needed.

The irregular forces were composed of Circassian and Laz fighters who were well known for their daring exploits, as well as Kurdish tribes which had already distinguished themselves by their brutality. Since these elements were not sufficient for the tasks ahead, they were joined by convicted criminals and murderers who were released from prisons, fugitive Kurdish tribal leaders who were granted pardons in return for their cooperation, and Hamidiye Kurds.

All of these efforts were against Russia. However, the Turkish government had become so audacious that it prepared for war not only against Russia, but also Great Britain and France. It did not reflect on the bloodcurdling nature of its undertaking.

On 14 October, 1914, the Turkish government announced the abolition of the Capitulations. These were the series of concessions which European countries had gained by treaties over the centuries to protect their nationals in Ottoman Turkey. As was mentioned earlier, the Young Turk government rescinded these privileges with one stroke of the pen, thus challenging Europe, especially France, Great Britain and Russia.

These developments were accompanied by relentless pro-German propaganda in the Ottoman Empire. Many such newspaper and telegraphic reports were spread throughout the country while French, British and Russian sources were censored in Constantinople and not allowed to be sent to the provinces. Turkish newspapers were full of exaggerated and embellished reports of German victories. Opposition papers, especially Armenian and Greek newspapers, were self-censored and remained muted.

Such propaganda had great impact in the Ottoman Empire so that those who wavered in their support of the state were heartened, those who doubted became supporters, and those who already supported became fanatical. These developments were accelerated by a number of Russian failures on the German front.

One has to stress the importance of such propaganda because Ottoman mobilisation had been very unpopular in many circles, including amongst ordinary people. For example, on the border with Russia, in the provinces of Van, Bitlis and Erzeroum, the Muslim population was against both mobilisation and Ottoman participation in the war. This was not only the case in the villages but also in the big cities. The Muslim population had a high regard for the Russian government and army, and they doubted they could oppose a Russian advance for even one day. They were against the war that was looming on the horizon.

According to Armenian sources, Muslims, including Kurds, approached their Armenian neighbours in towns and villages with the offer: "We will defend you if the government oppresses you, and you will protect us if the Russians occupy our lands." They tried to win over Armenians in any way they could and wanted to remain on good terms. They were convinced the Russians would win if there was war.

Not only ordinary people, but also government officials were against the war, and there were many cases where Turkish officials expressed their absolute opposition to the war and the general stance of the Young Turks' political party. For example, as Nazaret Mardirosian, the former secretary of Moush prelacy and correspondent to Constantinople newspapers related:

> On August 4, Sdepan Vartabed Baghdasarian, the Vicar of Sassoun prelacy and abbot of Bedros Arakel Monastery and I were with Asad Bey, the kaimakam of Sassoun, when he received the telegram announcing mobilisation. At that time I was the treasurer (*sandegh emini*) in Kabiljoz and was very close to the kaimakam as his employee. The kaimakam was an Ittihadist of Albanian origin. When he read the telegram, he exclaimed in great distress, *"Bu hiukmat patajak!"* [This country will be destroyed]. He then threw the order on a table and added, "Our government borrowed money from the French to look after its needs at home, and now it is buying guns with that money to fight the French." He kept repeating himself in such a negative tone, against war and mobilisation, *"Bu hiukmat patajak!"*

This Ottoman kaimakam spoke out in such a manner during the mobilization as did other officials. The exceptions were some high officials and a few of their Turkish supporters who had strong ties to the Ittihadist party in Constantinople and were encouraged by Germany.

The war started in Europe and with it began German propaganda in Constantinople. The Young Turk propagandists went to the provinces, and official and unofficial German agents flooded the country with telegrams and newspapers with one-sided news in favour of Germany. They covered all corners of the country and excited the people who started to believe in the extraordinary power and invincibility of the Germans.

However, before discussing the actual outbreak of the Russo-Turkish War, we should examine developments in the Caucasus.

Chapter VII

The Volunteer Movement

During the 18th and 19th centuries, especially the 19th, the fate of Armenians was tied to the success of Russian arms in the Caucasus. The more successes the Russians had, the more security and well-being Armenians enjoyed.

Starting from the beginning of the 17th century, the Armenians of the Ottoman Empire and Persia turned their orientation towards Russia, which was a rapidly expanding Christian state at the expense of its two backward Asiatic neighbours.

Since Armenians in the Ottoman Empire and Persia could not find opportunities to cultivate their ancient cultural identity, they looked to Russia, under whose protection they could make progress. This was why, starting from Peter the Great, Armenian secular and religious leaders supported the Russian expansion against the Persians and Ottoman Turks.

For example, Israel Ori, Archbishop Hovsep Argoutian, Nerses Ashdaragetsi and others appealed to Russian rulers to free Siunik and the lands of Ararat from Persian rule and to establish an Armenian principality under Russian protection.

During the 18th century, with the Russian advance and occupation of the northern and western shores of the Caspian Sea as far a Baku, Russia established a foothold in the South Caucasus. In the 19th century, they occupied Siunik, Georgia, and later in 1827, 1856 and 1877, the khanates of Yerevan and Nakhichevan, the regions of Alexandropol and Kars, and the south-east of the Black Sea.

Every time there was a Russo-Persian or Russo-Turkish War, Armenians gave their full support to the Russians, not only by guiding them through enemy territory, but also passing information about their adversaries, welcoming Russian armies with crosses and holy standards, and often providing material supplies. Armenians even organised volunteer groups to join the advance units of the Russian forces. Throughout these developments, Armenians were acting in their own interests.

Several times in the past, groups of Armenian volunteers joined the Russian army, but such contributions were only really noted during the occupation of Siunik and the Ararat regions.

During the 1827 war, Nerses Ashdaragetsi, the prelate of Tiflis, left all spiritual work and entered the conflict, agitating Armenians at the head of volunteer forces. The 1827 volunteer movement started in Tiflis and many Armenians, both from the city and the wider province, entered it. On April 13, volunteers drilled at Ghabakh Square, now called the Aleksandrian Garden, with Nerses Ashdaragetsi on horseback encouraging them. On May 28, in a grand ceremony at the mother church of the monastery, Armenian volunteers took the oath and had their flag anointed. This actual flag, as far as known, is now kept in Echmiadzin museum.

The Armenian volunteer group was issued arms by the government, had its own uniform, and received support from the treasury. The families of the volunteers were free of all taxes. The military unit was led by Armenian officers who received pay according to their rank from the treasury.

Nerses Ashdaragetsi, who headed the volunteer movement and called on all Armenians to support it, expected something in return. He not only wanted the liberation of Armenians from Persian rule, but also the autonomy of the lands of Ararat as an Armenian province. This was Nerses Ashdaragetsi's vision, which was never realised.

So, the birth of a volunteer movement at the beginning of the present war [1914] in the Caucasus was not unprecedented. However, while appearances were similar, the circumstances were different.

During earlier wars, both Persia and the Ottoman Empire were despotic countries where Armenians were subject to persecution and misrule. During the latest war, the Ottoman Empire was a constitutional state and Armenians were in an incomparably better position than at earlier times.

On the other hand, Armenians in the past had enjoyed the Russian government's flattery and encouragement, though in the last two or three decades, the same government's – or more accurately – the Caucasian administration's attitude towards Armenians had changed. This change had been sudden and extreme, as the Golytsin regime's authoritarianism had led to the closure of Armenian parish schools and the confiscation of church properties whose income supported the schools. Armenians had also experienced the Armeno-Turkish clashes of 1905–06, and the persecutions of 1909, when many members of the intelligentsia throughout the Caucasus had been accused of being members of the ARF and imprisoned or exiled. Some were sent to penal colonies, many escaped abroad, and others chose to work in the Ottoman Empire, where they were not only free from persecution but even courted by Ottoman officials.

Such were the conditions in the Caucasus until the middle of 1912, when the Russian embassy in the Ottoman Empire took a new interest in Armenians. By the middle of 1913, the Russian government changed its tone and presented the European powers with a reform plan for Ottoman Armenia. It thus revived the Armenian reforms plan exactly at a time when the anti-Ottoman alliance in the Balkans had collapsed and the former allies – Bulgaria, Serbia, Montenegro and Greece – had turned against each other.

During the following two years, Armenian intellectual circles and their press in the Caucasus were preoccupied with the Armenian Question in the Ottoman Empire. The subject was examined at special meetings and in the press, as well as by official and unofficial bodies. Nothing else seemed to matter.

Soon, the Armenian issue was once more raised in diplomatic circles and engaged the embassies of the Great Powers in Constantinople. The Russian Embassy defended the Armenian Reforms plan and the Russian Foreign Minister did not miss an opportunity to discuss it, even in the State Duma. In a word, the disposition of Petrograd's high officials towards Armenians suddenly changed, including those circles which had advocated keeping the ARF under close scrutiny three years earlier.

The Caucasus was now ruled by a clever diplomat, the best representative of the Russian bureaucracy, a man known in Russia as a free thinker. He was Count Vorontsov-Dashkov. None of the former viceroys or governors of the Caucasus had understood the Caucasus and the interests of Russia as well as Vorontsov-Dashkov.

He did not resort to the whip or any other force. He was a gentle and good governor. Not only that, he was not an oppressor of different nations, nor an advocate of crude and forced Russification: he was a tender governor who achieved a great deal in the Caucasus – and a great deal for Russia. If everything he did was put to one side and only one thing he did for Armenians was to be recalled, it would be the return of confiscated church properties and the opening of parish schools. And if one considers the positive attitude of Armenians towards Russia today, one can see how clear-sighted Vorontsov-Dashkov had been. His genius as a Russian official was reflected in the brilliant report he presented to the Tsar about the Caucasus and Armenians.

Only time will tell how genuine Vorontsov-Dashkov was in his support of the actual interests of Armenians. This matter is debatable and will need time for a clear answer, but it cannot be denied that the Count had particularly friendly relations with Armenians, especially the high clergy.

The friendly attitude shown by high authorities in Petrograd towards Armenians, combined with a wise state official like Vorontsov-Dashkov in the Caucasus, meant that the Armenian upper classes and clergy, who had been demoralised and reserved, could now assume leading positions in Armenian affairs in the Caucasus.

Armenians formed a national body in Tiflis, and it was later called the "National Bureau." Similar bodies were set up in other cities with large Armenian communities. The representatives of these bodies often held meetings in Tiflis and focused on the question of Armenian reforms. This subject was examined from different perspectives and in great detail. The Tiflis body liaised with Echmiadzin, Armenian communities in Moscow and Petrograd, as well as certain well-known Armenians and friends in Europe. The Tiflis committee, which was considered the main organising centre, was not a legal entity, though its existence was well known and the government clearly knew of its activities.

This committee gradually gained a following because the government did not put any obstacles in its way. Many members of the intelligentsia sat side-by-side with rich merchants and clergymen at its meetings. All of this was possible because of the government's positive attitude towards Armenians, who even asked high officials for the pardon of convicted or exiled Armenians, such as ARF members who had escaped abroad.

It was under such conditions that the European War broke out in 1914. Germany threw down the gauntlet to Russia, while the Ottoman Empire showed its appetite for war.

Soon, the Armenian contribution to the last Russo-Turkish war [1877–78] was invoked, as the authorities tried to tap Armenian support. Following the wishes of the National Committee in Tiflis, they even allowed the return of a number of ARF activists who had been exiled from the Caucasus.

With the outbreak of the European War, there were new possibilities concerning the resolution of the Armenian question, and a final settlement became more likely. The realisation of Armenian dreams was now tied to the victory of Russia, France and Great Britain – a victory that promised to be quick. The solution would be to the advantage of Armenians and Russia, with Armenian participation in the war helping to speed up final victory.

Common interests and a series of guarantees led a number of activists to organise the beginning of the volunteer movement in the Caucasus.

This is not the place to examine the organisation of the movement in great detail but it should be noted that the heroes of Caucasian Armenians stepped forward: these were people who had led demonstrations against the confiscation of Armenian properties by Tsarist authorities, fought in the Armeno-Tatar clashes [1905], or participated in the Persian revolution [1905-11]. Such heroes were allowed by the Russian authorities to become the leaders of volunteer units. They were:

1. Antranig: Antranig Ozanian from Shabin Karahissar, the hero of Sassoun.
2. Dro: Drasdamat Ganaian from Igdir.
3. Keri: Arshag Kavafian of Erzeroum, an old guard.
4. Vartan: Hero of Khanasor, Arshag Mehrabian of Shoushi
5. Hamazasb: Hamazasb Srvantsdian of Van.
6. Tashnagtsagan Khecho: Khachadour Amirian of Old Nakhichevan.
7. Ishkhan: Hovsep Arghoutian, of Tiflis.

Thus the crucial time had arrived. Armenians had to show their valour, and the final resolution of the Armenian question was dependent on their actions.

The National Bureau's call to the Armenian people could be summarised as follows. Young Armenian men, most of whom were army reservists, were quick to join the above-mentioned leaders. The treasury of the National Bureau received donations from everywhere, even large contributions from Europe and the United States. The Russian state gave arms, uniforms, and other materiel so that a number of strong units were quickly set up under their commanders, captains and lieutenants. These ranks included the rich and the poor, the urban dweller and the villager, the intelligentsia and the low-bred. People of all backgrounds came to shed their blood in the red flood that the 20th century brought in such haste.

All of these developments took place openly and everyone could observe them, including the Muslims in the country. Such news soon reached Ottoman Armenians and their government, thus adding to the antipathy of the Young Turks towards Armenians of the Ottoman Empire.

The Ottoman government was amassing its forces at its border, Russia was doing the same on its own side with the support of Armenian volunteers, and the condition of Armenians in the Ottoman Empire was becoming increasingly unbearable.

During this period, the Ottoman government, under the pretext of pursuing Armenian deserters, began entering villages and burning down houses, confiscating properties and even killing people. In the Van region, for example, there were serious incidents in

Antranig   Dro   Keri

Vartan   Hamazasb   Khecho

Ishkhan

Armenian Volunteer
Group Commanders.

GOMIDAS
INSTITUTE

Shoushants, Aliur and other villages over a brief period. There were also murders of ARF activists such as Nazaret Chavoush of Zeitoun, who was incarcerated and strangled in Marash prison. Similarly, the ARF activist Kalousd of Yerevan was killed after being followed from Van to Old Bayazid.

But these were individual killings and there was a need for more systematic steps against Armenians. The Turkish press in Constantinople obliged by publishing provocative anti-Armenian articles, and the Tsar of Russia's call for Armenian support presented a good occasion for them. The Turkish press did not care about the nature of the call or its content: the fact that a call was made provided the pretext for provocative articles against Armenians.

One can see the impact of these developments on Ottoman officials, the military and most importantly, the ignorant Muslim masses. One can also see the terror generated in the hearts of Armenians in the Ottoman provinces and Constantinople as reflected in the following two reports published in the newspaper *Horizon*:

> The more we see of the preparations for war, the greater we fear being massacred, gripped by our throats and wasted away. We can clearly see the danger approaching from afar, as it assumes a real shape and becomes something tangible. And from the skies above, we see skeletal hands reaching out to drag us away by our collars. It will throttle us. Help us, help.

> I am not a madman, nor subject to hallucinations. I can see the monster with my own eyes. I can smell it and feel its presence. This all reminds me of the days before the 1895 and 1909 massacres. They are making preparations, and the signs are there. Whoever has ears, let them hear. Those who can take precautions, let them begin.

These were the conditions in the Caucasus and the Armenian inhabited areas of the Ottoman Empire at the end of October 1914 – on the eve of Russo-Turkish hostilities.

Chapter VIII

The Russo-Turkish War

The outbreak of a Russo-Turkish war was not surprising, given the preparations that had been taking place in the Ottoman Empire. However, the prelude to the war was unexpected. Even on October 28, 1914, the Ottoman government gave Russia friendly overtures. They sent direct messages through Giers, the Russian ambassador in Constantinople, and Fahreddin, the Ottoman ambassador in Petrograd, reassuring Russia that the Ottoman Empire was not going to war and wanted to maintain strict neutrality. That was the sweet eastern melody which the Ottoman government was playing as its warships left the Bosphorous and sailed in a quiet and deceptive manner toward the Russian shores of the Black Sea.

On October 28 and 29, 1914, the main warships of the Ottoman navy, the *Geoben*, *Breslau*, and *Hamidiye*, sailed for Odessa, Theodosia and Novorosisk, where they aimed their big guns at shore positions and started bombarding those cities. The inhabitants fled in terror, as a few buildings were damaged in Theodosia and Odessa, and the fuel storage tanks at Novorosisk were set ablaze. The warship *Donets* was sunk near Odessa, as were the troop carriers *Yalta* and *Kazbek* near Kerch. By the time the much surprised Russian Black Sea fleet came out to meet the enemy, the latter had returned to Turkish waters. This plan was possibly drawn up when Germany first sent its two warships to the Bosphorous.

Russian fury exploded. "Do not spare the devious enemy!" roared Russia, while Russian diplomats showed no interest in hearing an explanation from Constantinople that the attack was carried out without the knowledge of the Ottoman government and that it was a provocation prepared by the German navy. Russia declared war.

The Russian declaration of war was greeted with great fervour:

> Germany and Austro-Hungary, in their failing campaigns against Russia, with a wish to expand their powers by any means, turned to the Ottoman government and led Turkey, which they had themselves blinded, into a war against us. The Turkish navy, led by the Germans, dared to attack our Black Sea shores. Immediately after these attacks, we ordered the Russian ambassador in Constantinople to leave the territories of Turkey with all consular and embassy staff. Russia, completely unruffled and trusting in God, now accepts the new challenge from the old oppressor of Christianity and Slavic peoples. This will not be the first time Russia's powerful forces defeat the Turkish hordes, who will be crushed yet again, as our homeland's audacious enemy.

As the official statement was made, Russian forces received orders to advance on all fronts against the Ottoman Empire, from Batumi to Maku and Lake Ourmiye. The Russians crossed into Ottoman territory on November 1 and their progress was swift.

Between November 2-4, 1914 the Russian forces occupied Id from the direction of Olti; the Zivini fortifications as well as Ardos and Khorasan villages from Sarikamish; the Karaderbend Pass from Kaghizvan; and Bayazid and Diadin from Igdir.

Between October November 4-9, they occupied Keopri Keoy in Pasen, Toprak Kale, Karakilise and the Tapariz heights in the Alashgerd and Bayazid valleys, as well as the Khanasor Pass from Dilman.

On November 15, they occupied Toutagh, on the way to Arjesh and Manazgerd.

At the same time, the Russian navy bombarded Trabizon, as well as Zongouldak. The latter supplied coal to Constantinople.

Between November 18 and 28, Russian forces had a minor setback on their way to Keopri Keoy and pulled back. The Turks sustained significant losses in the fighting and their 28th, 29th, 33rd and 34th divisions suffered heavy casualties.

On December 2, the Russian forces in Persia scattered the Turkish army and its Hamidiye units and occupied the centre of Hekkiari, Bashkale and Saray.

Thus, within one month, the Russians were able to push forward on the entire Turkish front and occupy Keopri Keoy, Alashgerd, Toutagh, Tapariz, Saray and Bashkale.

Armenian volunteer groups (or battalions) fought alongside the Russian forces. They were familiar with the layout of the country and often formed the advance units.

Keri and Hamazasp's battalions moved from Sarikamish; Dro's moved from Igdir; and Antranig's from Dilman. Their successes were noteworthy. Keri and Hamazasp's battalions occupied Toprak Kale; Dro's advanced on Kavre Shamé village of Abagha (where Keri was wounded); and Antranig reached Molla Hasan via Saray, a few hours from the village of Arjag.

Thus Armenian volunteer units and their commanders, fighting in the front lines of the Russian army, came face to face with Ottoman troops. The Ittihadists, who led the Ottoman forces, undoubtedly noted the presence of Armenians in the Russian ranks. Armenian soldiers in the Ottoman army – that is, soldiers who had suffered greatly under Ottoman autocracy – also came face to face with Armenian volunteers in the Russian army and saw their own salvation in those ranks.

The Ottoman army began blaming Armenians for their defeats, while Ottoman-Armenian soldiers, seeing the Russian army and its Armenian volunteers, were increasingly demoralised, stopped shooting, and deserted, often crossing over to the Russian side. These developments eventually led to the mass persecution of Armenians and the greatest deportation and massacre in Armenian in history.

The thing that concerned the Ottomans most, especially the Young Turks, were the Armenian volunteers in Russian ranks. They exaggerated their importance, especially in the region of Van, where Ottoman authorities and Young Turk officers had approached ARF activists several times to halt the Armenian volunteers in Persia. One of those proposals was particularly interesting and is presented here in full.

The Russo-Turkish war had been raging for one and a half months when the representative of the Young Turks, Naji Bey, was in Bashkale. As already mentioned, Naji Bey, Boukhar-Eddin and Hilmi Bey had approached ARF representatives in Erzeroum for

Turco-German Attack on Russia, October, 1914

a special agreement at the beginning of the European War. Now, Naji Bey commanded irregular [*chete*] groups in Bajirgane stirring up trouble against the Russians in Persia.

On December 17, Naji Bey sent the following telegram to Vramian from Bajirgane.

Dec. 17, 1914, Bajirgane

To Ottoman Parliamentary Representative of Van, Vramian Effendi,

It seems clear to the Mosul army and the soldiers and chetes under my command up to the villages in Selham, that the promises made in Erzeroum and Van have been broken. If one were to look at the enemy that approached Bashkale and was forced back two days later, especially Smpad and his friends in Salmast, it becomes quite apparent that the Tashnags [ARF] are working with the Russians. The Armenians are making the mistake of dividing the lion's hide before killing it. I have in my possession a letter for Ishkhan, found in Fahki Osman's possession. Before revealing its contents to the Muslim and Ottoman press, I wish to warn you for the last time that your political party, which pays great heed to Karl Marx and Kropotkin, has become the instrument of Russian Tsarism. This is a most risible development in the 20th century. I will be treating your few hundred comrades in Persia as Russians.

Eomer Naji

PS Fahki Osman related everything to Uncle [the Russians]. He sends his greetings to Ishkhan. The letter was written in a very convoluted manner. I could not understand its meaning. I am sending it to you for translation. It was not written on paper, but on cloth, and then sewn into Osman's collar.

Same.

Vramian responded to Naji Bey's telegram.

We have no information about such a letter. It is possible that Smpad has written it on his own initiative. In any case, I am not aware whether he has any standing.

Perhaps, having gathered a few people around him, he is working on his own account. Their greatest anxiety might be the danger facing Armenians in this country.

They might have heard of the recent massacres at Bashkale; the destruction of Mantan and Heresan villages by irregular forces; the outrageous treatment and murder of Armenians by gendarmes who remain unpunished; the sacking of villages during the movement of Hamidiye troops; the disregard of protests sent to the government; the outrageous behaviour and barbarities committed against Armenian villages; and finally, the disarming of all Armenians in the gendarmerie and their dispatch to Bitlis. All of these developments have led to great disquiet. It is possible that they, having heard of what is going on, wanted to come to the rescue.

You should know that the ARF Committee cannot be the instrument of any state. Regarding Fahki's letter, though I have no information about it, I can confirm that Ishkhan Effendi has not had any communication with Uncle, nor could he have had any. It is possible that there may be a misunderstanding or that we are dealing with a false accusation.

If the government had acted as I suggested to you, we would not be in these difficulties now, nor would you be raising these questions with me. Anyhow, we have not lost our hope in you.

Vramian

A similar proposal was made by the governor of Van, Jevdet. As soon as the Russo-Turkish War had been declared, Jevdet transferred his duties to the mutasarrif of Bashkale and went to the front, as did some kaimakams, including the kaimakam of Shadakh. They went in the spirit of patriotism. During the end of September, Jevdet was in Saray, when he suggested to Vramian and Aram that they should ride to Salmast and disperse the Armenian volunteer groups. Vramian and Aram responded by stating that they were ready to do so on the condition that Ottoman-Armenian volunteers were allowed to serve near their homes with their weapons. Jevdet did not accept this suggestion and Vramian and Aram remained where they were.

Indeed, while Turkish officials were trying to win over Ottoman Armenian notables to stop the Caucasian volunteers, they were also persecuting Armenians.

Turkish officials first accused Armenians of being traitors and disarmed Armenian soldiers. These were not isolated cases but quite extensive.

In the middle of November, when serious fighting raged around Keopri Keoy and the Russian army in Persia was moving towards Saray and Bashkale, there were over 20 Ottoman *tabours* (battalions) in the province of Van – at Pergri, Abagha, Arjag, Khoshab and Bashkale. Significantly, when the Ottomans prepared to send these battalions against the Russians, they first separated and disarmed the Armenians serving in them. For example, they disarmed Armenians serving in the 4th and three other battalions in Pergri, the 15th and 16th battalions in Arjag, and the 17th and 18th battalions in Khoshab. They disarmed Armenian soldiers in many regions – demeaning, insulting and humiliating them in the process.

These Armenians soldiers were a large proportion of the above-mentioned battalions, often a third, so thousands of Armenians were disarmed. Afterwards, these soldiers were formed into the so-called *amalia tabours*, or workers' battalions. They repaired roads, dug trenched at the front lines, or worked as pack animals carrying supplies on their backs. They had to do all the menial work that was demanded of them. As if these tasks were not enough, regular soldiers were allowed to insult and mock them. After all, Armenians no longer enjoyed the confidence of the government and were considered as outcasts.

Such treatment might have been of no consequence if the men in question were not subjected to further mistreatment and given the means to survive. However, after being disarmed, Armenian conscripts were deprived of their uniforms and had to wear their own clothes while working. Their access to food and shelter was limited. They were kept in animal shelters and barns, with no

German postcard depicting the alliance between Germany, Austro-Hungary and Ottoman Turkey.

bedding or cover. They were only given bread to eat, infrequently, and often in the form of flour. The poor Armenian soldiers had to prepare their bread with no utensils or fuel for baking. It was no easy task to labour all day on an empty stomach with nowhere to sleep at night and no proper clothing. This was the background to the mass desertions that took place as the government simply looked on. The older soldiers started to flee from the day they were disarmed. It is surprising that the authorities did not take steps to stop it. For example, when the Armenian soldiers in the 15th and 16th battalions in Arjag were disarmed, many fled as the authorities watched.

When the Russian armies crossed into Ottoman territory, the abuse of Armenian soldiers was relatively minor, but the mistreatment became more acute after the declaration of *Jihad* (Holy War). Armenian soldiers, armed or disarmed, began to be shot under various pretexts, and the murder of groups and individuals increased. For example, in the middle of December, after the great battle of Keopri Keoy, when the Ottoman forces were defeated, around 50 Armenian soldiers took refuge in the village of Yeghan. However, only these 50 Armenians were apprehended in the region as deserters and shot. This mass execution, which was witnessed by a wounded Armenian officer, took place without any trial or charges. Such executions took place in several places and individuals continued to be killed every day under different pretexts. We know that such murders were part of a general policy because of the testimonies of eye-witnesses.

Boghos Balabekian, who was a medical doctor at a military hospital on the Persian border near Kotour, received a letter in the middle of January from Kiazim Bey, the commander of the mobile gendarmerie:

> The Kurds are attacking and killing Armenian soldiers on the roads. Do not send any Armenian soldiers away without the company of Muslims. I pity Armenians who are good, loyal, and invaluable soldiers, even if there are a few bad people among them.

Kiazim Bey's note concerned the movement of wounded Armenian soldiers who were sent home. This Muslim officer was undoubtedly relating confidential information when writing this letter to his friend, the Armenian doctor.

The same Armenian doctor, on his way to Van, also saw the suffering of disarmed Armenian soldiers who had to carry unbearable loads. They were beaten mercilessly with sticks and left to starve for days. He witnessed such incidents on his way, as did others, and could not hold back his tears as he related what he knew.

The Ottoman government's barbaric treatment was not limited to Armenian soldiers. It also extended to peaceful Armenian civilians in towns and villages. One incident amongst many others may be related here to compare to the cruelties under Sultan Abdul Hamid II.

With the declaration of war, the Ottoman government pardoned all murderers and thieves in prisons, as well as fugitive leaders of various gangs who had ravaged the country in the past. Among the latter was Bshare Chato, a well-known tribal leader from Modgan in Bitlis province.

This man was related to Seyid Ali, who was hanged after the Kurdish uprising in Bitlis in March 1914. Bshare Chato had become a bandit because the government was after him. Around 1913, the authorities had gone to his village with an armed force that included a cannon, taken his family prisoner, destroyed his village, but failed to capture him. A similar attempt to arrest him was made after the 1914 hangings in Bitlis, but Chato could not be caught. Worse, Chato captured a captain and ten soldiers. He had the soldiers shot and the captain hanged in response to the hangings that had taken place in Bitlis. Despite all this, Bshare Chato was pardoned by the authorities in 1914 and invited to the battlefield with his Kurdish followers.

Bshare Chato and more than 600 Kurds, half of them mounted and half on foot, thus came to Manazgerd at the middle of December. They were then armed by the authorities and made their way to Saray through Patnos, Arjesh and Pergri. This band resembled one of Sheykh Jalaleddin's gangs, except for their government issued weapons. They wore similar clothing and their needs were met by the villages on their way. It is not difficult to imagine what happened in the villages where Bshare Chato's gang lodged.

One Armenian eyewitness related how enraged Lieutenant Erza Bey, a friend of the captain who had been hanged by Bshare Chato, was when he saw the gang leader in

Manazgerd. Ezra Bey screamed, "This country is doomed! They are sending the robber who hanged a captain to join us against the Russians."

Thus, this criminal and his gang passed from one Armenian village to another, foraging and gorging on their way. Two such villages on the road to Arjesh were Hasbusinag and Haroutiun. Chato, who was not in a hurry to get to his destination, stayed in each village for a whole day. The inhabitants of Hasbusinag provided lodging, fuel, and plenty of food to avoid any complaints or incidents, but Bshare Chato also demanded a woman for his pleasure. However, when the head of the household, Setrag Agha, refused his obscene demand, he was punished as a result. His suffering became very well known. They beat the poor man so badly that he passed out. Not content with what they had done, Chato ordered skewers to be put into a fire and Setrag Agha's hands and face were burnt with the red hot irons. The local authorities did not intervene and allowed the torture to continue. Bshare Chato then proceeded with impunity and behaved in the same manner in Giuzag and Kordzout villages of Pergri, as well as at Daghveran in Arjag. The old barbaric regime was thus revived with such outrages.

As conditions got worse, the Armenian population in the war zones started to flee to the Caucasus and the centuries' old fate of Armenians – flight and migration – was repeated once more. "In the Armenian inhabited regions, where the fighting has been taking place, people are fleeing across the Russian border," stated an eye-witness. "Their caravans paint a sad picture, as they pass in their thousands, their carts pulled by donkeys and oxen, deprived of their homes, helpless. There is nowhere for them to stay and they remain cold, hungry and naked under open skies." Another observer wrote, "Kurds have attacked Khorasan village in Pasen and killed nine men and abducted 30 women." The persecution of Armenians thus gained momentum and pleased Muslims.

In late November [1914] the Ottomans developed a bold plan. They concentrated their forces on the left flank of the Caucasian front at Artvin, Olti and Sarikamish. They moved the entire Erzeroum garrison there, as well as new forces from Constantinople. They planned to push ahead with all their might, break through the Russian lines, and press into Russian territory through Ardahan and Akhaltskha, as well as into Tiflis through Sarikamish. After occupying these regions according to their strategy, they planned to raise not only the Muslim populations of the Caucasus and Daghestan in an uprising, but also the Georgians with whose help they planned to occupy the whole Caucasus.

Thus, on December 23, the Ottoman army went on the offensive. Their army was composed of the 9th, 10th, 11th and 12th corps, and Enver Pasha came from Constantinople to lead the attack, even though the commander-in-chief in Erzeroum was the well-known Turkish commander, Shoukri Pasha.

The 9th and 10th corps attacked Olti and broke through the weak Russian lines and entered Russian territory. From Olti, the Ottoman forces separated into two columns, one moving towards Sarikamish to occupy the railway line, and the other toward Ardahan. At the same time, a third Ottoman column moved through the Jorokh valley through Artvin and Ardanouch, and also advanced towards Ardahan. The few Russian forces on these fronts and the support given to the attacking Ottoman army by local Muslims meant that the attackers were able to reach Ardahan and Sarikamish with little difficulty, despite the freezing cold and deep snow that was prevalent in those regions.

The Ottoman attack led to much consternation in the Caucasus. The population of Baku, Tiflis and other cities prepared to flee, while state schools received orders to evacuate (some actually began moving to the north Caucasus). There was a danger of general chaos and confusion until the Russians regrouped their forces and stopped the enemy onslaught.

The Ottoman army was destroyed near Sarikamish on December 30, Ardahan on January 3, as well as at Ardanouch and Artvin. They then retreated to the Ottoman border with terrible losses. The roads and snow-filled valleys and slopes were covered in countless dead and frozen corpses.

The 9th and 10th corps practically ceased to exist, a good number having been killed and a large number captured by the Russians. The officers of the 10th corps were also captured, as was the commander of the 9th corps, Iskhan Pasha. The Russians pursued the Ottoman army for a few days and the remnants of the Ottoman army was destroyed and scattered. The Turks continued their flight the following day without regrouping in Erzeroum. The fighting stopped in the Caucasus.

The Turks had marched to Ardahan and Sarikamish very quickly and then, having been crushed, fled to their own borders equally swiftly. This was the reality of December 1914, and the Turkish-Armenian population on the borderlands suffered terribly as a consequence.

Chapter IX

The First Exodus

As already mentioned, at the beginning of the Russo-Turkish war, the Russians occupied a part of the Pasen plateau, Alashgerd, Karakilise, Toutagh, Tapariz, Saray, Bashkale and Ourmiye (Ourmia) as Armenians greeted them with great excitement. Then, on December 29, when the Ottoman army advanced towards Sarikamish and Ardahan, the Russian army was ordered to withdraw. From this point onwards, Armenians and Assyrians, who were left behind by the retreating Russians, experienced a new and far worse wave of violence.

Following the order for the Russians to retreat, Armenians could no longer remain on their lands. The Ottoman army, as well as the Hamidiye forces and Kurds, would turn all of their anger following their defeats on Armenians. This time they would not spare anyone. Armenians knew what was in store and when the Russians began to withdraw, they also retreated with them to the Caucasus. Thus the mass exodus began.

It was one thing to leave under peaceful conditions during summer, but it was very different to take flight, terrified by the enemy, during an icy winter over snow-covered plains and mountains. This was a daunting trek.

Some Armenians had left Pasen in November, when there had been bloody battles there, and settled mostly in the Sarkamish and Kars regions. Now the exodus was from other areas on the border.

On December 29, Armenians left Alashgerd, Toutagh, Karakilise, Diadin and Bayazid regions with the Russian army. They also left from the Saray and Bashkale areas. Later, Armenians and Assyrians were to leave the Ourmiye, Dilman, Khoy and Tabriz regions. Tens of thousands, old and young, men and women, abandoned their homes, fields, animals and belongings, even the food and clothing they needed, and set off on the frozen roads to the Caucasus. The Russian army was withdrawing, the Ottomans and Kurds were advancing, and the refugees were terror stricken.

On January 5, caravans composed of tens of thousands of frozen and starving refugees from Kaghizvan, Igdir and Julfa reached the borders of Yerevan province. It is difficult to imagine how they moved, what they looked like, or where they were heading. A dense mass of people from Kaghizvan, Igdir, and Nakhichevan was moving to Echmiadzin, to engulf Yerevan and its surrounding areas with poverty, hunger, nakedness, frozen faces and endless suffering.

These refugees were observed by the Armenian inhabitants of Yerevan province and Caucasian Armenian newspapers were full of reports of the refugees' plight.

> The Turkish *yataghan* has spread the assassin's terror in Alashgerd and Pasen. It is pure terror. An old sledge of refugees, full of children, has to cross the Euphrates and gets stuck. The river carries off one of the children, then the

second and third. People naturally dive into the water, grab whoever they can, but the river takes its share. The stones cry for the mothers who lose their children.

At Ardzap village, on the other side of the border, four poorly-clad children are crying behind a wall. The eldest is a 12-year-old girl. I approach and inquire after them. She says [quoted in her distinct dialect], "Our mother died on the road; we were left behind; find a way for us, brother, do not leave us, we'll come with you."

We are near Arhaj village, near Igdir, and there is an unburied corpse on the ground. It is of an elderly person. It seems the poor man had just died, holding onto a rock with his hands. He appears to have struggled with death, trying to stand up, to live. But alas, he perished, and his face bore the imprint of the terror of his life.

These sketches were from an eye-witness account entitled, "Some Droplets from the Sea of Suffering."

Upon reaching Igdir, I witness an indescribable, horrible scene. The flow of refugees has become a flood of weary people. They are all wet and covered in mud. It is a cacophony of screaming and shrieking children, wailing women, and men shouting and yelling. Some lie under walls lamenting and cursing their miserable fate. During the panic everyone tries to save themselves. Parents forget their children, children their parents, sisters and brothers. Some mothers leave their suckling children on the road, unable to carry this most precious of loads. Hundreds of parents have lost their children.

One commentator gave the following description in Igdir.

It is late at night. Nothing can be seen in the dark. The mud is awful. I am going home. I can hear some sounds ahead of me in the dark. "Sir, I implore you, brother, we are left here in the mud. Do you have nowhere for us, no means? We lost our friends and family." I turn my oil-lamp in their direction and I can see some dark shapes moving under a wall in the mud. Gradually they stand up, a woman and someone else, holding a child, a man carrying a great load, and then a second woman with children, five and six years' old. They are all blackened, burnt by the cold, their clothes muddy and torn. The man and woman carrying the child are a couple, and the children are their own. The other two women have lost their husbands and remain alone. I try to find them a place to stay, but all houses are full of refugees. There is nowhere for them and I stare at them, confused.

Another eye-witness gave a similar description from Igdir.

A new dawn breaks. We are all standing. We have chosen the school as a centre. It is on a road, 100 paces from the huge bridge on the Arax river which is crossed by refugees. Yesterday's refugees exit the houses and come onto the streets.

"Sir. My children are starving. Give us a little bread."

"I do not need bread, I can stay hungry, but please give some hay for my animals. They are dying of starvation."

"My husband is ill. Give us a little sugar so that I can give him some tea."

"My wife has survived, sir; she wants a spoonful of hot food."

These poor destitute people ask for a thousand and one things and repeat themselves – bread, hay, bread, hay – and we try to help them somehow.

While those who were in the village move on to Echmiadzin, disorderly and confused, in a racket of the creaking carts and children in tears, a new wave of refugees crosses the bridge. An hour later, the flow becomes a torrent. They come in droves, with their noisy carts. They sit on animals, some are on foot, following each other in a file, sometimes holding hands. The mud, the terrible mud, has made them forget everything else. Men, women and children arrive covered in mud, frozen and blue. The endless, tired caravan marches in step, without a beginning or an end. They move in a monotonous manner. Among them are women who are pregnant, or simply old, or carrying children. This sight of a lifeless plodding caravan is sometimes broken with the passage of rented or military supply carts full of refugees. The situation often seems completely chaotic and pitiful with the intermingling of people, animals and carts.

I then notice a carriage full of children, poor children, around 30 of them, who have lost their parents. Some people stop and give them bread out of pity. The children grab the bread and devour it.

The day passes, and the flow of refugees continues unabated. They try to shelter these people in the village, as the convoy stops in its muddy streets. Within an hour, all of the houses are full of the poor refugees, yet the flow continues and new people arrive.

The men working on foot are now hungry, tired and impatient, but continue as expected. As dusk approaches, the flow of people slows down, and the different groups and carts are somehow settled down, with the expectation that there will be no more arrivals. Yet more carts arrive, 5, 10, 15, 20 and then 24, mainly full of women and children. The carts do not stop but continue to an open field on the other side of the village. There is no suitable space for them and many in the column of 24 have to remain outside. It is the middle of January and we feel awful that so many women and children have to remain in the open. But there is no other way. We, more than 15 men, pick up 10 loaves of bread and 10 quilts and cross the muddy streets to the other side of the village. We distribute the bread and quilts and return with sadness. We do what we can, what is possible, but whatever we are able to do is only a drop in the flood that we see all day long.

These were the descriptions of the flood of Turkish-Armenian refugees in this cruel world. But there were also refugees in a worse condition, such as those in Saray, Bashkale and Adrbadagan [north-western Persia] who suffered more terrifying ordeals as they fled. This is how one eye-witness described their condition.

Adrbadagan was emptied of its Armenian population. People from Maragha, Ourmiye and Tabriz, and finally Salmast and Khoy took to the Caucasus. The terror spread by Turkish and Kurdish neighbours forced Armenians to flee. Everyone had one thought, to save themselves.

After the battle of Miandap, people fled overnight from Maragha to Tabriz, and whoever was able continued towards Julfa. Ourmiye was suddenly emptied. The approach of the Turks and Kurds hastened people's flight towards Salmast. Tabriz was quite prepared for these developments, but Salmast did not have the means and its people joined the long and miserable caravan to Julfa. This latter caravan was joined by refugees from Ourmiye, Khoy and Aghpag, presenting the most pitiable spectacle.

Crossing snow-covered Saray, battered by freezing winds, the convoy of Armenians found itself under cruel skies, in abject poverty and facing uncertainty. The oxen and buffalo of the people from Salmast, forced out of their warms stables, grunted and groaned in agony, as they froze to death along the way. The poor animals could not carry the children, the infirm and other loads placed on their backs. Oh, the misfortune of those lifeless creatures. Unfortunately, it was not only the animals which froze to death. There were many elderly people and children who also froze to death and found their final resting place under a white blanket of snow.

If the Tabriz-Julfa route saw only small misfortunes, the Ourmiye-Salmast-Khoy-Julfa route became the Golgotha for tens of thousands. This route was lined with corpses, the bodies of multitudes who were not afforded proper burial.

A population register dated February 12, 1915 recorded the following information concerning Armenian refugees who had come to Yerevan province and the region of Kars from the Ottoman Empire and Persia between November and December [1914].

From Ottoman Turkey		
Province	Households	People
Pasen district	1,551	12,914
Narman district	84	655
Bayazid district	224	1,735
Diadin district	130	1,111
Karakilise district	781	6,034
Alashgerd district	956	7,732
Bashkale district	385	2,897
SUB-TOTAL	4,111	33,078
From Persia		
Tabriz-Khoy	341	1,809
Salmast region	514	2,816
Ourmiye region	426	2,601
SUB-TOTAL	1,281	7,226
GRAND-TOTAL	5,392	40,304

Alongside Armenian refugees were also Assyrians who numbered 1,325 households or 8,061 people.

These were the remnants of Armenians from a few areas – over 40,000 people from Ottoman Turkey and Persia who had lost everything. They came under dreadful conditions – freezing weather, filthy mud, hunger, open skies – forced to abandon children, the elderly and the infirm, and leave behind the corpses of the dead.

While it is true that Armenian volunteers were helping them, as were Russian Cossacks, such cases were single drops in an ocean of suffering refugees.

Chapter X

The First Stage of the Massacres

Though devastated by their losses, Armenian refugees came to the Caucasus and somehow settled down. The local Armenians responded generously to the many calls for help. They donated large quantities of food and clothes. In some places special organisations were formed to give assistance, such as the so-called committees of "Fraternal Help." Ordinary Armenian men and women also stepped forward to help. The peasants opened their doors and let in the frozen refugees, warming them at their hearths, scrubbing down their grime and putting hot soup in front of them so that the unfortunate people could forget their suffering for a moment. What about those who were not able to flee and had to remain behind in the Ottoman Empire? Their story was the saddest part of the developments discussed here.

The Muslims, excited by their temporary successes with the retreat of the Russians, unleashed unspeakable violence on the remaining Armenians. There was no limit to their ferocity, with the plundering in some cases turning into huge massacres, not only by Kurds but also the army. The following cases are a few examples of the abuse, plunder and murder of Armenians at this time.

On February 7, 1915, Vramian, who was a member of the Ottoman Parliament for Van, presented a detailed note to the Minister of Interior. It was composed of the following points.

A. The Massacre of Armenians in Bashkale and Surrounding Areas

This incident took place in the third week of December 1914, immediately after the Russian retreat, when Tabur Aghasi Ahmed Bey and 160 gendarmes, as well as 150 Hamidiye troops under Sharaf Beg of the Mazrig tribe, plundered Armenian homes and set them ablaze. They then had all men above the age of ten killed and their bodies thrown into streets and gardens. Ahmed Bey and his men seized attractive girls and left hundreds of other women and children naked and hungry in their ruined homes. The villages surrounding Bashkale were treated in a similar manner, with the Armenian men of the villages of Baz, Arak, Pis, Alalyan, Alas, Soran and Ralim [Rasulan] massacred in a field at Arak.

Following the occupation of Bashkale, the local authorities arrested Vahan Aslanian, Hagop Safoian, Jochagha Tosounian, Minas and Hapet Seferian, Tavit Algatian and others, totalling 11 people. These men were told that they would be sent to Van but were killed on the road outside the city.

B. Boghazkiasan (Arjag)

This incident took place on Wednesday, December 9, starting with the murder of Garabed Sarkisian and the parish priest's wife. Afterwards the church and village were ransacked, with material losses estimated at 4,000 liras. Details of this incident were given to the governor's office.

C. Akhorig, Hasan Tamran, Kharabasorig, Tashoghlou Massacres (The Kaimakam of Saray)

This incident took place around January 12,1915, when gendarmes under the command of Abdul Kadir, Yaver Eomer and Rasim Effendi went to Akhorig and announced that they were ordered by the kaimakam to gather all Armenians and take them to Saray to rebuild the military barracks. A day earlier Saya Tahar Bey from Hiuseyin Bey's village had already given rise to suspicions when he locked up the Armenian peasants of that village in two houses.

The gendarmes picked out the youngsters amongst the men and sent them away surrounded by Kurds. A second group composed of elderly men were also sent away in the company of gendarmes. As soon as the first group got to Avzarig, the Kurds shot them down in the presence of gendarmes and Yaver Eomer. An eyewitness counted 28 bodies in Avzarig. Other participants in these murders were two aghas, Tahar and Mustafa Begs, plus Mahmet Ali and his son. After this mass execution, while Yaver, the gendarmes and the aforementioned Kurdish aghas were enjoying the hospitality at Soultan Agha's house in Avzarig, murderous Kurds dashed to the second group of elderly Armenians, chose the youngest four, and killed them in front of the others. The remaining 14 in the group were taken to Saray and later related their awful experience. The Armenian corpses remained unburied in Avzarig for a week, until Armenian women from Akhorig buried them in their own village cemetery.

While the atrocity at Akhorig was taking place, 10 Armenian households were massacred at Hasan Tamran and two at Tashoghlou. Seven people were taken from the village under the pretext of taking them to Saray and shot on the way. Six people escaped, two of whom were recaptured and shot on the spot. Women and girls were seized and distributed amongst the Kurds.

Needless to say, all of the wealth of those villages, such as sheep, wheat or household goods, was taken away by Kurds. The wealth of Akhorig alone was estimated at 10,000 liras, a small part of which was taken as a war tax.

D. The Massacre and Pillage of Hazara

This took place on 29 December 1914. The number of dead was seven men, one woman, and two girls. There was also one wounded. The pillage included the theft of 5,630 sheep, oxen, cows, buffalo and a horse. Also 5,900 measures of different cereals, 1,600 litres of oil, cheese, and yoghurt, 1,600 pieces of bedding, 1,000 utensils, 200 kilograms of wool, 150 boxes of goods and so on.

E. Satmants (Saray)

On October 3, 1914 an officer and three gendarmes came to the village and announced that according to orders from the governor, Armenians had to immediately vacate the village. That day, 90 people were forced to leave, barely managing to reach Krel in four

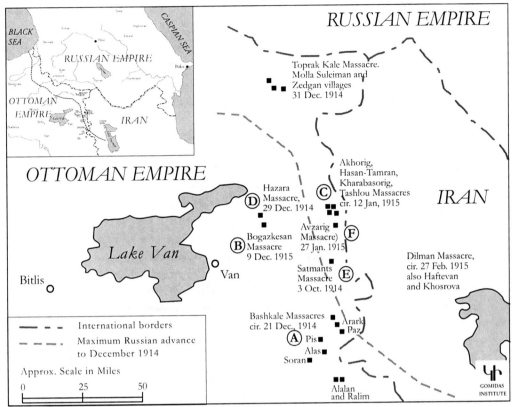

The First Stage of Massacres, 1914-15

days, when 12 children died from the cold. The remaining 120 people were locked up in a house, where three gendarmes and other Kurds ravished the poor defenceless people. A few days later, these people were sent away to Salakhane, Zarants and Farough villages. Eight of them died from hunger and exposure. Satmants was entirely pillaged.

F. Avzarig (Saray)

On January 27, 1915 Hiuseyin Beg of Akhorig and the infamous Molla Sayid visited Avzarig and threatened its Armenian population. Immediately after their departure, gendarmes came to the village and gathered all the Armenians in the home of the village headman [*reis*]. They then picked nine people and gave them containers of oil to carry to Saray on their backs. As they were taking the oil out of the village, the gendarmes shot two of them, Asbadour Khloian and Vartan Minasian, in front of the other villagers. A few villagers managed to escape at night and reached Shamshadin, while the rest disappeared without trace. Such violent episodes in the Bashkale and Saray regions were also repeated elsewhere.

* * *

There were 12 Armenian inhabited villages in the Alashgerd plain, one of which was the seat of the kaimakam, Toprak Kale. The larger Armenian villages were Molla Suleiman and Zedgan. The former was composed of 154 Catholic Armenian households and the second of 87 Apostolic Armenian households. When the Russian army retreated, these two villages were isolated and their inhabitants were unable to leave. They remained where they were, as did some of the Armenians in Toprak Kale. On December 30, the population of Zedgan, in fear of Kurdish attacks, took what it could and moved to Molla Suleiman. On December 31, the local Sipku and Zilan tribal Kurds surrounded Molla Suleiman. After some resistance the Armenians fled to Toprak Kale in the hope of finding safety, having left behind their considerable wealth as well as 10 dead. But Toprak Kale was soon surrounded and became the scene of pillage, destruction, as well as a terrible massacre, which a group of local women described as follows:

> Initially, the Kurds were busy pillaging, but soon everything was taken away and the massacre began. They took a large number of people out of their houses and packed them into the mosque. Then they picked out the men, took them away, and killed them nearby. The mosque was turned into a slaughter-house. The killings were carried out in a barbaric manner, in the presence of the terrified women and children. The first victims at Molla Suleiman were Hiurigan, the Catholic Vartabed, and Abraham, the Apostolic Vartabed of Zedgan, both of whom were hacked to pieces. They killed a few notables in a similar manner. After they murdered all of the men, they started to rape women and take people away. They carried off the attractive young women and girls, killing those who resisted. This treatment continued over three days while the women and children held at the mosque and other places remained in absolute terror. They did not notice their own thirst or hunger. When the killing of the men, the abuse of attractive young women and children, and other abductions ended, they released the survivors, who returned to their villages, though some dispersed here and there. Since there was no bread or flour left in the villages, the starving people had to open up the wells, take out their hidden supplies of grain, grind flour, and feed themselves. Terror made them forget everything and they lived like moles until the Russian army returned to Alashgerd.

The massacres in Persia were also described by a visitor returning from Persia as follows:

> After the retreat of the Russian armies, around 700 or 800 Armenians and Assyrians sought safety in Dilman. They had been hidden in the houses of Persians and, I have to say, all honour to the Persian people, because they carried out their neighbourly duties with great sacrifice.

Armenians were thus protected by Persians until February 27, when the Russians began advancing. The Turks, sensing that they would have to give way to the Russians, decided to kill all the Christians in Dilman, as they did in all the regions they had occupied. On the above-mentioned day, Rusdem Bey, the kaimakam of Dilman, instructed a town crier to announce that any Persian found to be hiding *gâvurs* [infidels] in their homes would be shot. Many Persians did not give in to such threats and sheltered Armenians. The governor at that point ordered soldiers to enter Persian homes and pull out any Christians. In their initial efforts, they apprehended seven Armenians and shot them on the spot. Thereafter around 700 people were found in different parts of the city. Seeing that it would be unseemly to shoot so many people in front of those who had sheltered them, the authorities took the victims to nearby villages, especially Haftevan and Khosrova, where they tortured and killed them in the presence of Turkish officers. The correspondent continued:

> I have personally seen hundreds of corpses in wells, whose stench could be detected in the whole region. I saw people's heads rolled in the mud having been cut off with axes, as well as dismembered hands, legs, etc. The two wells of Hakhnazarian, the one well of Khachadourian, and the three wells of the 'kaghtagan' Nshan were full of corpses. Most of the bodies had been hacked to pieces. There were more than 100 bodies in an orchard in Khosrova.

Another eye-witness said, "I saw five bodies under a wall. They had been tied together, butchered, and then the wall was collapsed on top of them." Yet another horrified eye-witness described the skinless faces and shattered bones of victims, as well as other atrocities.

Such was the fate of many Armenians who were left in areas the Russians relinquished to Turkish control. But did Armenians remain quiet and simply give way to the Muslim sword, or were there also cases of resistance, and even a thirst for revenge? We address this issue briefly in the next chapter.

Chapter XI

Armenian Resistance

After the Russo-Turkish hostilities had started, the Armenian provinces, especially Vasbouragan, were compelled to organise their own defence. This was natural given the conduct of the Ottoman government towards Armenians. The Ottoman authorities had disarmed Armenian soldiers, formed them into labour battalions, and made them work as pack-animals. They had made their provision of food and clothing almost impossible, and there had been cases of mass, as well as individual killing of Armenian soldiers. Such instances have already been discussed. It has also been noted how, following such developments, Armenian soldiers had deserted, so that Armenian villages were full of deserters. Furthermore, using the pretext of looking for deserters, gendarmerie and militia forces had descended on Armenian villages and carried out searches, committed outrages, shot people, and torched houses.

Consequently, deserters had had to secure arms and withdraw to the mountains and caves during the day, only descending to villages at night. The government, in its turn, had set up military cordons around villages. It was thus inevitable that the two groups would clash, though such clashes should have been limited to deserters and soldiers, were it not for the government harassing different communities.

Unfortunately, Armenian villagers were mistreated not only by gendarmes claiming to be after deserters, but also Kurds and irregular forces. The terrible deeds carried out by Bshare Chato's horde in the villages of Arjesh, Pergri and Arjag region, the barbaric deeds of gendarmes and Kurds in Bashkale, Saray and Alashgerd districts, or those in Dilman in Persia have also been described earlier.

Armenians could see what was happening around them. They could see how the Turkish government was preparing to repeat earlier massacres. And their sense for self-preservation led them to take appropriate action.

* * *

The Armenians in the six provinces had made significant material progress during the six years of the constitutional era [1908–14] and their communal life had improved. Their educational movement had made great progress, as well as their national self-awareness and collective sense for survival. The leading role in these developments was played by the main political party amongst Turkish-Armenians, the Tashnagtsoutiun (ARF).

The Armenian defensive strategy during the constitutional era was principally aimed at opposing Kurds and Kurdish brigands who raided Armenian villages, grazed animals on Armenian fields and pastures, or stole cattle and sheep. The central government, though it had tried to appear as a friend of the ARF, made excuses and did not intervene.

Given these developments in the Armenian provinces, especially in Vasbouragan, the ARF organised special committees and sub-committees to attract the best elements of the provincial youth into its ranks. There was great activity in schools and reading rooms, and the organisation of new defence units became the subject of fables. Books and weapons were the most appropriate response in those dark days, when Armenians had to take matters into their own hands and deal directly with neighbouring nomadic tribes and a weak government.

The Van Working House was built during this period. It was an impressive building, where there was a large theatre, several rooms serving as a library-reading room, an auditorium, the editorial office of *Ashkhadank* press and newspaper, and much more.

Aram Manougian from Shoushi

While the ARF had been involved in similar work before the Ottoman constitutional revolution in 1908, such efforts found more fertile ground in the more positive political climate of the constitutional period. Consequently, the Turkish government began to look at ARF leaders as the representatives of the Armenian people and maintained close relations with them, consulting and working with ARF leaders on all issues. These developments raised the prestige of the ARF and Armenians began looking at it as their representative, in a sense creating a government within a government.

These were the prevailing conditions in the Armenian provinces, especially in Vasbouragan, when the European War broke out. *Seferberlik* (mobilisation) was announced, a new Russo-Turkish War broke out, and the Young Turk government – finding the moment most suitable – reverted to the

Ishkhan (Nigoghayos Boghosian)
from Shoushi province

murderous anti-Armenian policies of Abdul Hamid.

The leading ARF members in Van at that time were Ishkhan (Nigoghayos Boghosian from Karasne village of Shoushi province) and Aram (Aram Manougian from Shoushi).

Both men had been active in the days of the Hamidian autocracy. While the former was a seasoned military activist who had withdrawn to a quiet life, the second was known as an organiser and educator.

Before the Russo-Turkish war, in the middle of September, 1914, the Ottoman Parliamentary representative Vramian (Onnig Tertsagian from Constantinople) came to Van. He was one of the leading activists of the ARF and, because of his reputation, had great influence not only in his party but also on government officials. For that reason, when he came to Van, he and Aram ran the party, especially Vramian, who had special standing as a member of the Ottoman Parliament.

Ishkhan also came back during this period and was mostly involved in defence work.

There was serious activity in the provinces as the defence groups tried to arm people and create some mobile units which could reinforce position wherever necessary. The ARF leaders instructed everyone that no occasion was to be given for incidents and clashes should be avoided. This was a difficult task because the government side gave cause for conflict every day.

There was an additional complication. The Russians were advancing quickly, the Ottoman forces were retreating rapidly, and Bashkale and Saray were about to fall. Russian artillery could be heard at Molla Hasan village and on the borders of Arjag district.

"Antranig has reached Molla Hasan." These words spread like lightning. One had to have experienced all of the abuses on one's skin, as the Armenians of Ottoman Turkey had done for decades, in order to understand how that one sentence lifted Armenian spirits. On the other hand, the news spread terror amongst the Muslim population. Some began to flee, including people from Van. They included government officials who lost their heads. An Armenian policeman in Aykesdan, Armenag Shadakhtsian, related the following story.

> On the morning of December 2, I went to the city as usual and went straight to the police station. When I entered the main office, I was amazed to see the pale faces of the policemen there, as if they were unwell. "The police chief asked for you" said the officers when they saw me, and I went to the police chief's office. There were two people there. One was police chief Vafik Bey from Salonika and the other was the gendarmerie commander Burhaneddin Bey. They seemed to be in an uncomfortable conversation. They were also pale-faced and looked so terrified that they were hardly able to speak. When I entered, they stopped talking and the police chief turned to me and said, "You know, my child, war is like a game of cards. Sometimes one side wins, sometimes the other. We know that the Russians like you [Armenians] and will harm none of you. I therefore hand our station to you so that it is not ransacked."

The police chief said these words with great alarm, hardly moving his lips. At the same time, the affluent Muslims in Van were hurrying to Avants in order to board a ferry. The following day it was reported that the Russians were retreating but the Muslims remained in a state of terror for a long time.

These developments took place at the end of November during the advance of the Russians, when Armenian morale was raised once more, following the tyranny of Ottoman authorities in the previous few months.

These developments also had several other serious consequences which were not planned and were often triggered by individuals. One such incident took place at Pelou.

A. The Pelou Incident

On the Gevash-Garjgan border was an Armenian village called Pelou. It was composed of 77 households. According to official Ottoman administrative divisions, this village was inside Garjgan, but it was also considered to be in the Gevash region in Armenian parish records. The village was placed under the watchful guard of eight gendarmes.

Around December 8 1914, when news came of the approaching Russians at Molla Hasan and the flight of well-to-do Turks from Van, a telegraph wire was cut near Pelou. The kaimakam of Vosdan, Shoukri Bey, went to Pelou to examine matters. Convinced that it was the work of Armenians, he proceeded on to Garjgan. Just at that moment, the Russians pulled back from Molla Hasan and the Turks were somewhat relieved.

After the departure of the kaimakam, a few armed Armenians of the local defence unit, led by Abraham of Nor Kiugh, came to Pelou. The gendarmes watching the village, who had often seen the armed Armenians and did not confront them, now surrounded the house where the men were staying and wanted to arrest them. The Armenians refused to surrender and a fire fight broke out with one gendarme being killed.

The kaimakam, who was in Garjgan at that time, gathered a large number of militia forces and Kurds and attacked Pelou. The Armenian fighters soon got backing from Asbo of Gevash and Mihran Chatoian with their twenty men. The defenders resisted the government forces for two days but, on the third day, on December 18, they could no longer resist the growing number of attackers. They therefore withdrew from the village, along with its inhabitants. The attacking mobs overran the village, killed the few remaining Armenians, plundered houses, and then torched the place. Hiuseyin Agha of Takhmants played the leading role in the destruction of Pelou.

B. The Atanan Incident

The destruction of Pelou shocked Armenians in surrounding regions, especially in Gevash, Hayots Tsor and Shadakh, which bordered on Pelou. The ARF had been very active in these regions, as it prepared young men to form mobile defence units with the help of new graduates from the school at Aghtamar. There was no reaction to the destruction of Pelou, but there was another serious incident at Atanan.

When Pelou came under attack and Armenians opposed the militia forces and rabble accompanying them, the government prepared to send the army to Garjgan. The Armenians, in order to block the advance of the army, cut the telegraph wire between Gevash and Hayots Tsor, arrested the seven or eight zaptiehs in Ankgh, and destroyed the bridge over the Khoshab river.

During this period, the *kadi* of Vosdan and another official were returning home from the war front. They were amongst a few Turkish officials who supported the holy war [*jihad*] that had been declared by going to the war front as volunteers. The kadi and his friend were carrying out their patriotic duty. They were now on their way home to rest and were passing through Atanan just as news of the destruction of Pelou had reached that village. Some young men in Atanan saw the approaching officials and recognised them. When they found out the two men were coming from the front, the youngsters went into a fit of rage and shot both men in the centre of the village, hiding their corpses afterwards. The killing was concealed.

A day after this incident, on December 19, two gendarmes who were taking the government post between Vosdan and Van were also killed in Atanan. When they were attacked, there was shooting and around 150 gendarmes, militiamen and Kurds were sent to Atanan and surrounded the village. At that time, the main spirit behind the resistance in Gevash – Kharagantsi Levon and his men – were in Atanan. Over 60 armed Armenians were on a hill next to the village and Sbidag Vank, which the gendarmes and militia forces wanted to cross to get to the rear of the village, a little to the south. Soon, heavy fighting broke out between these groups and lasted all day. The Turks could not make progress and pulled back to Vosdan at nightfall.

The fighting continued more intensely the next day and government forces received re-enforcements. The latter came from Pelou, after that village had been destroyed. Despite superior numbers, the enemy forces were not able to approach the village. The Armenian positions also held strong at Sbidag Vank. Levon remained the spirit of this resistance.

That day, a Kurdish notable called Khourshoud Agha was shot dead by an Armenian fighter in the Turkish Nor Shen quarter of Vosdan, which was very close to Atanan. His death spread fear not only amongst Kurds, but also among local government officials who requested an end to the hostilities through the intercession of the abbot of Sbidag Vank.

While Atanan was battling courageously against numerous Kurdish and militia forces, another incident took place in Shadakh. In this case, the telegraph wire was cut at Pesantashd and Armenian fighters blocked the road near Sivdgin. Over two days, Armenians captured eight to ten gendarmes who were going to Tagh (the centre of Shadakh) from Van and Vosdan. As Turkish-Armenians say, they put these gendarmes down, and all communications with Tagh were cut.

During this period, the shocking news from Tagh reached Van and both government officials and Armenian leaders found it imperative to send a special delegation to restore peace. On December 20, a delegation set off for Gevash with Vramian going on behalf of Armenians and Miunib Effendi on behalf of Muslims, both men being members of the Ottoman Parliament.

The peace delegation found the bridge at Ankgh destroyed and managed to repair it. They reached Vosdan when the fighting at Atanan had stopped, though the situation remained tense and the road to the village was blocked. Muslims, even government officials, did not dare to approach it.

In order to calm matters, Vramian went into Atanan and had the bodies and weapons of the gendarmes who had been killed sent to Vosdan, but he was not able to find the remains of the kadi and the other official who had been travelling with him. The

Armenian fighters confessed to killing the officials. Although the kaimakam had wanted the bodies of the two victims, Vramian managed to evade the issue and they set off to deal with the situation at Pelou.

The peace delegation passed through Atanan but the mood remained the same. The Armenian fighters did not abandon their positions, and Kurds and Turks were not allowed to pass through the village. When around 200 soldiers from Bitlis rested in Vosdan, they did not dare approach Atanan until Vramian returned from Pelou. It was only when Vramian came to Atanan with the kaimakam that the soldiers passed through the village.

This tense situation continued and even after a week Kurds and Turks, including officials, did not feel safe to travel through Atanan. There were occasions when officials travelling from Van to Vosdan would get a letter of introduction from Vramian so that the Armenians at Atanan would let them proceed on their journey. Such officials would approach the village, present their letters of introduction, and continue with some assurance.

This was the impact of the Atanan incident on Turks, Kurds and the government, and for a while there was peace in that region. The telegraph lines and Ankgh bridge were repaired, the captive gendarmes were released at Sivdgin, and Pelou was rebuilt.

If one discounted the resistance and destruction of Pelou village, the Atanan incident represented the most serious resistance in the whole region following mobilisation and the outbreak of the Russo-Turkish War. Indeed, as will be seen later, the Pelou incident showed that there was no hope for Armenians other than their own self-defence.

C. The Gargar Incidents

Shortly after the Pelou and Atanan clashes, there were serious incidents in Gargar, leading to the destruction of Armenian villages in that area. The destruction of those villages had a great impact on Armenians.

Gargar was a small mountainous sub-district that contained 18 Armenian villages with 3,000 inhabitants. The region was south of Gevash and Garjgan, on an eastern tributary of Khizan Sou. It was composed of two valleys called the upper and lower *gyalis*. The upper valley was in the Gevash region of Van, while the lower one was in the Khizan district of Bitlis.

On February 12 the local government official (*miudir*) of Shenitsor (Khizan) and 24 gendarmes came to the village of Yeghekis in lower Gargar and summoned the village elders, demanding that they hand over deserters. Since no deserters were surrendered, the elders were subjected to terrible beatings and torture. After punishing them, the government official led the gendarmes to the villages and ordered deserters to be flushed out. A few of the gendarmes went to Hougourtsou and Tsgor, where they committed outrages such as beating men, molesting women, and so on. The Armenian villagers responded with arms, killing four gendarmes in Hougourtsou and two in Tsgor.

News of these killings immediately reached the kaimakam of Gevash, who sent Haji Darvish, Seyid Ali's son, with a large militia force and Kurds to Gargar.

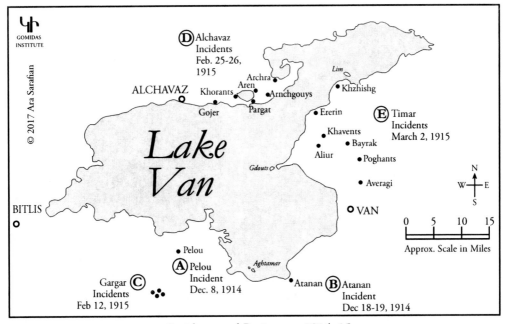

Incidents and Resistance, 1914–15

Meanwhile, the Armenian men made preparations to defend themselves in Gargar, under the leadership of Kalousd Boghosian (also known as Voushig Kalo), who was a heroic figure and the spirit behind the defence of Gargar.

Kalo, seeing the approach of a large enemy force, sent a message to Gevash asking for help. However, reinforcements arrived late, and despite the desperate situation, Kalo chose to oppose the enemy with his small force at Sanekri height. The fierce clash that ensued lasted for three days. The Armenian fighters retreated on the fourth day and the enemy occupied the Sanekri height. The nearby village of Hargents was also ransacked and torched. Although Lato and Mihran Chatoian and their men had arrived from Gevash by this time, the Armenian fighters only managed to relocate the displaced population of a few villages under their protection. Once more Kalo and his men faced the enemy alone and continued the fight, which now took place at the village of Voriz. The battle at this village lasted for two days and the Armenian peasants under Kalo's protection became fearful and began to complain. Kalo was offended by such talk and took his rifle, descended to his village of Tsgor – which was in enemy hands – and fought bravely to his last bullet. He had decided to die in his own home and fell like a hero, forever closing his ears to senseless grumbles.

The hero of Gargar, Voushig Kalo, was no more, and his men now lost hope. They retreated from their positions against the large enemy forces, taking with them the civilian population, all suffering heavy losses. The enemy pursued them and killed over 130 people – women and children – and looted, destroyed and burnt down all villages. The government did not put a stop to these developments but encouraged them, confiscating all animals in the name of the state. To celebrate their victory, the attackers cut off Kalo's head and displayed it on a stave.

The entire population of Gargar fled to Mogs and Gevash. They arrived in a terrible state and related new horrors which once more shocked people.

D. The Alchavaz Incidents

The incidents in Gargar were still fresh in people's minds when much more disturbing incidents took place at Alchavaz.

As mentioned earlier, Alchavaz was in the foothills of Mount Sipan to the north-west of Lake Van. It was one of the most significant Armenian populated districts of the area. The centre of this region was the old fort and city of Ardzge, which included 80 Armenian households. The kaimakam's seat was in this city, and there were 21 Armenian inhabited villages with over 6,000 people in the area. The principal villages were Yergou Sipan, Aren, Gojer, Archra and Arnchgouys.

Until mobilisation, the kaimakam of the district was an ethnic Armenian, Bedros Mokian. After mobilisation, when the political atmosphere changed, the Armenian kaimakam was sent to Van, and his place was taken by a Turk, Naji Bey.

Alchavaz had its own Armenian mobile defence force which, when needed, could muster more than 50 men. This unit was led by a brave peasant from Archra, Ohan Tarpinian. There was another brave man under his command called Mgo from Karakeshish, who was known by the name of Sev Hayou Dgha. When the Constitution was proclaimed, Mgo had dared to demand the return of his lands from Keor Hiuseyin Pasha of Patnos.

* * *

As was seen earlier, at the middle of December, Bshare Chato, starting from Manazgerd, had gone on a rampage in Armenian villages in Arjesh, Pergri and Arjag on his way to Saray. But his life was short lived in the war. He was killed near Kotour, when his band scattered, and his followers went home. This often happened with Kurdish gangs.

After Bshare Chato's death, his strapping 30 year-old son, Amare Chato, and his own brother, Hiuseyin, wanted revenge on the unbelievers (*gavurs*).

Though Bshare Chato had travelled through Manazgerd and Arjesh, his son Amare Chato went through Alchavaz and Arjesh. Thus the young Chato reached Ardzge with his followers on February 22. After resting for three days, he continued on his journey and reached the Armenian village of Gojer on February 25.

It is not difficult to imagine his gang's violence. Two months earlier, his father had arrived without the poison of vengeance inside him and had committed savage acts, including murder. Now his son arrived with the encouragement of the government to disturb Armenian villages – and Amare Chato came full of his father's vengeance. Unbelievers had killed his father, so unbelievers were to make up for it, and the unbelievers at hand were the Armenians. The news of Amare Chato's approach quickly spread throughout the region.

As commander Ohan of the mobile defence unit explained:

> I was in our village of Archra with my unit. It was after 10 p.m. when two Armenians from Gojer rushed in and asked for help. They pleaded "Come for

the love of God, there is no honour (*namous*) left. Amare Chato has lodged in the village, beating up the men and raping the women and girls. They are slaughtering the sheep and cattle, cooking and eating, despoiling everything. Come, our village has been devastated!"

These words, as they were uttered, pierced my heart. I rushed off with around 25 men. We did not know what to do because of our rage. I sent out word to surrounding villages and around 25 others joined us. We then set off towards Gojer with 50 men. The sun was just rising when we reached the Armenian village of Ghouzel. We were half an hour from Gojer, when two men came to us from that village and advised not to proceed because whatever was to happen had already happened in their village. The Kurdish rabble was preparing to leave. We remained in Ghouzel and prepared for the defence of the other villages. But where would the Kurds go next? They were halting at all villages on the way and completing a day's journey in three. Anticipating what lay ahead, we divided our group into two parts. I gave command of 15 men to Mgo and sent him to Aren, the largest village in the area, with a population of 177 households. I took 35 men and went towards Khorants. Aren and Khorants are situated on opposite shores of Lake Khorants. The village was to the west of the lake and Aren to the east. It was possible to go from Gojer to Aren on either the northern or southern lake shore. The southern route passed through Ghouzel, but the northern route didn't. I reached Khorants with my 35 men and picked a good position from where we could observe Aren. We took up our positions and waited. When the sun rose and there was light, we could see some of Chato's band. He was at its head. He was with his uncle and a few bodyguards, followed by scattered groups of five to ten men, some on horseback, some on foot. They continued northeast towards Aren but did not enter Khorants. We weren't wrong. They continued along the northern shore of the lake. We took the southern route to Aren.

At 10 a.m., Amare Chato, his uncle and some bodyguards reached Aren. The people of Aren had vacated part of the village, moving families to other parts of the village so that the Kurds could be lodged in the empty houses without coming into contact with the village women and girls. That way, Amare Chato and his band could be hosted without any unpleasantness. When Amaro reached the edge of the village with his group, two tall Armenians came to greet him from the village. They were Melik Apre and Reis Srko. Melik Apre was a member of the judiciary. He was a serious and brave man. He approached and greeted Amaro by putting his hand to his chest and forehead and stated that part of the village had been vacated for him and his men. Melik Apre invited them to dismount.

"What! Have you made these arrangements so that we do not see the faces of your women?" exclaimed Amare Chato, looking at Melik Apre as if he was offended.

Melik Apre, who knew how to keep his composure in such situations, turned to the Kurdish thug and said in a calm voice, "We have prepared, my lord, both lodgings and hospitality for you. You are here as our honoured guests, and if you are thinking about touching the honour of our women, we will not allow that."

Amare Chato was not pleased to hear such words. In fact, he was displeased and angry and gave a signal for a few of his men to fire their rifles in the air to spread terror. However, Melik Apre did not lose his composure but realised that they would not be able to avoid disturbances and violence. He therefore sent for Mgo, who had taken up position in Yeritsou Tavo's house and was waiting for news of developments. By the time Melik Apre reached the Armenian fighters, the latter had already heard the Kurdish gunfire, taken up positions, and responded. The Kurdish force was enraged by this development and turned its fire on anyone who could be seen in the village. The shooting continued, as the rest of Amaro's followers reached the village and the fighting intensified. The villagers escaped to Pargat and Arnchgouys, while the 15 armed Armenian fighters opposed a force of around 500 lightly armed Kurds.

Commander Ohan continued his account.

> When the shooting first started, we hurried and reached the village when our boys were in serious difficulties. Five of them had been killed, amongst whom were Sirouni Rasho, Cheloyi Asbadour and Parvani Mirzo. When we got there the boys took heart and the fighting intensified.
>
> The fighting continued until 5:00 p.m. First Amare Chato and a little later his uncle Hiuseyin were killed. They were in the front lines, under the direct fire of our boys near the church and school to the north of the village. The death of the leaders of the horde led to confusion amongst the Kurds, who began to flee, leaving behind eight dead. We followed them and shot ten more as they were running away. They fled all the way to Ardzge. Naturally, the situation became more serious. We returned to the village and led the population of Aren, Arnchgouys and Archra to Karakeshish and Vijgatsroug, which were well suited for defence. Meanwhile the population of Pargat, Khorants, Ghouzel and Gojer took to boats and the open lake. All of this happened on February 26, on the eve of Dyaruntarach [Candlemas].
>
> This incident also terrified the surrounding Kurds and government as well. The following day, when 25 gendarmes under the command of Davrish Chavoush arrived at the abandoned village of Aren, they did not dare enter it. They picked up the corpses of the Kurds and returned to Ardzge.
>
> During the following three days, no Kurd or official dared to step into our district. Only on February 29 did a large government force of militiamen and three cannon land near Pargat and Arnchgouys villages. While these forces prepared to attack us, the boat we had sent to Van returned with new orders, "Vacate the area and leave the civilians where they are. The government will not touch them." And that is what we did. We took our 60 armed men and set off for Timar by boat, while ordinary villagers returned to their homes.

This was captain (*khmpabed*) Ohan's account of developments which led to a powerful response in Timar.

E. The Events of Timar

Two weeks after the incidents in Alchavaz, there were further incidents in Timar. These developments were a continuation of what had happened in Alchavaz, where the government had not been able to apprehend the armed Armenians who had clashed with Amare Chato.

On the morning of March 2, Ohan, the commander of the Alchavaz defence unit and his 60 men arrived at Khzhishg. It was difficult to look after so many men in that village, so that they were divided into three groups. 25 men were sent to the village of Ererin on the lake shore, 15 went to the villages of Upper Timar, and the rest went to Van.

Nothing untoward happened for more than 10 days, but on March 15, an official with 25 gendarmes came to Ererin to collect the sheep tax. It was highly unusual for a tax collector to come with so many gendarmes. The villagers were worried and asked the armed Armenians to leave. The latter obliged, but as they were leaving with a local guide, they came under fire from three gendarmes hiding at a mill. The young guide was wounded in the foot, but the Armenians fired back and fled to the mountains. This seemed to be the end of the matter.

Two days later, on March 17, gendarmerie commander Burhaneddin and his men came to Ererin from the city. They entered the village and the abuses started. The village was ransacked, several houses were burnt down, and many men were taken to Van in chains. These atrocities spread terror amongst ordinary people and there was more to come.

The column that had wreaked havoc at Ererin went to the largest village in the region, Aliur, and then to Khavents, committing the same atrocities, including theft and arson, as well as the dispatch of many men to Van in chains.

Meanwhile, the commander of Lower Timar's defence unit, Roupen Israyelian from Van, sent word to the city and asked for further instructions. In view of the incidents at Alchavaz and Atanants, where the government only gave way to force, the central command ordered the Timar unit to resist if the army continued to commit atrocities. By this time the outrages at Ererin, Aliur and Khavents had ceased and there were no further complications, though there were other incidents elsewhere.

On March 22, a small mobile defence unit consisting of ten men under the command of Roupen was near Bayrak. Sghotskar rocks was half an hour south of this village. Twenty Armenian deserters from two neighbouring villages, Adnagants and Drlashen, fearing that gendarmes were in pursuit, were hiding at Sghotskar. Two neighbouring Muslim villages called Shkheni and Shkhkara were at the north-east of Bayrak. On this day, the militia forces in Shkheni and Shkhkara attacked Sghotskar rocks, after they had been informed of deserters hiding there. News of this attack reached the Armenian units in Bayrak, who went to the aid of the deserters. While on their way, they clashed with a militia force and then heard that Bayrak itself had come under attack. They returned to Bayrak and arrived at the same time as Turkish forces approaching it. Captain Misak and a few of his men managed to get to the village in time and a fierce fight ensued, lasting until evening. The Armenian casualties included one dead, the brave Mgo, while the Muslims lost over ten men.

When darkness fell and the Muslim forces retreated to their positions, the Armenian force of 20 men relocated the civilian population to Poghants, while they themselves moved to Averagi and waited for reinforcements from Van. On the morning of March 23, 46 men arrived from the city, including those who had gone to Van from Alchavaz. They went to Poghants, while Roupen and his 20 men remained in Averagi. As dawn broke, they could see a force of about 500 men and three artillery pieces deployed against them. They were under the same Burhaneddin's command.

While the armed column was approaching Averagi, fighting broke out at Poghants between Armenian and militia forces, and the column diverted to Poghants. As it proceeded, the Armenian forces followed them. When the government forces reached the valley of Malanoug, near Pognants, the Armenians opened fire at the front and rear of their enemy. Despite the use of cannon, the fighting continued all day, and the soldiers could not occupy Averagi. The Armenian forces moved the civilian population out of Poghants, suffering the loss of one man, two women and a child. Around 20 soldiers were also killed.

After darkness fell, the army moved towards Giusnents village, while the Armenian forces took the civilian population to Averagi.

On March 24, a peace delegation came to Averagi from the city at the suggestion of the deputy governor. One of the members of this delegation was an Armenian who was a member of the provincial administration, Kevork Jidechian. The other member was a Turk, the police chief Vafig Bey. At the suggestion of Jidechian, the Armenian defence units withdrew to Nabat, Mkhgner and Kizilja, while the peace delegation took the civilian population to Poghants. They then instructed Burhaneddin at Giusnents to return to the city with his forces. The delegation thus considered its work finished and returned to the city.

Burhaneddin, on receipt of his written instructions from the peace delegation, ordered captain Suleiman Effendi and 50 of his men to return to the city through Nabat, while the rest of his force, including the artillery pieces, returned via Geol.

While the main problems seemed resolved, a new clash broke out when Armenian units in Nabat saw Suleiman Effendi with his 50 soldiers. Doubt and confusion led them to think that these forces had been sent to trap them, and they opened fire on the gendarmes as they came near the village. The gendarmes responded and fighting ensued during which Suleiman Effendi and a few gendarmes were killed and the others fled to the city.

This was a new complication which also spread terror amongst Muslims. Consequently, on March 26, a new peace delegation came to Nabat. This time Aram was representing Armenians and the same Vafig Bey representing Muslims. Peace was established once more.

The incident at Nabat coincided with a telegram bringing news of the Russian occupation of Przemysl [Austro-Hungary]. These two incidents led to great excitement among Armenians in Van, while Muslims were so disheartened that the deputy governor tried to suppress news about the fall of Przemysl.

After peace was established in Nabat, the Armenian defenders went to Van, and everything seemed calm, though it was the calm that preceded a great storm; a storm that was to result in great suffering as well as the heroic deeds of Armenians in Vasbouragan.

Chapter XII

The Prelude Before the Terrifying Events

After the aforementioned incidents in Timar, there was a lull which was more of a cease-fire. Both sides calmed down and a mysterious silence ruled the city and the wider province of Van. Such an atmosphere had never been experienced before and everyone was anticipating a major development. There was a premonition of what was to come.

Immediately after the Timar incidents, there was a telegraphic exchange between Vramian and Jevdet, who was in Bashkale, while the mutasarrif of Bashkale, Shefik Bey, was acting-governor in Van.

On March 26, in the immediate aftermath of the events in Timar, Vramian sent the following telegram to Jevdet.

> First and foremost, I would like to pay my respects to you and ask you to accept my following requests.
>
> I would like to meet you and discuss the painful events in Timar. As you know I, as well as my comrades, wish such problems to cease immediately. It is regrettable that following the events at Garjgan, no thought was given to remove the causes of such incidents.
>
> In my January 9 memorandum to your Highness, I had outlined some steps to address the question of deserters, stopping the attacks of militia forces, and the criminal actions of gendarmes. I had also suggested steps to safeguard the life, property, honour and rights of Armenians.
>
> If the Armenians of Alchavaz were not forced to defend their life and honour, they would not have sought refuge in Ererin village, where they would not have encountered the gendarmes protecting the sheep tax, and they would not have come under fire. If due attention had been paid, Armenians would not have been accused of hiding outlaws and would not have been subjected to such brutal treatment, including the torching of a village school and the destruction of a church. I consider the latter fire and destruction to be an act of aggression against my nation.
>
> These developments were bound to bring turmoil to Timar. However, worse was to follow, as Edhem Bey and his militia forces further provoked Armenians when they went to Aghjaveran village, persuaded 15 people to approach them, and then shot them dead. If there is anything positive in all this, it is what acting governor Shefik Bey said, that Edhem Bey had acted on his own authority.
>
> We have managed to weather the dangers this time and I hope the incidents of the past few months prove to be a good lesson. I am sorry that the provincial authorities are in such a state of disarray that Shefik Bey and I saw fit to contact you and the eminent Talaat Bey.

I can give assurance on my honour that there is no intention to trouble the government in any way, as my actions have proved for many months. For these reasons and under the present circumstances I ask that the government takes the necessary steps to ensure the well being of Armenians.

First of all, the authorities should immediately solve the problem of deserters by allowing them to work on road construction in the province of Van and undertake agricultural work.

The militia forces should be given the work of gendarmes and only armed in certain places.

Edhem Bey and his friends should face a court-martial for the murders at Aghjaveran.

The government should give compensation of 10,000 gold pieces for material losses following the torching of Ererin, Drlashen, Adnagants and Bayrak villages in Timar district.

The gendarmes' illegal acts should be curtailed, and the people responsible for the violence and murder of Bedros in Khoumar in Shadakh district should be apprehended and punished.

With my respects to your highness and Naji Bey, I await your response.

Vramian.

Jevdet, who would have known about the Timar incidents, as well as those in Alchavaz from his deputy in Van, sent the following reply that same day.

26 March, Sourp Partoghimeos Monastery,

Vramian Effendi,

With the will of God, I will be coming to Van with the regular army and a large force tomorrow. I particularly thank you for your efforts to contain the news about recent incidents. I hope that with the arrival of the army the disorders will come to an end. When I get to Van we can have a serious meeting.

Let me comment on your advice and suggestions, in the name of patriotism. You are insisting on naive and impossible tasks without taking realities into consideration.

To you and our compatriots I would say that your suspicions and rejection of my repeated warnings have led to the removal of thousands of your people in accordance with Russian plans, condemning them to great hardship. They should have been moved in a different manner to safeguard the well-being of Armenians in Azerbaijan.

You should trust the government's honest and fair approach, and let the people know this. We will naturally examine the latest incidents very carefully.

I return your kind regards and look forward to seeing you. Be well.

Governor of Van, Jevdet.

This two-faced threatening telegram was unsettling. "With the will of God, I will be coming to Van with the regular army and a large force. I hope with the arrival of the army, disorders will come to an end." These were the main points of Jevdet's telegram.

What did Jevdet wish to say with these words? If his message was a threat, then why did he mention Vramian's patriotism and good work? What was the point of making threats? Was Jevdet's message meant to restrain the Armenians? Or were there more sinister designs?

Such misgivings weighed heavily on Vramian's mind until Jevdet's arrival.

On March 30 it became clear that Jevdet was returning from the field of battle. Officials prepared to welcome him and the Armenian prelate and a few merchants also joined them. Such a reception was not enough and Vramian and Aram also deemed it important to be present.

The presence of these two Armenian activists at Jevdet's reception had another purpose. Jevdet's two-faced threatening telegram had worried them, and they felt responsible for the very existence of their nation, as they were seen as the representatives of a political party that had created civil strife. These men thought it best to win Jevdet over, calm him down, and check the approaching danger implied in Jevdet's threatening telegram.

Jevdet, governor of Van

Thus the reception took place as planned, with a special committee going to Kouroubash village, an hour's journey from Aykesdan. Jevdet appeared in his carriage, wearing the khaki outfit of the irregular (*chete*) forces, followed by about 600 fine Circassians and three artillery pieces. This was indeed a threatening force complementing a threatening telegram.

Jevdet alighted from his carriage and greeted the reception committee which included Vramian and Aram. He then re-entered it to continue his journey. The reception committee accompanied him to his residence, where Vramian had a long meeting and then left, confident that he had calmed the governor down. Vramian was in a positive mood.

Two days later, the Easter celebrations started and everything was peaceful. Jevdet visited Vramian on the occasion of the celebrations and spent over two hours with him. Meanwhile, as Jevdet was expressing his firm friendship to the representative of the Armenian people, around 800 infantrymen were entering the city. Jevdet had brought them from the front, three days behind him by the same route. The Armenians did not foresee Jevdet's cunning plans regarding their own future.

Jevdet was a master of evil, conspiracies and deceit. He was a perfect Asiatic in his negative traits. While he was calling on Armenian leaders with friendly visits, he was also moving troops into the city. He was betraying the people he was visiting by organising a massacre, the like of which had not been seen in Armenian history. Nobody could foresee what was being planned.

Jevdet realised his plans as follows.

April 11, Sunday, Easter Day!

Suddenly, without warning, six teachers were arrested in Tagh, the centre of Shadakh. Among those arrested was a leading member of the ARF, Hovsep Choloian. As will be seen, this incident sparked the defence of Shadakh.

The arrest of the six men created a commotion among Armenians. Young people avoided being seen in town. Armenians residing in the outskirts of Tagh moved to the centre. Regardless of the fact that the market was to open the next day, mistrust against the government prevailed, and it did not open.

News of the Tagh incident reached Van, and Vramian and Aram were informed by the eight-member Defence Council. Jevdet was also informed of developments through the kaimakam. Hovsep Choloian's arrest had been unexpected in Tagh as well as in Van.

It should be noted that ARF members had been followed by government agents for some time. The official explanation was that these agents were doing their job looking for deserters and people who had not paid their military exemption tax. One thing was clear though: any Armenian – and especially an ARF member – could not have been arrested unless the order had come from governor Jevded himself.

As usual, Vramian went to Jevdet to discuss Hovsep's arrest. Jevdet feigned surprise and stated that the issue should not have any repercussions. He suggested a delegation should be sent to Shadakh to calm the situation.

Vramian returned to discuss developments with the All-Armenian Council. This body had been formed as soon as the Russo-Turkish war was declared and included different social and political segments of the Armenian population of Van. Of the fourteen members of the council, two were Vramian and Ishkhan from the ARF, Kouyoumjian and Roupen Hovnanian from the Ramgavars, Kaligian and Khachadour Cherpashkhian from the Hnchags, plus Terzibashian and several others representing the merchant class. Any important issue regarding Armenians was discussed in this council.

It was not surprising that the council always stressed the importance of acceding to the government and its demands. Armenians had to avoid any incident that might have complicated matters. Time was of the essence and everything had to be done to gain time.

This strategy to "gain time" came from the ARF leaders within the council. Conditions were critical and the well-being of Armenians in Van and its vicinity demanded such a policy. Any divergence could have had dire consequences.

However, the youth in Van thought differently. The majority were ARF members. They were sure that the government was preparing a sinister plan and waiting for the opportunity to act. Why should Armenians fall prey to such a plan? It was better to stand up and let whatever was to happen, happen! The resolute stance of these youngsters was contrary to the position of the ARF leadership. In other words, the youth were restless…

While such opposing views spread and challenged the Armenians of Van, Jevdet ordered all Armenian men of conscription age to register with the government within three days. Thus, even as the Shadakh incident remained unresolved, Jevdet presented a new challenge to Armenians.

A young man from Van, B. Pakradouni, described the situation in his diary as follows.

> We are extremely nervous. Yesterday Jevdet had the Chief of Police, Vafik Bey, call the headmen of the city quarters to a meeting where he demanded all Armenian men between the ages of 20 to 40 be conscripted and those between 18 to 20 registered for the army. Jevdet also poured scorn on the French and Russians. He once again stressed the three-day ultimatum and added that at the end of that period, those who were apprehended would face military courts-martial and the death penalty while their families would be driven to Baghdad and Syria. Immediately after his announcement, he began to act on his word. I toured the main street just after the meeting and saw some 120 to 150 Turkish soldiers and chetes who had taken part in Jevdet Bey's campaign in Azerbaijan enter the Haji Hamoud garrison.
>
> People are extremely concerned by developments around them. Everything seems clear after the massacres in Akhorig, Avzarig, Hasan Tamran, and Hazara villages, as well as the massacre of Armenian soldiers in the Turkish army. They obviously want to create the same situation in Van, where there is extreme excitement and anxiety among the youth. We have decided not to respond to the call of the government, nor to the suggestions and announcements of the arachnortaran [prelacy], because they want us to go to certain death.

Conditions were very serious.

The Armenian Council was still discussing matters with no end in sight. They continued for many hours and days.

"We must pacify Shadakh. We must give 400 conscripts, otherwise they will be executed," the council decided.

The meetings between Vramian and Jevdet continued with demands and promises.

"We have to send people to Shadakh quickly!" insisted Jevdet, "Otherwise, there could be complications."

The leaders thus discussed sending a delegation to Shadakh, especially as they were informed that unless Hovsep was released, the Armenians in Shadakh would attack the convoy taking him to Van and release him themselves.

April 14 and 15 passed under a dark cloud. On April 16 the decision was taken to send a delegation to Shadakh. Ishkhan was picked as the best man for the job. Jevdet agreed with the decision, though nobody knew his plans.

* * *

On the evening of April 16, Ishkhan set off for Shadakh. He was a well-known leader and an ARF military activist. Everyone knew him and he was not sent alone. Accompanying him were three young ARF members from Van: Boghos Toutounjian (Kotot), Vahan Khranian, and Mihran Der Markarian, a seasoned revolutionary from Tagh. Ishkhan was also accompanied by Vehib Bey and three gendarmes. Eight people, four from each side and all armed. The peace mission thus set off for Tagh. Everyone had doubts and nobody believed that the delegation would be able to achieve its task, especially the three young men – Kotot, Vahan, and Mihran – who were against such a delegation being sent. However, they were carrying out the orders of the ARF.

"Farwell comrades, we are being duped once again," murmured the Armenian fighters as they parted from their comrades.

Shadakh was far away and the delegation rested at the village of Hirj in Hayots Tsor. The village consisted of 30 Armenian and 70 Kurdish households. There were entirely Armenian inhabited villages in Hayots Tsor, such as Gem, Ankgh, or Kiziltash. However, Ishkhan decided to rest in Hirj, because he was familiar with the place. He had visited it many times to collect the tithe and was friends with Kyarim Oghlou Rashid. The delegation rested at Rashid Agha's two-storey house.

It was here, as the Armenians rested at Rashid Agha's house, that a nefarious plot was put into action. A number of Circassians, who had followed the delegation from Van, entered the premises and shot Ishkhan and his comrades dead. The peace mission fell victim to a perfect Asiatic conspiracy.

The four youngsters fell, sacrificed for the Armenian people, as Jevdet's bloody plans were set into motion. This was the beginning of a series of murders which led to the most horrific pages in Armenian history.

The Armenians in Van were unaware of what had transpired during that awful night. Vramian and Aram were not informed. But Jevdet knew well what had happened, as news of the murder had reached him first. Part of his plan had been realised and he now focused on the next steps. Shortly after daylight, he called Vramian and Aram to meet him. He telephoned both men around the same time, Vramian from the Post Office, and Aram from Arark police station. He invited them separately in order to entrap them both.

Vramian lost no time and returned home, where he emptied his pockets onto a table and wrote the following few lines:

"Aram. The governor has asked me to meet him. If he contacts you too, please don't go." He then took a carriage and never returned.

Aram got Vramian's note after a policeman at Norashen police station let him know about Jevdet's invitation. Aram never went to the meeting. Vramian's note saved Aram's life.

"Ishkhan and his three comrades have been treacherously killed at Hirj!" and "Vramian has been deceived by Jevdet and has disappeared!" These two pieces of shocking news spread like lightning across Van. People first reacted as if they were thunderstruck. Then came the roar of the people of Van and their horrified bodies.

"Treachery!" they exclaimed, as they took to arms. They were not unprepared. They had spent months planning for the unexpected and began to mobilise.

Communications ceased between the city and Aykesdan. The markets were closed, relations between the government and Armenians were severed, and Armenians in outlying areas moved to more central Armenian quarters in the city. The young people began their preparations to resist.

Pakradouni continues his description:

> Soon ARF groups were in a frenzy of activity. All those who had been organised
> into units of 10 were soon under arms and assumed their positions. These
> developments were triggered by Ishkhan's murder and Vramian's arrest. Captain
> (*khmpabed*) Misak's group, which was at our friend Shahenents' house on Great
> Kendrji Street, was soon prepared and went through the orchards to take up an
> important position. The ARF quickly spread news of any developments so that
> they were ready for all eventualities. By evening, all important positions were
> occupied by Armenian units. We had 50 or 60 men at key positions along the
> main street of Sghka. The same was also the case in Ararouts district. We also
> learned that the governor's office had wanted to capture Aram and Bulgaratsi
> Krikor, who had turned down the treacherous invitations. Following these
> developments, Armenian families in outlying quarters quickly moved to more
> central areas.

While Van was in such commotion, there were still those who believed in Jevdet's good
intentions and the value of negotiating with the government. Having been informed of
Vramian's arrest, the prelate of Van, Yeznig Vartabed, as well as the merchants Kevork
Jidechian and Avedik Terzibashian, went to see the governor. However, this time Jevdet
spoke to them in a very different and threatening tone. The Armenian notables listened to
the threats and returned convinced that all doors to the government had been closed.

On April 18, news came from Avants, that the previous evening some 50 gendarmes
had brought Vramian and put him on a boat to an unknown destination.

Ishkhan had been killed and Vramian was now removed. Only Aram was left but he
was not alone, as the whole of the Armenian youth of Van, as well as the Ramgavar and
Hnchagian parties stood with him. Armenians, however zealous and sharply divided
during peaceful times, knew how to unite as one during times of trouble.

As danger approached, the people of Van stood up and became a formidable force. All
credit to them.

There were endless meetings in which they organised defence, military, supply and
other committees. They appointed regional commanders and captains, prepared defensive
positions, and amassed supplies. Normal life was at an end as Van prepared for war.

Jevdet was also not sitting still. Always scheming, he tried to post soldiers inside
Armenian areas, organise offensive positions, and begin hostilities.

Pakradouni records in his diary.

> A little earlier, I was at the editorial offices of *Ashkhadank* newspaper. The
> American missionary, Dr. Ussher, came to see Aram and related Jevdet's wish to
> place 50 Turkish soldiers as guards for the defence of the American mission.
> Simon Agha Tiutiunjian, a wealthy merchant, Mampre Mgrian, a teacher of the
> Yeremian School, and Gaydzag Arakel, a seasoned ARF fighter were also there.
> They all told Dr. Ussher that Jevdet was trying to gain an advantageous position
> against Armenians and that it would require a lot of energy and resources to
> remove them. Mgrian and Tiutiunjian used strong words to remind Dr. Ussher
> about the dark days of 1896, when an old and experienced American missionary,

Dr. Reynolds, handed over Armenians sheltering in the American compound to the provincial authorities. Gaydzag Arakel and Aram ended the conversation by stating that Armenians would not allow Turkish soldiers to enter Armenian areas, especially the American and German compounds, where large quantities of supplied had been stored over the previous two days. Dr. Ussher left to inform the governor that Armenians would not allow him to place soldiers in the American compound.

While these negotiations were taking place, Muslim soldiers and militiamen were digging trenches in the open fields between Aykesdan and Varak. The Armenian men facing the fields could see these developments and made their own preparations. In one word, both sides were preparing for a terrible clash, though the fighting seemed to be delayed for some reason.

Soon it was the morning of Monday, April 19. It was an important day, a day of work, though nobody went to their workplace or the market. However, there was still a lot of movement about, as described by Pakradouni:

> It is morning and the commotion continues in the streets. I took some important items and bedding from our house to my uncle's hiding place and rested there. During this time, I received orders from the head of ARF forces, Bulgaratsi Krikor, to go to my position at the Belekian Avanes' residence on Great Kendrji street and oppose any attack from the two houses and garrison at Hamoud Agha. Soon Apel of Avants and five or six comrades came to support our position. Last night they had clashed with Turkish guards at Kyazge Pos on their way from Avants and captured them. A little later, Captain Ohanes also came and instructed us to strengthen our position with bags of soil, reinforcing the northern side of the roof and two rooms overlooking the Hamoud Agha houses and garrison.
>
> A little later, we had a visit from the newly formed Red Cross contingent of student comrades. They were Krikor Shiroyian, Ardashes Safrasdian, Vahram Terzibashian, and Askanaz Ararktsian, all secondary school students who had attended Red Cross courses and carried bags of medical supplies on their shoulders. A short while after their departure, Teos of Van arrived with his mobile group of fighters. He inspected our positions and left after giving us words of encouragement. Now morale is high in the streets, as armed groups and individuals move about. We have not seen any Turkish faces in the last three days.

It was in such a turbulent yet spirited atmosphere that the people of Van prepared to greet April 19. They took their last break on that momentous night before the terrible but also glorious morning which was to become one of the greatest moments in Armenian history. However, before discussing the fighting that erupted in the city of Van, we should say something about developments in the surrounding districts during this period.

Chapter XIII

The Horrible Massacres

On his return from the war front, Jevdet brought with him a heinous plan to exterminate the Armenians of Vasbouragan. No Armenian male above the age of 10 was to remain alive, whether a civilian, soldier, or a member of the *amele* groups. All were to be shot or killed by the sword, while women, young girls and boys were to be distributed among Muslims. Every *believer* was permitted to abuse, enslave or abduct any Armenian woman or child of his choice.

The appalling plan to destroy Armenians was devised in Constantinople, but this suggestion was made by Jevdet and members of the Ittihadist party.

The Young Turk government could not have found a better opportunity to continue the legacy of the murderous Sultan Abdul Hamid and his plans to wipe out Armenians. There could be no better time to do what they wanted. All of Europe was preoccupied by war and the titanic struggle had disoriented all. Which power could do anything for Armenians? The European states were barely able to look after themselves. The Turkish government knew the score and felt free to act.

As the Constantinople daily, *Turan,* wrote in a December 1914 editorial entitled "Russia and Armenians":

> If the Turks want to get rid of the Armenians once and for all, they could do so when there can be no outside intervention.

Yes, if Turks wanted to eliminate Armenians, they could do so now without any opposition. This was what the Young Turk government believed when it put such a plan into action. The order for the extermination of Armenians was given, but it was first applied to Vasbouragan.

"Van and its surroundings are preparing for a general uprising," said Jevdet. "Vramian and Aram are in secret communication with Armenian volunteers in Persia. We have in our hands written proof which was intercepted at our border," repeated Jevdet so many times. All of this was communicated to Constantinople and the murderers in the capital gave the order for extermination. The orders came from Talaat, Enver and Sanders – Sanders, Enver and Talaat. They were the criminals, and Jevdet returned from the front to carry out these orders.

At first, it seemed that Jevdet was only concerned with the city of Van and not the outlying districts. However, while he maintained good relations with Armenian leaders, he also prepared to massacre Armenians outside the city. For example, he set up road blocks at key locations in different districts and gave orders to Kurdish chieftains to be ready with their followers. The kaimakams also received secret messages with details of massacres that had taken place.

Although such plans were being arranged in great secrecy, Armenians in some areas were informed of what lay ahead because of warnings from Kurdish friends. Nobody could have imagined such massacres.

Example One: Avdal Hamze, one of the villagers of lower Pzhngerd in Hayots Tsor, was amongst the Circassians and chetes who had returned from Persia with Jevdet. When he went home on a two-day leave, he met his Armenian friend Aharon Der Mardirosian of Eremerou at Chllan mills in Gghzi village. During their conversation, Avdal warned his friend, "Armenians, fend for yourselves. Jevdet Pasha has come from Persia to kill all of your leaders."

Example Two: A Kurdish gendarme named Peno from Komer in Shadakh, who was amongst 10 gendarmes arrested by Armenians at Sivdgin in December and later freed by Azad, wrote the following to the latter prior to developments in Shadakh:

My dear friend Azad:

You have been so kind to me. I will never forget what you have done and I am writing these few lines to warn you. Please look after yourselves especially well these days. The kaimakam will come to gather Armenian conscripts. Knowing beforehand that Armenians will not join up, the government will use this refusal as an excuse to massacre Armenians.

Lazki is currently waiting in Hayots Tsor with 30 gendarmes. The governor has ordered him to remain there until skirmishes begin in Shadakh, when he will be allowed to wreak vengeance on Armenians for his father's death. The call to battle has been made and already the Yezdinan and Alan ashirets have gathered here. The Khoumar guard unit has also been called back for the same reason. The Khalilan and the Khavshdan tribes in Parvari and Nordouz have been ordered to send armed men. The battle will start when all are ready. Other than the militia forces here, other Kurds nearby have also received arms. In expressing my gratitutde to you, I ask that nobody knows of this letter other than God and us two.

Peno of Komer village

Example Three: Nouro, from Pirsolan in Pergri district was a loyal ARF messenger and a close friend of ARF activist Shirin Hagopian of Arjag. On April 16 he came to Kharagonis and related the following to Shirin:

Yesterday, Zia Bey, the kaimakam of Pergri, called all the village heads and leaders and warned them sternly that, should Armenians be massacred, no Muslim should dare hide or defend any of them, even those who wished to convert. Whoever went against these arrangements would be treated as Armenians.

Such friendly warnings indicated what terrible massacres were being planned against Armenians in the province of Van. All such information was communicated to Armenian political leaders who did not pay much attention to it. They were busy with developments in the city and could not deal with the outlying districts. One could say that the outlying areas were forgotten and left to their fate – especially after the murder of Ishkhan and his three comrades, and the disappearance of Vramian.

Thus, the outlying areas were left without leadership or direction and became the scenes of terrible massacres the like of which Armenians had never experienced before. It is true that in some areas there was resistance, and some small groups fought back and fell bravely, but the majority of Armenians in these areas were stupefied and simply put to the sword or shot without putting up any resistance.

People were gathered up by dozens, hundreds, and even thousands and detained in courthouses, prisons, churches, schools and private houses. Their arms were bound and they were led to riverbanks and lake shores where they were shot or killed by the sword. Their bodies were thrown into rivers and lakes, tossed into wells, or piled up and burned.

These massacres were planned for April 19, a day before the Feast of the Resurrection (Easter). It is true that in some places the massacres took place a day earlier, and in a few places a few days later – as it was impossible to start them all at the same time – but this infernal crime took place on that date in district centres, large villages, and the main Armenian inhabited areas.

It is impossible to describe every case of mass murder of hundreds of people, the abduction of women, enslavement of children, theft of animals, plunder of homes, and the destruction or torching of houses and villages in the different parts of Van starting on April 17. One would need hundreds of scribes, thousands of witnesses, and endless sheets of paper to record what happened to incense the world, prod the human imagination, and move the conscience of all mankind.

This author's pen is weak and unable to describe those awful and terrifying events. Only a few descriptions and images will be presented, as well as the words of several eye-witnesses, in order to give an idea of what happened in Armenian inhabited regions during those horrific days.

1

The following incident took place at the village of Hirj in Hayots Tsor on the evening of Sunday, April 18. Hirj consisted of 70 Kurdish and 30 Armenian households. Eight gendarmes had been stationed there over the previous few months. At the western edge of the village were two buildings. One was the Armenian church, which faced north, and the other was Kyarim Oghli Rashid's house, the only large, two-storey building in the village. The reception room was upstairs, while the ground floor consisted of a store room and two stables. Rashid Agha's house was considered the palace of Hirj. Between the church and the palace was a large tract of land that was the village square with a large well in the middle.

A group of women stood outside one of the houses. They were exhausted and had no life in their eyes. Among them were three widows: 50 year-old Yaghout and her two daughters-in-law, Kohar and Koulo. This was Melkon's house, where three men of the household had been murdered. They were Melkon, Yaghout's husband, and their two married sons, Avedis and Kasbar. Melkon's third son was with Antranig's volunteers; nobody knew whether he would ever return alive. There were three widows in Melkon's house, six young fatherless orphans and, as if by miracle, a fourth son, Tavo, who was 15 years' old at that time. This household reflected the reality of each Armenian house in Hirj.

The women related with tear-filled eyes and much bitterness what had happened in their village three months earlier, often pointing to Rashid Agha's house and giving their account in a candid manner in their own distinct Armenian dialect.

On Saturday, April 17, a black day dawned for us. Our Kurdish neighbours started to whisper to us before dawn that Ishkhan and his three comrades had been murdered by Circassians who had come to Rashid Agha's house from Van. Gendarmes were now watching the village and the Circassians forbade anyone to leave it. We were all terrified and could only speak to each other in whispers. Our men-folk did not leave their houses. We spent the whole day as if we were in prison. The gendarmes were patrolling the streets and keeping watch on people's houses. They were like wild beasts. The murder of Ishkhan and his companions had taken over our lives.

Sunday morning was upon us. A black Sunday. The gendarmes and Circassians spread out throughout the village and began gathering our men and taking them to Rashid Agha's house. They seized them all and none managed to avoid capture, except for those who happened to be away in the first place. In total, 46 men and boys were collected from 30 Armenian households and locked up in Rashid Agha's stable. Our men obeyed without any resistance and even remained quiet. We were very scared because of the murder of Ishkhan and his companions and the brutal faces of the gendarmes. We did not even dare to ask questions.

The terror of the previous day grew and we were all distressed. We forgot everything – home, hearth and nourishment. We huddled in groups at home and asked questions, but we could not make sense of anything. We were drained and the day passed in great suspense. We tried to go to Rashid Agha's home to see our men, to ask questions, to get information, but they did not allow us to get close. They cursed, threatened and pushed us away. They even refused to accept the bread we were offering.

Soon it was evening, but it was not any evening. It was especially stifling, oppressive and bitter. As we stood around, worried and depressed, thinking of what lay ahead, we were shaken by loud shots from Rashid Agha's house and began to weep. Regardless of the danger, many women ran out of their homes towards the agha's house. We were met by gendarmes who came out to stop us and push us back. We heard more deafening shots, as well as heart-rending and pitiful cries.

"They are massacring our men!" screamed someone, as the whole village burst into tears. They were executing our men in our presence and our whole world was falling apart.

A terrible night of mourning began, one that could never be reversed, and what a night it was. Thank God for keeping us alive. But it would have been better to die a hundred times than to live through that night. We could not find out exactly what had happened. The black night passed and the mourning continued on Monday morning. The same mourning and weeping, and the same laments in the streets. The gendarmes now blocked off the road to Rashid Agha's house. That slaughter-house had become a fortress.

Ishkhan and his three companions, as well as our 46 men, all shot and stabbed, were thrown into the empty grain-storage pit in the ground, near the church, and covered with soil. That soil now covered the future prospects of the whole village, the pillars of 30 households. It became our sacred site. Our weeping was not ordinary weeping, nor was our mourning ordinary mourning. It was a terrible lament that echoed in the mountains and valleys. We lamented for two whole days, until Tuesday, the morning of the Annunciation, when the general massacre of Hayots Tsor began, accompanied by fire and destruction. We forgot our own agony as we saw the attacks on surrounding Armenian villages, the rising smoke, and the seizure of women and children. Our own suffering of the previous day became even greater, unfathomable and pervasive, and since that day, Sir, we have been consumed by that whole experience.

Reshid agha's house was later burned to the ground. Only a few walls remained, including the long, blackened, stable walls riddled with bullet holes, with hundreds of bullets embedded in them from the time the men of Hirj were murdered.

To the north, towards the church, was the wide pit looking like the mouth of a wolf, where the 50 or so corpses lay buried until the Russian army arrived and the dead could be reclaimed.

Soon a stone mound appeared a short distance from the pit, to the south of the church wall, where 40 of the exhumed bodies were reburied. It was the fraternal gravesite of Hirj, where every evening the mourning women from the village would come to burn frankincense. But it was not ordinary frankincense, but one mixed with the grief of the mourners, as their tears flowed and watered the mass grave.

2

The following incident took place on April 19 in Agants, the centre of the district of Arjesh. This was the seat of the kaimakam, Ali Riza Bey, who was a Turk from Constantinople. Agants was an hour from the north-eastern shores of Lake Van. It was a township which was renowned for its vineyards and fruit trees and was composed of 300 Armenian and 700 Muslim households.

The following story was related by a fifty-year old father of six. He had miraculously survived a Turkish massacre and his eyes and expressions conveyed his agony. He was a builder by profession, hence his name, *Binaji* Simon.

The day before the Anunciation, a Monday, a government crier suddenly started announcing that all Armenian men above the age of 15 should gather at the *hiukmat* (government building). As the crier was making his announcement, a group of gendarmes started patrolling the streets and even entering people's homes. Over 400 men and boys were brought to the government building and locked in its prison and other rooms. They continued to bring more people over several hours: grown-ups and youngsters, rich and poor, city folk and peasants. Soon there was no more space left, so they began taking them to the *kshla*, [army barracks] which was to the south-west of town. There were more people at the kshla than our location.

We remained very worried all day long, as we did not know what was happening outside. We were impatient. We remained restless and nervous about what lay ahead. We had all sorts of ominous thoughts, though we could not have imagined what would actually happen.

We lingered all day suffering thirst, hunger, and a thousand and one worries. Soon it was evening and the town became quiet much earlier than usual as arrangements had been made for people to be indoors as soon as it was dark.

While some people contemplated worrying scenarios, others just sat or slept on the bare floor. Suddenly, the door flung open and Ali Effendi, the jail keeper, appeared.

He then took eleven people to the courtyard where they were made to stand side-by-side and then tied to each other. I was among these men. Then another eight men were brought and tied in the same manner. Then a third group of nine men were treated in a similar fashion. These were all the men who could be tied together with the available rope.

Following these steps, the warden gave orders to the eight to ten gendarmes who were there, "Bounlari siza teslim ettik, geotiuriun kshla" (we are surrendering these to you, take them to the barracks). These gendarmes led the three groups totalling 28 Armenians away.

I knew all of the Armenians who were tied together. For example, in my group were Vartan Agha and his two sons Kapriel and Soghomon, and Boghos Agha Boyajian and his two sons Roupen and Arsen. I also knew our gendarmes: Boyraz Iso, Shoukri Oghli Hekmat and Kouli Oghli Siuleyman.

The gendames led us away, but instead of taking us to the barracks as ordered, they took us on the road to the port on the lake. We walked in the dark and said nothing. We were so afraid that we did not dare utter a word. However, one of the men asked the guards to loosen the ropes as he was in great pain and a gendarme responded by hitting him so hard with the stock of his rifle that the man collapsed.

We left the city and were taken to the village of Khargen, half an hour away. The village was on a small but powerful river called Dara Zamin. They brought us to the river bank and we had no idea what they were going to do to us. Suddenly, the gendarmes took a few steps away, pointed their rifles at us, and opened fire.

People screamed and yelled "I am hit!" and grabbed each other. We all fell to the ground in small heaps. There was a mixture of heart-breaking cries and gunfire, as countless bullets penetrated the fallen bodies.

A few moments passed, the moaning and shots subsided, and the gendarmes approached the victims to see if any were still alive. I was out of my mind and did not know whether I was hit. I kept losing consciousness. I suddenly felt the ropes loosen and my arms free. I saw a light, as one of the gendarmes struck a match and looked at the faces of the fallen men. Whoever showed signs of life was shot in the forehead. They approached me. It was such a terrifying ordeal. It would have been easier to die many times than live that moment. I was waiting for my final fate, when more shots were heard nearby. Now there were new screams and cries and the gendarmes around us, fearing for their own safety, rushed off. There were several more volleys, as more groups were shot down, and we were forgotten.

I was still unaware whether I was shot. I moved a bit, examined myself, but felt no pain. I examined myself yet again and there was nothing. The bodies that had fallen on top of me had protected me and soaked me in blood. Those stains remain with me even today.

My first instinct was to run away, but I could not do so in my shoes, so I immediately put on a pair belonging to one of the dead and escaped. People are so quick when threatened by death. I was running at the speed of a bullet, without looking back, crossing streams, fields and hills. I was not aware of anything else, such as feelings of hunger, thirst or fatigue, though I had not had anything to eat all day. I could only hear the shooting and the hastening of my stride.

I walked all night and when daylight broke, I was on the snowy Alakaz mountain. Only then did I feel exhausted as never before. There was snow everywhere and I found a dry spot to sit and rest under a large rock, but I was overcome by fear once more when I stood up and noticed others people under different rocks. I soon felt relieved, however, as I recognised the others. There were 23 people including the priest from Sosgoun village. They had fled when they had heard about the massacre at Agants.

So, hungry and exhausted, I remained in the snowy ravines of Aladagh with those 23 people for another day and night, and then descended to Diadin, which was under the control of the Russian army.

A few of us miraculously escaped, but no other men were left behind in Arjesh. They were all shot or killed by the sword.

3

The following story also relates to the massacre that took place at Agants. The witness was Mgrdich Hovhannesian from Panon village in Arjesh. He was called Avedi Mgo in his village.

Mgrdich was a short, elderly man, who had witnessed Turkish atrocities before. Twenty years earlier, he had been married for three years and had a young wife and a one-year-old daughter. He belonged to one of the great families of Panon, a prosperous village of 40 households.

This village was destroyed in the 1896 massacres. Mgrdich's family also suffered many losses, including his wife and child, his older brother Aslan and his wife and two daughters, and his other brother Haroutiun and his sons and daughter. Following the destruction of his village and hearth, including the death of so many family members, Mgrdich took refuge on the Ararat Plain.

In the following 14 years, he got married again, had children and earned a living. He began to forget his earlier pain. Then came the 1908 constitutional revolution in Ottoman Turkey and encouraging news about the country. He remembered his ancestral village, felt the pull of his homeland and returned to Panon with his family, where he found five poor families of the former 40 well-to-do households. The village of Panon began to grow and prosper once more. As the village approached its former glory, the country entered the war and there were new massacres.

This is the story related by a very distressed Mgrdich who miraculously survived the massacre.

> On April 15 news spread in our village that *Onbashi* (Sergeant) Ali was coming with seven or eight gendarmes in search of deserters. We then heard that the gendarmes had reached the village of Kantsag. I was curious and naive enough to go to Kantsag, with the expectation that they would not harm me. However, as soon as I arrived, Onbashi Ali arrested me. As I was 48 years old, I was exempt from military service. I protested and stated that I was not eligible for conscription and showed my *hamidiye* (birth certificate). However, Onbashi Ali paid no attention to my protests or to my birth certificate. He simply put the paper in his pocket and set me alongside a number of men who had been arrested. He stated that his orders were to take all men above 18 to the city. Over 30 older men were brought to Pertagh. Two of them managed to escape at night and the headman of the village was severely beaten as a consequence. On the second day we were taken to Ororan as more men working in the fields were arrested on the way.

> We reached Agants and Lake Van and were led directly to the *kshla* (barracks). There were many Armenians there of all ages and new groups were still arriving. On the last day there were 700 to 800 people who were supposed to have been formed into "amali tabouris" [labour battalions].

> On April 18, we were taken in groups to the government building, where police commissioner Abdullah Effendi registered our names in special lists without listening to my protests. We were once again taken back to the barracks where a large number of Armenians were packed like animals. We were not provided with any food and ate what remained of the food brought from some people's homes.

Finally, a terrifying and fateful day began on April 19. At sunrise, gendarmes took me and seven other Armenians to work in the city. We worked on a fountain near the market, but our work did not take long, and they decided to take us back to the barracks two hours later. Our movements seemed odd and when we queried the gendarmes accompanying us we were informed that we were to go to Diyarbekir.

At the barracks, we were joined by 70 people from Abagha. Starting from midday, more people came from the city, including Der Yeghishe (the prelate's *locum tenens*), Nigoghos Effendi Shaljian and his sons Sarkis, Haroutiun, and Nshan, as well as Khosrov and Serop Effendis. The latter were well-known merchants from the city.

A large number of militiamen gathered in the main square of the barracks that evening, some young, some old. Then the kaimakam – Ali Riza Bey – addressed them and sent them in different directions before leaving himself. All this took place in front of us. We could see what was happening from the windows, but we could not hear what was said. We had no idea what they were planning and what was happening outside. However, we could feel that something serious was underway.

We soon learned that the authorities had arranged that nobody in town would be allowed outside after 8 o'clock (1 o'clock Turkish time). Our suspicions increased when we noted how many people had been packed into the large rooms of the barracks. After 8 o'clock there were whispers that the *locum tenens* and a few well-known people were taken outside the city and killed. The information came from a militiaman, Geoyli Zahar, who was known to an Armenian. We were all terrified but nobody suspected what was planned for us.

Suddenly the door to our room was opened and 50 people were taken out. The door was then closed and locked again. After a quarter of an hour, the door was opened again, and fifty more people were taken away. Where were they taken? What was happening to them? We had no idea. We approached the gendarmes near the windows and asked them questions. They all said that there was nothing to worry about, that the men had been taken to the port, on their way to Diyarbekir.

When the door opened for a fourth time, it was my turn and 50 more of us were taken away. Among us were Boghos and Asadour Goranian of Kantsag, Kevork Bedrosian, Hagop and Sahag Nahabedian, Hagop, Vartan, Mikael and Safar Ghazarian and, from our village of Panon, Kevork Manougian, Melkon Sarkisian and Khachadour Avedisian. Among us were also people known to me from Aghsraf, Pertagh and other villages.

Thus, when around 50 of us came out, gendarmes and militiamen fell upon us and tied our arms together. This was done quite quickly and we left the barracks under the direction of gendarmes and militia forces.

We were taken to Ororan village. Our guards were hasty and impatient, beating and cursing anyone who slowed down. They were taking us to a slaughterhouse, something we could not imagine, though we were terribly worried. There were fields with streams, furrows and two mills on the way to Ororan – and we went towards them. We went a long way, and even if it was not that long, it took us a long time. The ropes made us anxious. Finally, they took us to a stream called Karachi Yiurt, where they made us stop. It was quite dark but I noticed some corpses in the distance. I was terrified and confused, and my eyes went blank. I instinctively nudged the people next to me and pointed out the corpses. My companions were also petrified. We started whispering to each other and were all baffled. The gendarmes and militiamen noticed what we had seen and within seconds there was a thunder of shots fired at us. Many of us collapsed, pulling others down, so that there were heaps of bodies on the ground. I remained under such a heap. I am still unable to remember what happened next and how I escaped that hell. However, I can remember that I was running, out of breath, without looking back, crossing a stream, as well as mounds and holes in the ground. I also remember someone else escaping with me, someone I did not know, while the firing continued behind us.

I ran without stopping and covered a lot of ground. The following morning I reached my home, but it was impossible to stay there. We were getting terrible news from the city that no Armenian men were left there, that the surrounding Kurds were being mobilised, and that some villages had already been attacked and massacred. I waited until evening and escaped in the darkness towards Alakaz, leaving my wife and children to their fate.

4

Some massacres took place in the river valley of Bande Mahou in the region of Pergri.

Pergri was mainly composed of two plains which were separated by a range of mountains. One of the plains was the beautiful Abagha, in the north-east, and the other was Pergri Ova in the south-west, extending all the way to Lake Van.

The Abagha plain had many rivers and streams such as the Soroukh Su, Kanli Chai and Drshig Chai. There were also tributaries such as the Snt Chai and Chipoukli Chai, both of which joined Soroukh Su.

All of the rivers on the Abagha plain flowed westward, cutting through the mountains dividing the two plains, thus forming a long, meandering valley that crossed Pergri Ova and ended at Lake Van.

The river formed by all of these streams was called Bande Mahou, as was its 10-mile-long valley. This valley, which narrowed and broadened from place to place, was the route taken by travellers from Van to the Caucasus.

The river Bande Mahou presented quite a sight. In some stretches it was calm and mysterious, while elsewhere it was turbulent and noisy. In mid-valley, it crossed rocks, where it broke up into streams that formed a roaring waterfall. One could only marvel and be awed by the foam and spray that was formed by the waters.

But Bande Mahou looked more terrifying at the end of the valley. Here, it descended into deep rocks that had been cut into over the centuries, and then forced its way through a narrow exit, where it was at its wildest, and erupted like a dragon.

A small stone bridge was built at this narrowest point of Bande Mahou. The bridge was called Golod Bridge in Armenian, or Pra Kortk in Kurdish.

South-east of this bridge, around one mile or so further on, was the centre of the district – Pergri or Pergri Ghala. It was a poor town with a small market, as well as the remains of an old fortress on a hill to the west.

Pergri was composed of 110 Kurdish and 25 Armenian households. It was the seat of the kaimakam who, during the massacres, was a certain Zia Bey.

The following account was given by Moushegh Mgrdichian of the village of Yegmal in Abagha. He was a small framed man, around 25 years old, who had managed to escape the Turkish sword. This is what he related in a much distressed – and outraged – voice.

> There were very few men left in the villages of Abagha at the beginning of spring. Conscription had left very few men in their homes. The majority had been called to arms and then disarmed and placed in labour battalions (*amele tabour*s). However, some had escaped and remained in hiding.
>
> Regardless of this, gendarmes from Pergri Ghala went to the villages and gathered up the [remaining] Armenian men in the middle of April. I was amongst them. They were taking us to strengthen the labour battalions. That was what the gendarmes said and we did not know their real intentions. There were a few dozen Armenians from my village, Khachan, and other villages. We were taken to Pergri Ghala. At that time, the Abagha plain – part of Pergri valley – was still covered with snow and many disarmed Armenian soldiers, as well as other Armenians from the villages, were working on the roads. There were at least 1,000 of them. We joined these men. The gendarmes told us that a large number of soldiers would be coming this way, and that our job was to clear the way. However, that explanation was a pretext to gather all Armenian men over the age of 15 together and carry out their treacherous plans.
>
> We were working in groups of 50, 60 even 100 people. Although the road stretched a long way, we were working mainly in the valley. We were taken to town in the evenings and to road construction in the mornings.
>
> I worked for three days, that is, supposedly worked, as we were mostly killing time. We were quite naive and carried on.
>
> On April 19, a Monday, while we were quietly at work, Israyel Hovov of Chiboukhli village, who was with a group working quite a distance above us, ran to us in a distressed manner and let us know that around 25 men in his group had been taken away to an unknown destination and he suspected foul play.
>
> Half an hour later, someone else also approached us from another group further down and related in a terrified and anxious voice that 25 men had been taken away in their group to an unknown destination. Less than half an hour later two horrified people approached us and whispered: "Look after yourselves. They are

taking people to the riverbank, killing them, and then throwing them into the water."

Our group did not know what to do. It was not our turn to be massacred yet. If the gendarmes guarding us saw our anxious movements and whispering, they did not let us know. But it was not long before we noticed a group of gendarmes and militia forces approaching us. We thought we could hear shooting and wailing in the distance. Everything indicated that we were falling into a trap. Those of us who were working, as well as the gendarmes guarding us, watched the approaching gendarmes and militiamen. Two other men and I saw an opportunity and escaped. What happened next, I do not remember. I only remember that I had run up a high mountain on my own and could hear dreadful rifle fire.

I was in great fear and reached my village at midnight, having crossed several mountains and valleys. Ordinarily, one needed two days to cover the distance. The next day, around 15 deserters appeared one by one and related terrible things. Among them were Hovhannes Kholian of Khachan and Garabed Manougian, who had escaped from the Arjesh massacres and seen many corpses on the way. The Bandi Mahou had not carried all the bodies away. The gendarmes did not have the time to throw everyone into the terrifying river either.

Three days later Amer Bey, the gendarmerie commander, came to Khachan from Pergri Ghala. He wanted to wipe out the remaining Armenians. Around 30 of us were taking shelter in the mountains and did not descend at night. Our Agha, who was Kop Mahmad Bey's son, Tahar Beg, the head of the Hamidiye Corps, protected us by stating that there were no Armenians in his villages. However, Tahar Beg had to pay a high price for his action, as the kaimakam was informed that Tahar Beg was sheltering Armenians. The kaimakam, under orders, invited Tahar Beg for a meal at Nazarava village and poisoned him. Tahar Beg was sacrificed for us. We went to Maku and waited until the Russian army reached Abagha.

Over 1,000 Armenians were thrown into the Bande Mahou river. The village of Khachan alone, which was composed of 60 households, lost 80 people – one family, Ousta Mgo's household, losing 12 men.

The men murdered in Ousta Mgo's family included the head of family Mgo; his five brothers Avak, Isro, Matos, chorister Harten, and Balo; his two sons Sisag and Roupen; and Balo's two sons Hagop and Garabed. One household, 12 men, murdered.

5

The following account concerns the massacre at Golod Bridge over the Bande Mahou river.

To the north of Pergri Ghala was a small, unassuming and poor Armenian quarter. Shatri Hago lived in this quarter, in a typical poor village house composed of a narrow, damp room. His house had been robbed of all its furnishings. The room was lit by a small opening in the main wall. There were a few women there but no men. The scenario was the same as elsewhere and people's faces were pale and unhappy. Among them was a short woman with a tortured face. She was Zmo, Shatri Hago's wife. Alogside her was a woman with an intelligent face and pained eyes. She was Heto, Shatri Setrag's wife. These women represented the two halves of the same family. Both of their husbands and brothers-in-law had been murdered.

Zmo and Heto related what had happened in the presence of other widows who had lost their children.

It was the Feast of Annunciation, a day of joy for the world, but a day of mourning for us. We were naive and living as normal, when we were suddenly informed that gendarmes were arresting Armenians in the market and taking them to prison. Soon, the gendarmes appeared in our quarter and started entering our houses. They were dragging men away to the prison. No more men were left in our quarter. Until that point, we did not know what was happening elsewhere, but we soon discovered that the kaimakam and the gendarmerie commander had entered the villages of Bsdig and Kordzout with their forces and killed the men. A short while later we received more bad news from the valley of Pergri about the massacre of Armenians in the labour battalions and how their corpses had been thrown in the river. This news was brought to us by friendly neighbouring Kurds. They stated that all Armenians were to be killed. We were absolutely terrified and our cries and laments rose to the heavens. We ran to the prison and asked to see our men folk, but the gendarmes did not allow us to get close. The prison was surrounded by guards and we were all pushed back with insults. We had never experienced such brutality.

As the sun set, our men were still not released. We took bread to the prison and gave it to the gendarmes through the windows who then forced us away. We all returned home wailing and waiting for bad news. We continued to receive more reports of massacres in surrounding villages. Nobody slept that night. We spent the time in and out of our houses.

We rested a little in the morning. Our Kurdish friends told us that our men were still in prison and had become Muslim. They were to be spared for that reason. But why were they not released if they were to be spared? Such thoughts now started to torment us.

Our Kurdish informants and gendarmes consoled us by stating that the kaimakam had written to the Vali about the conversions and was awaiting a response.

But our men were not released even after eight days – and it felt like eight weeks, eight months and eight years. We suffered for eight days and nights, as did our men in prison. We could not see them, talk to them, or console them. The gendarmes continued to accept bread through the windows and force us away.

We did not know what was going on. We had never seen such behaviour. And we were receiving more news of killings and massacres around us, as well as of the bestial treatment of women and children. The government was not doing anything and every day our fears and suspicions were growing. We soon lost our faith in seeing our men alive.

One day, they captured around 20–25 Armenians who had been on Der Housgan Vortou mountain. These were men who had fled the massacres at Bsdig and Kordzout villages. There were now around 70 Armenians in prison, 32 of whom were from 25 Armenian homes of Pergri.

This was April 28, a Wednesday, the eighth day of imprisonment of our men. The gendarmerie commander returned that night but they still did not release our men. We were now expecting the worst and none of the 25 homes hung evil-eye amulets that night.

We were all unsettled and listening for any movement. It was enough for a dog to bark for us to look out with terrified faces. Well past midnight, nearing dawn, the dogs began howling and we began to be fearful. God, what kind of a night we had to endure! When that night was over, an unimaginable sense of loss descended upon us. The prison had been emptied and none of our men were left behind.

We started to lament, cry and run around in a frenzy, asking and begging the Kurds to tell us where our men were. The Kurds were frozen and could not answer.

"Golod Bridge" whispered some Kurdish friends. A few of us ran to the bridge and returned after seeing the stone bridge covered in fresh blood. Everything was over and a new helpless lament and sorrow took over.

A few days passed and the robberies and abductions started. People entered houses at will and did what they wished. Nobody was putting a stop to anything. There was no opposition. The abuses became common and the killings were considered normal. The gendarmes began telling stories about the murders they had committed, including one by militiaman Isa Telou, who descrbed how they had taken the Armenians who had been tied up in prison to Golod Bridge and shot, stabbed and then thrown over the bridge. He described how Kapoyi Panos and Hovsep were thrown into the river alive, how these two men clung onto the bridge stonework, and how they were eventually shot. They related that not one of the 70 men had remained alive to tell the world about that particularly brutal massacre at Golod Bridge.

Since that day, the Kurds have continued to bring news of how this or that man was thrown into the Bande Mahou at Pshi Koumpet village below Der Housgan Vortou Monastery. Such news was repeated over and over as more bodies were identified. We, the families of those unburied men, became numb, stone-like, and unable to cry any more. Our laments and grieving became overwhelming. We were consumed by grief.

These few descriptions of massacres are enough to provide an idea of what happened, how the massacre of Armenians in the province of Van was organised, and how they differed from earlier massacres, as they were now carried out with the participation of kaimakams, policemen, gendarmes and militias.

A-Do's appraisal of the Arjesh massacres and their aftermath (July 1915)

Such massacres took place throughout the province of Van, and in some places they were carried out in such a well planned and systematic fashion that practically not one man was left alive. There were many villages where every man was killed. There were also places where the killings were carried out by crowds of Muslims who were helped by the government and indulged in theft, abduction and arson. The destruction wreaked by such Muslim hordes, nevertheless, allowed some people to escape. Generally, no part of the province of Van remained free of such barbarous acts and murder, and practically all Armenian communities were destroyed or disappeared.

These actual killings were not the only calamity, as Vasbouragan experienced mass looting, destruction of foodstuffs, as well as the loss of means of livelihood, all of which took a further human toll. The destruction became so large that details were soon lost.

The loss of human life took three forms: firstly, the terrifying sword (*yataghan*) took away many of the men; secondly, the abduction of young women and maidens, even little boys and girls, to propagate the Muslim world; thirdly, the terrible deaths that followed the massacres, once foodstuffs and means of livelihood were destroyed and people had to go into exile. These developments also led to the spread of infectious diseases, which claimed many lives, especially among young children. What was not lost to the sword was lost to disease. The number of dead thus multiplied several fold.

It was not possible to make a detailed list of the lives and property that were lost over several weeks. One requires peace and much time to make such a list. However, in order to gain an idea of the human losses, a report on the district of Arjesh was prepared by this author three months after the massacres, during the temporary Armenian administration of the region, with a list of village names, the number households and their population, as well as those who were murdered, abducted or simply died.

No.	Village	Households	Population	Murdered	Kidnapped	Dead	[Total losses]*
1	Agants	304	2,078	413	5	467	[885]
2	Plourmag	96	645	187	22	40	[249]
3	Khargen	39	285	85	10	24	[119]
4	Irishad	29	304	98	3	57	[158]
5	Ororan	36	410	92	30	14	[136]
6	Papshgen	8	85	27	12	6	[45]
7	Majars	24	160	45	28	4	[77]
8	Chrashen	5	61	28	5	5	[38]
9	Hasbesinag	31	254	76	18	12	[106]
10	Haroutiun	22	180	63	14	16	[93]
11	Sosgoun	84	615	145	8	30	[183]
12	Khojalou	12	84	8		1	[9]
13	Aghes	3	31	3	1	1	[5]
14	Ardzvaperi Vank	20	120	26	2	20	[48]
15	Pay	5	46	22	9	1	[32]
16	Geoz Nerkin (Inner)	15	145	28	18	20	[66]
17	Geoz Verin (Upper)	11	105	34	35	7	[76]
18	Kalakiu	2	18	7	1	2	[10]
19	Gdradz Kar	32	250	44	2	12	[58]
20	Aghsraf	56	491	133	36	38	[207]
21	Kantsag	26	206	42	13	6	[61]
22	Joudgyah	38	390	129	39	36	[204]
23	Dzaydzag	28	211	36	6	24	[66]
24	Panon	29	180	25	2	2	[29]
25	Paykhner	34	273	63	25	14	[102]
26	Pertagh	7	78	21	12	4	[37]
27	Moy	44	318	55	9	8	[72]
28	Chakherbeg	5	49	31	11	1	[43]
29	Antsav*	5	37				[no info]
30	Piromar*	5	46				[no info]
31	Hakrag	7	85	16	3	6	25
32	Haghi	4	31	8	7	1	16
33	Kokn*	3	16				[no info]
34	Keyartis	7	110	29	7	6	[42]
35	Sinamesh	3	19	10	4	1	[15]
36	Inje Sou	4	55	31	7	4	[42]
37	Khacherov	12	110	21	16	8	[45]
38	Medzopavank	34	305	101	54	18	[173]
39	Tatalou*	4	23				[no info]
40	Zeve*	3	25				[no info]
41	Karachalou*	5	29				[no info]
42	Kozer	60	360	116	26	35	[177]
43	Shgavdian*	3	25				[no info]
44	Gelkan*	2	14				[no info]

* This column was added by the present editor. – A.S.

45	Komeshavan*	10	67				[no info]
46	Grakom*	50	411				[no info]
47	Madghavank	9	68	14	1	10	[25]
48	Dilan	9	67	13	6	7	[26]
49	Armizonk	26	240	30	8	4	[42]
50	Arjonits Vank	5	61	19	3	7	[29]
51	Kenapori Vank	5	37	4		4	[8]
	TOTALS	1,303	10,313	2,378	518	953	[3,849]

* The population of these ten villages simply disappeared. It is not clear how many were actually killed and how many died afterwards.

According to the above table, there were 1,303 Armenian households in 51 Armenian inhabited villages in Arjesh with a total Armenian population of 10,313 people. The number of people who were shot or killed by the sword during the massacres was 2,378. These were mostly young and middle aged men. A further 518 were abducted. These were mainly young and attractive women. Another 953 survivors succumbed to diseases and died during the following three months. An additional 90 households with 693 inhabitants simply vanished. The total number of people who were massacred, abducted, died of diseases or simply vanished in Arjesh was 4,542. These were the losses in Arjesh, so that it is not difficult to estimate the number of people who were lost in all 17 regions of the province of Van.

While the above massacres took place in the province of Van, the slaughter in other provinces and the general deportation of Ottoman Armenians – accompanied by massacres and other horrors – would take place one or two months later in June and July. It is still not clear why these killings and abuses were carried out. But the fact remains that massacres were first organised in the province of Van in April, at a time when everything appeared to be calm in the other provinces; if it is at all possible to use the word calm to describe those days. Given the present discussion, it is important to point out the following facts.

The general massacres in Alchavaz started on April 19. Gendarmes and militiamen, accompanied by local Kurds, attacked Armenian villages in an organised manner. One of these villages was Norshnchough, which was composed of 48 Armenian households. As soon as the massacre started in this village, 40 men managed to escape and take refuge in Kizil Yusuf village, which was in the neighbouring region of Manazgerd [Manzikert], which was populated by both Armenians and Kurds. Manazgerd was part of Bitlis province.

On April 26 and 27, after the massacres in Alchavaz had been completed and the bloody gendarmes and militias halted, the kaimakam of Alchavaz was informed that many Armenians from Alchavaz had escaped to Kizil Yusuf in Manazgerd. Therefore, scores of gendarmes entered that village and tied up the 40 Armenian men of Norshnchough village. They killed them after taking them to a remote place outside the village.

The Armenians of Kizil Yusuf immediately informed the *locum tenens* of Manazgerd, Father Hovhannes Der Avedisian, of what had happened.

Fortunately, the kaimakam of Manazgerd, the ex-Miudir of Tadvan, Ibrahim Halil, was a peaceful Turk from Baiburt. The treasurer (*sndgh emini*) of the town was an

Armenian from Moush called Nazaret Mardirosian. The *locum tenens* informed Nazaret of what had happened in Kizil Yusuf and they both went to see the kaimakam and protested against the killings, the influx of gendarmes from the neighbouring province, and the barbarities that followed. They requested steps to be taken to protect local Armenians.

The kaimakam, upon hearing the complaints of the *locum tenens*, stated that he had already telegraphed the incident to the governor of Bitlis and had received the following telegraphic response: "The developments in the province of Van are a matter of policy by an imperial irade (*irade seniye*). The gendarmerie forces there have the right to seek deserters and bring them to justice. Armenians harbouring such fugitives are also being punished. As for our own province, since we know of no Armenian movement, there cannot be similar incidents here."

The governor of Bitlis was thus testifying that the massacre of Armenians in Van was sanctioned by the central authorities. The massacres were sanctioned by law.

Chapter XIV

Resistance During the Terrible Massacres

The previous chapter recounted how the horrific massacre of Armenians spread rapidly and unopposed. It could not be stopped by loud protests. People died by tens, hundreds and thousands, as they were tricked, tied up and led to killing-fields to be slaughtered like cattle. It would have been appalling if everyone was killed in such a calm and submissive fashion. However, there were villages and entire regions which did not bow their heads to the executioners; instead, they protested, rebelled and took up arms against the Turkish sword. It is true that the struggle was unequal and many perished bravely, but they struck at the enemy, upheld the honour of Armenians, and ensured the continued existence of their nation.

A. Resistance at Arjag

Arjag was a small sub-district to the north-east of Van, well known for its lake by the same name. The east and north-east of this region was a plain, and the rest was mountainous, especially the western part, the most notable peak being Mount Kizilja.

The most important villages in this region were Arjag and Kharagonis, both entirely inhabited by Armenians, 180 and 230 households respectively. These villages were on the eastern shores of Lake Arjag and were only half an hour from each other. Arjag was the centre of the sub-district and the seat of the local *miudir*, a position which at that time was occupied by a Turk from Erzeroum, Shafik Bey, who was known as a peaceful man. He was answerable to the city of Van.

On April 16, a man called Shirin [Hagopian] was approached by Nouro from Pirsolan village in Pergri district. Nouro was a loyal and friendly Kurd who was a well known former ARF scout. He told Shirin that the Pergri kaimakam, Zia Bey, had called all the *mukhtars* (village headmen) and *rsbis* and warned them that no Kurd should dare shelter or defend any Armenian if massacres were to occur – if they did, they would be shot.

Two days later, on April 18, a force of about 150 mounted soldiers and infantry with a cannon came to Arjag from Saray. Entering the village, they asked for Shirin, who was in Kharagonis at that time. Two gendarmes were therefore sent to fetch him, but Shirin got suspicious and refused to go. The gendarmes left after threatening him.

The massacre of Arjag, as it later became apparent, was entrusted to the kaimakam of Saray, Kyamil Bey, who did not confide the massacre plans to the miudir of Arjag. The day the aforementioned force of 150 men was sent to Arjag to arrest Shirin, the kaimakam had enlisted Sharaf Beg of Khanasor, Naji Agha of Mougour and Arif Beg of Shaveh with many Kurds and marched on the village of Mandan. The village had made a name for itself in the past by opposing a bandit called Sayid Bey and now received the first blow from the kaimakam.

The twenty or so defenders at Mandan, not wishing to cause the destruction of their village, pulled back to Kharagonis before the expected attack, convinced that the inhabitants of the village would not be harmed in their absence – but the village was not spared. As soon as the Kurds entered, the atrocities began: around 15 men were killed, the houses were looted and the population fled.

After the destruction of Mandan, on April 19, the kaimakam led his horde onto Arjag. Some of the men in Arjag had already left the village, while others remained behind, relying on the protection of the *miudir*. At 1 p.m., the horde entered Arjag in a frenzied mood and started to kill and loot. This massacre was not the same as those in Arjesh. The Kurds and soldiers entered houses, dragged out the men in hiding, and immediately killed them in the presence of the women and children. They looted houses, raped women, and killed anyone resisting them. The atrocities continued until evening, when all remaining men in the village were killed (over 100 people) and many women raped. All of this took place in the presence of the kaimakam.

While these barbaric acts were taking place in Arjag, another group of Kurds led by gendarmes attacked Kharagonis. At that time there were 2,000 people in Kharagonis. Other than locals, the village was giving refuge to people from Hazare, Boghazkiasan, and Mandan villages. Hazare and Boghazkiasan had been evacuated in December and January, when Armenians were being massacres around Bashkale. There were some 100 Armenian men of fighting age from Mandan, Arjag and other villages there. Therefore, when the Kurdish forces approached Kharagonis, one of the Armenian positions around the village opened fire, and after several hours of senseless shooting, the Kurds returned empty-handed to Arjag, where the atrocities were still continuing.

On April 20, all the regular forces in Arjag with their cannon and many Kurds besieged Kharagonis.

The defenders opened fire on the attackers from their positions near the village and gardens. The army and its accompanying horde were enraged and the village came under fire – including cannon fire – from all sides. However, Kharagonis did not give way and the defenders held their positions. The fighting lasted till evening. The Armenian defenders did not yield and when it was dark the enemy pulled back to Arjag. The Armenians lost two men, one of whom was a brave fighter from Mandan called Sahag. The enemy lost several men. Despite the fact that the attackers had circled the village twice and failed to defeat the several dozen Armenian defenders, Kharagonis was still considered in great danger and the defenders decided to evacuate the villagers to Mount Kizilja on the northern shores of the lake.

During this period, they also sent a few men to Persia to give news of the massacres.

On April 21, the Kurds and the army came to Kharagonis once more and entered the village unopposed. Then the atrocities began with the looting of what was left, the arson of a few houses, and the murder of about 50 women, children and elderly who had remained in the village.

By this time massacres had also started in Timar and many more people sought refuge on Mount Kizilja from the villages of Ardavez, Koch, Adigeozal, Giusnents, Seti Bey,

Kharashig, as well as from Kyababig in Pergri. The kaimakam and the Kurds therefore moved against this position.

On April 22, some 300 Kurds tried to ascend Mount Kizilja from the north, through the Yalgouzaghach valley, but came under fire from Armenian defenders and were forced to retreat with the loss of a few men.

On April 23, the army and Kurds responsible for the destruction of Arjag and Kharagonis advanced to Nabat from the southern shores of the lake. The village was already giving shelter to refugees from Mkhgner and Chobanoghlou. As the army and Kurds advanced on the village, some defenders slowed their advance, so that the population of the village could retreat to the Chomakhlou peak of Mount Kizilja. This peak was also the destination of the people from Kizilja and Yalgouzaghach.

While the enemy forces were being strengthened, the hordes following them in search of loot were also becoming larger. It was impossible to look after thousands of Armenians on the mountain or return them to their villages. The defenders held back the enemy by every means available until it was dark and the enemy retreated. They then moved the civilian population to Averagi village on the road to Van.

Averagi had been completely deserted at this point because of the Van uprising which had started three days earlier. As shall be seen later, several villages around Van escaped to the city, including the people of Averagi and Shahbaghi. The Armenian refugees on Mount Kizilja settled in Averagi, as did those of Poghants and Bayrak villages, a total of 8,000 people.

April 24 was a difficult day. As soon as it was light, the village of Averagi was surrounded by the army and Kurds and a dogged fight ensued with the large enemy force and its artillery. The gunfire could be heard everywhere and the fighting around some positions became very serious, as in the case of Ttmakar to the south of the village. This position was defended by 12 brave men from Kyababig, under the command of Kiurd Ghazar and his son Alo. Their stubborn defence ended with their heroic deaths, having inflicted many casualties on the enemy. However, the loss of that position led to the loss of morale and the desertion of other positions around the village. The enemy thus got closer, the siege was tightened, and hostile fire was directed into the village itself.

There was great confusion among Armenians and some civilians ran out of the village towards Poghants in great terror. They were attacked by Kurds, who killed and robbed them, with the loss of 150 Armenian men.

At this time there was also heavy fighting around Mount Choban Oghlou, where around 40 armed Armenians opposed a much larger Kurdish force. The Armenians were forced to retreat to Mount Kizilja, with the loss of five men, including Aram Yeghiazarian and Manaser Asbadourian.

At this point some 40 Assyrian men from Kharashig village, who were rushing to Van over Khoshgyadoug, were stopped by the army and killed.

The fighting around Averagi continued as the enemy started to destroy the houses around the village perimeter and kill the people it captured, though the village was not overrun. The enemy also used cannon, killing and wounding people inside the village.

One shell hit the school and killed five people. The fighting continued until evening when darkness ended the fighting. The Kurds and the army pulled back as usual while the armed Armenian fighters led the 7,000 people under their care to Van – leaving behind some 100 dead in the village. During this period, the fighting in Van was in its second stage, when the strength of the defenders was made apparent, and it was possible to enter Aykesdan at night.

On April 25–26, the forces besieging Averagi turned their attention to Tarman and Goghbants villages, where some 3,000 Armenians from Zarants, Sevan, Ermants (Assyrians), Bakhezig, Farough and Vosgepag were seeking refuge under the protection of 70 armed Armenians. The Armenian defence was successful and they managed to retreat to Mount Varak, as shall be seen later.

B. The Defence of Hayots Tsor

When the kaimakam of Saray at the head of soldiers, Kurds and a cannon began the destruction of Arjag, starting from Mandan and Kharagonis and moving to other villages, Armenian defenders led civilian populations towards the city of Van. Similar developments were also taking place across Hayots Tsor.

Hayots Tsor was to the south of Van, in a long valley whose western border touched on Lake Van. The Khoshab river ran through this valley, with 35 or so Armenian inhabited villages scattered on its banks. The district consisted of Upper and Lower Hayots Tsor.

The villages of Eremerou, Angshdants, and Asdvadzashen were the main villages of Upper Hayots Tsor, while Ishkhani Kom, Kerdz, Bltents, and Nor Kiugh were the main ones of Lower Hayots Tsor.

As was seen earlier, on April 16, Ishkhan and his three companions were treacherously killed in Rashid Agha's house. On April 18, the 46 Armenian men in the village were also executed in the same house.

While these killings were taking place, government forces attacked Atanan. This was the village which had terrified the authorities in December [1914], when it blocked the movement of the army in Vosdan, until they were accompanied by Vramian and the kaimakam. Now, as Jevdet planned a general massacre of Armenians, he decided to first obliterate this village. Therefore, around April 16, the gendarmes and Kurds in Vosdan tried to quietly occupy Sbidag Vank and its village, which formed the rear defence of Atanan. However, eight armed Armenians noticed their movements and took up positions inside the village and monastery to stop the enemy's approach. These Armenians fought for three days and repelled the Kurdish attacks.

However, on April 19, an Ottoman force of 300 gendarmes with two cannons marched to Hayots Tsor under the command of Captain Edhem Bey and crossed the Khoshab river. The column halted by Bltents, where it fired a few artillery rounds into the village. A group of Armenian fighters at Heri Kamag responded to the attack, killing three Turkish soldiers and forcing the army to retreat. Soon re-inforcements arrived and Edhem Bey attacked the village with new vigour. As the Armenians realised that they would not be able to resist the new onslaught, they led the village population to Mount Geliesa, allowing the army to enter Bltents and begin the looting and arson.

After destroying Bltents, the army marched on Sbidag Vank, where the civilian population of the village and Atanants had withdrawn. The monastery thus came under attack from two sides, and the defenders resisted for a few hours and then retreated with the loss of one man – a young man called Kapriel from Bltents who distinguished himself during the fighting. When the defenders retreated from Sbidag Vank and Atanants, the two villages fell into the hands of the army. The hero of the December clashes, Levon of Kharagants, was not in Atanan at this time, so the Armenian resistance was weak.

After these developments in Lower Hayots Tsor, the population of Kerdz and Kiziltash, as well as some people from Atanan and others from Bltents who had fled to Geliesa, withdrew to Mount Kerdz. This mountain had very good defensive positions.

While these events were taking place in Lower Hayots Tsor, similar events were taking place in Upper Hayots Tsor.

During this period, communications between Upper and Lower Hayots Tsor were broken, as battalion commander Ahmed Bey and his 200 gendarmes and militiamen patrolled Upper Hayots Tsor, where they committed outrages while supposedly looking for Armenian deserters.

There actually were many deserters and they generally retreated to the mountains during the day and descended to the villages at night. This was the reason no Ottoman official dared to enter Armenian villages after dark.

The Armenians in Upper Hayots Tsor did not know what was happening in Lower Hayots Tsor or even in Hirj village when, on April 18, Lazki, the son of Shakir Agha, the tribal leader of the Krav Kurds of Nordouz, arrived. He had come after he had raided the Armenian villages of eastern Shadakh.

The villages of Angshdants, Eremerou and Gghzi were on the left of the Koshab river, half an hour from each other. The first two villages were entirely Armenian populated, one with 67 households, and the other with 82 households. The third village was mixed, with 44 Armenian households and 12 Kurdish ones. Angshdants and Gghzi were set among mature trees.

The road from Nordouz first descended to Angshdants, and then separated to Eremerou to the right, and Gghzi to the left.

On the morning of April 18, Lazki descended on Angshdants with his numerous horsemen. His men looked like a classic oriental expeditionary force. First came eight to ten riders as the advance guard, followed by Lazki and his aides, and then his cavalry and accompanying rabble.

There were 20 armed Armenians in the village who, upon noticing the approaching Kurds, separated into two groups. One group of 12 men went to the only two-storey building – Safar's house – and the other group of eight to Polat Haroutiun's house in the lower quarter of the village. While the Armenian defenders were making preparations, a group of eight to 10 older men under the leadership of Reis Mourad came to the edge of the village to greet Lazki. The advance guards arrived first, followed by Lazki with his aides. The villagers greeted him with the words "Sar-saran sar-javan" (on our heads and eyes). They took the reins of the horses and led them into the village. When they reached the village square called Nakhradegh, Lazki gave a signal and a few volleys were fired by his men. The Armenian villagers who had greeted him became his first victims. Among them were Reis Mourad, Aved Sakhoian, Avanes Hokhanian and a few others. The Kurdish volleys led to a thunder of gunfire from the second floor of Safar's house. Now, lying next to the Armenians who had been killed moments earlier, lay the bodies of a number of Kurds. The Kurds were taken by surprise and took cover behind garden walls and a battle ensued.

The fighting continued until midday. The Krav Kurds could not make progress against the Armenian positions and retreated. Part of their forces separated and went towards the village of Eremerou. Although ordinarily this village also had around 20 armed defenders of its own, they were away from the village at that time. They had gone to the city to avoid capture by gendarmes and had not yet returned. For this reason, the Kurds were able to enter the village unopposed, breaking into houses, pillaging, killing and raping. There was only one armed young man in the whole village, a 25 year-old youth called Sahag Kaprielian, with a Mauser pistol. This young hero was not intimidated and did not flinch; he simply picked up his automatic and took up the best position in the village – the Banirian house – and opened fire. The Kurds surrounded him but he did not surrender. He remained at his well-fortified position and continued to take a toll on his enemies. According to some, he killed seven Kurds, the bodies falling all around him. He terrorised his opponents so much that the attackers, after pillaging part of the village and killing some people, did not approach Sahag's position and retreated to Angshdants at nightfall. When it was completely dark and the attackers had pulled out, the young hero came down from his post, gathered the villagers, and took them to Kouroubash. They left around 80 dead in the village streets, including some women and children.

The attack on Angshdants restarted with new vigour in the afternoon and the shooting continued until evening. The Kurds picked up their dead, around 20–25 corpses, as they besieged the village. They did not want to allow the young Armenian defenders to escape under the cover of darkness. But they were not successful. As soon as it was dark, the defenders came out of their positions, concentrated their forces, and managed to break through the siege and disappear. The following morning was terrifying, because there were no defenders left in the village. The attacking Kurds overran the village unopposed and were in a frenzied mood. The massacre that had been planned now included personal revenge so that the houses and streets of Angshdants became the scene of unimaginable pillage, murder and rape. Over 70 men were killed, as well as women and children. The survivors fled from the village in absolute terror towards Asdvadzashen and then Varak. A few fled to Demgos village, to seek refuge amongst familiar Kurds. Angshdants was thus destroyed and bore the imprint of Lazki's barbarities.

Angshdants, as well as Eremerou were destroyed, and Lazki moved onto Gghzi. Mahmad Sharif, a Kurd with an evil past, lived in this village. However, he was now considered to be a friend of Armenians. Lazki and his entourage visited Mahmad Sharif at home. The latter assured the Armenians that he would not allow any abuses in his village and Armenians believed him. Several witnesses have stated that, during their meal, Mahmad Sharif pleaded with Lazki to spare his village, but the latter explained that the orders had come from above and concerned all Armenian villages. The meal was finished, the leader of the horde was satiated, and the command was given. The village leaders were killed first, then the young people, around 60 individuals. Among them were Hovsep Aloian, Haroutiun Garabedian, Vartan Manougian, and the village priest, Der Mgrdich, all of them harmless and peaceful people.

Eight young people survived in that village because they had weapons and retreated to Sevoyi Hovhannes' house and resisted. The Kurds surrounded the house and one local Kurd got onto the roof and tried to point out the whereabouts of the defenders from the sky-light. However, he was shot through his jaw and killed by one of the Armenians. The Kurds were enraged and wanted to smash the house door down but two more of them were shot. When they realised that the defenders would not give themselves up easily, the attackers set the house ablaze. The thick smoke began to overpower the Armenians and one of them suffocated to death, but the others soon made an opening in a wall and escaped next door to Zozani Mouse's house, where they continued to resist until nightfall.

When darkness fell, the boys came out of the village and clashed with some Kurds guarding the roads to the village. There was heavy gunfire in the darkness and two Kurds were killed and the others fled. The Armenians then went to Pertag village and later to Varak, saving their lives and weapons, which were so important in those days.

The villages of Gem and Ankgh, located to the north of Khoshab river, in Lower Hayots Tsor, were noted for their size. Each was composed of 108–110 households, and on April 20, they also became scenes of much savagery.

The sun had barely risen when Lazki and his horde, including Jihangir of Pzhngerd with his men, Sandoul of Kharnourd and his militia forces, and two cannons moved towards Gem. At this time the village was giving shelter to a considerable number of people from Mousgaven, Kiziltash and two other villages, including around 60 armed young men.

The Armenian defenders were deployed as follows.

Yeghishe Kadoian and 15 men took up positions at a place called Shalalgod to the east of the village.

Arshag Gagosian, Khachig Mayilian and Misak Kasbarian and thirty others took up positions on the mountainside above the village.

Kevork Soneian and the others took up their positions near the church.

These forces were supervised by Hovsep Khleatian, an organisational committee and Mgrdich Adomian.

The enemy approached the east of the village, where Yeghishe Kadoian and his group were positioned. The attacking force was large, the opposition weak, and the young men had to retreat to the haystacks at the edge of the village. The enemy occupied the abandoned Armenian positions, placed its cannon there and began bombarding the village. The Armenian positions collapsed under the first salvos, partly because the mobile defence units of Hayots Tsor, under the leadership of Mashdagtsi Kasbar Khaboian, did not come to the aid of the village as expected. The fighting, therefore, did not last long, only about an hour, as the young defenders abandoned their positions one by one. Arshag Gagosian also abandoned his position, though he did oppose a powerful onslaught of the enemy and inflicted 10 dead in their ranks. The attackers gradually approached the village, as the cannons took their toll, wounding or killing people left and right. The boys who were fighting lost hope, the commanders were not able to carry out their tasks and the Armenian villagers began running to Ankgh, as did some of the defenders.

The situation got very serious. While some unarmed villagers desperately rushed into the valley and made for the plain to Ankgh, the armed men went up the mountainsides and the enemy followed them. The horde attacked the unarmed people and embarked on merciless massacre and plundering. Around 250 bodies of men, women and even children covered the bottom of the valley up to Ankgh. While the unarmed people were being massacred, a large group of horsemen cut off the Armenian defenders moving up the mountainsides. There was no chain of command left in the Armenian ranks and the men broke up into small groups and disappeared.

Arshag Gagosian and Mgrdich Adomian and 12 young men followed the Shamiram stream and managed to reach Asdvadzadzin Monastery in Ankgh. The Kurds who were following them surrounded the monastery and a desperate fight ensued. The young men fought to their last bullet and were all killed, as were a few of the enemy. One of the Kurdish casualties was a well-known religious man, Molla Fayim of Kharnourt. Arshag Gagosian distinguished himself in this fight, as he had in Gem.

Yeghish Mgrdichian followed Shamiram's stream with 15 men, moving towards Ankgh and then crossing the Khoshab River towards the hill of Sourp Dziranavori Tar. The Kurds following them surrounded the hill and there was a desperate fight. Three of the young men were killed, as were two Kurds and three horses. After a long resistance, Yeghish and 12 of the boys broke through to Mount Kerdz.

Hovsep Khlghatian and about 30 men, who were followed by the Kurds, made for the slopes of the mountain above Ankgh and the bridge over Shamiram stream. Khlghatian was seriously wounded by a bullet smashing both of his knees. However, he managed to save his rifle and gave it to one of the young men. Unable to move, he took out his Mauser and began firing at the enemy until he was killed. He thus made up for his shortcomings at Gem. Hovsep and eight other men were killed on the shores of Khoshab River between Ankgh and Mashdag. The rest fled to Ishkhani Kom.

However, a great massacre took place in the village of Ankgh. The government had eight men stationed there, and the leading men of the village – including Reis Krikor, Haroutiunian Hovhannes, Ousda Mardiros, and the village teacher Arshag Ghazarian – trusted the authorities. They even suggested that the 20 armed young Armenians leave the village, which they did. On the other hand, as people from Gem fled to Ankgh followed by an attacking horde, the army and other Kurds – along with the gendarmes already stationed in the village – a terrible massacre, robbery, rape and arson ensued. The victims were the leading men of the village, ordinary peasants and later, women and children –

more than 27 people. Additionally, around 300 people fled to the Khoshab River in order to cross it to the other side. However, the Kurds caught up with them and started a massacre. Around 100 were killed at this spot and their bodies were dumped in the river.

Thus, one of the worst massacres was carried out at Gem, between Gem to Ankgh, and from Ankgh to the banks of the Khoshab River. About 700 men, women and even children were killed at these locations on that day. Such unprecedented savagery came to an end with the clash at Ishkhani Kom.

Many people escaped to Ishkhani Kom after the massacre at Ankgh. They came from Gem, Ankgh, Mashdag, Atanan, Bltents, Marks, Khorkom, Kharagants and Kiziltash-Keoshg. About 80 armed Armenians also arrived, though Kasbar Khaboian and his men were absent.

At midday on that same day, April 20, after the massacre at Ankgh, the huge enemy force moved to Ishkhani Kom. Edhem Bey with his two cannons and militia force, which had been in Bltents and Atanan, also descended on Ishkhani Kom, so that over 1,000 Kurds and militiamen plus four cannon were concentrated on this village.

The Khoshab River was one or two versts [1.3 miles] to the south of Ishkhani Kom. To the west and north was Shamiram's stream. There was a run-off from Shamiram stream, meandering and watering the fields and gardens to the south and east of the village. Edhem Bey set up two cannons to the south of Khoshab River and started to bombard the village, while the horde from Gem and Ankgh took another two cannons and approached the eastern part of the village. Seeing this movement, the Armenian defenders also concentrated in this part of the village.

A force of some 80 armed men thus took up positions in the gardens and trenches dug east of the village. They were led by Hovhannes Baroian of Khorkom, Setrag Shaghoian of Kharagants, Armenag Moukhsi-Pokhanian of Kiziltash, Hagop Kahana and Hagop Mounoian of Ishkhani Kom. Thanks to these five people the Armenian defenders carried out their duties in an exemplary fashion. In the distance was Lazki and his horde and Satoul Agha with the militia forces and two cannon. They felt confident after their experiences at Gem and Ankgh and approached Ishkhani Kom accordingly. They continued their advance, and when they were a few hundred steps away, the defenders opened fire from the gardens and trenches. The Kurds and militia forces had to retreat with the loss of a few men and horses. The enemy was now more cautious and set up its cannon near the Mashdag mills and began bombarding the village. Meanwhile, Edhem Bey's two cannons bombarded the south of the village. The enemy was encouraged by these developments and began to advance once more. The defenders could still withstand the bombardment and managed to stop the enemy advance. The people in the village moved to its western part, which was not under bombardment.

The four cannons and around 1,000 rifles opened fire on the village. The fighting continued the whole day and over 150 shells fell on the village. However, they did not cause any serious damage and the enemy was not able to enter the village. The Armenian commanders were effective, the defenders remained calm, and not one position was abandoned to the enemy. The fight continued until 10 o'clock at night, when darkness fell and the enemy pulled back with a few casualties. The people in the village were saved. The defenders only had one casualty, Sarkis of Takhmants village, who fell victim to his own audaciousness. He had converted to Islam during the 1896 massacres and had returned to the Armenian Church after the constitutional revolution.

The enemy withdrew, the fighting ended, and the young men came together and held a meeting. Would Ishkhani Kom be able to continue its resistance in the same manner? The answer was possibly, if there was a supply of ammunition; but there was little to be had and the Armenians decided to leave the village. Unfortunately, their glorious resistance was marred by this unfortunate decision.

The defenders led around 800 Armenian boys and young men towards Varak, which they reached safely, while the remaining population went to Ardamed, the seat of the miudir, thinking that with the departure of the armed Armenians, the rest of the population would be spared a massacre. However, they were wrong again and were massacred in Ardamed, where about 300 were killed. Only after this third great massacre did the group of over 3,000 people disperse, most of them going to the city and Varak.

In this way, Hayots Tsor was cleared of its Armenian defenders, as well as its civilian population, with Armenian villages destroyed and survivors fleeing to the city of Van, Varak and other places. A small number also went to Kerdz Mountain where, as we have seen, others had fled from Bltents, Kerdz, and Sbidag Vank, as well as some from Kiziltash and Atanan.

Close to 2,000 people remained on Kerdz Mountain for around three weeks. These people would descend to Kerdz from the mountain at night and return in the morning. Armed Armenians defended the positions on the mountain. After a while, the Kurds could no longer be seen and the siege of the village ended. Twice the Armenians attacked Kurds transporting wheat by cart and seized the loads. Six Kurds were killed in one of those attacks.

This state of affairs continued until the morning of May 11, when the kaimakam of Vostan marched on Kerdz with around 200 militiamen. The people who were in the village withdrew to the mountain and were followed by 50 militiamen. However, when the latter saw the armed Armenians at their positions, they pulled back.

That day, four Armenians from Kiziltash, who were returning to their village, got into a fight with some Kurds and were killed. All four were from Moukhsi Pokhanian's family. One of them was Armenag, who had fought at Ishkhani Kom. Among the dead was Armenag's 15 year-old son, the gallant Hapet, who fought with his Mauser pistol until the last bullet.

The kaimakam of Vosdan entered Kerdz and confiscated the village's entire stock of grain. Deprived of their food supply, a small number of Armenians fled to Van and Varak that same evening, while most went to Pesantashd, where a large number of people from Garjgan and Gevash had sheltered – as shall be seen later – under the protection of armed Armenians.

C. Resistance at Timar

The region of Timar was to the north-west of Van. Its mountainous terrain extended as far as Lake Van and formed a peninsula. The island monasteries of Lim and Gdouts were nearby. Timar had a large Armenian population with over 30 Armenian and about 20 Kurdish and Turkish villages. The most important Armenian villages were Aliur, Marmed, Ererin, Khzhishg, Giusnents, Poghants, Khavents and Janig. Timar was composed of two parts, Upper and Lower Timar.

During the massacres, little resistance was offered by four of the villages. These were Asdvadzadzin or Diramer and Khzhishg in Upper Timar, and Aliur and Marmed in Lower Timar. The region of Timar that had resisted so well in March did nothing this time.

The incidents started in Pergri, when the first massacres took place at Bsdig Kiugh and Kordzout. The bloody horde that carried out the killings here moved on to Diramer and Janig, followed by Aliur and Marmed. The present account thus starts with Bsdig Kiugh and Kordzout.

Pergri was one of the regions with very few Armenians inhabitants. In that historically Armenian area there were now barely 700 Armenian households which were dispersed on the plains of Abagha and Pergri Ova. Bsdig Kiugh was one or two versts [around a mile] to the south-east of the town of Pergri. Kordzout was 10 versts [6.6 miles] to the south of the town, near the border with Timar. Both had large Armenian populations, one with 74 and the other with 128 households. These two villages were attacked during the Pergri massacres, which took place at the same time as the killings in Bande Mahou valley.

On the afternoon of April 19, the kaimakam of Pergri, Zia Bey, and gendarmerie commander, Amar Bey, accompanied by 200 gendarmes and Hamidiye soldiers, came to Kordzout to massacre the inhabitants of that village. In order not to forewarn the victims, they also brought Der Manvel with them, the abbot and vicar of Der Housgan Vortou monastery.

Following appeals by Der Manvel, the villagers gathered 10 rifles and 50 gold coins and presented them to the kaimakam. The simple Armenians gave the 50 gold coins for protection. After taking the rifles and gold coins, the kaimakam ordered the men to be rounded up. The gendarmes locked up the men, all 86 of them, in Manoug Meloian's house, who was a merchant from Van. After this step, the kaimakam left the village. Der Manvel also left and went to Pergri, where he remained overnight. Realising what was going on, he then went to Khourshoud of Malbat village for protection but was murdered there.

The Armenians of Kordzout remained locked up in Meloian's house overnight, completely unaware of what was in store for them. On the morning of April 20, the gendarmes and militia forces tied and chained these men and marched them south to a place called Yeghounatsor, where they were massacred as in other places. After the massacre of the men, they turned on the general population and began the usual bestial abuse.

On the same date, April 20, Suleiman Agha of Irishad village in Arjesh, accompanied by 300 militiamen and Hamidiye forces, entered Bsdig Kiugh, gathered the men – around 120 individuals – and took them to the village threshing fields where they were shot and killed. This was not an organised massacre as in Kordzout; the killing was carried out by a mob, and about 60 people, some wounded, managed to escape. Some fled to Pergri and sought the protection of the well know tribal leader of Kop, Mahmad Bey, who could not protect them. Gendarmes took the Armenians who had been seeking shelter in his house and massacred them outside the town. Another group of survivors escaped to the mountains, but they were caught within a few days, brought to Pergri and, like the Armenians there, shot on Golod Bridge over Bande Mahou. Their bodies were thrown into the raging waters of the river. The corpses of the Armenians killed in Bsdig Kiugh were robbed and left under the sun in their naked state for six days, until heartbroken women came, dug holes, and buried their relatives where they had fallen.

After the destruction of Kordzout and Bsdig Kiugh, the blood-thirsty mob attacked Giuzag, Sourp Tateos, Antsav and Panz villages, sacking houses and murdering people. The whole area was pillaged. About 60 men who had escaped fled to Trkashen, seeking the protection of Arif Bek, the tribal leader of the Shavi tribe. However, Ali Bek, Arif's brother, turned them over to the Kurds who had been following them. The latter dragged them to a place near the watermills and put them all to the sword.

After this episode, which took place at dawn on April 21, Commander Amar Bek, along with the Shavi tribal leader Arif Bek, as well as many militiamen and Hamidiye forces surrounded Diramer in Timar.

Diramer was known as a powerful village with 35 armed defenders who could have defended the village if they had been prepared. However, their leaders – four aghas – had gone to Pirgarip village a day earlier to consult with other defence forces in the region, while 10 of the defenders had gone to Lim monastery in the absence of their leaders. There were thus 20–21 defenders in the village without any leadership.

When the attacking horde appeared, seven of the defenders in the village under the leadership of Yenovk Khachadourian rushed to the west of the village to occupy positions in the rocks near Khach Aghpiur. By the time they got there, however, the Kurds had already occupied the rocks. The Armenians thus came under fire and two were killed – Avedis Mgrdichian and his son Arshag. The remaining five defenders returned to the village and tried to go to the other side and occupy the rocks called Poughoum, but they too were already occupied by Kurds. The Armenians once more came under fire and lost three of their number, including Yenovk Khachadourian. The remaining two could only escape to Lim. Five defenders also managed to escape from the south of the village and save themselves. Since there was no leadership, the men did not know what to do. The people in the village congregated at Der Kevork's and surrounding houses. Meanwhile, the enemy opened fire and advanced into the village. 13 young men armed with pistols at Pasho's house, at the north-east edge of the village, rushed into the open without realising that they were surrounded by the enemy and were all killed. Afterwards, the enemy occupied the whole village and began looting. They also moved into the areas where the village population had gathered.

At such a distressing moment, the remaining four defenders in the village – the teacher Smpad Aloian, Haroutiun Amirian, Tavit Tanielian and Mardiros Manasian – ascended the only room on the second floor of Der Kevork's house and began firing at the approaching mob. A few Kurds were killed but there were many others who continued to advance from all directions and set the defenders' building on fire. The four heroes continued to fire and a few more Kurds were hit, including the agha of Aren village in Pergri, Zeynal Bek, who was hit by Smpad's bullet.

The frenzied fight continued all day. When one of the walls of the defenders' upper room was destroyed by bullets, the men inside could not come into the open and had to descend to the lower floor. Meanwhile, the Armenian villagers began escaping in all directions, as the enemy closed in and set the defender's house on fire. They also killed any Armenian men they found. The Armenian defenders, unable to fight the thick smoke, made a hole in one of the walls of the house and went into neighbouring Sarkis Der Aprahamian's house and continued to fight from there. It was only when their ammunition ran out, having inflicted a few more casualties on their enemy, that they were overrun and killed. Over 70 people were killed in Diramer, 10 of whom were women and children.

While the resistance and massacre at Diramer was taking place, a large militia force and Kurds came to Janig. The local miudir, Mahmad Efendi, who resided at Janig, advised Armenian men to move to the caves near the village, until the militiamen and Kurds had passed through, but that did not save them. The attacks and massacres took place both at the caves and in the village. 73 men were killed at these two locations without any resistance, and then the pillage and cruelty started.

The whole region was overcome with terror and people fled to Lim monastery, where they always sought shelter when under threat. Starting from April 21, over a whole day and an evening, thousands of people came to the shores of lake Van from Pirgarip, Sosrat, Shahgyaldi, Janig, Diramer, Norshen, Kochani, Norovants and Koms – turning the lake-shore into an extraordinary place of anguish.

Here, too, Armenians were not left alone, and on April 22, the murderous mob that had attacked Diramer and Janig moved towards the shores of Lake Van. Trsi Doun of Lim monastery and Khzhishg were on the shoreline some distance away. Between these two points were several hills which were considered the lake's ramparts. The people moved to the lake shore and waited for boats to take them across to the monastery, while armed young men took up positions on the hills. The number of defenders was a few dozen, and they were bolstered by the arrival of Ohan and his group – the leader of the Alchavaz defence group – who had dismissed the pleas of the people of Alchavaz and left for Lim two days earlier, thinking that his departure would spare the unarmed population from massacre. The weight of the enemy assault fell on Trsi Doun and Khzhishg village, where the defenders had established themselves. The fighting was intense and continued all day. It was fierce and bloody, and both sides lost men, the enemy losing 40. The

Typical sailing boat on Lake Van

outlaw Sltane, who was infamous for his conduct at Abagha, was killed here. He had been pardoned at the outbreak of the war and joined the government's murderous forces. The Armenians lost eight men on that day.

When it got dark, the enemy retreated and did not return. Their losses were great and they moved elsewhere. The people were ferried by boat to the monastery over the following two or three days. The terror and distress was great as around 12,000 Armenians gathered on Lim. There was a lack of supplies, bread ran out quite quickly, and eventually everyone was given two handfuls of wheat which they cooked on fires and ate simply for survival. This situation lasted for a few days until the Russian army arrived.

These clashes in Timar did not simply end in this way. On April 25, the murderous mob organised by the kaimakam of Pergri, Ziya Bey, which had killed many people and destroyed the villages of Upper Timar, surrounded Aliur, the largest village of this region. The village was set amongst trees and had a population of 343 households. Other than the local Armenian inhabitants, there were also about 150 families who had escaped to the village from Arayg, Adnagants, and Drlashen during the events of March. At that time there were around 160 fighting men in Aliur, under the command of Apisoghom and Sarkis Mardoian from Aliur and Mihran from Khavents.

These defenders were divided into several groups which took up key positions and waited for the enemy's arrival. The latter surrounded the village just after dawn and attacked so that a serious fight ensued until evening. The enemy was powerful but the

Armenians managed to resist heroically and stopped the attackers from coming close to the village. The enemy lost 17 men that day, one of whom was Shavi Hsei Gorjo of Dampat village. The Armenians had one man killed, Der Garabed of Khavents.

The besiegers retreated to the Muslim village of Molla Kasoum at night and, not having any hope of taking Aliur, resorted to a trick. They prepared a letter and handed it to Captain Ismail of the militia forces to deliver to Aliur the next day. He arrived with the letter held high in his hand and presented it to one of the leaders of the village, Reis Giulamir and Armenag Chamanigian. The letter stated that, if the Armenians disarmed, Aiur would not be harmed.

This led to questions in the minds of the people. Some thought they should hand over their arms, others disagreed. The disagreement continued and the majority of the fighters picked up their weapons and left. The Turks then occupied the village unopposed. The Armenians had been tricked. As soon as the militia forces and Kurds entered Aliur, they started to gather up the Armenian men and imprison them in the church. The villagers who saw this development fled and the 160 prisoners remained in the hands of the Muslim forces. The village was pillaged and destroyed. The men who were captured were kept in the church for two days and, early in the morning on the third day, April 28, they were tied together and taken to an isolated spot called Yekya Bagh and killed.

The day after the destruction of Aliur, April 27, a bloody horde, under the leadership of Ali Bek of the Shavi tribe, came to Marmed. The madness here was even more complete. Reis Hovhannes, relying on his fellow townsman called Manoug, went to Avants, made a plea to Commissar Shiukri and received a banner from him. He then returned and placed the banner in the middle of his village and asked the 60 or so armed Armenians to leave. The men left as requested.

As soon as Ali Bek entered the village with his men, they arrested any Armenian men they came across and herded them to the church, as in the case of Aliur. The general population started to flee, as well as many of the men, but around 100 of the latter fell into the hands of the Kurds, including the local leaders. These men were tied up that same day, taken half an hour westwards to Jaghatsi-Tsor, and killed. About 25 other men were also brought to this spot from Jirashen and killed.

After the destruction of Aliur and Marmed, they destroyed many of the villages in Lower Timar, scattering their large Armenian populations. Some of the latter fled towards Avants and the city [Van], while others to Pesantashd. Many women were abducted and enslaved.

Gdouts hermitage, which had given shelter to thousands of people during previous massacres, was not able to shelter even one person on this occasion because the government placed a unit of 15 soldiers there, and the Armenian defence forces of Lower Timar, which could easily have removed them and turned the island into a haven for many people, did not receive orders to do so. Consequently, the sizeable Armenian population of Lower Timar had many losses and scattered in all directions. As for the Armenian defence forces, over 100 of them simply went into the Timar mountains, where they remained until the Russian army arrived.

While the massacres and abuses at Aliur and Marmed were continuing, new incidents were taking place in Kordzout village in Pergri, where, as already discussed, there had been earlier massacres.

A few words should be said about these new developments.

After the first wave of massacres, many people from Giuzag [Angiuzag], Sourp Tatos, and Chakhmakh villages fled to Kordzout, so that there was a large number of people in the village. Among them were around 300 men, 50 of whom were armed. On April 25, a large number of Kurds from surrounding villages came and took the wheat held in underground stores. This was when the armed Armenians fired on them and killed approximately 10 Kurds. Consequently, the remaining Kurds fled and Kordzout was left in peace for 10 to 12 days.

However, on May 7, the gendarmerie commandant in Pergri, Amar Bek, appeared with several hundred Kurds and a battle ensued. At the centre of the village was the church, and in order to shield the general population, the defenders prepared 8 to 10 houses to shelter people, while they went onto the roof of the church and began firing. The enemy occupied the houses at the edge of the village and continued firing but was unable to overpower the defenders. They therefore decided to trick the Armenians. The commandant forged a telegram supposedly pardoning the Armenians and showed it to the Armenian defenders. While the latter did not credit the note, there were murmurs among the population at large, some believing in its authenticity. During the disagreements that followed, the 100 or so armed Armenians left the village. Amar Bek then approached the church without opposition and the people in the church let them in. Then, the 100 or so men in the church were taken to Meloian's house and killed. This happened on May 10 and five days later, on May 15, when Armenian volunteers entered Kordzout, they found the corpses of the villagers piled up in the main square.

D. Resistance Around Varak

An hour to the east of Van stood the twin peaked Mount Varak. One of the peaks was high and imposing, the other one less so. These peaks were aligned in such a manner that, looking from Van, the smaller peak was outlined by the larger one. The large eastern peak was called Kalilea, and the smaller western one, Shoushanits Sar. Between the two peaks, on the foothills of the larger one, were the heights of Upper Varak, from which two deep valleys opened up to the north and south. In the northern valley was Sourp Krikor monastery, and on the southern face of the tallest peak was Varak Monastery – the eagle's nest of Vasbouragan. To the north of Varak, near Sourp Krikor monastery, were four villages: the entirely Armenian inhabited villages of Goghbants and Tarman, the mixed village of Tsorovants, and the Muslim Turkish village of Zrvantants. The village of Shoushants was located on the western slopes of the small peak.

Varak Mountain, because of its geographical location, surrounding valleys and monasteries, played two important roles during the massacres. First, several thousand people fled to this area from nearby villages and Hayots Tsor for protection. Second, and most importantly, Varak was regarded as a key station on the road to salvation. If Van had been overrun and its inhabitants abandoned the city, their principal direction during their flight would have been towards Varak, because the mountain's northern and southerns slopes led to Arjag–Persia and Khoshab–Bashkale. For example, during the 1896 incidents in Van, when Armenian revolutionaries under the leadership of Bedo, Avedisian and Mardig had to leave the city, they first went to Varak and then took the road to Persia (though they were killed on the way).

Considering these two important factors, the government placed 30 gendarmes in the monastery. Armenians also moved in this direction, so that with the outbreak of violence, Armenian fighters from Shoushants, Kouroubash and Nor Kiugh prepared to remove the gendarmes and free the monastery. On the night of April 20, when the fighting had already started in Van, the gendarmes realised their difficult position and killed two of the monastery's monks, Arisdages and Vrtanes, as well as four servants, and then escaped. At this time, the massacres had also started in Hayots Tsor and many Armenians were pursued to Varak by Kurds. Varak, by now, was in the hands of Armenians led by Captain Toros. When news came that Kurds had cut off the route to the monastery near Nor Kiugh, Captain Toros led a group of Armenians to Nor Kiugh, where they clashed with the Kurds. Two of the latter were killed and the rest fled, so that the Armenian refugees were able to enter the mountain fastness.

By now the fighting had already started in the city of Van. Varak was in Armenian hands, and it was important to clear the roads to the city for the movement of people at night. One of those routes was hindered by Tsorovants and Zrvandants villages, and on April 25 Armenag Yegarian, Hovsep Kouyoumjian and Zaven Gorgodian were sent to clear that route. Accompanied by armed men from Tarman and Goghbants villages, they attacked Tsorovants, where the Turks had concentrated their forces. The Armenian attacks weren't successful during the first two days, but they succeeded on the third. By that time, however, the kaimakam of Saray had destroyed the Armenian villages of Arjag and had come to help with his army and a cannon, while the civilians of Tarman, Lim, Zarants and Sevan had also come to Varak. Given the uneven forces, the Armenians retreated, including the people from Tsorovants and Tarman villages.

Goghbants, Shoushants, Sourp Krikor and Varak monasteries remained in Armenian hands with their supplies, and around 6,000 Armenian refugees from surrounding villages and districts sought shelter there. The night-time communications with Van continued, and Varak remained the last point of contact with the outside world for the city.

Naturally, as this state of affairs troubled Jevdet, who could not subdue Van with his forces that included artillery pieces, he decided to destroy Varak at any price. After a few unsuccessful attempts, on Saturday May 8, he moved a large army from Haji Bekir garrison and other places to Shoushants village. His forces consisted of 300 cavalrymen and over 1,000 infantry *chetes* [irregulars] and militiamen with cannons.

The Armenians also had substantial forces which were divided over three positions. Goghbants village and Sourp Krikor monastery were defended by Captain Hagop Belengoian with 50 men; those at Varak monastery by Captain Toros and 250 men; and

Shoushants by the commander of Arjag, Shirin Hagopian, with 250 men. The entire enemy force was directed at Shoushants.

When the defenders at Shoushants noticed the enemy's movement before daybreak, they rushed to take over the position called Drovkyol. The enemy opened fire on them and the defence at that position crumbled after a minor fight. The loss of Drovkyol was decisive in the loss of Shoushants, as the enemy advanced towards the village with three cannons and many rifles. Many shells and bullets rained on the village, while the defenders did not realise their real capacity to fight. Shoushants fell quickly and the defenders gradually withdrew to Varak. After occupying Shoushants, the enemy torched all houses.

Following these successes, the attackers tried to climb towards the Armenian defensive positions at Varak, but the Armenians advanced and pushed the enemy back to Shoushants. However, defeat was in the air, and the loss of Shoushants led to the loss of Goghbants and Sourp Krikor monastery. After the occupation of Shoushants, some of the enemy moved towards these latter two Armenian positions and the defenders, after resisting for a few hours, retreated to the heights of the mountain and allowed Goghbants and Sourp Krikor monastery to fall to the enemy and be burnt down.

Night-time allowed Armenian civilians to retreat to higher ground, while the Armenian fighters assembled at Varak to confer with each other against a background of enemy gunfire and some desertions. Under these circumstances, instead of concentrating their forces and trying to reoccupy their lost positions, there were many suggestions but no agreement. This was a result of the loss of Shoushants and other disappointments. Soon, it was midnight and the enemy withdrew, leaving the road to the city open. Some defenders went to Van with a number of civilians. This effectively started the evacuation of Varak and its impregnable positions. The remaining fighters and civilians also left Varak the following night, and the enemy occupied and burnt down the monastery. Two days after the loss of Varak, the Armenian defenders on the heights around Varak, as well as a place called Asdghagan Pert, also left for the city.

Thus, entire districts were overrun, this or that village was defeated, as was the fastness of Varak, the impregnable last link to the outside world. All Armenian forces were now concentrated in Van, which continued its dogged fight. Here, in Van, the Armenians reorganised their resources and showed their determination to mount a heroic struggle for an honourable and sublime Armenian victory against the Turkish government.

Chapter XV

The Heroic Struggle of Van

Before discussing the heroic struggle of Van, one should comment on the city's topography, ethnic profile and strategic setting. Only then would it be possible to understand the remarkable resistance Armenians mounted in their epic struggle of April, 1915.

The city of Van comprised two sections: one was the old city [commonly referred as "the city"], and the other was Aykesdan. The city was to the west, on the lake-side, and Aykesdan to the east. It was a rather small urban area that was devoid of vegetation. Its houses adjoined each other and its streets were narrow and irregular. This was where the main market, state institutions and the military warehouse were located.

Aykesdan, in contrast, was spacious, with houses surrounded by gardens and vineyards and its streets remarkably ordered and wide. One could not miss its wide thoroughfare which began in the city and crossed Aykesdan. The majestic poplar and willow trees on both sides of this street gave great pleasure to travellers. In its entirety, it was called *Sghkayi Jadda*, but its different segments had more specific names. At its mid-point was a small cross-shaped square called Khach Poghan or Khach Poghani Square. Aykesdan, with its clean air and water, attracted many people, especially the wealthy, to live there.

To the north of the city was the huge, historic barrier called Shamiram's Rock, with its cuneiform inscriptions and citadel. One could still see on the other sides, where it had been protected by ancient walls, some traces of these structures. The only place these walls still stood firm were around Tabriz Gate on the eastern side.

Aykesdan was new and had no protective walls because it had no need for them. It was surrounded by vineyards, gardens and orchards. Its only natural barrier was to the north: a small mountain chain, where the well-known Zmzm Maghara [cave] and Mher's Gate were located. The Muslim village of Agrpi and a chapel were also located there.

The two parts of Van were separated by a largely deserted area known as the Haygavank quarter. It had once been inhabited by many Armenians, but was later practically abandoned and fell into ruin.

Van had a population of 41,000 people, 23,000 of whom were Armenian and 18,000 Muslim.

Around 3,000 Armenians and 1,000 Muslims lived in the city, totalling 4,000 people. The rest of the population lived in Aykesdan, Haygavank, Glor Tar and in the more remote quarter of Shamiram.

One should remember that over the years there was an exodus of Armenians and Muslims from the city, with Armenians going to Aykesdan and Muslims going mainly to Shamiram.

Armenians were predominant in the eastern parts of Aykesdan, which extended onto a wide plateau that stretched all the way to Varak, while Muslims were mainly concentrated in the western regions. For example, with very few exceptions, the Arark, Norashen and Hangouysner neighbourhoods, with their different sub-divisions, were entirely Armenian. Arark had a large area called Ararouts Square, which was surrounded by shops and was the second busiest market in Van. Extending to the north of Ararouts Square, up to Khach Poghani Square, was a wide road called Nalband Oghlou. To the west of this road were the main Muslim quarters, but most of the people living along the road itself were Armenian. Neighbourly contacts between these communities therefore started on this street. Norshen to the north and Glor Tar to the south were also mixed neighbourhoods. During the fighting in April, these mixed communities separated, with Armenians moving to solid Armenian areas and Muslims moving to Muslim ones, and the fighting taking place across the cleared zones. No Armenians remained in Glor Tar during the clashes, as it was densely populated by Muslims. The same was the case with the Sourp Hagop neighbourhood of Norshen.

The eastern half of Aykesdan's main street, which stretched to the city, was in Armenians hands, while the western half was in Muslim and government hands. Because of these circumstances, the Armenian communication lines between the city and Aykesdan were broken during the unrest.

The Armenian-populated quarter of Haygavank, which was in the desolate region between the city and the western Muslim quarters of Aykesdan, was evacuated to the old city. Historically, this quarter had always been the first to suffer casualties during massacres of Armenians, as it was not able to defend itself. It was for this reason that the quarter was gradually abandoned by its Armenian inhabitants.

There was also another quarter, to the south-east of the city, called Shamiram, which was inhabited by Muslims and did not experience any fighting or massacres.

The Armenian quarters of Aykesdan were thus surrounded by Muslim areas to the west and north-west, and free of Muslims to their south, east and north-east. Consequently, the Turkish authorities built garrisons in these open areas to circle the Armenian quarters. For example, the Haji Bekir garrison was located to the south-east of Ararouts quarter and the Armenian parts of Glor Tar. Toprak Kale garrison was situated to the north-east of Hangouysner quarter and Hamoud Agha garrison was located at the centre of Hangouysner quarter, quite a distance above Khach Poghan, on a square at the end of a large street. The garrison was built in 1904 for the specific purpose of intimidating the Armenians of Aykesdan. The homes of a few well-known Muslims were built next to this garrison. The occupants of these houses moved to Muslim quarters during the April fighting because they were either threatened by Armenians or felt in danger.

We can see from this brief sketch that the two parts of Van – the city and Aykesdan – would be separated from each other during any massacre or conflict, each left to its own fate. This is what actually happened during the fighting of April 1915. For these reasons, we will discuss the fighting in these two parts of Van separately, starting with Aykesdan.

Before discussing the actual fighting, however, we will present the context in which the fighting took place, by describing the organisation of Armenian defensive positions and their leadership, the approximate size of forces, and the relative strength of the Armenians of Aykesdan against the superior forces of their enemies.

The front-line defences of Aykesdan were divided into primary and secondary positions with their own armed units. These were divided into seven sectors.

Sector 1

This sector stretched from the so-called Mandabouri Mesha woods to the south of the front lines, from Nakhri Street to the Charchi Baghdo position. Its centre was at Ararouts Square. This front was therefore called the First or Ararouts sector. There were 16 units as follows:

Sector commanders: Nshan Nalbandian and Garabed Saroukhanian

No	Position	Unit leader
1	Mandabouri Mesha	Minas Baloian
2	Khaligian residence	Choghagha Salakhian
3	Boleian residence	Dikran Pneian
4	Dhertsi Sarkis residence	Nshan Res-Melikian
5	Yaghoupian residence	Dikran Nordouztsian
6	Dhertsi Nerso residence	Dikran Dhertsian
7	Salo's coffee house	Ghevont Zhamgochian
8	Panour's bakery	Tavit Chraghatsbanian
9	Der Mgrdichian residence	Ardashes Hiusian
10	Asho's coffee house	Dikran Chitjian
11	Potikian residence	Nazaret Sabounjian
12	Kolod Tavit residence	Yeghia Boyajian
13	Kartalian residence	Kalousd Mirijanian
14	Fargouzatian residence	Armenag Areghtsian
15	Misakian residence	Adom Sabounjian
16	Charchi Baghdo residence	Tateos Bjigian

The Dhertsi Sarkis, Dhertsi Nerso and Yaghoupian positions distinguished themselves at Ararouts Square as they came under heavy enemy artillery fire.

The enemy had four main positions on this front. These were:

1. The police station or *markyaz* [centre] at Ararouts Square. This position was much strengthened.
2. Ararouts School, where the government had placed its forces before the fighting broke out.
3. Ararouts church and its school, which passed into enemy hands.
4. Glor Tar quarter, where two cannons continuously pounded Armenian positions. One of those cannons was later moved into the church grounds.

Sector 2

This sector, which was a continuation of the first one, started at the Piroumian house and ended at Simon Terlemezian's position, including Nalband Oghli Street through Ararouts Square, and Khach Poghani Square with its surroundings. There were 18 units in the following positions:

Sector commanders and aides: Panos Zhamgochian, Roupen Israyelian, Karekin Vosgerichian, Nshan Zhamakordzian

No	Position	Unit leader
1	Piroumian residence	Ghasab Arshag
2	Polis Apo residence	Manoug Barsamian
3	Chachal Mirzi residence	Vahan Hatsakordzian
4	Sounatjian residence	Chochagha Alamgalamian
5	Natanian's Tatlough	Yeprem Chrpashkhian
6	Sahag Bey residence	Aram Bournazian
7	Tovmasian residence	Aram Shaljian
8	Pale's coffee house	Arjeshtsi Knel
9	Maksabedian residence	Nshan Aghanigian
10	Kaligian residence	Armenag Zhamakordzian
11	Yavrouian residence	Hovhannes Ghazarian
12	Noramirian residence	Solgar Dikran
13	Smsarian residence	Armenag Sarkisian
14	Hotel	Hovhannes Ashjian
15	Nalbanian residence	Mardiros Gotoian
16	Sarajian residence	Kamsar Paylian
17	Simon Terlemezian residence	Tavit Chavoush
18	Mouhasabajian residence	Vartan Bandigian

The Polis Apo, Sahag Bey, Tovmasian and Maksabedian positions played a key role in the defence of this sector. Against them were:

1. The large central Muslim quarter with its armed positions and an artillery piece. The Topal Khoja and Hamze positions were especially menacing.

2. The British consulate, located in i dechian's three-storey house on the eastern side of the street, in the Armenian quarter. Around 30 gendarmes were posted there.

The large two-storey Nalbandian house – the Hotel – played an important role on Khach Poghani Square, which was at an important intersection between the main quarters.

Against them were the telegraph office and, after it was burnt down, the ruins next to it. An artillery piece was positioned in Shahbaghlian's house.

These two sectors were major battle fronts as they were on key lines of contact between the main Armenian and Muslims quarters.

Sector Three. Misak Simonian (1) and his ARF volunteers
who were organised before the fighting in April, 1915

Sector 3

This sector started at Zrvantian's house and ended at Shaghoian's position including
Shanoyi Tar, Pos Tagh, Shan Tagh, and Kheran Tagh of Norshen. They stood against the
Muslim sections of Norshen, as well as Sev Kar and the Muslim village of Agrpi on the
other side of Hangouysner stream. There were 20 units in the following positions:

Sector commanders and aides: Melikset Eynatian, Misak Simonian, Hovhannes
Manougian and Vartan Kasbarian

No	Position	Unit leader
1	Zrvantian residence	Kerim Chavoush
2	Terlemezian residence	Vahan Kaylian
3	Torkomian residence	Mgrdich Pehrizian
4	Vzvzian residence	Vozments Hampartsoum
5	Torkomian residence	Ghevont Aboubabayakian
6	Berberian residence	Hovhannes Sarkisian
7	Kuyumjibashian residence	Nerses Mardirosian
8	Yeghigian residence	Sahag Pokhsrarian
9	Malaghian residence	Avedis Margosian
10	Topal Ohanes residence	Ghevond Ghazarian
11	Shmavonian residence	Aram Shaljian (teacher)
12	Bournoutian residence	Vahan Sosoyan
13	Katakjian residence	Bedros Roupenian

14	Mrodian residence	Mgrdich Manougian
15	Tnglchoian residence	Yeghishe Vartanian
16	Sanoian residence	Senekerim Sanoian
17	Iso's residence	Kasbar Mgrdichian
18	Mrodian residence	Mihran Mousoian
19	Khrimian residence	Hovhannes Zabarian
20	Shaghoian residence	Garabed Barigian

The following positions played a key role in this sector:

1. The Zrvantian and Vzvzian positions against the Friars' School occupied by government forces with a cannon.
2. The Shmavonian position against the Muslim Lavant Oghlou position.
3. The Shaghoian position which sometimes came under cannon fire from Sev Kar.

Sector 4

This sector started at Janoian's house and ended at the Chantigian position and included the north-eastern parts of Hangouysner area called Tari Kloukh and Chavoushbashi quarter. There were nine units in the following positions:

Sector commanders and aides: Kalousd Dantsoian, Garabed Der Haroutiunian

No	Position	Unit leader
1	Janoian residence	Yeghishe Nalbandian
2	Amirkhanian residence	Vozmetsi Hovsep
3	Manaserian residence	Apel Haroutiunian
4	Shahbenderian residence	Mgrdich Mgrdichian
5	Shegoian residence	Markar Hiusian
6	Aghanigian residence	Roupen Hiusian
7	Shiroyian residence	Boghos Gotoian
8	Der Khachadourian residence	Erzroutsi Sarksian
9	Chantigian residence	Vozmetsi Vartan

Four positions – Shahbenderian, Amirkhanian, Der Khachadourian and Shiroyian – played key roles in this sector. They faced a large number of Kurds at Toprak Kale, as well as the Toprak Kale garrison with its large Kurdish detachment, soldiers, and two cannons. Sometimes large scale attacks were made and were successfully repelled, especially at the Shahbenderian position, which overlooked the bridge over Hangouysner river and the road leading to Toprak Kale garrison. The position came under heavy bombardment and even fell into enemy hands at one point. Across the river from this position were the church, school and cemetery of Hangouysner, all in enemy hands.

Sector 5

This sector started at the Kreshtsian residence and ended at the Derjoian position. It included the Tezkargeh street and its orchards. The sector was defended by units in nine positions:

Sector commanders and aides: Nazaret Bournoutian and Hagop Bazigian

No.	Position	Unit leader
1	Kreshtsian residence	Garabed of Arjesh [Kavor]
2	Deli-Batman residence	Zaki of Mantant
3	Deli-Batman residence	Hovhannes Ardamedtsian
4	Hatshamaroghian residence	Manoug Vozmetsi
5	Dabbagh Khero residence	Baghdasar of Gavar
6	Aghvanian residence	Kapriel of Ganknar
7	Hiusian orchard	Hagop Bazigian
8	Hiusian orchard	Armenag Mazazian
9	Derjoian residence	Avedis Trchounian

The most important positions in this sector were the Hatshamaroghian, Deli-Batman and Dabbagh Khero's residences and the Hiusian orchard defending the sector against the forces located at Toprak Kale military base bombarding the Armenian positions with artillery fire. The sector also had to defend the city from any incursion by the mobs that had gathered on the adjacent plain.

Secor 6

This sector started at the Khiyak Parsegh residence and ended at the Haji Malkhas position. It included Avo's street where the German and American institutions were located, and Miravi Chader Street. There were four units in the following positions:

Sector commander: Raphayel Der Khachadourian

No	Position	Unit leader
1	Khiyak Parsegh residence	Dikran of Bltents
2	Solakhian residence	Hagop Gandalian
3	Der Khachadourian residence	Avedis Gandalian
4	Haji Malkhas residence	Madteos D. Hovannesian

This sector had to defend the plain leading to Varak and was involved in great battles.

Sector 7

The sector started at Miravi-Chagher and ended at Mandapouri Mesha. There were three units holding the following fortified positions:

Sector commanders: Ales Barsamian, Krikor Bazigian, and Mihran Khranian

No.	Position	Unit leader
1	Pasho residence	Melkon Kasbarian
2	Adle residence	Mihran Janoian
3	Ayijoghlou residence	Haroutioun of Lorto

The three positions in this sector accomplished a great deal by defeating the enemy. There were sections within the plain, where enemy forces could easily infiltrate the Armenian lines, especially from the Haji Bekir garrison, which was considered the strongest military compound in the city of Van. The artillery located in the compound continuously bombarded the Armenian defences. Moreover, there were at least six hundred Ottoman soldiers and militia fighters there. During the first days of battle, the enemy deployed most of its resources against this sector to break through the Armenian lines. The Armenians, however, conducted a tenacious defence. It was for this reason that these defensive positions were known as "Dardanelles" and "Kum Kale."

The 79 positions thus started from Mandapour and extended as far as Ararouts Square, then to Nalbandoghlu Street to Khach Poghani Square, then to Little Kantarji, Norshen Street and the Hangouys River, Chavoush Bashi, Taza Kyahrez, Avoyitar, Miravi Acher, Yeni Mahalle and finally back to Mandapour. This constituted a powerful bulwark, a compact ring, forged for self-preservation against a terrible enemy.

Aside from these seven sectors, there was one more area that was of extreme concern to all Armenians. This was the Hamoud Agha garrison, which was located at the centre of Hangouysner district inside the Armenian defensive ring.

There were also three large Turkish houses near Hamoud Agha garrison, which were considered to be part of it. In order to contain this enemy bastion behind Armenian lines, it was necessary to create the following positions:

1. The Madoian, Dzhikian and Balakian positions to the south
2. The Chichoian position to the south-west
3. The Pilavian and Khorenian positions to the west
4. The Shaghoian and Khrimian positions to the north
5. The Doghoian position to the south-east

The fighters in these nine positions were successful in torching the garrison and adjacent homes and were then deployed in the defence of the outer ring.

So, what was the military strength of Armenians in Aykesdan in this unequal battle? The Armenian forces were not great, but one should remember that the outcome of such battles are determined not by numbers but the quality of the forces deployed. The people of Aykesdan were in a fight for survival, as the prospect of massacre hung over their heads like the sword of Damocles. Death was seemingly inevitable, so why not choose an honourable end? There was another factor. After centuries of servitude, Armenians were now standing up, at the end of their tether, and resorting to arms – would they now simply put down their weapons? The answer was certainly not, and this spirit led to many miraculous deeds and outcomes.

When the battle started in Aykesdan in the middle of April, the Armenians had the following weapons:

1. 200 Mosin, Mauser, Aynali and Berdan rifles with some 70,000 cartridges
2. 300 Mauser parabellum pistols with 40,000 cartridges
3. 200 pistols of various types with 20,000 cartridges

Total: 700 firearms with 130,000 cartridges

The number of firearms almost doubled during the course of battle. As will be seen later, this was because of the arrival of groups of Armenian fighters among refugees fleeing to Aykesdan from adjoining regions during the fighting in the city.

Sector Five. Nazaret Bournoutian (1) and his group

Sector Seven. Ales Barsamian (1), Lorto (2), Khachig
Khranian (3) and Sahag the Assyrian (4)

AYKESDAN MILITARY COMMAND
(*Left to right*) Bulgratsi Krikor, Gaydzag Arakel, Armenag Yegarian

Despite this, it was not the number of rifles and pistols that determined the outcome of the great battles. It was military strategy, organisation, and discipline. The Armenians of Van showed great self-discipline and courage during the city's defence. All internal differences were immediately put aside, inter-party rivalries were forgotten, and all came under the control of the military leadership, promising unwavering allegiance to it.

A responsible military body was formed, which later became known as the "National Self-Defence Body" [*Azkayin Inknabashdban Marmin*]. The members of this provisional military command [hereafter the Military Command] were:

1. Bulgaratsi Krikor [Krikor the Bulgarian]
2. Gaydzag Arakel
3. Armenag Yegarian

All three were seasoned military men. The first two were members of the Armenian Revolutionary Federation [ARF], while the third was a member of the Ramgavar Party.

Panos Terlemezian, a photographer by profession, as well as others were also called to join the Military Command. They were:

1. Hmayag Manougian
2. Hovhannes Mkhitarian
3. Armenag Pokhanian
4. Hrant Kaligian
5. Garabed Ajem-Khachoian
6. Kapriel Semerjian

Aram Manougian, the future governor of Van, became an ever-present and influential adviser to the Military Command.

Other than the Military Command, three other bodies were also formed and played a major role during the fighting. These were the:

1. Red Cross Committee
2. Military Supplies Unit
3. Foodstuffs Committee

A whole people was resorting to arms: the dead and wounded were beginning to arrive, and there was a need for medical assistance.

Hundreds of fighters had left their homes and were expected to remain at their positions under fire, day and night, and it was necessary to feed them.

A mass of people were arriving from the surrounding districts, robbed of their belongings and without any means of livelihood. It was necessary to organise relief.

Consequently, the abovementioned three bodies were formed to meet these needs:

The elected members of the Red Cross Committee were:

1. Dr. Sanfani (Kh. Chitouni)
2. Dr. Khachig
3. Varaztad Deroian
4. Vartan Kzartmian
5. Arshavir Avedaghian
6. Armenag Vouvounigian

Some 30 secondary school students were also invited to help the committee.

The following locations served as hospitals:

1. The Norashen School
2. The Der Parseghian residence
3. The Sosian residence
4. The Vartabedian residence

The elected members of the Military Supplies Unit consisted of:

1. Kevork Soujian
2. Mgrdich Ajemian
3. Hagop Zhamakordzian
4. Simeon Shiroyian
5. Hmayag Tarpinian
6. Tavit Bandigian

Supporting members were:

7. Sahag Shegoian
8. Garabed Parseghian
9. Ghevont Vosgerichian
10. Garabed Meykhanajian
11. Kevork Hovnanian
12. Dikran Berber-Seferian

The elected members of the Foodstuff Committee were:

1. Sebouh Khanjian
2. Set Kapamajian
3. Ghevont Janigian
4. Mikayel Minasian

5.   Mgrdich Cherpashkhian
6.   Bedros Mozian
7.   Aghabeg Hamparian
8.   Roupen Shadvorian
9.   Father Arshavir
10. Garabed Karakhanian
11. Hovsep Bochovian
12. Hagop Papazian
13. Mardiros Khanoian

Aside from these committees, a special group was appointed to help the Military Command to procure arms and armaments:

1.   Garabed Beylerian
2.   Tavit Papazian
3.   Vahram D. Boghosian
4.   Dikran Terlemezian

This was the overall military strength and organisational structure of the Armenians of Aykesdan as they responded to the terrible – yet glorious – call of April 20.

Chapter XVI

The Heroic Battle of Aykesdan

In chapter 10 we related how Jevdet started to unveil his cunning plan on April 14, 1915. He demanded the surrender of all Armenian men of conscription age and stationed government soldiers in the previously vacant Hamoud Agha garrison in the Armenian quarter. He then had Ishkhan and his three comrades killed in Hirj on April 16, and, on the following morning, he summoned Vramian to a meeting and had him arrested and sent to an unknown destination.

The Armenians considered the above developments as signs of an imminent massacre and began to mobilise for their self-defence. Contacts between Aykesdan and the city came to a halt and the markets were shut down. Communication and other ties between Armenians and the government ended and Armenian families living in the suburbs of Van started moving to central quarters. Armenian defence units assumed their previously designated positions, windows were barricaded and trenches dug in certain places, and everyone awaited the much-anticipated danger.

Jevdet also prepared his forces. The Haji Bekir and Toprak Kale garrisons bordering Aykesdan were reinforced with the placement of cannons. Government soldiers patrolled the plain leading to Varak and dug trenches in various places, while soldiers assumed positions in the neighbouring Muslim quarters.

The Armenians of Van were thus in a resolute mood as they rested during the night of April 19 in anticipation of the terrible morning that awaited them. It was to be a morning that would prove to be one of the most celebrated sagas of Armenian history.

The momentous night slipped away and the sun arose on April 20.

It was morning and some Armenian women were going to Aykesdan from Shoushants. When they reached a place called Ourpat Arou, one of the Ottoman sentries, who had been patrolling the plain stretching to Varak over the previous three days, assaulted the women. Two Armenian defenders at the Avoyi Tar position, Yeghia Nakhshounian and Hagop Tourzian, saw the incident and ran to intervene but were gunned down before they could do anything.

Herr Spörri, the director of the German orphanage, sent the following letter to Jevdet through the offices of the Italian Consul General the day after the above incident:

> Your Excellency,
> Jevdet Bey,
> Governor of Van,
> Very dear friend,
> When I talked to you last Sunday, I was hoping that the problems between the Armenian community and the government would be resolved in a manner acceptable to both sides. Unfortunately, my hope was not realised. On the

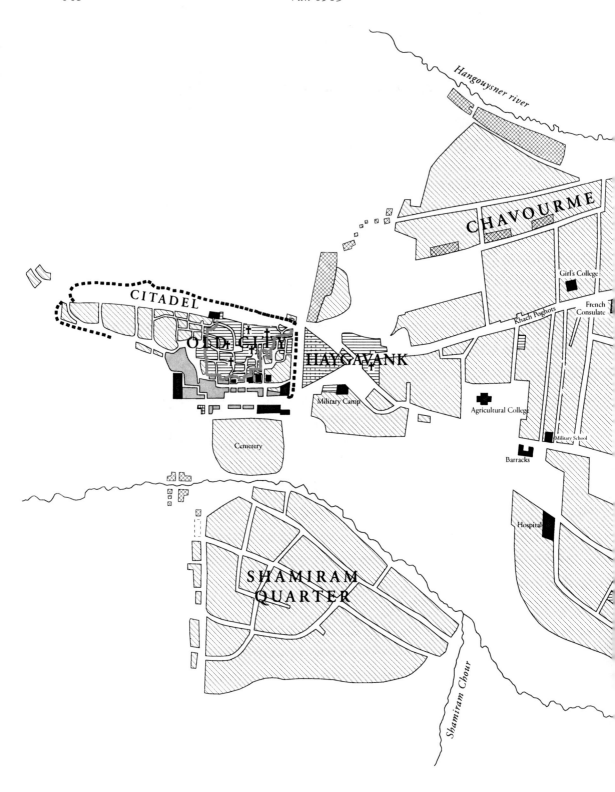

CITADEL

OLD CITY

HAYGAVANK

CHAVOURME

Girl's College

French Consulate

Rhach Poghots

Military Camp

Agricultural College

Military School

Barracks

Cemetery

Hospital

SHAMIRAM QUARTER

Hangouysner river

Shamiram Chour

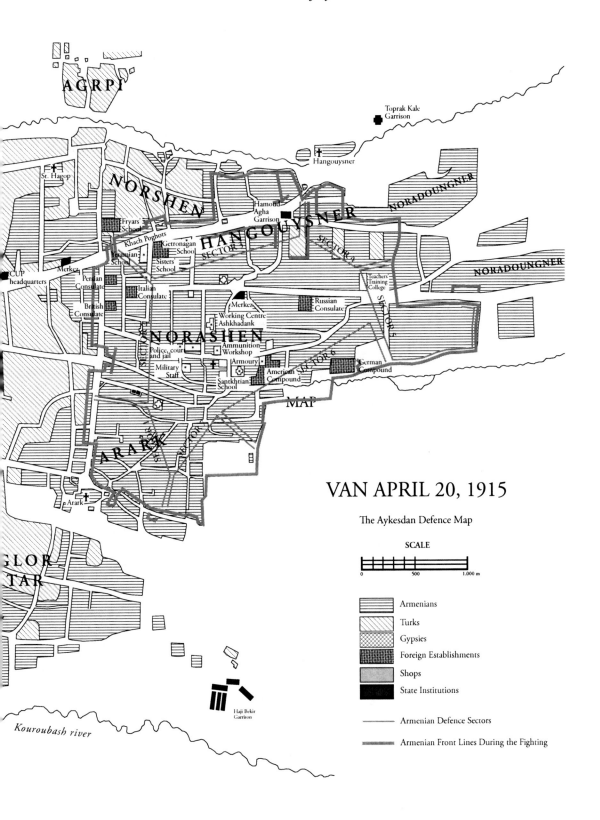

AGRPI

St. Hagop

NORSHEN

Fryars' School

Khach Poghots

Yesanian School

CUP headquarters

Merkez

Persian Consulate

British Consulate

Getronagan School

Sisters' School

Italian Consulate

SNORASHEN

Merkez

Working Centre Ashkhadank

Police, court and jail

Ammunition Workshop

Military Staff

Armoury

Santkhtian School

ARARK

Arark

GLOR TAR

Hamoud Agha Garrison

HANGOUYSNER

SECTOR

Toprak Kale Garrison

Hangouysner

NORADOUNGNER

SECTOR 2

NORADOUNGNER

SECTOR

Teachers' Training College

Russian Consulate

American Compound

SECTOR 6

German Compound

MAP

Haji Bekir Garrison

Kouroubash river

VAN APRIL 20, 1915

The Aykesdan Defence Map

SCALE

0   500   1,000 m

Armenians

Turks

Gypsies

Foreign Establishments

Shops

State Institutions

Armenian Defence Sectors

Armenian Front Lines During the Fighting

contrary, it seems events took a turn for the worse. And it was the army that is to blame for this outcome.

Yesterday morning, a little after 6:00 a.m., a few [Armenian] women, who were apparently being followed at Kouroubash, came to the city from the village of Shoushants to find refuge. When they had to cross a line of soldiers on guard duty, a young woman, who was one of our former orphans and a little deranged, was attacked by the soldiers. That woman, whose husband was conscripted at the beginning of the war, managed to free herself by abandoning the bundle she was carrying and a donkey. The soldiers then started to shoot and others joined in.

These events happened across our compound and in front of our eyes. We are very sorry to have seen all this. Last night they opened fire on our compound in a very frightening way. We were subjected to great danger. Fortunately, nothing more happened. Three bullets hit our building. One of our teachers was almost killed. I cannot believe that all of this was done deliberately.

(Signed) Herr Spörri,

The incident near Ourpat Arou immediately echoed from one end of Aykesdan to the other and the fighting started.

Thus the battle begun. What had been expected for weeks, months, years, and even centuries, now became a stunning reality. The city was divided into two enemy camps: on the one side was the government with an army and religious fanatics, and on the other stood the subjugated slaves of many centuries.

The attack near Ourpat Arou and the killing of two Armenians led to some shots from Armenians at Avoyi Tar. The next reply came from the Haji Bekir garrison, as over 300 well-armed soldiers and militiamen rushed out and divided into two columns. One quickly advanced towards Glor Tar to attack Ararouts quarter, while the other advanced northward towards the open fields and occupied the stream flowing to a mill. They took up positions in trenches that had been prepared beforehand. The Armenian defenders of the seventh sector and Pasho, Adliye, and Ayijoghlu positions watched what was happening and opened fire. Their attack was followed by firing from the garrison and the trenches in the fields.

While these developments were taking place, a similar move took place at Toprak Kale garrison. Soldiers marched quickly in the direction of Hangouysner church, where they took up positions in and around the church and adjacent cemetery. The Armenian Shabenderian position opened fire on them.

As soon as the first bullets were fired at Ourpat Arou, a commotion started in the garrison inside the Armenian defensive ring. Several soldiers took up positions on the roof of the main building while others came outside. The Armenian forces at Chitjian, Shaghoian, and Toghoian residences opened fire. The soldiers outside retreated into the building, taking several of their wounded with them. Other soldiers started firing at the Armenian positions from the windows.

The sound of gunfire reached Khach Poghani Square. As bullets whizzed in every direction, a guard at the telegraph office looked out of a window and was immediately shot dead.

Soon the firing spread to the Glor Tar position and along Ararouts Street. Shooting also started on both sides at Norshen Street, and extended to Khach Poghani Square and all of Arark and Nalband Oghlou Street.

Armenian Defence Forces in Van

The firing thus spread to all 79 Armenian positions, as several hundred defenders opposed three garrisons full of soldiers and militia units, as well as dozens of positions manned by hundreds of other soldiers. The government forces soon started to use artillery too. The bombardment started from Haji Bekir garrison and was joined by Toprak Kale garrison, and then the Sahag Bey position where Hamze mill was located. Four cannons roared from those three positions and their projectiles landed everywhere.

Within three hours of the Ourpat Arou incident, there was shooting in all directions, and the cannonade continued incessantly. Aykesdan was encircled by a ring of fire while inside that circle stood the former slaves. All credit to the now awakened Armenians.

As the fighting continued, all Armenian positions opened fire, with no indication of what lay ahead; a spectre that weighed heavily on the shoulders of Armenians. The first day was a trial. Armenians initially thought the fighting would last two or three days, if that. Jevdet, especially, thought two days was enough to punish the rebels. He had already sent Vramian a threatening telegram from the border, "I will soon arrive there with regular troops and am more than confident that I will put an end to any issue."

However, the first day of battle showed that it was not easy to subdue a people who had lost all patience and resorted to arms. Soon weary hearts gathered courage, unaccustomed hands got used to weapons, and heartening announcements of early victories nourished the will of the people in a battle for survival.

As Armenian fighters clutched their weapons and followed the movement of their enemy through loopholes at their positions, the small press at *Ashkhadank* newspaper quickly printed and distributed the following announcement.

Communication No. 1:

Victory!

April 20, 1915, morning,

Turkish soldiers opened fire on Armenian women coming to the city from Sghka. Our forces responded. Three soldiers were killed and two mules were confiscated. One Turk was killed at Khach Street and another at Ourpat Arou. There were no casualties on our side.

That announcement – which deliberately did not mentioned the two Armenians killed at Ourpat Arou – was immediately sent to all Armenian positions. The news spread like wildfire among the people and boosted morale. It did not matter that these were minor incidents; they created excitement, because they were the first successes in a great battle.

Gradually the number of clashes increased, the attacks and resistance became greater, and the information bureau received more reliable news of victories leading to a second announcement at midday:

Communication No. 2

1. Three Turks were killed at the Ayij Oghlou Street.
2. Two more Turks were shot at the Tovmasian position.
3. Another armed man was killed in front of the Der Nersessian residence.
4. A militiaman was killed at the Arark Merkez position.
5. The garrison at Hamoud Agha is surrounded by our forces. The soldiers inside have neither bread nor water. A Circassian has been killed there. We have procured a rifle and a horse.
6. The telegraph office on Khach Street has been taken with all its equipment intact plus a rifle. The telegraph line and telephone is not operational.
7. We have one killed and one wounded during the fighting near the German building.
Conserve your ammunition!

This second announcement created even more euphoria. Not only had Armenians taken over Turkish positions at Khach Poghani and the telegraph office, but they had surrounded the Hamoud Agha garrison, the very garrison that was at the centre of Aykesdan and the cause of much alarm.

In the subsequent excitement, young people joined the band of the Armenian Teacher's School and marched through the streets with a fanfare of flag-waving and singing.

It is interesting to note how heightened Armenian morale led to further desertions from Turkish positions. It seemed that the music and fanfare were having a great demoralising influence on the Turks and the army.

It was during such jubilation that a third communication was printed that same night:

Communication No. 3

The Turkish people do not want to participate in the fighting.
1. The artillery round that hit our position at Sahag Bey only scattered the sandbags that had been erected by our fighters. Upon the arrival of our new forces, the enemy stopped its attacks and suffered four dead.
2. The Turkish fighters at Khach Street set their own position ablaze and fled.
3. One Turk was killed at the Apo position.
4. We lowered the Turkish flag at the Sisters' school.
5. The militiamen attacking the Ayij Oghlou position suffered several deaths from the artillery shells fired from their own Haji Bekir garrison.

6. We killed another Turk at the entrance of Hamoud Agha garrison.

7. We killed three militiamen in Pos quarter.

8. Our comrades respond to the thousands of enemy bullets with one bullet.

This third announcement, like the others, also passed from hand to hand at lightning speed and created further excitement. News of even the smallest of victories boosted the morale of Armenian fighters while the uplifting music animated the general population. Thus, as darkness fell on April 20, all positions received the following message from the Military Command.

Comrades:

The artillery fire injured only unarmed Armenians. Please escort the civilian population to safe places.

Be strong. We have already attained victories on all fronts.

The password for tonight is "Tsoren."*

With regards,

The Military Command Body

The first day of fighting ended with a string of Armenian victories and peoples' confidence in their own arms was further strengthened. However, it was an extraordinary night with continuous rifle and volley fire, as well as the roar of cannon from enemy lines. Nevertheless, these attacks were no longer terrifying. The first night of fighting passed and the second morning of battle began. Daylight also brought the following announcement from the information bureau.

Compatriots,

Last night's bombardment and the hundreds of thousands of bullets wasted by the enemy were meant to frighten our people. However, there were no casualties in our lines, or the loss of any position. Our defenders did not even respond.

There is no need for alarm.

The announcement, which was intended to comfort both civilians and the fighters following the previous night's bombardment, actually emboldened Armenians even more.

On that day, the enemy bombarded Arark, Glor Tar, and Vzvz sectors with its cannon at the Friars' School. The artillery at Haji Bekir garrison also targeted the Armenian positions in the seventh sector.

Enemy cannons were thundering from different positions, as they were moved from one place to another. The artillery rounds constantly destroyed walls, windows, doors and sandbags, but the enemy was not able to overrun Armenian positions. The only position they were able to take control of was Shahbenderian, which was across Hangouys Church. That position came under heavy artillery bombardment from Toprak Kale garrison and its cannon. It was a difficult position to defend.

The forces at Hamoud Agha, in order to establish a link with Toprak Kale, opened a passage in the rear wall of their garrison, entered the Tabkoian residence nearby, and proceeded to move southwards through houses and gardens towards the Shahbenderian

---

* *Tsoren* (Armenian) = Wheat – A.S.

position. The Armenian defenders were in a difficult position, and in order not to be encircled by the enemy, they first fought their way to the Shegoian and then to the Toghoian residences. Turkish soldiers thus occupied the Shahbenderian position. The situation at this sector was now dire. Meanwhile, throughout the day, despite bullets flying around, young boys distributed announcements from the information bureau:

Communication No. 4

April 21

1. Our fighters at the Shiroyents position killed two Turkish artillerymen.

2. One militiaman was killed on the roof of Hamoud Agha garrison.

3. We burnt down the Turkish position at the Loroyents residence.

4. During the fighting at the Shahbenderian and Toghoyents positions we killed eight Turkish soldiers and two artillerymen.

5. We killed one militiaman at the Nalbandian position.

6. We killed an artilleryman inside Hamoud Agha garrison.

7. We killed two soldiers from our position at Ararouts.

8. Several "Cross of Honour" medals were awarded to fighters who distinguished themselves during the most dangerous moments of battle.

Be strong. Victory will be ours! Conserve your ammunition!

Communication No. 5

April 21

1. We killed two Turks from our Der Hagopian position. One was a *mullah* [Muslim clergyman] and the other a militiaman.

2. We killed one Kurd and injured another at the Solakhian position near Haji Bekir garrison. We also killed two oxen laden with weapons and ammunition.

3. We killed an artilleryman from our Taza Kyahrez position.

4. We killed a Turk who was trying to escape with a mule in front of the Friars' School.

5. We killed a Turk who was trying to escape with a mule at the Khach Street position.

6. We killed two artillerymen stationed at the Friars' School from our position at Vzvz.

7. Because of their lack of care, a boy, a woman and several others were wounded from Turkish gunfire.

Always be on guard and ready!

Communication No. 6

April 21, night

Conserve your ammunition.

1. We killed six militiamen from the Shiroyian position.

2. We killed eight soldiers from the Taza Kyahrez position.

3. Ten to 15 hand grenades were thrown at our Ararouts position but they had no effect. We killed one militiaman from that position.

4. We killed three Turkish soldiers from the Nalbandian position.

Armenian Defence Forces in Van

5. At exactly 7:30 p.m. the Turks embarked, in vain, on an offensive between our Sahag Bey and Khach Street positions. Their aim was to concentrate new forces at the British Consulate. We killed six soldiers of the attacking force and by 9 p.m. the building was burnt down. So far, we do not know how many were killed or injured in the building.

The second day of fighting thus ended with the failure of the hopeless Turkish attack on the Sahag Bey and surrounding positions and the destruction of the British Consulate by fire.

The British Consulate, as we saw earlier, was behind Armenian lines and occupied by 30 gendarmes – thus posing a threat to the second sector. Consequently, from the first day, Armenians tried to torch the building and succeeded during the evening of the second day. The attack took place in the dark, when fire-bombers approached the main entrance and attacked it. Soon the building was in flames and most of the soldiers inside managed to escape, leaving a few corpses inside the building. The fall of the British Consulate balanced the loss of the Shahbenderian position.

Other than the attack on the British Consulate, there were several other heroic operations that day. These were all possible because of the heightened morale following the successes of that first day of fighting. The Military Command, in order to raise spirits further and encourage the fighters, established the first medal for valour. It was a small silver cross with the abbreviation "Arm. Rev."[*] This medal was called the "Cross of Honour"[†] and became a symbol of victory. Soon, several fighters in Aykesdan started wearing these medals on their chests.

However, the second day of fighting created serious problems and alarmed the Military Command.

---

[*] *Hay Hegh.* or *Hay Heghapokhoutiun* (Armenian) = Armenian Revolution –A.S.
[†] *Badvo Khach* (Armenian) = Cross of Honour –A.S.

The battle was not going to end soon. The skirmishes of the previous two days indicated that it was going to last several weeks and the Military Command was worried about the supply of ammunition. This concern was reflected in its 4th to 6th communications with the message, "Conserve your ammunition!"

There was another problem of equal importance. The enemy was using cannon and countless projectiles were exploding and causing damage in different places. It was necessary to repair the damage, reinforce positions, and dig trenches under enemy bombardment. Therefore, bricklayers, carpenters and workers were formed into so-called "amrashen and amalia" teams who thus played a major role in the battle of Aykesdan.

A construction committee was also formed under the direction of:

1. Shavarsh Hovivian.
2. Azad Khorenian.
3. Haroutiun Gakavian.

Naturally, the mason Krikor Banirian and his partner joined this group. Their tasks were tough, relentless and dangerous, and could only be undertaken at key moments. These teams dug trenches between positions and homes, often across exposed streets. These networks continued to amaze visitors after the fighting. Thanks to these communication channels, Armenian fighters, carriers of military supplies and food, as well as the little couriers could move about freely. The construction workers repaired damaged positions by dim candlelight at night time, creating secondary walls and fortified positions with wooden posts to withstand enemy artillery bombardment. How did they manage all of this? These were all the achievements of a people fighting for their salvation, and their enemies were both amazed and demoralised by such resistance.

The torching of Hamoud Agha garrison was also to the credit of these *amrashen* and *amalia* corps.

As we saw earlier, Hamoud Agha garrison was a major source of concern behind Armenian lines. It was built in the middle of the Armenian quarters. This arrogant 120-man garrison of Abdul Hamid and the Young Turks spread fear among the Armenians of Taza Kyahrez, Chavoush Basi, and Aghvanian districts, as well as Shan and Kherani quarters. Such fears increased after the fall of the Shahbenderian position and the establishment of communications between Hamoud Agha and Toprak Kale garrisons. The situation got worse when soldiers tried to burn down nearby Armenian houses. They entered the Shaghoian residence and burnt it down, and then attempted to tear down a wall and enter the Kordzounian's residence. This was when Armenian defenders realised what was happening and threw a bomb into Shaghoian's burning house. The soldiers, who were busy digging into a wall, fled after the bomb exploded.

The threat from the garrison, however, remained and had to be removed. This problem was of major concern to the Military Command and one of its members, Bulgaratsi Krikor, undertook to resolve it.

They say that Krikor had no rest for three days, holding consultations here and there, and drawing up plans and sketches to blow up the garrison. He finally came up with a plan.

Armenians were to dig a tunnel to the foundations of the garrison and blow it up with dynamite. But how feasible was such a plan? The answer lay in a group of craftsmen known as *kankan*s among the amarashen and amalia workers.

Van, and especially Aykesdan, was well known for its abundant water, and each quarter, even smaller areas, had their own waterway or *kyahrez*. These waterways beneath the streets were built by master-craftsmen called kankans. For this reason, nobody knew these underground tunnels better than the kankans.

These kankans informed Krikor that when the garrison was constructed, there was a waterway from Aykesdan to the garrison. When they were building the garrison's foundations, they had to divert the waterway and fill in the tunnel under the garrison. Therefore, it should have been easy to approach the garrison's foundations through the old tunnels.

Thereafter, a few experienced kankans started digging at the Khorenian residence and tunnelled to the main square and the former waterway. Then they took Bulgaratsi Krikor to the north-western foundations of the garrison.

While this work was carried out, the third day of battle started on the morning of April 22, with the same gunfire and explosions as during the previous two days. Once more, several announcements were released, one after the other.

Communication No. 6 (sic)

April 22

Comrades,

In order to be quicker and more accurate in our work, please note the following points when you communicate with us:

1. Write your messages in a concise, clear and simple language.

2. Try to check all incidents carefully and inform us as quickly as possible under the signature of your captains [*khmpabeds*], noting the place and time. We will not accept verbal communications. Khmpabeds will be held responsible for inaccurate reports.

Return all shovels and construction equipment at your positions.

Don't waste ammunition. Each bullet you fire should serve its purpose. Those who waste even a single bullet will be punished. Send us all used cartridge cases.

The excessive consumption of *arak* and wine is prohibited.

You are not to insult the religion of the enemy.

Communication No. 7

April 22

1. We were able to take over a Turkish position in the Ararouts sector, next to Dhertsi Sarkis's residence, and seized a large cache of cartridges.

2. We seized more than 300 cartridges when Turkish soldiers fled from the Maksabediants residence.

3. We killed some firemen at Hamoud Agha garrison.

4. A 12 year-old boy called Hmayag snatched a fur-cap which a Turkish policeman had set up to make us believe that there were soldiers there. The boy returned safely to our positions.

5. Our fighters at the Nalbandian position wounded a Turkish gendarme.

6. A *chete* was shot from our Chachal Mirzi position.

7. We killed a militiaman from the Piroumian position.

8. A militiaman was killed by Turkish bullets from Haji Bekir garrison.

9. At about 9 a.m., a group of some 30 Turkish militiamen advanced towards the upper garrison at Hangouysner to attack us. We repelled them and killed three Turks.

10. We killed three Turks at the Sahag Bey position during the fighting yesterday and today.

The Military Command Body

While the fighting continued and the information bureau quickly spread news of every positive success, Bulgaratsi Krikor was continuing his underground work. He was placing explosives under the foundations of the garrison and setting his fuses until everything was ready. Then, at 4 o'clock, he looked at his watch, lit the main fuse and quickly moved away.

Ten minutes later a huge explosion shook the garrison. The soldiers at the garrison were bewildered and some ran to the roof of their building to see what was going on. However, the garrison stood firm and the explosives did not have the desired effect.

Were the explosives of poor quality, or were the tunnel and other passages the problem? Nothing was clear, except that the explosion had no effect. Krikor expressed his anger by shaking his fist and leaving. But he was not one to give up and went home to gather his thoughts and come up with a new plan.

While he was up all night working on a new plan, a few hours after midnight, at 3 a.m., Aykesdan was suddenly lit up by a huge fire. People ran outside and marvelled at the sight of Hamoud Agha garrison in flames.

Krikor's efforts were a success. While the explosives had not managed to destroy the garrison, they had started a fire under the floorboards of the building. The fire had smouldered and then engulfed the whole building. The soldiers in the barracks escaped into the night towards Toprak Kale, leaving behind the corpses of a captain and five soldiers. The palace of the dictatorship had fallen. The amazing view of the burning building was recorded by one eye-witness as summarised below.

April 22, Thursday evening,

We were now impatient.

The delay of the job [explosion] began to make us a little despondent, though we had kept such feelings at bay since that happy moment when we received our orders to go to our positions; especially after we fired our first shots from Ourpat Arou and forced the Turks to retreat. All of our attention was now on the project undertaken by the man from Rusjuk. After the loss of the noble Ishkhan and his comrades, as well as the unforgettable Vramian, Aram and the man from Rusjuk were the critical links to the great task ahead – Aram, with his commanding presence and instructions and the man from Rusjuk with his deeds. We so admired the work of the latter, who had become so much more important at that moment. We expected a great deal from him in the heroic struggle of Van which started on April 20. Wasn't he, after all, an old revolutionary of the underground days? He had remained active and dedicated to the cause, and we expected him to rise to the challenge for the good of his people at such a critical moment.

After a long wait, we were informed that the underground operation to destroy the garrison had failed. If one could only see our pained faces at that moment, and our shame and sorrowful return to our positions!

It was night.

Our position sent out some supporting fighters as we had been ordered. The enemy's heavy gunfire had abated, but we could sometimes hear the explosions of artillery projectiles which had little effect on our fortified positions. The fighters we sent out did not return. Our sentries were watching carefully and our impatience had no limit. It was now 3 o'clock. Suddenly, to the north of our position, a bright red light overcame us. Hamoud Agha garrison, the nest of murderers in those years, was finally engulfed by fire and was turning into ash. The dynamite under the ground had done its job.

Aykesdan was elated. Happy cries and national revolutionary songs could be heard everywhere. We stood for hours marvelling at that den of the dictatorship.

Hamoud Agha was in flames. Long live the Bulgarian!

Thus the fourth morning of battle started and shortly thereafter came the 8th announcement from the information bureau:

> Yesterday, during the evening hours, a tunnel was used to plant explosives under the foundations of Hamoud Agha garrison and the glorious result was seen at 3 (8) o'clock when the whole garrison burnt down.

Hamoud Agha garrison was destroyed, as were three positions around it. The soldiers in the garrison fled towards Hangouysner River and Toprak Kale garrison. The Armenians no longer had the Shahbenderian position to stop their escape and catch them in crossfire. The Turkish soldiers were so scared that they even abandoned their Shahbenderian position.

Indeed, the Shahbenderian position fell silent. There was no gunfire from there. But the Armenian defenders who had earlier come under heavy fire and retreated to the Toghoian position from Shahbenderian thought it was a trap. Nevertheless, they decided to reconnoitre the position by climbing over the high wall encompassing the garden, descending into the garden itself, and carefully approaching the house. If the house was not empty, any scout would definitely have been seen by those inside the two-storey building. Who would be that one person in a thousand who would undertake such a mission? A 19 year old woman who had worked at the Shahbenderian residence. She was short, shy, and had a baby face with fiery black eyes. She was Srpouhi Hampartsoumian or Kyankar Khampo's daughter, Sevo. She cooked for the boys, bandaged the wounded, and dodged bullets to carry messages to the Military Command and ammunition to the fighters. On top of everything else, she carried a Mauser pistol, which she fired at the enemy from Armenian positions during her free time.

Nobody believed that the Turks would abandon the Shahbenderian position, or that anyone sent there to investigate would return alive. Sevo, the daughter of Van, also thought so and removed her pistol from her shoulder strap and handed it to the boys: "Keep my ten-shooter. If I am killed, at least my pistol will be saved and remain useful to you." She then disappeared. While the boys worried and waited, the brave Sevo returned to report that the position was abandoned. She had descended from the high wall, examined the orchard and the two-storey house, and returned under fire from far away. Her clothing had a bullet hole in it, but her life had been saved by a miracle. The Armenian defenders re-occupied the Shahbenderian position and Sevo was awarded the Cross of Honour.

God only knows how many Sevos were needed in those difficult days at Aykesdan.

The Hamoud Agha garrison thus fell into Armenian hands along with three positions around it. Armenians had once more occupied the Shahbenderian position and these successes strengthened the resolve of Armenians in Aykesdan.

Sevo - Iskouhi
Hampartsoumian

The fifth day was noted for the torching of a powerful enemy position in the third sector. This was the Hamza position, across from the Armenian Sahag Bey position. The Hamza position was a major enemy base. There had already been an attempt to approach it through a tunnel and blow it up. The work had started swiftly with tunnelling for three days across the wide street between the two positions. However, when the tunneling reached the enemy position, the excavators were astonished to discover that their opponents were also doing similar work. Therefore, the Armenians stopped their work and decided on a direct attack by crossing the street in broad daylight and firebombing the main entrance which, like all of the entrances on the street, was kept shut. And so they proceeded.

Two brave men, Vagharshag Shirvanian and Tovmas Krikorian were the first to move forward, followed by two others behind them. They crossed the street in the blink of an eye, set fire to the entrance using petrol soaked rags, and returned to their lines under enemy fire. During this operation the Armenian fighters at Sahag Bey gave covering fire by shooting at the windows of the Hamza position.

A little later, the fire spread to the whole building, the enemy lost hope, and the position fell. With the destruction of the Hamza position, the third sector also experienced a small victory, which completed a series of triumphs over those three days.

Not surprisingly, during the third, fourth and fifth days, there was great excitement among Armenians in Aykesdan, especially among the fighters, all of whom displayed an appetite for bold operations. This spirit was echoed in the following call from the Military Command.

Compatriots,

During the four days of our heroic battle we have stood our ground against thousands of shells, hundreds of thousands of bullets, a barbarian horde and hopeless soldiers.

From Ayij Oghlu to Arark, and then to Khach Street and the cruel Hamoud Agha garrison, our forces stand tall and victorious. They have no fear of death, though it hovers over all of our heads.

The number of enemy losses to our individual bullets is now countless. The desertions and hopelessness in their ranks seem obvious.

It is now clear that the enemy is suffering a huge number of desertions. They have heard the delusional talk of their chief executioner, Jevdet, to turn our homeland into a slaughterhouse within 24 hours.

Every day our fighters go from victory to victory. There is a burning desire in their souls, and it is growing from one day to the next, to defend their homeland. They have decided to die for you, for your defence, and your ultimate freedom.

We are not afraid of the greater number of our enemy or the knowledge that we will die today or tomorrow. No! We want to embrace death in its godly essence. We want to show other nations in this world conflict that in the depths of the east, the centuries-old oak tree, the Armenian nation, knows how to die, weapon in hand, standing over the countless corpses and ruined fortresses of its enemy.

Armenians! We will continue the battle we have begun to the end, until the last drop of our blood is shed, or the final defeat and destruction of our savage enemy.

Armenians! Be brave. Victory is ours, whatever happens.

Let our fighters' spirit of resistance resonate in you.

Do not leave the huge burden of resistance on their shoulders.

Everyone has a role to play, including old and young, women and girls. We should all share the burden side-by-side with our young fighters.

This fight is not only our battle for survival, but also for truth and justice. Let everyone fight for justice. Let all long for the victory of truth.

Be positive and brave, and continue to work quietly and fruitfully for new victories.

Marvel at the smouldering garrisons and countless enemy dead.

Marvel at the epic struggle of our fighters and prepare with hope and action for the celebration of our national rebirth in the coming days.

Long live Armenian soldiers!

Long live the Armenian people!

April 23, Van National Defence Body

Strength, faith, and spirit. This was what Armenians had gained in the first four to five days of battle. This was the atmosphere in Aykesdan in the first phase of the fighting. But what was happening in the old city? To answer this question, we should digress from our current narrative, and look at developments there.

Chapter XVII

The Heroic Battle of the City

What role did the old centre of Van play in the communal life of Armenians?

As we saw earlier, the old city was the original location of Van, shielded to the north by Shamiram's citadel on a chain of vertical cliffs, where people had built new fortifications, while on the other three sides it was surrounded by fortified walls. Most of these were destroyed over time, but the city had earlier been the centre of political life in Vasbouragan. Consequently, it was also the location of ancient Armenian churches, as well as a few famous mosques built by invading rulers. There was a continuity of life in the city from ancient times.

The modern era created new conditions. There were cultural shifts, the fortified walls lost their purpose, the wealthy and powerful classes left the confines of those walls for new suburbs, and the former buildings gradually fell into disrepair and were destroyed.

As Vasbouragan's capital gradually declined and lost its former glory, Aykesdan was born, expanded and prospered.

However, the main market remained in the old city. The state institutions also remained, including the Armenian prelacy, though they became less relevant as most people, especially the wealthy and able Armenians and Muslims, left the city, leaving behind a very small and impoverished population. In our times [1914], of 41,000 people in Van, only 3,000–4,000 Armenians and 1,000 Muslims remained in the old city.

Under these circumstances it was only natural that the city would gradually cease to play a vital role in the lives of Armenians in Van. In this context, by the lives of Armenians, we mean their national-revolutionary lives. This was because the autocratic state created an intricate link between "national" and "revolutionary" in the minds of Armenians. During this period, all issues, even innocent ones relating to Armenian national life, were subject to official harassment. Since Armenians were incapable of living without a national ethos, they turned to secret activities and revolutionary paths. The only place they could undertake such underground, revolutionary activities was in Aykesdan with its gardens and orchards, a thousand and one hiding places and defensive positions among the trees, even under the nose of the government. It was not possible to have such a clandestine network in the cramped conditions of the city.

Indeed, the city centre became even more neglected after the 1908 constitutional revolution. Prior to 1908, the local prelacy, as well as the national council attached to it, were recognised by the old regime as the representatives of the Armenian community and were consulted by government officials regarding Armenian issues. Members of the national council also lived in the city, which was the real hub of communal activities. However, with the arrival of the new regime in 1908, the prelacy and its national council assumed a secondary position.

The Armenian Revolutionary Federation (ARF or Tashnagtsoutiun), the strongest political party within the Armenian *millet*, was now legalised and treated by the new government and its Young Turk officials as representing Armenians. Thus all issues were discussed and negotiated with the representatives of the ARF, who were based in Aykesdan rather than the city centre. Previously, during the Hamidian years, Aykesdan had been a hiding place for ARF leaders. After 1908, even the prelate and the national council would hold talks with government officials in Aykesdan rather than the city centre, since almost all ARF leaders resided in Aykesdan.

The city centre thus ceased to play a central role in Armenian communal affairs and the government did not bother it. Even during the 1894–95 massacres, Armenians living in the city centre were left unharmed, while their brethren living in Aykesdan and other suburbs were ill-treated. It is true that the Armenian market was sacked and burnt down at that time, but no physical harm came to Armenians who lived inside the city walls. The city played no role in the upheavals of Armenian communal life until the fighting started in 1915.

When fighting broke-out in the outlying districts of the province, it was Aykesdan which addressed the issue with the authorities. When it was necessary to approach the government, it was Aykesdan that did so. When it was necessary to have the presence of the prelate or hold a meeting of the national administrative council, the prelate would be invited to Aykesdan. When the government wanted to consult Armenians, they approached Aykesdan where the ARF leaders were based. Similarly, when major developments took place and Aykesdan was in upheaval, the city seemed quiet. However, as soon as the fighting started in 1915, both Aykesdan and the city exploded like volcanic eruptions.

So, was the city really inactive till then?

The answer is no. The city was active, but in a quiet manner.

The ARF had an executive body in the city composed of local cadres. It was a seven-member sub-committee under the authority of the central committee in Aykesdan. Their relations were good and they maintained good communications. The city received its orders from the central body.

Secondly, the sub-committee was composed of powerful, able and dedicated people. They included an Armenian teacher, a tradesman, a merchant and even a property owner. The political persecutions led to the emergence of such a group. Their common interest, given the persecution of all Armenians, was the defence of their nation. This body represented the ideal for the defence of Armenians, and it was to direct the fighting in the city with the unquestioning support of all classes until the very end. The Armenians of the city carried out heroic deeds that even surpassed those of Aykesdan.

So, who were these people?

1. Levon Kaljian, a young graduate of Yeremian School and a merchant by profession.
2. Mihran Toromanian, a graduate of Yeremian School and the owner of a soap factory.

City Military Command

1.	2.	3.	4.	5.	6.	7.
Levon Kaljian	Mihran Totomanian	Tavit Sarkisian	Haygag Gosoian	Mihran Mirzakhanian	Haroutiun Nergararian	Sarkis Shahenian

3. Tavit or Tavo Sarkisian, a serious and courageous man and the owner of a small business

4. Haygag Gosoian, a graduate of the Kevorkian Seminary (in Echmiadzin) and the headmaster of the Hisousian-Shoushanian [Jesuit] School. He was the spirit directing the Armenian defence.

5. Mihrtad Mirzakhanian, a graduate of the Yeremian School and a landowner.

6. Haroutiun or Haro Nergararian, a coppersmith, who was a talented individual and a seasoned fighter.

7. Sarkis Shahinian, a Yeremian School graduate and a merchant by profession.

This committee, which was called the Military Committee when the fighting started, had two important aides. They were:

1. Taniel Vartabed, the abbot of Aghtamar Monastery, who happened to be in the city and could not return to the monastery when the troubles started

2. Mirzakhan Mirzakhanian, a lawyer and a member of the Social Democratic Hnchagian Party

The headquarters of the Military Committee was set up in the prelacy building, where the prelate Yeznig Vartabed resided.

The European War was a catastrophe that blew up in the heart of Europe in July 1914 and quickly spread. It soon drew in new countries and devoured them. Ottoman Turkey and its weak government could not avoid this catastrophe and soon the danger loomed over Armenians who could not avoid small disasters even in peaceful times. All of this was obvious to Ottoman Armenians, as well as the people of the city.

Starting in October, when the nightmare reached the Russo-Turkish and Turko-Persian border, the local Military Committee placed the old city into a self-defence mode. It made every effort to procure arms and ammunition; it advised people to arm themselves through their own means; it began reviewing the different quarters of the city, its streets, homes and bulwarks, and it prepared the young people for what was to come.

The Military Committee made plans for the defence of the city.

The Armenian parts of the city started at Tabriz Gate and stretched to the government granary, with its back to the sheer cliffs of the fortress stretching for over a mile to the east. The two ends of this area stretched southwards, forming a semicircle towards the market.

The Armenian areas bordered Turkish quarters to the south-east, west and south-west, while the market and government buildings, as we have already mentioned, were to the south. Therefore, in case of unrest, the Armenian quarters were bound to be completely surrounded.

Taking these factors into consideration, the Armenian defensive lines started from the eastern edge of the fortress, stretched southwards, and formed a semi-circle reaching the government granary or the fortress' cliffs at the halfway point. The citadel and its military might were perched above the Armenian quarters of the city.

The defensive perimeter was over a mile long and was divided into four sectors, each one divided into a set of defensive positions. These sectors from the east were:

1. Tabriz Gate Sector: This sector contained the old city walls that were still standing, including Tabriz Gate itself.

2. Tekalifi Harbiye Sector: The Tekalifi Harbiye (Military Requisitions) headquarters and depot were located here.

3. Khanidag Sector: This sector used to have several khans and commercial buildings, though only their collective name remained.

4. Ampardag [Amparidag] Sector: The government granary was situated in this sector. It was a huge building that towered over the quarter.

The following positions were important during the fighting.

1. Tabriz Gate Sector.

The first position to see action was the Mardiros Maroutian residence. This position suffered major damage from artillery bombardment over six days of fighting. The defenders eventually torched their position and retreated. The other positions in that sector were:

No.	Position	Captain [Khmpabed]
1.	Apro residence	Avedis Vartabedian and Baghdo of Haygavank
2.	Shishgoian residence	Moukhsu Vahan
3.	Der Boghosian residence	Sahag Jangoian
4.	Gaghoian residence	Mihran Hovagimian and Shadaghtsi Avo

5.   Laz Ali residence   Sgherttsi Nshan
6.   Shahen Agha residence   Shahen Agha and
                                  Dikran Kndaghjian

These positions opposed:

1.   The artillery battery in the old fortress
2.   The artillery battery at Haygavank cemetery
3.   The mosque located at Tabriz Gate
4.   Aram Gaghoian residence rented by a Muslim family
5.   Katirji Mosque
6.   Mahmoud Effendi residence

2. The Tekalifi Harbiye Sector.

No.	Position	Captain [Khmpabed]
1	Goghad residence	Goghadi Mardiros and Garabed
2	Keoloz residence	Tateos Nalbandian
3	Vartabedian residence	Asadour Minasian
4	Tekalifi Harbiye building	Mogatsi Hovhannes
5	Sp. Dziranavor and Tsetsian residences	Armenag Mirzakhanian (wounded) and Levon Gosoian
6	Hiusisian residence	Haroutiun Ashekian

These positions opposed:

1.   The artillery battery located in the old citadel
2.   The artillery battery located in the Muslim cemetery
3.   The municipal building
4.   The mosque located at the south-east
5.   The military depot
6.   The Kaya Chalabi Mosque

3. The Khanidag Sector.

The first position to enter action here was the Mirzakhanian Khan. It was destroyed after five days of battle. The remaining positions were:

No.	Position	Captain [Khmpabed]
1.	The Alexanian residence	Garjgantsi Manoug Agha
2.	Boya Khan	Hovhannes Pirkalemian
3.	Yazmalou Khan	Drtad Der Manouelian
4.	The Khanidag position	Manoug Paylian (who was killed), Kapriel Yeghiazarian, Manoug Toromanian, and Zinvor Zohrab
5.	The Kharpertsis residence	Mardiros Saroian and Shalji Haroutiun

These positions opposed:
1. The second artillery battery located in the old fortress
2. The artillery battery at Solgrnots
3. The artillery battery at Kiamil Kharabas
4. The Akif residence
5. The Kurshun Mosque
6. The Aziziya Garrison

4. The Ampardag Sector.

The first to go into action were in this sector were:
1. The Der Hagopian residence
2. The Atashgarian residence
3. The Karageoz residence

The Der Hagopian position fell during the first day of battle. The Atashgarian and Karageozian positions fell on the fourth day. The remaining positions were:

No.	Position	Captain [Khmpabed]
1.	Yunus residence	Shadakhtsi Ohannes and Haroutiun Kishmishian
2.	The Gakavian residence	Armenag Bazigian and Set Aslanian
3.	Ampardag, 1st position below the granary	Garjgantsi Manoug and Armenag Melkonian
4.	Ampardag, 2nd position below the granary	Vartan Der Vartanian

These positions opposed:
1. The artillery battery at the Khorkhor position in the old fortress
2. The artillery battery at Kiamil Kharabas
3. The Ulu Jami Mosque
4. Residences adjoining Ulu Jami

Local leaders and aides were appointed to each sector. These men were members of the Military Committee. They were:

1. The Tabriz Gate Sector: Tavit Sarkisian and Levon Kaljian. Tavit was wounded and was replaced by Sarkis Shahinian and Mihran Hovagimian.

2. The Tekalifi Harbiye Sector: Haroutiun Nergararian and Sarkis Shahinian. After Tavit was wounded, Sarkis Shahinian replaced him at the Tabriz Gate sector and Levon Kalajian replaced Shahinian at the Tekalifi Harbiye Sector.

3. The Khanidag Sector: Mihran Toromian and Manoug Sarkisian.

4. The Ampardag Sector: Mihrtad Mirzakhanian, Mihran Nergararian, and Armenag Bazigian.

The Armenians had the following weapons when the fighting began:

100 Mosin, Mauser, Madrid, and Pertag rifles with 30,000 cartridges

90 Mauser pistols with 15,000 cartridges.

120 assorted pistols with 15,000 cartridges.

In total, about 310 weapons with no more than 60,000 cartridges.

Aside from those involved in the fighting, the other committees were not as complex as in Aykesdan. The main bodies in the city were:

1. The Military Committee, which has been discussed.

2. The Logistics Committee, which looked after the needs of the fighters and poor families through fund-raising and the government granary. This body was composed of:

1. Prelate Yeznig Vartabed
2. Hovhannes Ayazian
3. Tarzi Manoug
4. Samuel Kasbarian
5. Janig Samarjian
6. Mardiros Mayilian

3. The Red Cross Committee was responsible for the treatment of the wounded and transformed the Isajanian residence into a hospital.

1. Roupen Nshanian
2. Souren Ararktsian
3. Melkon Hakamian
4. Senekerim Shaljian
5. Manoug Hovagimian

Such planning, material supplies and organisation underpinned the Armenian position as the city went to battle with the lofty goal of self-defence. But before discussing the actual fighting, let's discuss what happened in the city beforehand.

On the morning of April 17, a Saturday, news spread in the city about the murder of Ishkhan and his three companions and everyone became fearful. Some merchants who had opened their shops in the bazaar quickly closed them and returned home. Two hours later, news spread about Vramian's arrest. People felt overwhelmed and communications between the city and Aykesdan ceased.

The prelate, Yeznig Vartabed, who had just returned from Aykesdan with Taniel Vartabed, rushed to see Jevdet upon hearing of Vramian's arrest.

When Yeznig inquired about Ishkhan's murder and Vramian's arrest, Jevdet, the low Asiatic satrap who had been flattering the Armenian representatives two days earlier, now talked in a different tone about his orders to have Ishkhan killed and Vramian arrested, adding that the Ottoman state would not be the plaything of a few young men.

Jevdet's words were firm and final, and Yeznig Vartabed left the meeting in a depressed mood. The Military Committee and a few leading figures who were waiting for him at the prelacy became deeply worried when they heard what Jevdet had said and saw Yeznig's mood.

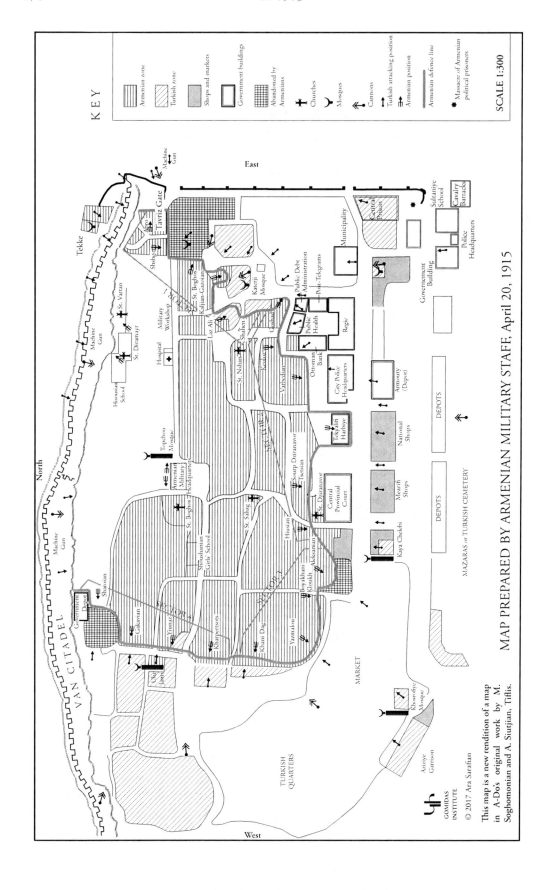

KEY

Armenian zone
Turkish zone
Shops and markets
Government buildings
Abandoned by Armenians
Churches
Mosques
Cannons
Turkish attacking position
Armenian position
Armenian defence line
Massacre of Armenian political prisoners

SCALE 1:300

MAP PREPARED BY ARMENIAN MILITARY STAFF, April 20, 1915

This map is a new rendition of a map in A-Do's original work by M. Soghomonian and A. Siurjian, Tiflis.

© 2017 Ara Sarafian

GOMIDAS INSTITUTE

MAZARAS or TURKISH CEMETERY

TURKISH QUARTERS

VAN CITADEL

North

East

West

MARKET

Tekke

Tavriz Gate

Machine Gun

St. Vartan

St. Diramayr

Hisousian School

Topchou Mosque

Shabogh

St. Boghos

Kalian-Gazoian

Katerji Mosque

Laz Ali

Shaben

St. Nshan

Koloz

Varbedian

Gloshag

Public Debt Administration

Post-Telegrams

Public Health

Regie

Ottoman Bank

City Police Headquarters

Municipality

Central Prison

Sultaniye School

Cavalry Barracks

Police Headquarters

Government Building

Armoury (Depot)

DEPOTS

DEPOTS

National Shops

Mearifi Shops

Central Provincial Court

St. Dzranavor

Tekyalih Harbiye

Ssurp Dzranavor Tserisin

Hussian

Aleksanian

Boyakhan Kloukh

Kaya Cheleki

Khosrofiye Mosque

Azizije Garrison

Sharoian

Gakavian

Yumza

Kharpertsots

Khani Dag

Yarmalou

Chji Jami

Machine Gun

St. Sahag

Shoushanian Girls School

St. Boghos Headquarters

Armenian Military Headquarters

Military Workshop

Hospital

Machine Gun

Government Depot

SEVORA

VICTORY

SEVORA

This map is a new rendition of a map in A-Do's original work by M. Soghomonian and A. Siurjian, Tiflis.

The situation remained tense all Saturday and Sunday. Nobody left their neighbourhoods and there was no trust in the government. Despite these conditions, Yeznig Vartabed approached Jevdet once more on the advice of the Military Committee in order to calm matters down and discuss Vramian's release.

Jevdet received Yeznig Vartabed in a bellicose manner and spoke in a threatening tone, responding to Yeznig's persistence with the words, "This country will either belong to Armenians or Turks, but the two people cannot live together."

Jevdet uttered these words when the orders for a massacre had reached the surrounding districts and the infernal work had already begun.

Yeznig Vartabed returned to the prelacy more depressed than ever and stated that nothing good could be expected. These were heavy and hopeless words, but the preparation of many months and years took over and the Military Committee went into action. The final arrangements were made and all fighting units went to their positions and prepared for the moment they had been anticipating for months.

The hours passed slowly. Sunday was coming to an end, daytime was becoming night, and then it was Monday morning. It was a working day but the market remained closed. Nobody came to the city from Aykesdan and the people in the city behaved like a besieged army that didn't know what was happening elsewhere. Although the siege had not started yet – one couldn't see any armed guards – the distrust was so strong and relations so bad that Armenians and Muslims no longer had neighbourly contacts. Armenians living at the edges of their neighbourhoods moved to more central areas. The situation was very dangerous and everyone was on the lookout and waiting for the order to fight.

It was under such circumstances that on the morning of Tuesday, April 20, the first shots were heard from an area near Aykesdan.

As the sound came from some distance away, it was not possible to pin-point the exact location of the shooting. It was even thought that the shooting was between the police and Muslim deserters in the Shamiram quarter. Such deserters could be found everywhere at that time.

This was when Jevdet tried to trick the Armenians in the city by sending two gendarmes to Yeznig Vartabed and letting him know that there had been a minor clash in Aykesdan and that Armenians in the city should remain calm. The situation was so tense, however, that the gendarmes who came to the edge of the Armenian quarters did not proceed and simply passed on their message for the prelate to two Armenians they encountered.

Meanwhile, the noise from Aykesdan began to sound like a serious firefight. Soon, one could also hear deafening artillery fire as well, so that section commanders hurried to the prelacy where the Military Committee was located. They soon returned to their positions as the gravity of the situation was now quite obvious.

As they ordered, "Men, take your positions. The fighting has started in Aykesdan," the armed units, which had remained out of sight in houses near the front lines, went forward and assumed their positions.

While the units started to block windows and passages, and created small loopholes to shoot at the enemy, the following incident took place at Ampar. The defenders had just taken up their posts at Karageoz position when they noticed about 30 armed Kurds and militiamen at Karageoz Kharabas [wastelands]. They were acting in an unusual manner and the Armenians followed their movements. The enemy, who had no idea that Armenians in the opposite house were watching them, exchanged a few words with each other and separated into two groups. One group went to Ulu Jami and the other towards the government granary. When the Armenians saw that their opponents wanted to occupy the government granary, they fired a few shots into the air. These were the first indecisive shots fired by Armenians and were not aimed to kill. The Kurds and militiamen immediately withdrew to their positions in the wasteland and returned fire. The Armenians, in turn, also returned fire and soon there was more shooting from Ulu Jami, and the whole city roared. These developments took place at 9:00 a.m., three hours after the fighting had started in Aykesdan.

The fighting erupted with great ferocity, as the two unequal sides clashed. On the one side were a handful of Armenians with 300 rifles and pistols at the most and on the other was the Ottoman government with its massive military organisation, artillery and fanatical Muslim masses. Many positions in the east, south and west were manned by soldiers, militias and Kurds belonging to the Avdo tribe, while to the north stood the fortress, which was supposed to defend the city from external enemies. On this occasion, however, its guns were firing on the city. The western half of the fortress rose to a great elevation, where there were ramparts, military supplies, barracks and a mosque with a minaret. Some artillery pieces had been sited at the two edges of this area. On the eastern stretch, the fortifications consisted of sheer cliffs, along which was a wall with firing positions. This part of the fortress was immediately above the Armenian quarters. The soldiers and *chetes* hiding behind these walls completed the encirclement of the handful of Armenians in their defensive positions.

The first day's fighting, which was very intense, continued all day in all four sectors, but was mostly around Tabriz Gate, Tekyalifi Harbiye and Ampardag.

The Der Hagopian residence, which was located at the Ampardag sector south of Ulu Jami on the border of the Muslim quarter, was to play an important role in the Armenian defence. The first Armenian priority was to secure that residence, and the regional commander and ten men were ready when the firing started at Karageoz Kharabas and Ulu Jami. Despite the dangers, the Armenian forces occupied the residence unopposed, followed by serious clashes when Kurds and militia forces destroyed the garden wall at the rear of the residence and advanced. The Armenian defenders then opened fire and killed two of their opponents, while the rest ran away. However, the difficulties at that position were not eased as it remained under fire from three sides, as well as the cannon on the western edge of the fortress. The bombardment was intense and the upper floor of the building was in danger of collapse. Two hours later it was not possible to remain on the upper floor because of the damage. The resistance continued for another two hours, when the defenders torched their position and retreated. The other positions stood firm and continued their stiff resistance.

There was also heavy fighting around Tabriz Gate. The two-storey Mardiros Maroutian residence was a prime defensive position as it was at the edge of the Armenian quarter near the city walls, dominating a Turkish position to the south as well as a square located outside the city walls. For these reasons, the enemy attacked the Maroutian residence continuously for six days. It was also the enemy's second target to break into the Armenian quarters.

One of the defenders at the Maroutian position gave the following description of the fighting there:

> We, three soldiers at the Tabriz Gate sector, went forward. When we entered the Shishgoian house and proceeded to the Maroutian position from the fortress and the fields on the eastern side, we encountered heavy fire from Turkish positions. We then went to the upper floor of the Maroutian house and started to fire on the Turks. Just then, 50–60 mounted Circassians and policemen appeared from the south-east and threw themselves into trenches 400 metres away from us and started firing. They also brought up a more modern cannon and placed it at the old cemetery at Haygavank. We started to fire in that direction too and immediately killed two artillerymen. Just then the cannons in the fortress started to roar. The first two shots caught us by surprise and destroyed the defensive walls behind us, covering us in dust and soil. The fighting continued while we thought about capturing the cannon that was placed near us. After changing the cannon's position twice, the enemy cannon was nowhere to be seen by midday. They then started using it at the front once more. Their second shot cut off Avedis Vartabedian's foot and he died a few days later.
>
> The Maroutian position had three rifles and two Mauser pistols. When Avedis was wounded, we needed reinforcements, especially because the Turks twice tried to burn down the main entrance of the building. The local commander Tavit Sarkisian finally arrived with another soldier. However, he was shot in the face before he reached the upper floor of our position. This was a terrible blow to us, but we were not discouraged and were able to defend ourselves despite the hail of bullets.

One can appreciate the scale of fighting at the Maroutian position from the fact that the five or six defenders there drew the fire of two enemy cannons and many rifles.

However, the fighting at the Tekyalifi Harbiye position was even fiercer. As already mentioned, its regional commander, Haroutiun Nergararian or Haro, was a tough man and a coppersmith by trade. He had some 50 to 60 men armed with rifles and pistols under his command and was charged with an audacious task.

There were four large two-storey buildings in this region, and a number of state institutions were located there. These were, from west to east:

1. The Jidechian Khan, whose second floor served as the provincial courthouse, while the lower floor consisted of shops.

2. The Tsetsian residence, whose second floor served as the offices of the Tekyalifi Harbiye. Here, too, the lower floor consisted of shops.

3. Hilmi Effendi's residence, the second floor of which was occupied by the police force, while the ground floor had shops at the front and the Tekyalifi Harbiye depot at the rear.

4. The large Terzibashian-Piroomian Khan, the upper floor of which included (a) the Ottoman Bank's offices; (b) the Quarantine headquarters; (c) the offices of the Public Debt Administration; (d) the Tobacco Regie; (e) the Post and Telegraph office. The lower floor of this building consisted of many shops as well as the Tobacco Regie depot and the Public Debt administration's salt depot.

Haro had to occupy all four buildings with his limited number of fighters. The task was a colossal challenge given the means at his disposal. The plan became impossible as the last two buildings were always occupied by policemen, gendarmes and guards. It was therefore decided to take over at least the Tekyalifi Harbiye and Jidechian Khan. However, when the fighting started, even these plans were no longer realistic because three of these buildings were occupied by the army. For these reasons the fighting in this sector was particularly fierce.

The first priority was to take over the Tekyalifi Harbiye building, which was connected to neighbouring houses to its south. The main door of the building was on its eastern side, opposite the police station. The regional commander and a group of fighters stood nearby at the Mirzakhanian residence, when news came that Kurds and militiamen were taking up positions at Tekyalifi Harbiye. This was when the Armenians rushed to that building. However, seeing that it was impossible to approach the main entrance near the police station, the Armenian

Mrs. Aghavni Vartabedian

commander changed direction and entered the building from the back with the help of an Armenian woman. She was Mrs Aghavni, Solgar Mgrdich Vartabedian's wife. She was a modest, middle-aged, pretty woman with lively eyes. She had six children, four boys and two girls. Her eldest son, Khachadour, was 18 years old and a good fighter in that sector. Master Mgrdich and his large family rented the back of the Tekyalifi Harbiye or Tsetsian building. Mrs Aghavni knew that building well, including the little doorway that linked the two parts of the building. She therefore led the Armenian fighters to the entrance, which was mostly covered by a pile of wooden planks. These were immediately cleared, the small door was smashed down, and the fighters rushed into the small courtyard of the main building. They climbed onto the balcony of the second floor, entered the building through the windows, and quickly occupied the premises. The few officials who were there barely escaped with their lives. Then the enemy started shooting through the windows of the Tekyalifi Harbiye from the police station and elsewhere, but it was all too late. The position was now held by Armenians who started shooting back.

While taking over the Tekyalifi Harbiye building, the regional commander also arranged for Armenag Mirzakhanian and his group to take over the Jidechian Khan, where the courthouse was located. They assumed that the khan would be easily occupied, especially as its guard was an Armenian called Chouro. However, Jidechian, the wealthy Armenian merchant, had earlier ordered Churo to deliver the keys of the building to the police chief as soon as any fighting started. The simple-minded Chouro did as he was told. As soon as the first shots were fired, he ran to the police station and handed over the keys. That was the last that was heard of him. Afterwards, as captain Armenag and his group approached Jidechian Khan, they came under fire from the upper floor of the building and barely managed to escape without any losses.

Thus only part of the great plan was realised. The Jidechian, and Terzibashian-Piroomian Khans, as well as the police station, all remained in Turkish hands.

The Turks could not accept the fact that the Tekyalifi Harbiye building was under Armenian control. That Armenian position dominated over them and they were greatly troubled. They therefore decided to destroy it. While they rained bullets on the few dozen Armenian defenders at that point, they also planned to burn the whole building down. So, at exactly midday, when the fighting continued with no respite and the two dozen Armenians were firing from loop holes on the two floors of the building – barely holding the enemy at bay – one of the doors at street level was set alight. Now there were two enemies, both of them wild and threatening. The situation got more complicated as the fire started to spread quickly. It was impossible to see outside and the fire was soon inside the building. The whole building was in danger and there was a desperate need for water to put out the fire.

The defenders shouted "Water!" as they battled the smoke around them and fired at the enemy outside. The people who had gathered in the building, where Solkar Mgrdich lived, did not dare leave the safety of the building's walls as bullets whizzed past them. Time was of the essence, the need for water was desperate, and someone brave had to step forward and lead by example. Such a person soon ran to the water-well, pulled two containers and filled them with water. She then rushed towards the fire without paying attention to the bullets buzzing around her. A chain of people were soon taking water to put out the fire and returning for more until it was extinguished.

When the fire was out, one could hear people everywhere exclaiming, "Long live Mrs. Aghavni. If it was not for her, this place would have turned to ashes."

The fire was out, the position was saved, and Mrs. Aghavni was now a heroine. There were many such brave women who stepped forward during those days in Van.

The Tekyalifi Harbiye was saved and continued its heroic defence. All attempts to approach it, burn it down, or take it over resulted in enemy losses. The enemy lost 18 men at that position and the Armenian forces had two wounded, one of whom was the regional commander, Armenag Mirzakhanian, who had returned to the Tekyalifi Harbiye building after failing to take over the Jidechian Khan. The other was Sghertsi Israyel.

Nevertheless, the situation remained serious. The Jidechian Khan, the police station, the Terzibashian-Piroumian Khan and finally, the military depot, which were all powerful enemy positions, turned on the Tekyalifi Harbiye on three sides and continued their attacks. The potential loss of this position was a greater threat to the rest of the Armenian quarters than the loss of all of the other positions combined. It was imperative that those surrounding buildings be burnt down, otherwise it would have been impossible to continue the resistance. This became the main task that night.

When night fell, the heavy gunfire and bombardment diminished, as there was no point wasting gunpowder in the darkness. This was the time for Armenians to act.

At 9 o'clock, the regional commander went on a reconnaissance with a few men and reached the north-western corner of the Jidechian Khan. They had to go right up to the building, pour kerosene on the doors and windows, and set them alight. This was a critical mission and was not without considerable risk. It was at such moments that unexpected individuals rose to great challenges, often from lower classes or people of ill repute. Aram Gabarougian, an 18 year-old, was such a person, who came from a family with a bad reputation. His father worked in a Turkish coffee house and entertained customers, while his elder brother was a complete rascal who suffered the consequences of his actions. Aram, because of his family, had also set off on a bad road.

Yet this young man rose to the challenge at that critical time in the life of his people, despite his family background and social standing. While the Armenian defenders gave him covering fire from the upper windows of their building, Aram proceeded under intensive fire towards his target with kerosene and matches. He carried out his mission and returned.

A few minutes later, the flames erupted and quickly spread to the entire building, while the soldiers and Kurds inside fled in confusion. An hour later, the entire building was aflame. The wind soon blew the fire onto a row of shops belonging to a Turkish school and destroyed them.

While the Jidechian Khan lit up its surroundings and drew everyone's attention, the regional commander set off on a new mission with his fire-bombers at the north-eastern corner of the Terzibashian-Piroomian Khan. Here, Aram Gabarougian went forward to the large building with his kerosene and matches. He stopped at one of the eastern doors of the Quarantine Administration and tried to set fire to it several times. This time he was unsuccessful and was followed by two burly brothers, Garabed and Mardiros Mouradian, who went to the Post and Telegraph office door in the same row of shops. One carrying kerosene and the other an axe, they soon broke the door down and entered the building. They then covered the wooden stairs to the upper floor with kerosene and set it ablaze. The whole interior burst into flames, as the wind fanned the fire. The building, with its shops, storage-rooms, offices and government institutions lit up the whole city. The soldiers and Kurds who had been inside, fled.

It was then about midnight and the same group of fire-bombers approached the police headquarters. Having gained experience in engaging enemy soldiers and burning down their positions, this latest target was destroyed quite easily.

Van Old City Walls, 1916

The building housing the police station had doors on both its southern and northern sides and it was decided to set the northern ones ablaze. Once more Aram Gabarougian approached these targets under a hail of bullets and set both entrances ablaze at the same time. A short while later the police station turned into a burning torch and the Armenians pulled back.

The night passed quickly and the results of the fighting became evident the following morning. It was not possible to hide anything. The torching of the armoury was postponed. Much had been achieved, much more than during the day. Three buildings – three powerful enemy positions – were no more. The Tekyalifi Harbiye position was free of danger, and the great plans for the first night of fighting were successful.

The second day of fighting began early in the morning. Apparently the torching of government institutions had infuriated Jevdet and he ordered the Turks to begin their furious attacks on Armenians from all sides. These attacks were repelled with great losses to the enemy.

The Turks had been confident of their strength and derisive of Armenian military prowess. They often attacked without much thought or planning. On the other hand, the Armenians, who had little experience and feared their opponents a day earlier, were now firing directly at the enemy and forcing them to flee, leaving their dead in the streets.

These scenes were more noticeable in the Tekyalifi Harbiye area, where the enemy lost some 30 men that day, including the leader of the militias, Captain Ismayil Altay Oghli and Commissioner Molla Karsli. The Armenian defenders' achievements at Tekyalifi

Harbiye that day were so effective that their opponents, who had entrenched themselves in a row of shops, could not resist and fled after torching their own positions.

The second day of fighting was also fierce in other sectors. At the Ampardag sector, the enemy tried to overrun the Armenian lines from Paghgants Street. A small house used to defend this street was called "Satan's position." It was the post of two fighters, Shadakhtsi Ohannes and his comrade who forced the enemy back and showed exemplary courage.

The fighting was also relentless at the Tabriz Gate sector. Throughout the first day, the Maroutian position came under heavy enemy fire, including artillery bombardment. Despite the gradual destruction of the upper floor of the building, it remained in Armenian hands as the defenders bravely resisted the enemy.

The second day of frenzied clashes resulted in two incendiary attacks, both to the advantage of Armenians.

There was an old government post office opposite Shahen Agha's in the Tabriz Gate sector which had been turned into a Turkish fighting position. When it was dark, the men at Shahen Agha tried to attack and occupy it. They approached the post office and tried to break down its door, while the Turkish defenders resisted. However, when the latter realised its weakness, they burnt the place down themselves and fled.

The second incendiary attack took place in the Tekyalifi Harbiye area and was the final part of the earlier incendiary attacks. The government armoury still remained there, with the government's best soldiers shooting at the Tekyalifi Harbiye building. When it was dark, the fire-bombers carefully approached the armoury through the ruins of the police station and opened fire. The soldiers stationed there were taken by surprise, especially by the concerted nature of the attack, and abandoned their positions. Just then, the hero of the first day, Aram Gabarougian, approached the target with his supply of kerosene and set the doors of the building alight and returned. The armoury caught fire and the second night was lit up by another government building in flames.

The third, fourth, fifth and sixth days of fighting continued with the same ferocity. The shooting and bombing started early in the morning and ended late at night. The Turks were using ammunition without much thought or regard to their stocks. They had no concept of conserving ammunition and kept shooting as much as possible. Furthermore, seven cannons were firing continuously on Armenian positions. Three of these were on top of the citadel, and four of the latest models were located in different places outside the walls of the city. These latter pieces were moved about to bombard different targets. Sometimes several were used to attack a single target, such as the Maroutian residence near Tabriz Gate or the Tekyalifi Harbiye position. Seven cannons and many rifles were thus in continuous operation over many days.

The Armenian position was different. They were under siege with no ties to the outside world. They had no hope of receiving military supplies from elsewhere. For that reason, the conservation of ammunition was a major concern from the first day of fighting.

"Each evening we will ask you for an account of the number of bullets you fired and the number of enemy you killed."

These words were constantly repeated by the regional commanders to their soldiers.

"No bullet should be fired without good reason."

Given these circumstances, one can understand why the hundreds of shots from the enemy were met by just a few dozen from the Armenian side. Despite everything, the Armenians put up an honourable defence and in a few places created difficulties for their enemy.

The third day of fighting assumed a brutal character around the Katirji Mosque near Tabriz Gate. An enemy cannon was placed near this location and created great difficulties for the Armenians in the Shahen Agha and Laz Ali positions. The Armenians charged the Mosque, reached its door and set fire to it. Soon the mosque was in flames and the defenders abandoned their position and escaped with their cannon. The Armenians lost one man during the attack. He was Tavrezi Garabed, a brave 28 year-old illiterate young man. He was shot in the street during the attack. According to witnesses, he died singing Armenian revolutionary songs and exhorting his comrades to carry on.

The fighting intensified at the Ampardag sector on the fourth day. The Atashgarian-Karageoz positions were subjected to terrible attacks. The enemy attacked in large numbers and then retreated. The fighting continued for a long time, and the defenders lost one important man at the Gakavian position – the brave Vartan Der Vartanian – who was on his way to help the defenders at the Karageoz position. He had rushed out of his own position and tried to hurry through Ampar Street, where he was shot dead. Vartan's death led to a certain loss of morale. The men there resisted until 4 p.m. and then set the two positions alight and retreated.

As if that was not enough, the enemy tried to continue its offensive and take over the granary, which was a strategic location dominating that quarter. The granary was an important target for the Turks and they didn't spare any effort to capture it. However, the Armenian Military Committee was able to send reinforcements and the Turks retreated.

The torching of the Atashgarian-Karageoz positions was a blow to the Military Committee and there was a reassignment of Armenian forces that day. Two fighting units were sent to that sector and the Armenian lines were strengthened.

The fighting escalated at Tabriz Gate on the fifth day. The Maroutian position had already been under five days of bombardment and its upper floor was completely destroyed. The defenders were now positioned on the ground floor and continued fighting under difficult conditions. Their prospects were poor.

Furthermore, the Turks had breached the city walls and broken through. There were no Armenian positions to oppose them, which was the reason the enemy had concentrated its attack on that area. When the Military Committee got news of those developments, it sent around 20 fighters who occupied Abro's house near the walls. There was strong resistance but the enemy soldiers fled, leaving behind two dead.

By this time the situation at the Maroutian residence was hopeless, barely holding back the enemy mob. Soon the Armenians were quite aware that they could not defend the position and set fire to it. They retreated and created two new positions which remained in Armenian hands until the end of the fighting. These were the Abro and Shishgoian positions.

The sixth day of fighting was marked by a huge fire-attack in the Khanidag sector. The Mirzakhanian Khan was in a prominent position in the market, with two rows of wooden shops, and a long covered passage between them. This khan was one of the Armenian defensive positions which fought the enemy continuously for six days. However, the enemy forces managed to set this position alight and the Armenian defenders could not put it out. The khan burnt down and the defenders retreated to set up two new positions at Yazmalou Khan in Boyakhane.

There were no large fires after the torching of the Mirzakhanian Khan, nor any major changes in the battle-lines. There were no significant advances nor losses of positions. The defensive lines remained fixed, the fighting assumed a stable and continuous character, and the Military Committee issued a statement accordingly:

> Comrades in Arms!
>
> This is the sixth day we are facing the enemy and fighting bravely. Despite their thousands of rifles and cannons, they have not been able to break through our lines. We have decided to defend our life, honour and rights with dignity and should be prepared for many new surprises. Jevdet's mobs have been humiliated by heavy losses and shocking blows. The proof is in front of your eyes.
>
> Soldiers! In order to continue our resistance under these conditions, we ask all of you to remain calm, resolute, disciplined and sparing. These are the bywords that will make our resistance methodical, effective and honourable.
>
> Soldiers! As we have always said and repeat again, be frugal! Safeguard your lives and look after your ammunition and weapons. These are the essential elements which will prolong our resistance. And the longer we resist, the more hope we can have of succeeding. Be bold and brave but also cautious, and look after yourselves. Safeguard your ammunition, ammunition, ammunition! Let the enemy waste their own, as much as they wish, but we should respond sparingly. We'll need the ammunition in the coming days. Each bullet should claim the life of one of our enemy.
>
> A.R., Military Committee of the City

The first six days of battle were over. This was the first period when Armenians and Turks got a measure of each other. The Turks were finally convinced that the Armenian *reaya* – yesterday's slaves – were no longer the fearful cowards they could kick around. As for Armenians, they gained experience and faith in their own strength.

Six days of fighting demonstrated the importance of the defensive walls, gardens, and firing positions. Here, too, as in the case of Aykesdan, Armenians formed amrashen-amalia groups which rushed wherever necessary to repair walls damaged by bombs, build new ramparts, strengthen roofs with timber reinforcements, and block the entrances to streets. The Armenian defenders improved greatly in such work, especially as the defence work was shared by all, including women and children. They worked like ants so that walls damaged by the bombardment were immediately repaired and made even stronger than before.

Because of these collective efforts, the Armenians had considerably fewer casualties than the Turks and were on more solid ground than the government. In addition to their ability to fight, they had also gained a moral strength which was expressed in their vigour, faith, and spirit.

They showed such characteristics in Aykesdan, as well as in the city. This was the common disposition of the two isolated sections of the people of Van.

And what was the mood of the government of the Muslims, especially their treacherous representative, Jevdet?

It was all doom and gloom. Their sense of doom was as profound as the positive spirit of Armenians. Jevdet was feeling great indignation at his inability to deal with a handful of people, despite his military organisation, limitless military supplies, and even heavy weapons. His plans were ruined, as Van was turned into a slaughterhouse in a matter of days. And, seeing that it was not easy to suppress Armenians with arms, he resorted to new dastardly tactics, starting with Aykesdan.

First, he tried to disarm Armenians through trickery. He sent three letters to his personal friend, the Italian consul Spordone, mentioning the crackdown in outlying districts and stressing the peaceful conditions that prevailed in villages which obeyed the authorities – something that was not true. He repeated several times that Armenians should hand in their weapons and obey the government, otherwise there would be a general attack resulting in the destruction of the city. He wrote these letters to Spordone in the conviction that they would be read by Armenians.

Here are his letters, as well as their responses, challenging much of what Jevdet said.

Letter No. 1:

Dear Spordone Effendi,

The troublemakers who appealed to you in order to gain three or four days have succeeded. On Monday night, the youngsters who bore insignias on their arms and sang all night long killed the guard at Hamidiye garrison, cut telephone wires, and occupied the telegraph office on Khach Street. Needless to say, our vigilant troops also responded in kind. However, I did not allow our guards to respond for an hour, but when I discovered that the unrest was widespread and the policemen who had been to the prelacy in the city had come under attack, I ordered our units to shoot. Now there is fighting everywhere. Those who betray the state during such a major war will get their just punishment. The armed villagers in the city torched all government buildings and yesterday evening burnt down the market. I will take all necessary measures so that none of these murderers can get away with what they have done. The same will happen with those who dared to blow up the Hamidiye garrison with dynamite and celebrated with music the fire that resulted by the – thank God – harmless explosion. There is no doubt that those who threaten our existence will be crushed. I am very sorry that your building was hit by bullets. It is all because of the detestable work of Armenians who think of all sort of diabolical schemes to appear just to the world. As you know, other than the soldiers at the British Consulate, we do not have others troops in those neighbourhoods. As for the poor besieged guards, they respected your flag to the end.

The rebels who killed a few of those guards also burnt down the consulate. These traitors who endangered themselves are convinced that they can put pressure on the government by such action. They have raised their weapons and you can see that the violence continues with all its horrors. The only way to end this terrible disturbance is for them to hand in all weapons and pledge absolute obedience to the state.

Let these murderers, who are convinced that the Russians will arrive one of these days and try to support them, know that the Russians will not be able to take any step inside our borders. I am sorry for the people who will be hurt by this conflict. I do not have the time to write anything more detailed. I'd like to see you but advise against it as I fear the Armenians will hurt you and blame the army. I advise you to always fly your flag and show your colours in your windows during our forthcoming attack. The location of your premises has been shown to our units, but you must appreciate that the situation is complicated and it is important to hang your flag everywhere, because our attack will be extremely vigorous and decisive.

I ask you to give shelter to Monsieur Algardi, the director of the Tobacco Regie, and other officials who remain there. On the first night the trouble-makers burnt down the Public Debt offices, the bank and the Regie. They even attacked government offices with bombs but were forced to retreat. When the Public Debt building was set alight, they also tried to rob the bank vault but failed. Mr. Algardi should not be worried as the vault is empty. Those who attacked the government in Shadakh – our gendarmes, officials and the Muslim population – were exterminated by our units. Some rebels are still surrounded in the church and a few places. Today I expect news of their just punishment. Our army is coming from Bashkale and Saray and subduing the rebels who are trying to cut communications. I hope to crush them soon. With my respect and regards to the women.

Governor Jevdet

Governor of Van

His Excellency Jevdet Bey.

Your Excellency, Jevdet Bey,

I have the honour to inform you that I received the letter you sent me yesterday. I am very sorry that you think my acceptance of the position of an intermediary between the authorities and the [Armenian] committee might have been a ploy to gain time. You can be certain that the only reason for my actions was the desire to help both the government and civilian population, if possible, to avoid the recent incidents.

During my conversations with your excellency, I have often had the honour to point out that regrettable incidents might take place, as Mr. Spörri has also mentioned in his letter, if the militias were not to carry out your excellency's instructions to the letter and instead act in a tactless manner.

However, I still have the firm conviction that given your excellency's caring and humanitarian nature, which I have known for 12 years, you will be able to find a way to defuse the current situation and stop the bloodshed. I have faith in your abilities and great experience, and your ability to make such an offer that will be accepted to the other side.

As to your proposal that Armenians should hand in their weapons and accept unconditional surrender, I do not think such a proposal would yield results in the current situation.

The Armenians have resorted to arms in the conviction that the government wishes to use the conscription issue as a pretext to exterminate them. They do not expect or hope for any assistance from the Russians and are resolute in defending their families.

Like you, I also regret the destruction of the British Consulate, as well as the gendarmes who were killed there, but according to the information I have gathered, the guards at those premises were the first to open fire.

I can also inform your excellency that the Russian Consulate was hit by an artillery shell which exploded on the premises. Consequently, the local gendarmes and kavasses were forced to leave. I took the necessary steps to stop anyone from entering the consulate. Five bullets also hit our own consulate but fortunately they only caused material damage. I was pleased to hear that your excellency will give the necessary orders that no bullets or artillery shells should be fired towards our consulate.

According to your instructions, I ordered flags to be put around our consulate, to make it more visible. I have the honour to inform you that in order to give protection to my nationals and others under my care, as well as various employees and their families – as your excellency knows, out consulate is not large – I had to rent two houses next to my own. I have the honour to inform you that I will also be draping those buildings with our flags.

I will forward your message to Mr. Algardi. He will respond to you directly. Given the cramped conditions at my house, I cannot provide shelter for him, or the families staying with him. I therefore request, as he does of your excellency, that you allow him to put a flag on his house for his security as well as that of others sheltering there.

Mr. Limin is at my house. Mr. Hiuseyin Bey has already written to you that he is at my consulate with his family. I considered it necessary to give him shelter and protection after the bombardment and fire at his house.

I ask your excellency to protect the Roux family, as well as Mrs. Sanfort (the former French consul's wife).

The American mission has related the content of your letter to them.

According to reliable information, there are no armed men on their premises, as in the case of the German premises – only women, children and the infirm. They assure me that no shot has been fired from those areas, and I therefore request that the necessary steps are taken to protect them.

Since I was not able to find anyone to bring you this letter under the current circumstances, I had to ask Dr. Ussher to get one of his patients to do so. The latter is coming to the city by choice. I assure you that the release of the patient has nothing to do with creating space for the Armenian wounded at the

American hospital. To reassure my standing, I ask you to allow the courier of this letter to return, as well as the patients sent to you yesterday. This would please me a great deal. Your excellency can also be assured that their places at the hospital remain unoccupied and that they will continue to be treated like the other soldiers.

In order not to lead to misunderstanding and stop the future movement of patients, I ask of your excellency to suggest a simple way of communicating with him.

Italian Vice-Consul, Van

Spordone

Van 24 April 1915

Letter No. 2:

Italian Consul

Spordone Effendi,

Your response to my letter has astonished me. I did not say you tried to win time for the rebels. I said that the rebels exploited our relationship by playing the role of victims and declaring their obedience, thus gaining them three days. And that is actually what happened. Nevertheless, thank God they did not succeed with their plans. They are now keeping us busy. I have ordered all roads to be cleared, and most Armenian positions in the mountains and elsewhere have been defeated, thank God. I also hope to end the unrest here soon.

As long as we do not see the concentration of armed men, our artillery will not fire. Those are their orders. Mr. and Mrs. Sanfort are very well and comfortable at their home. The government knows its duty. I should be hurt at the idea that you think they may be under attack. Until the rebels show their complete obedience by handing in their arms, I am obliged to continue with their punishment.

The government can not sign agreements or accords with trouble-makers. You must surely appreciate this point. Other than the consulates, there should be no other flags flying anywhere. Please convey this message to your neighbours. With my kind regards.

Van, 26 April 334

Jevdet

Your Excellency,

It is my honour to acknowledge the letter you sent me two days ago. I considered it useful to share its contents with a few people.

I understand from your excellency's letter that the peaceful population enjoys the protection and consideration of the government. Unfortunately, the news reaching here is about the abuse of unarmed people in the villages. Such news has undermined the confidence of Armenians in the government and they are convinced that the authorities have plans for a general massacre. This is why they have chosen the path of self-defence.

Coming to the bombs hitting the American church, I personally verified what happened and saw that the American missionaries were in the right. I can assure your excellency that the latter are keeping strict neutrality.

Italian Vice-Consul, Van

29 April,1915

Spordone

Letter No. 3:

Spordone Effendi,

Thank you for the letter you sent me on the occasion of the enthronement of the Sultan.

Our forces advancing from Bitlis and Gargar are punishing the rebels blocking our communication lines while protecting the well being of villagers who show their loyalty. Our units advancing from Timar have reached Aliur village after destroying the rebels who had gathered in Diramer. The population of Aliur and a few villages around it who declared their loyalty were protected on the condition that they surrendered their weapons and presented their youth for conscription into the army. The population of Avants has shown complete loyalty and is enjoying the good will of the authorities. The forces coming from Saray and Arjag are punishing foolish rebels who have dug trenches across roads to stop the movement of government forces. Today, the rebels at Tarman and around Goghbants will also be punished. The trouble-makers in the city, many of whom have congregated from the villages, have been suppressed. The remaining few groups of rebels holding out in the church, the prelacy and one or two houses beneath the citadel will be neutralised later today. These traitors, despite many warnings, repeated that the Russians were coming and did not allow their families to leave. They publicly stated that their rebellion aimed at helping the enemy. Naturally, they will all receive their just punishment. Any talk about a bomb falling on the American church is undoubtedly a fabrication of the American missionaries to help the rebels. We see that the rebels are shooting from Sahag Bey's house in Arark in order to overrun the Muslim quarters.

Naturally, there will be a general attack on these disloyal murderers who will do anything to help the Russian campaign and wait for their arrival. We will strike them wherever they concentrate their forces, including at the American or German orphanages, in order to defeat and punish them. With the help of God, this problem will be solved. In Diyarbekir they have managed to collect many arms and bombs, as the people pledged their loyalty and identified the *komitaji*s. Consequently, the malevolent murderers were arrested and imprisoned, and the problem was resolved peacefully.

As for the people of Van, they are making absolutely every effort to aid the *komitaji*s and Russian designs. Consequently, they will all be punished. The sight of Armenian bodies mutilated by our cannons naturally disturbs us. But the government, seeing the threat these people pose to its existence, has to fight to the end, since the rebels do not offer their unconditional surrender.

We have just been informed from our Aykesdan headquarters that a house opposite the Nalbandians was torched as soon as it raised an Ottoman flag. I believe that the people living in that house wanted to show their loyalty and the rebels burnt their premises down as soon as they found out. If my understanding is correct, there is no hope for peace with these barbaric rebels. I wrote earlier that if Algardi Effendi could come, he should do so. I received no reply. The house he is staying in is dangerous because it is surrounded by rebels. Please be so kind as to let him know that he should not remain there if he is unable to come to our side.

30 April 331

Governor Jevdet

While writing these lines to the Italian consul, Jevdet resorted to another ploy, which was to subject Armenians to a famine.

"We need to put more pressure on their resources. We have to push masses of women and children from surrounding regions into Aykesdan, so that their supply of foodstuffs is depleted in a few days and they have to deal with a famine" thought Jevdet.

Thus a throng of women and children – hungry and naked, having survived massacres – started to arrive. They came in waves and increased pressure on resources.

One of the members of the relief committee, A. Hamparian, recorded:

In the first days of fighting, there were only a few destitute people. Barely four or five days later, a few hundred people needed help. The imperative was now the conservation of resources, giving enough for their needs so that they could just survive. It was decided to give each person one piece of bread per day. The number of needy grew exponentially, 200 to 400 to 800 and so on. After 15 days, one saw the arrival of famished groups of women, children and elderly fleeing from massacres. They generally travelled at night and entered Aykesdan in the early hours of the morning, having only saved their lives from the bloodthirsty Turkish and Kurdish mobs.

The problem of looking after the starving people arriving in Aykesdan became so acute that the Military Command's supply and relief committees had to deal with it. The problem was serious and it became necessary to limit the nourishment of not only the civilian population but also the defenders on the front lines. The situation was desperate.

And so, on April 25, the Military Command issued the following communiqué.

To all fighting units.

Comrades!

There are many refugees from surrounding regions in the city. If our comrades are not careful with the consumption of food, we will face the greatest enemy – famine.

Comrades, be prudent!

Henceforth, each group has to appoint a trustworthy and conscientious comrade who will have authority to take a modest amount of food from the central supply committee for his unit every day.

Armenian families who escaped to the city

We will supervise this process strictly and those who act in an inappropriate fashion will be punished. You are to forward the name of your candidate immediately to the central supply committee.

You must ban the entry of unauthorised people at your positions.

If you do not need the spades and axes in your possession, you should return them to us immediately.

25 April

Military Command

To the Armenian people,

To alleviate the lack of bread among the people, it has been decided to purchase prepared wheat, barley and some excess flour in advance at the following prices: Wheat (according to type) 60–70 ghouroush; annual measure 50; a measure of barley 40; a litre of flour 10–14 ghouroush.

It is requested that all those who can sell some of their stocks – or who know who has some – be so kind, for humanity's sake, to approach the Committee and have them registered. The Committee holds a meeting every day at 6–5 hour (2–10) in its office on the upper floor of the Protestants' pharmacy.

26 April, Aid Committee

While attempts were being made to control people's consumption of foodstuffs and regulate it, other developments had an impact on people's behaviour. As the continuous enemy attacks on April 23, 24, 25 and even 26 slackened, the Armenian defenders started to get used to the new pattern of fighting and began to relax as if the dangers had passed. Several unfortunate incidents, part of ordinary life, also took place. This always happened when defenders observed the enemy's slackness.

We can see the developments in a series of announcements of the Military Command.

To the people,

We strictly forbid entering and looting houses. Those caught doing so will be sentenced to death.

April 23, Military Command.

To all units,

Seeing many unfortunate incidents, we absolutely forbid you to consume alcohol. If you have obtained wine or *oghi* from houses in your areas, or know where it is available, immediately contact the Supply Committee.

April 23, Military Command.

Warning!

We advise all our comrades that when armed, they have no right to enter the American and German areas. Those who disobey this order will be subject to severe punishment.

April 24, Military Command.

Warning!

We have heard that certain individuals, without our knowledge, have dared to take weapons from the hands of this or that person.

We strictly warn that, without our stamped order, no individual or group has the right to disarm the holders of such weapons. Inform us who is armed or not in front-line positions and moving about, or people who are concealing their weapons.

25 April, Military Command.

Important notice!

For the knowledge of everyone, we announce that the Central Supply Committee, with the knowledge of the Military Command, has the right to requisition all necessary items or foodstuffs. So, you must not give anything to other unauthorised persons or bodies.

[no date] Military Command.

To all local commanders,

No soldier at any post has the right to leave his position without written permission from his group leader. Otherwise they will be disarmed and subjected to the strictest punishment.

28 April, Military Command.

The relative peace had three consequences. For example, ordinary arguments broke out among the people, often minor issues, sometimes even old arguments and demands. The military command had no time to deal with such things, so it felt it was necessary to create a judicial body whose task was to examine and adjudicate over such matters. To do so, it chose a three-person judicial body with the following members:

President: Hovhannes Gouloghlian

Members: Roupen Shadvorian, Hrant Kaligian

Important notice

We declare that a judicial body has been created under the jurisdiction of the National Self-Defence Committee which has the right to investigate and pass judgment on all questions of abuse and crimes which are not of a military nature. All questions must be addressed to this above-mentioned body which will hold its sessions every day from 9:30 until 2:00 (from 4:30 until 9:00) in Garabed Shirvanian's house.

April 29, Military Command.

At this time, two other bodies were formed, both linked to the judicial body. They were:

1. Police Administration.

2. Municipal and Health Administration

The force was composed of the following individuals:

Police chief: Garabed Aidjian

Members: Krikor Jonian, Khachadour Zenopian

There were also 40 policemen appointed

The Municipal and Health Administration was made up of the following:

Mayor: Bedros Mozian

Members: Mampre Mgrian, Hagop Yazoian, Avedik Der Kasbarian, Raphayel Der Atamian, Ghevont Khanjian.

After forming these bodies, the Military Command issued an order to the Police Administration which dealt with the important events of those days.

To the National Self-Defence Police Administration,

Gentlemen,

Under the current circumstances it is imperative for us to have harmonious relations between individuals. This harmony may be guaranteed by preventing and forbidding every kind of crime.

It is obvious that in the current crowded circumstances even the smallest dereliction from cleanliness must be regarded as an important crime, because such an act may endanger lives. Other misdemeanours, obviously, under the above-mentioned conditions, will be considered to be crimes worthy of severe punishment.

This is why the Military Command accepts the importance of the formation of a Police Administration to deal seriously and quickly with the following crimes and, where necessary, to surrender convicted individuals, along with a written report, to the military court.

1. Forbid people assembling in the streets in order to prevent tragedies due to artillery attacks.

2. Swiftly examine and punish people spreading rumours (be they good or bad news).

3. Examine and resolve all offences except criminal ones, which are to be handled by the military court.

4. Take measures to preserve good relations between different families living in the

same building and, if necessary, to order punishments. Protect empty houses.

5. Punish those who profiteer from the sale of foodstuffs, clothing etc. and inform the appropriate committee.

Having presented you with the outlines of your jurisdiction, we await your vigilant action.

1 May, National Self-Defence Military Command

The Armenians of Aykesdan thus continued their armed self-defence and maintained order. This in itself demonstrated how much faith they had in their own strength and how, even in a state of siege, they were ready to take positive steps to continue with their lives.

One should not think that the fighting had stopped while these arrangements were being made. No, shells continued to land and explode: death and destruction continued every hour of every day. There was only one difference: the attacks were less intense than the attacks of the first few days, and if they had not diminished, they simply did not terrorise people as they had done before – the Armenians had become accustomed to the dreadful noise.

As to how the second stage of the battle was progressing, we present the following announcements, as they were issued sequentially by the Military Command:

No. 9, April 26

1. A Turk was killed at the Toutounjian position last evening.

2. Three new positions were captured at Ararouts centre yesterday evening. We killed four of the enemy and burnt their advanced positions.

3. After a short skirmish on the Adnagan Bridge we captured eight boxes of military supplies.

4. We killed a Turk in the Shan quarter today.

Military Command.

No. 10, April 26

1. We killed a Turkish soldier in front of Haji Bekir barracks on Saturday night.

2. Two Turkish soldiers were killed yesterday at the Ararouts position.

3. We killed a Turk at the Vzvz position.

4. We killed a Turk at the Khach Poghots position and, on Saturday, a muleteer and a militiaman.

5. Yesterday we killed a Turkish soldier in front of Haji Bekir garrison from the Ayij Oghlou position.

Military Command.

No. 11, April 27

1. Yesterday we killed a militiaman from the Pos Street position.

2. We also killed a militiaman at our Shmavonian position.

3. So far we've found six bodies of *chetes* [irregular soldiers] under the ruins of Hamoud Agha garrison.

4. One of the Turks most powerful position, Topal Mollah's house, opposite the Toutounjian position, was burnt down after we tunnelled under it and blew it

up. The Turks tried to do the same to our position at Toutounjian but thankfully were too late. We captured two rifles and two *kasaptourd*s and a great quantity of other items.

5. We killed several Turkish soldiers from our Hotel position: three on Thursday, one on Friday, one on Saturday and one on Sunday. We also killed a soldier from our Nalbandian position on Tuesday, and another on Thursday. Only an 11-year old girl was killed on our side.

6. The Arark first sector information bureau informs us that there were no signs of movement by the enemy yesterday. The plan to torch Turkish positions was successfully completed. One brave man was decorated with a Cross of Honour. The fire spread as far as the nearby coffee house, which was an enemy position. Military Command.

No. 12, April 28
We killed a militiaman at the Shiroyian position yesterday.

A woman messenger carrying a white flag in accordance with rules, as well as a letter from the Italian consul to the governor, was shot dead by the Turks as she appeared from the Armenian trenches.

The enemy made attempts to use artillery today, firing about 20 shells at the Sahag Bey position. The shells, as usual, weren't able to cause any damage. Our comrades continue to mock the artillery strikes. We killed a Turk from this position.

Military Command.

The tenth day of fighting ended on April 29 with Armenian victories and good fighting spirit. The morale of the people was high and the fear of being overrun and massacred had mostly passed. This mood found expression in the following call from the military:

Ten days (April 20–29)
The struggle we have continued for ten days against the dishonourable enemy is the most wonderful and sacred fight for our national liberation. More than anything else it is the people's struggle. The enemy, insidious and treacherous, committing massacres and barbaric acts, bloodthirsty and wild, wants to put an end to our individual and national existence. But we decided to fight, to fight for our lives and property, faith and honour, our violated mothers and sisters, and for our national existence. Our fight is against the 600 year rule of bloodthirsty barbarians. Our fight is against the criminal Jevdets who stand against all human and political rights. They are all thirsty for Armenian blood and tears; they preached *jihad* [holy war] against the external enemy and began by massacring all Christians, be they women or children, young or old, able-bodied or disabled.

Armenians of Vasbouragan,

Ten days have passed during which we have struggled with all our individual and national efforts. It is a struggle that will be seen as a singular event, and not just in our own national history, but across the world. It will earn the admiration of the civilised world in these days of global conflict. Let the whole world see how a handful of braves, the greatest Armenian heroes, struggle with astonishing energy in the name of sublime justice.

May the God of vengeance fly above the heads of our warriors and may the spirit of legend speak through all of us.

We have completed ten days. May we remain victorious as we prepare for new victories and struggles.

Military Command.

The second phase of fighting lasted from April 29 until May 4. This is how the Military Command pictured it:

No. 13, May 9

Fires: Our soldiers continue their night-time work. Our Armenian fire-bombers tonight burnt Bojge Ahmed's house in Shan Tagh. This was an enemy position.

The first sector (Arark) information office made it known that tonight, at 1 o'clock (6 o'clock) the Armenians succeeded in setting fire to the Ararouts central police station, one of the enemy's most important positions. The fearless fire-bomber and his accompanying comrade armed with a ten-shot gun have returned safely to their positions. The fire stopped near the local coffee house.

Our fire-bombers tonight successfully burnt the Khoul house on Khach Poghots. They were also able to capture the Saradjian position, which was in enemy hands yesterday.

Enemy Losses: Our riflemen at the Shiroyian position killed a militiaman this morning.

We also killed a militiaman at the Isro position in Shan Tagh.

Enemy Advance Repulsed: At 10 o'clock (3 o'clock) today, after heavy artillery bombardment and much rifle fire, the enemy mob took to the streets and attacked the Sahag Bey position. But the firing from our positions forced the mob to flee, leaving behind three dead. The heavy bombardment continues.

Movements on the Lake. Five boats were seen on the lake sailing towards Tadvan and two coming towards Van.

Military Command

No. 14, April 30

Towards last evening a militiaman was shot dead in front of the Lavant-Oghli house.

They were able to retrieve the corpse in front of our position at Pos Tagh.

After yesterday's mindless attack on our Sahag Bey position, the enemy's bombardment succeeded in destroying part of our upper position. Today, however, we were able to repair the damage and make the position more secure. We killed a Turk from this position.

We killed a Turk at the Sahag Bey position in the morning.

A powerful bombardment began at 9 o'clock (2 o'clock) focusing on the Sahag Bey position and the whole of Aykesdan. It was quite pointless and harmless. We killed one artilleryman and then three soldiers who came to retrieve his body.

The two cannons in the citadel began the heavy bombardment of the city centre at dawn. They ceased two hours later.

This morning a force of about 200 cavalry and infantry advanced in three columns towards our Shoushants-Varak positions from Haji Bekir garrison. They were put to flight by several volleys fired by our comrades and left several dead behind. The column retreated towards the barracks.

Tsorovants. At 10 o'clock (3 o'clock) this evening our comrades entered Tsorovants. There they found a loaded rifle abandoned by the hastily retreating enemy. Household articles remained as they were left, and they were all confiscated, including some wheat. Our comrades have now surrounded the Turkish village of Zrvantants.

The night password is "dants" [pear].

No. 15, May 2

The enemy's intensive artillery bombardment of Sahag Bey and Tovmasian positions over the last few days has meant that over 400 shells have been fired, most of which have fallen on various parts of Aykesdan and hurt several people. It is clear that our clever enemy's wish is to hit the American and German buildings with cannon fire. Several shells have hit them successfully.

Yesterday several bullets from the Nalbandian position killed a militiaman who was cutting down a tree.

At 5 o'clock (10 o'clock) last night a general attack began from all directions against all of our posts. The enemy did not leave its positions and the fusillade hurt no one.

We killed a militiaman in front of our Shan Tagh position at 5 o'clock (10 o'clock) this morning.

The enemy began a fierce artillery bombardment on our Khach Poghots positions starting this morning.

The enemy began a general assault at 10 o'clock (3 o'clock). They were able to set fire to weaver Nazaret's shop located west of our Khach Poghots position. They fired countless shells and their fire ceased after our comrades responded and killed eight militiamen (and succeeded in extinguishing the fire). At the same time, a force of over 200 cavalrymen attacked all our Taza Kyahrez positions. The enemy also aimed their cannons there. However, as they began to advance, more than 10 of their number were killed by our fire which hit them from all directions. They fled in terror and disarray through the gardens. We also exploded two bombs which did what they were supposed to do. We only had one wounded.

Hundreds of enemy soldiers are attempting to advance from the Kouroubash direction towards our positions at Shoushants. They have all been repulsed.

We killed two militiamen at the Chachal Mirzi and Der Khachadourian positions at 12 o'clock (5 o'clock).

Yesterday we killed two militiamen – one at our Sahag Bey position and the other at Pos Tagh.

The enemy continues its bombardment of the city centre. There was very fierce rifle fire as well.

The information bureau of the 1st (Arark) sector reports: For over half an hour now the enemy has been bombarding the Dhertsi Sarkis position from the Glor Tar gardens. Many of the shells were fired indiscriminately and landed in various places. Five, however, landed on the aforementioned position, piercing the outer wall and falling through it. No one was hurt.

The bombardment continues. The latest news is that the enemy advance from Sofi-Dehne towards Shahbenderian has been repulsed from our position. The enemy ran away, leaving 10–12 dead.

The Turks lost a man at the Sahag Bey position.

Military Command.

No. 16, May 3

The enemy has continued its attacks after its futile efforts yesterday. Towards evening, it tried to set fire to our Hotel position on Khach Poghots, but thanks to our efforts, the fire was put out without any losses to us. The enemy lost 8–10 dead at the Shiroyian position and fled.

Towards evening, a Turkish officer and a soldier were shot dead in front of Avak's position from our Dbaghkhero position. The enemy pulled the bodies behind their lines using long skewers. The night passed relatively peacefully.

The enemy appeared weak this morning. Although they tried to attack our positions at Taza Kyahrez at around 10 o'clock (3 o'clock), they were repulsed and left 4–6 dead.

The information bureau of the 1st (Arark) sector informs us that at 10 o'clock (3 o'clock) in the evening, the Armenians succeeded in setting fire to the remaining part of the central police station at Ararouts, as well as the nearby coffee house. The fire-bomber and his comrades returned to their positions unharmed.

Yesterday we killed two Turks at the Smsarian position.

We killed a Turk at 1,650 paces using three bullets from the Hadji Malkhas position.

Yesterday we killed one Turk at the Dan Tagh position and three at the Shahbenderian position.

We killed a cavalryman at the Pos Tagh position this morning. The enemy retrieved the body.

We killed a militiaman and a soldier at the Taz Kyahrez position this morning and captured one rifle.

Military Command.

No. 17, May 4

About 30 Kurds tried to enter our Lavant-Oghli position yesterday. Three were shot dead from our position.

The information bureau of the 1st (Arark) sector tell us that at about 6 o'clock (11 o'clock) yesterday evening the enemy, piercing the south-eastern corner of the church cemetery wall, began to bombard one of the positions it had deserted a long time ago. But after five precise shots by our comrades through an opening

(Two left columns) "The Thirty Day Conflict - Day by Day." Republication of Report No. 16 dated May 3, 1915 in *Ashkhadank* (17 June 1915).

at their position, the enemy stopped its attack. The enemy began sporadic but fierce rifle fire at about 9 o'clock until 3 o'clock in the morning (2–8 o'clock) on all the southern positions, but had no effect. We only had one man wounded.

The enemy began bombarding the Amirkhanian position at 10 o'clock (3 o'clock) today. Four shells also hit the Shahbenderian position. All the shells were explosive. We had no casualties. The enemy left 10–12 dead in the river and in front of their positions.

100 artillery shells were fired at the Sahag Bey and Tovmasian positions yesterday without causing any losses. We threw a bomb before dawn from the Sahag Bey position on to the sentries in the burnt enemy position opposite. The results are obvious.

Last night the enemy initiated intense rifle fire on all our positions. This firing, having no objective, showed that the enemy was firing in panic.

The enemy carried out a fierce attack on the Shahabenderian position at 11 o'clock (4 o'clock) today. After demolishing the garden/vineyard wall with artillery fire, a crowd of Kurdish *bashibozuks* [irregulars] forced their way into the garden. They were under the command of an officer who, drawn sword in hand, advanced. Our soldiers began firing on these advancing plunderers who, after some fighting, withdrew from the garden. During this attack the enemy lost approximately 15–20 dead. Afterwards, they recovered the bodies under cover fire from their artillery and rifles.

Today the enemy set up an artillery piece behind the Catholic mission's wall and began to bombard the Vzvz position in Pos Tagh. They fired more than 20 exploding shells, demolishing the walls of the upper floor. Our workers have already started to reinforce the lower walls to resist artillery fire. Two shells also exploded at our Khachge Mno position.

The Kurdish mob attacked our positions in the Hiusian garden, firing a hail of bullets. Our sentries counter-attacked the mob from the edge of the field. The enemy lost four dead during the fighting. We had one or two minor casualties who had been hit by fire from the Toprak Kale garrison.

The enemy made a fierce attack on our Meolaji Markarents position today. Our soldiers repulsed the mob with great speed, killing 8–10 people, two of whom fell into the river.

We killed a Turkish soldier at the Smsarian position last evening, after the enemy failed to set fire to our position at Hotel.

Enemy artillery continued to fire shells at the Tovmasian position today.

There was a fierce attack on the Khachadourian position today. Our forces and the enemy were 20 paces apart behind the walls.

Military Command.

The Military Command periodically recorded events in terse, often condensed sentences. This left many incidents unexplained and consigned heroes to oblivion. But it was important to emphasise their importance and draw attention to them. One of the events that took place over five days and merited special attention was the torching of the Ararouts Square central police station.

As we've seen, the government had concentrated a considerable force at Ararouts Square. First, there were government forces at the police station that was located on the western side of the square in two two-storey houses. These had shops on the lower floors and had been strengthened just before the fighting started. Second, they had stationed troops in the Ararouts school building, which was on the south side of the square in the church courtyard. Third, the army had taken over a line of shops and the church on the southern side of the square. In this way they were able to fire continuously at Armenian positions on Ararouts Square from the police station, school and the church, thus threatening the entire quarter.

The enemy position that caused the most concern, and at the same time was the nearest, was the police station. But it was difficult to capture it with a direct assault. It was only possible to neutralise it by setting it ablaze. It thus required the efforts of a very brave and rebellious soul, the likes of many who had been born in the Turkish Armenian world.

The mild-mannered Dikran Apraham, better known as "teacher Dikran," had once been a schoolteacher in the village of Avants. Turkish rule didn't permit him to live his life as a peaceful teacher. He was persecuted and became a wanderer. One day he could be in one place, another day somewhere else. He occasionally went to Persia and the Caucasus as a revolutionary courier. Sometimes he would travel through the provinces as a peddler. So the peaceful teacher left his family and became a vagabond because of persecutions. Enraged, he became a rebellious soul and turned into a vengeful force against the oppressive government.

"I'm going to set fire to the central police station," he told the men at his position and set to work.

He rested during the day and worked at night, preparing the necessary items for a fire-attack. He soaked a bundle of hemp strings in kerosene and, when it got really dark, he put the hemp bundle on his back and disappeared. One man accompanied him but stopped a short distance away from the police station and kept guard.

Dikran carried out this kind of night-time attack four times: he started on April 29 and continued until May 2. Of course, not all of his attempts were successful; he burnt the police station one part at a time, with the final, large fire on May 2.

On that final day, he approached the remaining two shops with very great care, as the enemy was very vigilant. He took the bundle off his back, loosened it, and piled the oily hemp in front of two doors and lit it. The hemp immediately caught fire, lighting up the square as if it were daylight. There was now no way he could hide. He then threw himself into the centre of the square – he himself didn't know why – and began singing as he ran away. Volleys were fired from all four directions; bullets flew in every direction but, under that hail of bullets, the brave fire-bomber returned to his position unscathed. He had achieved his aim: the police station was ablaze and there were no troops there any longer.

The torching of the police station was the last fire which Aykesdan witnessed that day. The fire was so great and fierce that the Military Command felt it was important to issue the following statement:

To the Aykesdan units,

Fighting comrades,

Today the hopeless enemy, after thirteen days of mad attacks, launched a general attack on all positions which only demonstrated their weakness and our magnificent victory. They ran away from our bullets in panic, leaving more than 40 dead everywhere.

This was the enemy's latest hopeless offensive which you were destined to resist at any price.

Be brave comrades and defend your positions with the greatest vigilance.

Whenever you shoot during fighting, always hit your target and save your ammunition.

May 2, Armenian National Self-Defence Body.

Thus the second phase of the fighting ended. It was a period during which the valiant Armenian nation gained new experiences.

At this point we should interrupt our narrative a little and turn to what was happening on the battlefields of the Caucasian border and especially in Persia. This is important because events on this front had great repercussions on the progress and tactics used in the fighting in Van.

At that point, the battle in Van was in its second phase and Armenians had produced brilliant results. The first six days of battle were characterised by stubborn and endless fighting. The Turkish government, on the other hand, personified by the treacherous Jevdet, was resorting to new methods to break the rebellious people and turn Aykesdan and the old city into a slaughterhouse. During this critical period, there was also a major battle around Dilman between the Russian and Turkish armies.

After the events of December, when the Turkish army under Enver's command had broken through the Russian lines and advanced in the Olti direction as far as Ardahan and Sarikamish, the Turks had been subjected to a terrible defeat and scattered in disarray. During this Turkish advance, the Russian army had to withdraw from certain Turkish and Persian areas, so that the fighting stopped for two or three months. While it's true that some small clashes took place between advanced units, there were no major battles.

This apparent lull in fighting did not mean that the opposing sides were asleep. No, they weren't sleeping, just making their quiet preparations. After being crushed near Ardahan and Sarikamish, the Turks turned their attention to Persia. They concentrated significant forces in the Ourmiye region by bringing an experienced division from Constantinople, to which they added about a division's number of Hamidian regiments with new artillery pieces and machine guns. That army was under Khalil Bey's command and it advanced towards Dilman on April 27–28. The Turkish forces were much larger than those of the Russians, and it was for that reason that the Turkish advance was made in great confidence. The two armies clashed on May 1 near Dilman and the battle began. The Turks were victorious at the beginning and moved their forces with some skill. But that didn't last long. The battle swiftly turned to the Russians' advantage and the Turks were destroyed on May 3. The 1st Armenian Volunteer regiment under Antranig's command distinguished itself during this battle. The massacre of May 3 proved decisive for Khalil Bey's army. He left 3,500 dead in a small area of the battlefield and escaped in a panic, pursued by the Russians.

At the same time another Russian army, which included 3,000 to 4,000 Armenian volunteers, was moving towards Van from the Igdir-Pergri direction.

Jevdet, who was busy subduing the Armenians of Van during these critical days of the main war, received daily telegrams updating him with the latest news of the war from Khalil Bey.

Khalil Bey's army was defeated near Dilman with the enemy in pursuit, while another Russian army was moving from Igdir. Jevdet, the treacherous Asiatic who oppressed the powerless, received this news. Given the latest developments and seeing that the attacks and innumerable artillery shells fired over two weeks had not been able to cow the Armenians – indeed, Armenians had gained experience and learned new tactics making them more and more unbeatable – Jevdet attempted, for the last time, to resort to treachery and base means, this time promising to pardon Armenians after issuing false reports and threatening to sap the morale of their women and children.

Jevdet once more used letters, while increasing the severity of his attacks on both parts of the city.

The fighting that took place in the city after April 26 was relentless and received a new impetus during May 2–4. The artillery bombardment became heavier with the addition of older guns called *havanoutop* which fired large calibre explosive shells. The attacks increased in ferocity, especially at the Tabriz Gate area which the enemy regarded as a weak point and easier to overpower. They sited several artillery pieces opposite the Gazoyian and Der Boghosian positions, having pierced several walls for the purpose, and on May 2 they began to bombard these positions from a distance of 15-20 metres.

At midday they were able to destroy a wall from top to bottom at the Der Boghosian position and, reciting the *salavat*, 30-40 soldiers attacked the position. But the area commander – the hero Avo – encouraged his men to emerge from the ruins of the wall and pour a hail of bullets on the Turks, who retreated swiftly, leaving 3-4 dead behind. This incident was related by an eye-witness.

Mihran Hovagimian, a taciturn but very dedicated man, died heroically during this battle. Despite this loss, the Turkish assault was repulsed.

The attacks on other positions continued with constant firing from every direction. The battle was stable for three days. Then, at midday on May 3, at the height of the fighting, the enemy asked for parley from at their Telo position in the Tabriz Gate area, opposite the Der Boghosian position. One of the defenders, Avo, a brave elderly man, went to one of the openings at that position to hear his opponents.

"I've been sent by Jevdet," a Turkish military man said from the opposite lines, "Jevdet wants to end the fighting and arrange a truce. He wants you to offer your terms."

"We have our leader, Aram Pasha. Let Jevdet approach him. We're not the people to propose terms," Avo replied.

"Let the leader, Aram Pasha, stay where he is. You are a group leader. Lay down your terms."

"I'm just a clumsy fighter and don't understand very much. If you want to hear my terms, here they are: Bring me Jevdet's head and one of his wives, then we'll agree to a truce," Avo replied. The military man was offended and went away.

On May 4, one day after this incident, again at midday, two women carrying a white flag approached the Shahen Agha position. They were Armenian women who had been behind the Turkish lines. One was a half-mad woman from Haigavank, with the surname Touman. They brought the following letter addressed to the Armenian leader from Jevdet.

To the Locum Tenens,

Yeznig Vartabed,

The rebellion which the Committee started in Shadakh also began here when the Hamoud Agha garrison sentries were fired upon and martyred. Now there is fighting everywhere and much bloodshed. All of Hayots Tsor and Arjag, as well as most of Timar received their just punishment. I gave the people seeking sanctuary on Lim Island a time limit. If they surrender, they will naturally be completely free and their women and children will not be destroyed.

I issued strict orders on the day the fighting began, that the rebels' fire was not to be returned. But when I saw that the madmen were firing to the accompaniment of music played by a band parading through the streets, and that they were not going to stop, I ordered that the Armenian fire should be returned. So you can see that is what we are doing. It was at this point that I spoke by telephone to Burhaneddin Bey, definitely surmising that thanks to your intercession, there would never be firing in the city. I wanted to remove the guards at the Tabriz Gate and various points throughout the city and summoned *mounedigs* [drumming heralds] to announce that the government would defend the population that wasn't involved in the fighting. The guards, however, were suddenly fired upon. Several travellers and policemen were killed or wounded by fire from the Maroutian house. I then understood that preparations had also been made there and we moved appropriately and began firing using cannons and rifles. The Armenians of the city did and continue to do whatever they can against the government, and it pains me that these children of our homeland, who can fight so bravely, do not have an Ottoman spirit. It is evident that there are many villagers in the city and I am convinced that this whole [Armenian] plan is a sign of madness.

The leaders of the Armenian people are, without doubt, responsible before God and their people. We will naturally examine these questions in detail, later.

I've sent several officials so far to offer surrender terms, but they've been answered by bad language and bullets. We became sterner – and will become even more so – although we are thinking about the women and children. We have prepared every means to complete our task. I've begun to shell the city and will continue to do so until it is in ruins. We completely destroyed the bandits who tried to capture Khosh Gediug a week ago. I had 385 bodies buried above Averag. We've captured the village of Tarman and Goghbants and were victorious over 123 armed rebels who were there. We captured and burned the whole of the area above Aykesdan from Hamoud Agha garrison to Khach Poghots. We captured one of the quarters from the Arark direction, sparing the people who were running away from Varak-Shoushants. But I haven't given the order to attack Shoushants. I left two companies of soldiers from Saray near the village of Tarman. I would suggest surrender, and if this offer is refused, I will put the forces at Kouroubash and Tarman into action.

Khalil Bey's division, having cleared the Russians facing him, has entered Khoy, followed by our forces located in the Godol area. So there is no possibility of salvation under current conditions. Although until recently we have honoured the Armenian element of the population as the light of our eyes, we have only seen treachery from them. They will be punished but what is the guilt of their families? If you don't pity yourself, at least pity those poor innocents. My suggestion therefore is:

1. Hand over all weapons.
2. Trust the grace of the government and show a convincing sign
   of your submission.

If these terms are accepted, I promise that I will be able to intervene so that you receive Imperial clemency. Don't spill blood for no reason; spare your families. If you refuse, all blame will be on your heads, be sure of that, and you will all be destroyed!

4 May 331 [1915]
Governor Jevdet.

Jevdet's letter was read in the presence of the Military Committee and several other people, and the following reply was returned through the same women:

To the Governor of Van,

His Excellency Jevdet Bey Effendi,

I received your letter and I want to state that we are not rebelling against the Ottoman government and have always been – and will be – obedient to government laws. So we ask you to send two honourable persons to receive our reply.

Yeznig Vartabed.

In writing this letter requesting two negotiators, the Military Committee hoped to send people to Aykesdan, not to discuss the question of surrender but other issues. The real aim was to find out what was happening in distant places and conditions in Aykesdan. This was the Military Committee's aim, not surrender, because everyone knew that Jevdet wanted to turn the city into a slaughterhouse.

The bombardment stopped after the letter was dispatched and two women brought the following message.

Yeznig Effendi,

I've sent Kalousd Effendi Jidechian with Major Ahmed Bey. I ordered a stop to the bombardment and shooting. Please meet Kalousd Effendi Jidechian and be completely reassured that you may come out. I can assure you that none of you will be hurt while you meet him. If you can persuade the people – good. If you can't, return to your houses and exactly one hour later the clashes will resume. I give my firm word on this.

Governor Jevdet.

Handing over the letter, the women said that the people Jevdet had sent – Kalousd Effendi and Ahmed Bey – were in Aram Gazoyian's house on the Turkish front-line and were waiting for the prelate.

After a short discussion, the men sent by Jevdet were told by the women intermediaries that it wasn't possible for the prelate to come to Gazoyian's house and that they should meet at a different place. The delegates appeared shortly afterwards, but instead of Jidechian coming with Ahmed Bey, who might well have paid the price for his previous sins, Jidechian came with the education inspector Sherif Bey.

The negotiations took place in the open. Five chairs were placed in a narrow street in front of the Shahen Agha position. On the Armenian side the negotiators were the Prelate Yeznig Vartabed, the abbot of Aghtamar Taniel Vartabed, and the lawyer Mirzakhanian.

The discussion didn't take long because the Armenians put forward the following previously agreed condition: Yeznig Vartabed would be allowed to go to Aykesdan with one other person to discuss the truce proposal with the Armenians there, while two honourable Turks would be held as hostages pending their return.

Hearing this condition, the two negotiators returned, taking the following letter with them:

To His Excellency Jevdet Bey Effendi,

I called a meeting of some people who are in the centre of the city and are aware of the current situation. Having considered the possibilities ahead of us, we came to the following conclusion. We cannot make progress in the city on an individual basis, as no force can disarm people who have left their brothers, fathers and families in Aykesdan and the villages and taken up their own self-defence. Apart from this, calling the present situation a rebellion, despite our age-old loyalty and sincerity, raises doubts over any Imperial pardon.

As your Excellency will know, I cannot, in my present official position, prevail over anyone individually. I would like to draw your attention to this fact. If your aim is to free this poor country of its present difficulty and to spare those who are absolutely blameless – women, children and others – then, believing in my right-mindedness, honour and clerical esteem, give the order that I be allowed to be in contact with Aykesdan for one hour. Great men should be frightened of history. You can quench flames with water. I am ready to give my life for this much-damaged fatherland. May God above grant me my reward. I would ask you to believe one hundred percent that the general situation could become peaceful in accordance with your proposals. To that end, I have spoken in detail to the education inspector and Jidechian Effendi – who can relate matters to you themselves. I thus appeal to your excellency and send my special respects.

Locum-tenens Yeznig Vartabed.

A day after this letter, on April 22, the two women appeared once more and brought the following letter from Jevdet:

Yeznig Effendi,

If you and Taniel Effendi cannot persuade those in the city, then you can do nothing outside. I informed those in Aykesdan, through Spordone Effendi, of my proposals. I sent the education inspector Sherif Bey to you at your request. You appreciate that there cannot be long accords between the government and its subjects. If you accept the Sultan's grace and surrender, I said I would intercede. I repeat this. Otherwise, I will order the army to destroy everyone to your last soldier. I will wait until 6 o'clock (1 o'clock) tomorrow for your final answer.

Governor Jevdet.

It was decided that any new objections to Jevdet would be superfluous. His treacherous plans became obvious and the letter remained unanswered. Furthermore, one should record the following additional incident at this point.

During those days, when the above-mentioned treacherous letters were sent by Jevdet, a gendarme approached the Armenian positions. He was initially thought to be a Turk and the soldiers wanted to shoot him. But the gendarme, with great difficulty, was able to persuade them that he was Armenian and was allowed to proceed. When they allowed him in, it became clear that he was from Khnous and was called Hovhannes. There were six other Armenians serving in the Van cavalry and they hadn't suffered in any way up to that point, but on that day they disappeared one by one. Seeing that his comrades hadn't returned – a sign that they had been killed – Hovhannes escaped and came to the Armenian part of the city.

When the fighting started, there were 180 prisoners in Van prison, among whom were several teachers belonging to the Hnchag [Social Democratic] party. The latter were Apraham Proudian, Tantoyian and Ardashes Solakhian (Aso). Gendarme Hovhannes said that the Turkish and Kurdish prisoners had been drafted into the army, leaving only the Armenians in jail. On April 29, there were orders to massacre them.

On that day, they began to tie up and remove these Armenians from prison to a field not far away. There they cut them down and dumped their bodies in previously prepared pits. They didn't use bullets, just cold steel – swords and daggers – to kill them. It was for that reason that gendarme Hovhannes and his comrades, who were in the cavalry barracks not far away, did not hear bullets being fired but the Armenian prisoners' dying screams, the quivering sounds of their voices, and pleas. They heard the heartbreaking sounds and were tortured themselves, not being able to even speak of that barbaric act.

This was the same Jevdet who could arrange such crimes while writing letters to Armenians suggesting reconciliation with promises of forgiveness and saving the lives of women and children.

Having waited for one day without receiving a reply to the letter he sent to Yeznig Vartabed, Jevdet ordered the resumption of the bombardment of the city with greater intensity.

On the other hand, not despairing of his treacherous ideas, he also dealt with Aykesdan at the same time and in the same manner as the city. If the city refused, that didn't mean that Aykesdan would do the same. This was what Jevdet thought. He dispatched the following letter to the governor of the Ottoman Bank, Algardi, convinced that the latter would get its content to the Military Command through the Italian Consul and other people. It was obvious that Jevdet intended to fool Armenians with his lies and false information, as could be seen in the letter he wrote. Here is that letter.

> To Algardi Effendi,
>
> I received your letter and was naturally pleased to learn that you are well. As it is not feasible for you to come to me, it will be fine for you to go to the orphanage.
>
> Today I had the city centre bombarded with mortars. The shells exploded in houses and totally demolished them. For that reason, when I saw that children were running from one street to another crying and screaming, I offered a truce. I sent the educational inspector, Sherif Bey, to negotiate with Yeznig Vartabed. I hope they will declare their obedience by handing over their weapons and trust the Sultan's grace. In this way the women and children will not be destroyed underfoot. The Aykesdan *palikar*s continue to play music. We'll see how long that continues.
>
> According to telegraphic news, the Germans have decisively defeated the British and Belgians at Ypres with a major advance. The remaining enemy forces – 15,000 men – have become prisoners of war. The Austro-German divisions in the Carpathians continue to advance. I congratulate them.
>
> Khalil Bey's division located in Khantakht in the Ourmiye and Salmast region have scattered the Russian divisions and captured three cannons.
>
> We've completely punished, thanks to God's grace, the stupid peasants who attempted to cut our communications. There is no longer any danger from them. I asked Khalil Bey not to send the prisoners they captured to Mosul via Sheno, but to send them here. I'm going to make them march past Dr. Ussher's fortified premises. Let the doctor who, like the rebels, always expects the Russians to arrive, see the prisoners and be happy.
>
> I hope that Armenag Effendi is a thoughtful official who thinks of the actual well-being of the nation. When we meet, I will naturally make some arrangements for him. I've nothing to do today and my spirits are high (*ishim yok, kefim chok*). So this is a long letter to you, Algardi Effendi.
>
> 22 April, Governor Jevdet.

While writing the above message, Jevdet also sent letters to the provincial translator Armenag Sarkisian and the director of the German orphanage, Herr Spörri as follows.

> To Armenag Effendi,
>
> I had sent someone to immediately fetch you and Algardi Effendi, but unfortunately the rebels, having captured all positions, opened fire. For that reason it was impossible to approach your house and give you news.

It was good that you withdrew to the orphanage. If you can manage it, please give my respects to the Shabaghlian brothers. It is most unfortunate that such people have been tried by certain vagabonds.

22 April, Governor Jevdet.

To the director of the German orphanage Herr Spörri,

I received your letter. Both Schwester Martha and Mrs McLaren are well and continue at their posts. I'm very pleased with them – thank you. The Armenian boys serving in the hospital have been handed over to their care. I appointed a cook for them. Their comfort has been assured in every way. I'm having enquiries made in Vosgepag concerning the animals belonging to the orphanage. You may be assured that none will go missing.

22 April, Governor Jevdet.

Jevdet's duplicity and false humanitarian feelings are evident in these letters too. One letter was trying to draw people to him so that he could understand the general disposition of the Armenians and the other tried to demonstrate his kind attitude to Armenians in public service.

Treachery and duplicity, duplicity and treachery... these considerations preoccupied Jevdet's mind, but they never achieved anything. The Armenians attached no credence to Jevdet's words. They didn't enter into negotiations with him. They put their hope in the strength of their arms and continued the battle.

Now the third phase of the fighting began. On Jevdet's side it was a time of anger, while on the Armenian side it was one of hope. Jevdet, after his unsuccessful attempts at deception, resorted to desperate, hopeless fighting, while the Armenians fought a decisive battle for victory. Both sides prepared for the final confrontation but only one side could be crowned with success.

Serious fighting broke out simultaneously in both parts of the city, but it was fiercer in Aykesdan, which was considered more likely to be subdued.

The cannons used during this phase of the conflict were augmented with additional cannons, one of which was of a particularly large calibre, sited some distance away on a hill to the south of Shamiram quarter. It was aimed at the city and could only fire explosive and shrapnel shells. It caused serious losses at various positions. It was to this artillery piece that Jevdet referred in his letter to Yeznig Vartabed.

Apart from this weapon, great use was made of mortars, which were mentioned in Jevdet's letters to Algardi. These were short-barrelled, large calibre artillery pieces, more like cup-shaped cannon which had been left in Van citadel as antiques. There were others things in the citadel that had the patina of age, such as large antiquated bombs. It was possible to fight using the mortars and large bombs at close quarters. The shells used were filled with gunpowder and pieces of iron. Once the shell's fuse was lit, it was fired at the city. One or two of these mortars were located on the citadel; another was sited in the Tabriz Gate area, just behind the old wall. Their shells were fired at Armenian houses, sometimes exploding and sometimes failing to do so. Those that exploded made a deafening sound and created shockwaves and destruction where they landed. Sometimes bombs were thrown without the use of cannon. They were spherical and weighed between two and four poods [around 70 and 140 lbs]. They were brought to the precipices on the citadel and rolled down. This part of the citadel hung over the Ampar area, where the large bombs landed.

Thus Jevdet used everything that was available to him, whether they were in the garrisons or citadel, new or old, good or bad.

In their turn, the people under siege devised corresponding measures and acted bravely to thwart the enemy's efforts. The work of the amrashen and amalias also continued and increased, as they devised new kinds of defences, with subterranean passages, double defensive walls, and a chain of roof defences which covered the city and made it impenetrable. As to the large bombs and mortars falling from above and exploding thanks to their lit fuses, the besieged people found ways of neutralising them and utilising the gunpowder inside the projectiles.

The bombs would blow up a short time after landing, once the lit fuses reached the gunpowder. That meant that swift hands were capable of reaching such bombs and cutting off the lit fuses, but it was dangerous work. Who could say that the bomb wouldn't explode just as courageous hands approached to neutralise it? But the besieged people, just as in everything else, demonstrated marvellous, heroic self-sacrifice. There were many people who followed the trajectory of the bombs, snipped the fuses and neutralised them.

Who were these people? Were they fighters who had became experienced in battle? No! Were they fighters who had gained experience in the defensive positions? No! They were young boys of 15, 14, 13 and even 12 who, living through the dreadful battle and bombardment, and seeing their parents' and relatives' exuberant activity, weren't able to stay crouched down. They looked for something to do to help. Most of the work, such as acting as messengers, getting food to the defensive positions, distributing ammunition and so on was done by such young boys. Now a greater opportunity arose and their numbers gradually increased to such an extent that a strange sort of competition developed. The little heroes kept watch for hours and days to see where the bombs landed and, as soon as they did, several would rush and cut off the fuses. Then they would carry the unexploded bomb, if it was small enough, to the munitions store. If it was large, they would make a hole in it, empty out the gunpowder, and quickly take it to the workshop where cartridges were being filled. They would then return. Therefore, the majority of the bombs not only ceased to cause losses, but their contents added to the stock of gunpowder.

We append descriptions of some of these little heroes to complete our account of the heroic people's fight against their tyrannical government.

14 year-old Aslan was Antranig Aslanian's son. He was a pupil in the fifth class of the Yeremian School. His father was a cloth seller. Aslan operated in the Ampar area, where his family's house was located. This was a place where large bombs were dropped from the citadel. He also acted as a messenger.

(*left to right*) Aslan Aslanian, 14, Vosdan (Asnoush's son) 14, Papgen Isajanian 12.

14 year-old Vosdan was *Dzour* Anoush's son. His surname was Ourous. His father – Haroutiun – had emigrated to Russia long ago, where he had died. Vosdan survived thanks to his mother's work. She was a very poor woman who worked from her home. Because of their poverty, Vosdan never went to school.

12 year-old Papken was the son of the landowner Garabed Isajanian. He was a pupil in the fifth class of the Jesuit School. The cartridge-filling and weapons' repair shop was in their house, as was the hospital.

Ardashes Mardirosian was the son of a telegraph official and was a shop assistant. He was a special messenger and visited almost all the front-line positions. He was very quick and high-spirited. When he went to the front-line positions, he brought news of victories, encouraged the men and then left. He always brought joy and high spirits to any position he entered. For that reason he was given the nickname "Vosgi" [Gold].

These young heroes of the city also had their losses. They were the ones who worked in the streets – the ones who moved about under the bombardment – so it was inevitable that some would be killed. Some of those losses were:

16 year-old Hovhannes Vosgerichian. He loved his people and was killed on Sourp Vartan Street by a bomb from the citadel.

14 year-old Mardiros Keoloshian. He was a shoemaker's son and a pupil in the fourth class of the Jesuit School. He was killed on Maroutian Square by a bullet.

While some little fighters of the city continued their heroic work by rendering bombs harmless, grown fighters became messengers to Aykesdan. It was very important for the people in the city, besieged on all sides, to establish links with Aykesdan and let the people there know their situation, bring back information about Aykesdan, and raise awareness of what was happening in the outside world. This issue was best described by someone who was involved in this work.

> The best way to start the journey to establish a link with Aykesdan was from the Tabriz Gate area. On two occasions – once on foot and the other mounted – we sent someone out from Aykesdan, but because of the double siege lines and the hail of bullets, they couldn't get there and had to return. We sent Setrag of Alchavaz on a third occasion, armed with a Smith and Wesson pistol, but he too found himself among Turkish tents and returned. However, he managed to knock down a night sentry with his staff and took the Turk's rifle before coming back. There was no hope after that of establishing any links with Aykesdan. Therefore, the Military Committee, after a long discussion, decided to construct a tunnel from Abros' house to the Maroutians and to link it to the watercourse that ran under it, thus bypassing the siege lines. The work began and continued relentlessly day and night. We were in this underground work when, on the morning of May 4, a four pood [145 lbs.] bomb fell in our position's courtyard and exploded, demolishing the nearby wall from top to bottom. We were surprised, not knowing where the bomb had come from. A few hours later spies told us that a mortar section had been sited behind the wall, very near the Tabriz Gate, and that they were bombarding us from there. Towards evening a bomb exploded to the entrance of our tunnel and destroyed our ten days' work. There was therefore nothing else we could do. The only way we could communicate with Aykesdan was by very risky attempts.

The besieged people produced two more self-sacrificing men – Shalji Haroutiun Hovsepian and the shoemaker Krikor Tashdoian – who were successful in cutting through the siege lines and delivering letters to Aykesdan as we shall see below.

So, as the besieged Armenians of the city continued their dogged resistance and attempted to forge links with Aykesdan, Jevdet tried a final ploy to overcome the city.

Before noon on May 9, a line of 20–30 Armenian women and children approached the Tekyalifi Harbiye position with uncertain steps. They were from the villages of Timar and had lived through many horrors. They were covered in ragged and dirty clothing. The men at that position allowed them in but soon another group of women and children appeared and they too were let in. Then there was yet another group, followed by others. The men at that position took no more in and immediately sent word to the Military Committee. The military body inspected the newcomers and became very troubled. It was dangerous to let them in. On the one hand there was the question of feeding them, and on the other were serious concerns about the loss of morale and desertions. Then there was the possibility of treachery, as well as other uncertainties. Not to accept them was also difficult. After long discussions it was decided that they would not be allowed in but sent away from the Armenian defensive lines even by force of arms. That caravan of poor women and children circled round and then approached the Tabriz Gate, but they were also refused entry there.

"This is another plot created by the debased and treacherous Jevdet," everyone said, refusing the refugees' entry into the city. For two days and nights those poor people, comprising several hundred individuals, remained exhausted and hungry under the city walls. They weren't able to move on or return to the Turkish lines. They were threatened with being shot by both sides. The Turks, seeing that they couldn't influence the Armenians in that way, resorted to barbarous methods. For example, two women were thrown from a Turkish position on Der Khachadourian Street. They physically abused and killed them, and then threw the bodies on the street. They carried out this lewd and animal-like act before the eyes of the men at Abro's position. Similar filthy acts were carried out with only one aim: to break the hearts of Armenians and get them to admit the crowds of women into the city. But the Military Committee's decision was firm and the crowd was not admitted. Individuals in the Armenian positions threw them bread, but there was no way in which the hunger suffered by so many could be satisfied. As they remained without aid under the walls, many of these people died, several killed by bullets. It was after these scenes that the Turks drove them to Aykesdan.

The city's Armenian population fought fiercely for its survival, not knowing what was to come in the following days. The Military Committee and two church leaders, whose main concern was the defence of 3,000 people, decided with heavy hearts and crises of conscience, to allow the deaths of the starving women and children under the ancient walls rather than to give way and endanger the defence of the people. Oh, filthy Jevdet, what treacherous plans you hatched to defeat the Armenians.

The struggle for survival thus continued in strange and unusual ways, as the third phase of fighting ended along with the month of April [old style].

These were the conditions in the city as Aykesdan waged its own struggle as follows.

The first phase of fighting in Aykesdan were the initial 5–6 days, when, as we saw, the Armenians of Van had their baptism of fire and demonstrated the prowess of their most competent forces. The second stage of the fighting were the following 7-8 days, when unrelenting resistance forced Jevdet into more treacherous methods. The third period reflected Jevdet's anger and last-ditch efforts following his failed attempts at deception, characterised by a final clash of the two sides.

For Aykesdan, the third phase was one of an all-out call to arms. Twice messengers were sent to the Caucasus, both times calling for assistance from fellow-Armenians. However, the messengers never returned and help didn't arrive, nor did the menacing Russian army. Thus, no end of the fighting could be predicted. The only option open to Armenians was reliance on their own strength by summoning all resources to resist and prepare for continuous battle.

In actual fact, when one follows developments at that time, one is amazed at the way a peaceful people suddenly became a fighting force and adapted its physical, intellectual and creative talents for war.

As the judicial body was carrying out its duties, the police force and civil authorities functioning as needed, and the purchase and requisition sub-committees distributing essential supplies, the Military Command released the following notices and commands.

To all units,

We bring to the attention of all units the following critical orders which should be carried out at once.

1. The labourers deployed by the fighting groups must be allowed to return to their centres without fail so that they can receive food and nourishment.

2. All extra spades and shovels held at front-line positions should be returned so that others may use them as necessary.

3. If units need labourers and experts, they should request them in advance so that arrangements may be made during the day to provide the necessary number at night.

May 5, Military Command.

To regional commanders,

The enemy remained treacherously quiet today in order to attack us at night. You should remain especially alert tonight.

May 5, Military Command.

Important notice,

With this announcement we state, for the last time, that all refugee villagers and locals must hand over their weapons and any military supplies they might have to the military supplies sub-committee by tomorrow evening (Friday, May 7).

If weapons are found after the deadline, the owners will be severely punished.

May 5, Military Command.

To all groups

Comrades,

Please let us know the names of those who were killed or wounded at your positions during the present clashes (from April 20 until today), including the following details.

1. Name and surname.

2. Birth place.

3. Age.

4. Position.

5. Day and time.

6. How were they killed?

7. When did they die?

8. Life and other details.

Write clearly and neatly and send your answers to us by the evening of May 8, addressing them to the information bureau. Thereafter, send such information on a daily basis,

May 6, Military Command.

Notice.

Every individual has the duty to participate in current self-defence work in any capacity. All those who remain inactive in houses or coffee shops, by gathering at street corners, or trying to hide in the German-American areas to escape any duty that is appropriate to their abilities will be arrested by special officials and brought before the military tribunal.

May 7, Military Command.

The Military Command followed the fighting in great detail and issued important notices and orders to the fighting men and civilian population, while several workshops produced military stores and ammunition with great enthusiasm. These workshops were:

1. The arms workshop in the Nazaretian house on Bournoutian Street. A group of skilled tradesmen worked there and continuously repaired damaged weapons and made the necessary parts for them.

2. The cartridge factory in the Shahbazian house next to Norashen Square. Skilled tradesmen and adults worked there, as well as young boys and youths who not only cleaned empty cartridge cases with singular enthusiasm, but also filled them with gunpowder, secured the completed bullets, and put them in ammunition boxes.

3. The gunpowder factory in Barber Vartan's house on Taza Kyahrez Street. This house was turned into a real chemical laboratory and the storage for various items. Great quantities of sulphur, charcoal and saltpetre was collected in houses and shops, while the sulphur and saltpetre were piled up and stored in school chemistry laboratories. The director of the teacher training school, who was the chemist Prof. Minasian, worked there with former hunters Manoug and Mgrdich Pagheshtsian, as well as a villager who had worked in the Bulgarian government gunpowder works. They carried out experiments and produced ordinary and smokeless gunpowder. There were no efforts made in Aykesdan to make saltpetre as the supply of its constituent parts were very meagre. The fighting was lasting a long time, thousands of bullets were fired each day, and the amount of gunpowder available wasn't great. It would soon be exhausted and the factory made great efforts to procure more.

But the most striking project was the cannon foundry.

It was an ordinary forge which was on Ajem-Khachoian Street in the Norashen quarter with one door opening onto the street and another onto a yard. It was the fate of the owner of the forge, Tokmadji Markar Garibjanian, to become Aykesdan's Krupp. A great quantity of yellow copper tools and other items were brought to this forge where they created the mould for a cannon. After two weeks of effort, the "Armenian Cannon" was cast with a sufficient number of bombs. The idea for this cannon belonged to Aykesdan's hero, Bulgaratsi Krikor, who had tried to blow up the Hamoud Agha garrison. He didn't try to cast a few cannons with the expectation of neutralising the Turkish guns. Krikor, who was the spirit of rebel enterprises, aimed at firing everyone's imagination and succeeded doing so. The newly-cast copper cannon was brought to the sixth sector on May 4 and was sited in the Der Khachadourian position near Solakhian's house. It was then aimed at the Hadji Bekir garrison. The first shell was fired with a roar and it exploded in the air 400–500 paces away without reaching its target. That did not demoralise the creator and he soon cast a second one.

The Armenian Cannon

But how did the "Armenian cannon" oppose the government's cannon? Was Bulgaratsi Krikor able to pierce the enemy lines with his cannon shells? Of course not, but the cannon became the symbol of Aykesdan's martial spirit. It infused the struggling people with enthusiasm and hope.

The enthusiastic work in the workshops continued, as did the fighting. As to how the fighting progressed, we can present the occasional news sheets which appeared at that time, as they reflected the special circumstances of those days.

No. 18, May 5

Yesterday's Glorious Victory: As we wrote, the enemy made its strongest attack on our entire north-eastern front, penetrating the orchards. After clashing all day, they retreated with great losses. According to our military comrades' information, the enemy had 50–60 killed without counting the injured. The majority of the attackers were Kurdish looters who, shouted "loot, loot," as they rushed to secretly destroy the fruits of honest Armenian labour.

A Heroic Death: A heroic scene took place in the Shahbenderian position yesterday. A young man – Aram Boghosian – three times ascended to the top of a ladder at that position and killed three of the enemy. The enemy fired at our young marksman's position, but he still went up again to the loophole, wanting to kill a fourth man. His comrades' begged him not to do so, as an enemy cannon was now aimed at his position. The pleas had no effect. Aram went up again with a heroic gesture but a cannon shell shattered his legs and knocked him down. Aram didn't lose his head and retained his sangfroid. He only asked his comrades to sell his 10-shot pistol to pay for food so his mother and sister didn't go hungry. He asked his comrades to look after the living. After these loving filial words, he sent his greetings to his comrades and closed his eyes forever a few hours later.

An Enemy Cannon Exploded: When the artillery piece located at Toprak Kale, which earlier fired explosive shells at our positions, went to fire again, only smoke rose into the air and four artillery men were killed as a result of this explosion. Soldiers ran from the lower garrison and other places and took the bodies away. One body was removed on a stretcher, showing that he must have been someone of importance.

From the Information Bureau of the First Sector: The enemy began to bombard our positions from two places in the church yard. Several of the shells hit two of our positions, causing some damage. Thanks to our accurate fire on the artillery positions, they were forced to cease fire.

Yesterday morning it was observed that a body dressed in women's clothing was taken away from the enemy side.

Pointless enemy rifle fire resumed at 10:30 a.m. (3:30 p.m.) on all our southern positions. Our side replied sparingly.

From Dardanelles: Early this morning militia forces at Karashar Tar gradually entered trenches around Ourpat Arou. Thanks to their advance today, they were one more field closer to the road. At 10:30 a.m. (3:30 p.m.) they opened fire at our positions from the stream at the water mill near Haji Bekir garrison. We had no casualties and they made no advance at all.

From the Chantigian Position: We killed two of the enemy from our position during an attack yesterday and our group defended itself vigorously in the subsequent night attack. We only had one man injured.

Starting at 9 o'clock (2 o'clock), 60 shells were fired by the enemy from the upper position of their garrison, but only five shells reached their target without causing any damage. Then a Kurdish mob rushed forward through the Der Khachadour and Zrvantants orchards, firing thousands of bullets at us. We defended energetically and killed six Kurds. The enemy was barely able to retrieve the bodies of their dead under covering volley fire. Our morale is high and we suffered no casualties.

The shells fired from the cannons located at the Dominican Friars' school aimed at our positions at Pos Tagh and mostly missed their target. A few of them slightly damaged our defences. We suffered no losses. Our supporting forces at Pos Tagh fired several times at the enemy trying to enter the orchard and killed a militiaman. Thereafter the enemy began to retreat.

Enemy Advance Repulsed: Yesterday, at around 5 o'clock (10 o'clock), the enemy horde came out of their positions at Jashouni field and attempted to advance through an orchard, but our guards opened heavy fire on them. The enemy, disoriented and confused, took shelter in the orchards and lost four men. After firing 1,200 bullets, they tried to retrieve their dead but lost four more of their number and then completely disappeared. They managed to retrieve their dead at 10 o'clock (3 o'clock) under a hail of covering volley fire.

Unbridled shooting: Last night at 10-11 p.m. (3–4 a.m.), there was continuous shooting on all fronts for over an hour. The enemy remained behind their walls and other positions and their fire had no effect on us. Now that such bluffs are so clear, our men only respond by mocking them. The enemy fire expended 10,000 bullets on all fronts.

Important: We ask everyone to send all printed news items and announcements to the Military Command using the address of the Information Bureau.

No. 19, May 6

Yesterday's Developments: Yesterday, throughout the day, the enemy remained quiet on all fronts and showed no movement.

Report from Dardanelles and Davaboyne: At around 10 p.m. (3 p.m.) the enemy started a barrage against our positions without harming us or moving a step forward. This morning, starting at dawn, they started shifting their forces, emptying Karashar and putting guards in trenches.

At 2 p.m. (7 p.m.) the enemy started a barrage of heavy rifle fire that lasted until 3:15 p.m. We responded with pistols and single rifle shots. The enemy made no progress and we had no losses.

Report from Sahag Bey Position: Tonight around 2–3 o'clock (7–8 o'clock) we attacked and burnt down Adaloukhian Haji's house opposite Chacal Mirkian position and on the right bank of Hamzi Pos. On this occasion we captured a Martini rifle, 1,000 cartridges (Mauser-Martini), 100 Mauser cartridges and 143 Martini cartridges.

The enemy losses are considerable. An hour and a half after the shooting, one of our men was shot dead through an opening at our position. We had no other casualty.

After the operations at Adaloukh, the next plan was the attack on Sahag Bey Hamzi's house, which took over an hour. The Armenians made a brave attack on the enemy position, threw their bombs and went forward. However, as it became light, they were ordered to retreat and so it ended, with heavy gunfire from both sides. The bombs had their intended effect, but we could not see the results from close quarters. We had two wounded.

Arark (First Sector): Yesterday the enemy placed its cannon in the orchards of Glor Tar and began to pound our positions again. Only a few of the shells had their intended effect, piercing two walls with no other damage. We managed to kill the artilleryman and noticed his unusual uniform when he was taken away. The cannon also became silent afterwards.

Tonight there was again some rifle fire from certain places with no real result.

Information from Dardanelles: There are hardly 20-25 people in the trenches around Karashar. This morning, 60-70 cavalrymen and foot soldiers descended from the barracks towards the city. They were carrying loads but we do not know their content. Seen from another position, the people moving towards the city appeared like Kurdish women and children.

Military Committee.

No. 20, May 7

Good News From the City: Tonight two messengers from the city managed to get to Goghbants village with important news.

According to the lies of our chief executioner Jevdet, the city was destroyed and in ruins many weeks ago with great losses. It was supposed to have surrendered and been pressed into obedience to the bloody government. Despite what Jevdet says, the messengers say that the people in the city are entirely free. All positions inside the city walls are in our hands. All of the enemy positions and buildings are burnt down and destroyed. They have managed to burn down the post-telegraph office and certain government buildings.

According to what can be seen from Shoushants, yesterday, starting at 4 o'clock (9 o'clock) the enemy once more started to bombard the city. Towards 5 o'clock (9 o'clock) rising smoke was observed on the Bit Bazar side towards the lake.

Enemy Movements: A report from Shoushants informs us that around 200 of the enemy set off towards Hayots Tsor two days ago.

The enemy forces that advanced from Haji Bekir barracks had to retreat immediately as they came under fire from our sentries. These forces moved to the Kouroubash gullies and started their pointless and timid shooting. For two days, their strength is noticeably weak in that area. Two days ago, the enemy was more numerous above Sghka-Taza-Kyahrez. That front was also weak yesterday.

Tonight a force of over 200 militiamen went up the mountain from Kouroubash. As if in a military exercise, they returned from three directions.

Over 200 men went to Shahbaghi from Toprak Kale and then to Khosh Gediug.

All Positions Report: Tonight, starting at 9 p.m. (2 p.m.), the enemy began its usual cowardly firing on our positions. Without trying to go forward on any front, they continued to waste bullets until dawn, when they were tired and went silent. Our comrades responded with some small pistols or not at all.

Yesterday I went to the ruins of the bakery from the Nalbandian position and we shot a militiaman who was looking out of their positions.

They inform us from the Dardanelles position that early in the morning, around 100 Kurds passed in front of Haji Bekir garrison. Afterwards porters carried loads to the city on 20 horses.

Today at 10:30 (3:30) our comrades managed to capture the Hatshamroghner position from the enemy. The enemy fire did not harm us.

Information Bureau

No 21, May 8

The Turkish attacks on Aykesdan have stopped for four days. Yesterday a total of three bombs were fired into Aykesdan without any effect. Yesterday at 11 o'clock (4 o'clock) we killed a militiaman and wounded another in the ruins of Adaloukh. Last night passed peacefully.

In the morning enemy forces set off towards our positions at Shoushants from Kouroubash-Sghka. Our sentries showed them little resistance and were forced to retreat. In order to avoid being encircled, our comrades decided to abandon the village – and to take new positions and fight from the heights above the village. The enemy set some building in the village alight, including Garmro Monastery. Around 100 unarmed women and boys managed to escape from the attacking horde and reached the city. This minor unexpected enemy success has not demoralised us.

In the morning, our comrades followed the enemy towards the village of Sghka and cleared them from the heights above Taza Kyahrez. The enemy retreated to Sghka village after losing two of their number. At 2-3 o'clock (7-8 o'clock) there was heavy fighting around Shahbenderian and Taza Kyahrez. We are using our cannon there. The enemy has suffered three losses.

We killed a militiaman from our positions at Shan Tagh.

Latest News: At 6/11 o'clock, a Turkish force of 80 men attacked our positions at Taza Kyahrez. Our comrades mounted a successful defence and killed a gendarme. Our sentries fired upon an enemy force approaching from Ourpat Arou and forced them to retreat. We killed a gendarme from our position there.

Information Bureau

No 22, May 10

Yesterday at dawn, Armenian refugees from Shoushants-Varak poured into the city.

Another wave of refugees came tonight. We do not have information about the enemy's losses in the fighting at Shoushants.

There has been no fighting at Varak. Some of the armed villagers have come to the city, while a significant number are defending the mountain. The enemy, taking advantage of the absence of armed Armenians, entered the monastery and burnt it down at around 12 noon (5 o'clock) yesterday. They also robbed it of valuables and drove off all of the sheep towards Hayots Tsor.

The city has been under heavy enemy bombardment over three days. On the other hand, the enemy remains inactive against Aykesdan.

Yesterday, towards evening, the enemy started bombarding Sahag Bey and Der Tovmasian positions. After firing from the Siunetjian position, their cannon remained silent for four hours.

The officer in charge of that cannon was shot dead from our Toutlough position. A militiaman trying to recover the body was also shot.

Yesterday evening, one of our guards shot a militiaman in a trench in front of the entrance to Zrvantants Keoshk. The corpse remained where it fell until morning. They later managed to snatch it away.

We killed a Turk today from the Mrodian position in Shan Tagh.

From the Information Bureau of the First (Arark) Sector: Yesterday, the enemy attempted to bombard our positions from the direction of Glor Tar. None of the shells had their intended effect.

Yesterday morning we killed a Turk in front of Keyrat Kyahrez in the Glor Tar area.

Today we shot a Turk from the Peotigian position. He was next to Tavo's entrance. We also killed a Kurd beneath the walls of the Solakhian orchard.

An hour ago the enemy sent refugee women and children from Hayots Tsor and Ardamed. They entered our lines at Ararouts.

Information Bureau

No 23, May 11

This morning four cannons near Toprak Kale started to bombard our positions at Der Khachadourian, Dbagh Khero, Shiroyian, Chantigian and Shegoian positions. Only the upper floors of the Shiroyian and Der Khachadourian positions were destroyed. The enemy forces attacking the Chantigian position scattered after we threw a bomb at them.

We lost two soldiers and one worker. Two civilians were also wounded. Other than its wounded, the enemy lost around 20-25 men during its heavy assaults.

There were also cannon-balls fired at Shahbenderian position where there were no casualties.

Dhertsi Sarkis' house in the Ararouts area was also bombarded. The explosive shells did not cause any damage.

The Sahag Bey position came under periodic rifle and cannon fire.

Report from the Chantigian Position: Yesterday and tonight were comparatively peaceful, but starting at dawn this morning, the enemy lit fires behind all of the orchard walls and the keoshks to our north. Groups of Kurds and Cherkez are regrouping into larger units. The enemy has also dug trenches overnight and placed cannons at five locations above the barracks. We are expecting a battle today.

From the Information Bureau in the First Sector, May 10: Today, at 2 o'clock (7 o'clock), the enemy started an attack from the orchards at Glor Tar with two cannons against three of our positions on the southern front, especially against the Dhertsi Sarkis position, which was hit by over 10 shells. These shells made holes in walls and destroyed a semi-ruined stable. One of the cannons was firing explosive shells.

After the bombardment, the enemy tried to attack our comrades from a neighbouring house, but we suffered no casualties.

We killed an artilleryman from the Bneian position and our comrades saw his corpse being dragged away by the feet. We killed an enemy militiaman.

Yesterday we killed a militiaman from our Dardanelles position.

Information Bureau

The fighting continued in the same fashion until May 11, and on May 12 the Military Command made the following call.

Comrades!

We are informed from different positions that the Turks are in disarray and are abandoning their lines. Therefore, you all have to strengthen your positions and go forward in small groups to see whether the reports are correct or the enemy is preparing a trap for us.

May 12, Military Command

The following communication was released a day after the above call.

No 25, May 13

Nalbandian Position: Yesterday we were ordered to prod enemy positions. In order not to suffer any unnecessary losses, we planned a game instead of a military operation. We hung a bucket full of smoking-fire around a dog's neck and made it run down Khach Poghots, while we fired a few shots from a Smith revolver and shouted "Hurra!" as if we were attacking. The enemy, thinking that we were charging their positions, opened fire with around 500 shots. It was clear that there were only a few people at their positions and the shots were coming from further afield.

Information Bureau of the Fifth Sector: It was completely quiet in our sector yesterday, with occasional fire from the enemy. There were only two or three shots fired from our side until evening. The enemy was enraged when we started to set the body of a dead Kurd alight in front of the entrance to Sahag Bey.

The day before yesterday our position was hit by artillery fire with no serious consequences. On the same day one of our soldiers in a trench was lightly wounded on his hand.

In the evening the enemy started heavy gunfire without coming out. We responded with a few old rifles. The firing continued with some breaks throughout the night. It has been quiet since morning.

The enemy has not fired a single cannon on Aykesdan since yesterday, yet the bombardment of the city has intensified.

Information Bureau

It appeared that the Turks were leaving Aykesdan where the bombardment had ceased.

The Turks were also leaving the city, though they were still subjecting it to heavy bombardment.

"The heavy fighting continued until May 12 when during the day we saw Turkish women and some wounded and sick in hospital garb going to the port of Avants" wrote a soldier, adding:

> The captain (*khmpabed*) at Abro's position stood up and fired – and a Turkish woman fell down. The news was immediately communicated to the Military Command. Haygag Gosoian and Taniel Vartabed came to check the initial signs. The flight was continuing when, the following day, we heard from other positions that a large number of Turkish women and children were fleeing to Shamiram quarter, and then towards Ardamed and Vosdan. This news really encouraged us, but we received an order from the Military Command that the flight of Turks should not diminish our vigilance: we should remain more vigilant and careful because the apparent flight might have been part of a well-organised trap.

In actual fact, the Turks were fleeing because the Russian army was approaching Van. After destroying Khalil Bey's army at Dilman, the Russian army – including Antranig's units – had occupied Bashkale and was marching on Van, while another column including other Armenian volunteer units under the leadership of Vartan, Keri, Dro, Khecho and Hamazasb had reached Pergri.

Jevdet, who was kept informed of the advance of the Russian army, had lost himself and was evacuating Van. He was preparing to flee without putting up any resistance. But the Armenians, who remained under siege in Aykesdan and the city, did not know what was happening elsewhere and thought the evacuation was part of an elaborate trap.

It is noteworthy that at that time the Military Command at Aykesdan did not foresee the flight of the enemy as it was creating new local information bureaus, continuing the work of strengthening positions, making a register of weapons and supplies, and cautioning its forces.

It is useful to reflect on some figures here to give an idea of the military strength of Aykesdan in those days. According to a register dated May 13, the number of weapons in the hands of the political parties and individuals were as follows:

1. Rifles – Mosin, Mauser Model, Aynali, Gapakhli, and Berdan – 480 with 68,000 cartridges
2. Pistols – ten shot Mauser – 520 with 42,000 cartridges
3. Pistols – different makes – 265 with 11,000 cartridges

Total: 1,265 weapons with 121,000 cartridges

As we noted earlier, at the beginning of fighting the number of weapons was 700, but this number grew as fighters from Hayots Tsor, Timar, Arjag, Shoushants, and Varak retreated in the face of superior enemy forces and came to Aykesdan with their weapons. The quantity of ammunition also increased due to careful use and refilling empty cartridges for re-use.

Jevdet was preparing to escape, but not all of his forces at once. The first to leave were civilians – and thus the Turkish quarters were emptied. The cowardly satrap was afraid of Armenians following and massacring his forces. He therefore kept moving his troops around in his last two days before his escape, repositioning his cannons, sometimes attacking the city, sometimes Aykesdan with heavy bombardment. These manoeuvres were meant to cover up his escape plans. These were the final convulsions of a dying enemy.

The morning of May 16 seemed like a normal morning, as the besieged Armenians greeted the day with their weapons at hand and the Military Command released the following news.

No. 26, May 16

May 15. Report From the Sixth Sector and the Plain. At 1:30 (6:30) two enemy cannons started to bombard all positions in our sector with explosive shells. Most of the attack was pointless. One shot hit the upper floor of the Der Khachadourian position, four hit the American building and its flag, one hit the German building, and eight to ten fell in the direction of the Malkhas-Solakhian trenches. There were no casualties among our comrades. A little girl was killed by chance, as she was walking near our positions.

Yesterday, on May 14, Gasha, a well known Assyrian fighting priest was shot in the head and killed as he was passing through our trenches at Shahbenderian.

The First (Arark) Bureau Reports: Yesterday at 11 o'clock (4 o'clock), the enemy started bombarding from the trench in front of Haji Bekir barracks using explosive shells. After bombarding the whole eastern front at Aykesdan, it turned its fire on some of our other positions around 5 o'clock (10 o'clock) and blew holes in a few places without further damage. After some damage to certain positions, the enemy started a general bombardment of all quarters. Three men were wounded, one of whom died.

Yesterday, at around 6 o'clock (11 o'clock), we killed a Turk in a trench from our Zeitoun position.

The Seventh Sector (Dardanelles) Bureau: Yesterday's bombardment took place between 10–6/3-11. The artillery was joined by rifle fire. 100 cannon shells were fired. We only lost one of our fighters. There was much movement in enemy ranks within the city and from the city to the garrison, including the movement of carts. The enemy forces remain the same. There is no movement on the plain.

Refilling cartridges in a workshop

10 vessels appear on the sea, but their direction is not clear. We heard from people coming from Lezk overnight that the enemy is evacuating families by boat, and that the departure of men is prohibited for now. The people moving are Kurdish families.

The soldiers at Toprak Kale barracks are leaving one by one with bags and cases and going towards Sghka and the lake. The enemy positions opposite our lines are silent today. When our soldiers entered an orchard at an enemy position, they found a corpse with 40 Mauser bullets and a sword. The identity papers revealed that the corpse belonged to a *chete* from Erzeroum.

Today they began bombarding the Der Khachadourian position from Haji Bekir garrison. A few cannon shells fell on the American compound but none caused any damage. We noticed that some transports were leaving Haji Bekir garrison on the Kouroubash road towards Hayots Tsor.

The movement on this line is becoming greater. Government forces and families from Nor Kiugh, around 200 people, are on the move, but it is not clear where they are going.

Information Bureau

This was the last report, which appeared on May 16, and marked the end of the great resistance.

Often great events take place in unexpected ways and have mysterious beginnings. May 16 marked the end of an epoch for the people of Van, the last day of their struggle, as well as a great day of victory and salvation. But the Armenian people did not realise nor foresee what was happening. The Military Command's May 16 report was inconclusive and did not predict that it would be the last one.

Meanwhile, as the besieged people of Aykesdan continued their peculiar existence during those days of fighting and reading the reports of the Military Command, Jevdet was sitting in his governor's armchair, writing his farewell message to the Italian Consul, Spordone.

> Dear Spordone,
>
> I am leaving the city because of developments in the war. The situation is truly painful, ruling a country in rebellion. Our pity for children prevented us from undertaking night attacks. The Russians profited from this situation. May God punish the disloyal *komitaji*s. When the enemy invades, it is natural that there is endless fighting. My regards to Algardi Effendi and all friends, and my respects to the ladies.
>
> 1915 May 16
>
> Governor Jevdet

After writing this letter Jevdet began his last set of convulsions, the convulsions of a dying Turkish government, and re-started the furious bombardment targeting three points – Haji Bekir garrison, Glor Tar and Sahag Bey. The roar of the artillery and exploding bombs reached proportions which were not seen in Aykesdan during the fighting. 29 people were killed or wounded from the bombs on that day. One bomb hit the Khanigian Street, close to the Hiusian home, and killed or wounded 10 people. One of the dead was a young messenger. The bombardment was accompanied by rifle fire.

This period continued until 4 o'clock. Then the bombardment lessened and gradually ended, as did the rifle fire. The last shots were from the rocks of Zmzm-Maghara, like the final chords of a piano.

For a moment, the men at their positions lost themselves and were intoxicated by the magical sound. They did not realise what was happening and froze where they stood. Then, they suddenly awoke as if from a deep slumber. They felt the peculiar silence, saw the abandoned surroundings, and suddenly shouted, "Comrades, the enemy has fled!"

Those were the words that were repeated at the Armenian positions in Aykesdan on May 16, as the defenders leapt like tigers and attacked the Toprak Kale and Haji Bekir garrisons, the two symbols of tyranny. There were a few final skirmishes between the attackers and the remnants of the fleeing soldiers and a few more lives were lost. The two garrisons were then set alight and marked the victory of a people in arms.

But the city was also part of this victory bonfire. Since early morning the city had also been bombarded like Aykesdan, but not as heavily. Both artillery and rifle fire were less, but the firing continued until 6:00 pm, when the noise suddenly stopped, even though the rifle fire and bombardment usually lasted until 7:00 or 8:00, and sometimes longer. This unusual development was seen as an enemy ploy, especially because the garrison in the fortification high above was not lit up.

"The enemy is surely preparing a trick" thought the Military Committee and instructed the units to remain where they were.

The city was puzzled when smoke began to rise from Toprak Kale garrison, but the uncertainty continued as the Haji Bekir garrison remained intact and no smoke was rising from it.

Hours passed, heavy and anxious, as Armenians peered at Haji Bekir garrison from the roof of the prelacy. The final answer to the uncertainty was going to be seen there. Finally it was midnight and the Haji Bekir garrison started to burn and light up the sky. The news was instantly related to the Military Committee, and then the men came out of their positions and approached the enemy positions, which they found empty.

"The enemy has escaped" they shouted from the Turkish lines as the fire and smoke spread in all directions.

May 17 was a day of revenge, foolishness and great excitement. Aykesdan was covered with smog as fires sent clouds of smoke into the air. There was also fire and smoke in the Turkish quarters of the city. The Armenian fighters were burning Turkish homes without sparing anything. The terrifying enemy of the previous day could not be seen anywhere. They had disappeared like hyenas.

May 17 began with an extraordinary development which was the kiss of foolishness. A group of fighters arrived in the city from Aykesdan and embraced with the fighters greeting them. They kissed each other. Gradually the number of men reaching the city grew, people embraced each other left and right, and the Armenians of one part of Van welcomed the others.

Among the fire and flames were excited fanfares full of foolish play, with two dozen men approaching the Van fortress from two sides and occupying it – the fortification that had terrified them – and placing a flag at Tntanoti Kar (Cannon Rock), a rock overhang with a cannon emplacement immediately above the city. The flag they raised was not anything grand, but its symbolism was, as it represented the rebellion of Armenians. A people who had been enslaved for centuries had entered into an unequal battle and achieved a glorious victory. The flag was a symbol of a people on the road to freedom.

Afterwards came the plunder and arson, and those two words became the motto of Armenians in Van on May 17. It was the eruption of a long accumulated need for revenge. For two days they burnt down Turkish quarters and homes with no exception. The Armenians, who were used to peaceful work, were now engaged in destructive activity. The Armenians, who were used to only creative work, were now demolishing and destroying. This is what the behaviour of a barbaric Turkish government had done to them. There was no other way for Armenians and they became thieves and wreckers.

These were the conditions in Van on Tuesday, May 18, when two scouts from Van led an advance column of Armenian volunteers in the Russian army to a smouldering Aykesdan. Their ranks included the Russian officer Ozol and Captain Khecho.

The Armenians of Van greeted the Russian advance unit with flowers and bouquets. Thousands honoured them and there were celebrations in the streets of Aykesdan – never to be forgotten by the people of Van.

Old City of Van, 1916

General Nikolaey was also met with the same enthusiasm on May 19, as he arrived with the Russian army. He entered Van with the Armenian volunteer units under the command of Vartan, Keri, Dro and Hamazasb. That evening there was a great banquet at the mansion of Simon Tiutiunjian to honour the Russian army and Armenian volunteers.

The celebrations of the Armenians of Van between May 16 and 19, following the flight of Turks and the arrival of the Russian army, was truly reflected in the last request of the Military Command to the Armenians of Van on May 19.

ARMENIAN PEOPLE

We conclude a month of struggle and glory, the death and resurrection of our nation, the first bright spring of Armenians.

A month ago, today, when the enemy unleashed a terrible battle against civilisation and justice, against us, we placed our faith in our weapons and felt in the depths of our soul that victory would be ours, because our fight was against darkness, ignorance and tyranny, and in defence of truth and justice.

We thus raised our arms and faced the enemy bullets and bombs which were supposed to deal the final blows to destroy us. They wanted to destroy our nation making our youth kneel before them.

We faced the fanatical and arrogant gestures and attacks of the enemy, but at no time did the enemy see our soldiers in disarray or our defensive positions in neglect during our epic struggle.

We now enjoy the fruits of this month-long struggle – which we conducted gloriously and honourably – with the Armenian people elated by their victories.

Our soldiers' enduring martial spirit has shown the enemy that the spirit of freedom flows in our blood. This is consecrated blood that knows how to scatter the once arrogant, powerful and today cowardly and low enemy.

We have been celebrating for three days, intoxicated by the sight of the burning garrisons, the destruction of the den of executioners.

We are intoxicated by a God-driven madness because the people who plundered, extorted and crucified us are fleeing from us – we are now the ones plundering, massacring and crucifying those who plundered and crucified us for a thousand years.

It is the vengeful but just God who is inside and above us.

It is the call for revenge that we hear right now. It is the heartbreaking voice of generations of Armenians killed by the sword, children thrown into fire-pits, and virgins raped and terrorised.

Today, in the course of a thousand years, it is the first time that the Armenian flag flutters on top of the historic citadel of Van, under the bright sun of Armenian freedom. Today, for the first time, it is the tyrant – with his family and belongings – fleeing from the bullets of the Armenian soldier. Today, for the first time, it is the Armenian army that is coming to the aid of its kindred militant youth.

And today, with the glorious struggle behind us, we know the taste of real victory and look forward to the freedom ahead in the knowledge that we can hope for a brighter and happier future for our race.

With our heroic struggle, we have already laid the foundations for that great freedom, which our people and their great thinkers only dreamed of, sacrificing millions of lives over 30 years of struggle; a freedom whose dawn is rising over the proud mountains of Vasbouragan.

Today, therefore, is a celebration of not only our month-long struggle and victories, but also a celebration of the freedom of Armenians from the claws of tyranny.

Long live Armenian freedom,

Glory to the fallen,

Long live the fighting youth of Vasbouragan,

Long live the Armenian army.

The Military Command of Vasbouragan.

19 May

A LIST OF THOSE KILLED IN THE CITY DURING THE 27 DAYS OF FIGHTING

1. Karekin Atashgarian
2. Yervant Maksoudian
3. Hagop Sharoian
4. Mihran Hovagimian
5. Payel's wife
6. Margos Kiurigian
7. Manoug Baylian
8. Vartan Der Vartanian
9. Vahan the fire-bomber
10. Mardiros Keoloshian

11.   Hovhannes Azkaserian

12.   Miss. Keoloshian

13.   Dndes Yeghishe

14.   Dndes Serovpian

15.   Souren Janoian

16.   Hius Manas

17.   Salakh Toum's daughter

18.   *Bakhal* [shopkeeper] Kaspar

19.   Chilinger Garabed

20.   Shamam's son-in-law

21.   Hovhannes Pirghalemian

22.   Simeon Soltigian

23.   Mardiros Ardamyatsian

24.   A village youth

25.   Mrs. Kaprielian

26.   Keor Khacho

27.   Mrs. Ayazian

28.   Mrs. Jonavedian

29.   Hagopig Krikorian

30.   Miss. Yeghisapet Gafafian

31.   Miss. Hovagimian

32.   Shervantsi Saro

33.   Garabed Tavrezian

34.   Khachig Charchi-Avedian

35.   Haygavanktsi Mikayel

36.   Kevork Aslanian

37.   Churo (guard)

38.   Tovmas Ghazarian

39.   *Frnji* [baker] Adom's son

40.   Avedis Varbedian

41.   Tovmas Ghazarian's wife

42.   *Siuriuji* [driver] Hagop

43.   Daughter of Kh. Mardirossian

Other than the above 43 names of those killed, 15 of whom were fighting men, there were also 71 wounded.

As for those killed or wounded in Aykesdan, the numbers were incomparably greater, but we could not get a list of them.

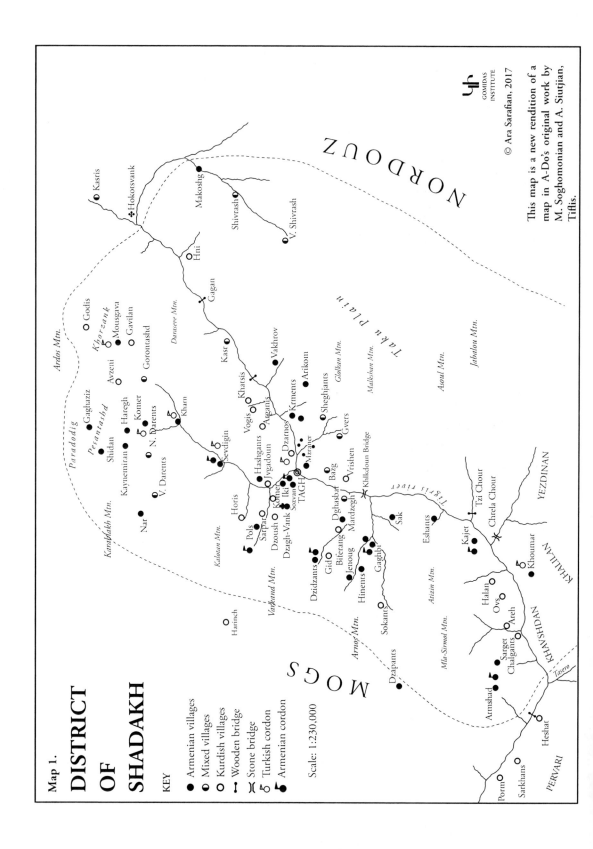

Map 1.

DISTRICT
OF
SHADAKH

KEY

● Armenian villages
◐ Mixed villages
○ Kurdish villages
⌶ Wooden bridge
)(Stone bridge
⌐ Turkish cordon
◢ Armenian cordon

Scale: 1:230,000

This map is a new rendition of a map in A-Do's original work by M. Soghomonian and A. Siutjian, Tiflis.

© Ara Sarafian, 2017

Chapter XVIII

The Heroic Battle of Shadakh

While the Armenians of Aykesdan and the city remained isolated for weeks, as they heroically resisted the Turkish government, Shadakh also took to arms and continued with its own dogged fight.

If Armenians, demoralised after centuries of oppression, managed to achieve heroic victories in Aykesdan and the city and opened a new era in their history, a greater deed took place in the mountains of Shadakh, where the struggle started earlier and lasted longer. That 40-day unequal fight was won by the brave people of Shadakh who managed to stand their ground.

We should start by saying a few words about the region of Shadakh.

As we saw earlier, Shadakh was a mountainous region to the south of Lake Van. Along with Mogs and Gargar, Shadakh was a maze of mountains and valleys, most of it unknown even in those days. They were simply called the mountains of Shadakh, Mogs and Gargar. The most notable region among them was Shadakh itself.

The northern boundary of Shadakh was marked by the peak of Mount Ardos. To the west was Mogs, with its Arnos peak marking the boundaries between them. To the east was the district of Nordouz, and the southern boundary was the Eastern Tigris and its valley.

Shadakh was a mixture of impregnable mountains and many valleys. Across the entire length was a huge valley, where the Eastern Tigris rose and smaller valleys joined it. Two other valleys started at the north and north-east of the district, one beginning on the southern slopes of Mount Ardos and stretching southwards, with the other starting on the southern slopes of Mount Pashed and extending south-west. The first valley was called Sivdgin Valley, where the Sivdgin river flowed, while the second had several names, and the upper Tigris flowed through it. These two valleys joined each other in the centre of Shadakh, where the Sivdgin and Upper Tigris rivers ran into each other and flowed down a deep valley southwards.

Shadakh was composed of 100 villages, 50 of which were Armenian inhabited. The central town was Tagh, which had 220 households, all of them Armenian. Tagh was located at the confluence of Sivdgin and the Upper Tigris, at the conjunction of three sheer-sided valleys. It was the seat of the district administration and its head (kaimakam).

The Armenian villages were mainly in the north, on the Sivdgin and Upper Tigris rivers, and extended down to Tagh and a place called Khlkdoun, where the main bridge to the south was located. There were also Kurdish villages in the north, but the major separation occurred south of Khlkdoun bridge. On the right bank of the Tigris were Armenian villages, Kurdish ones being on the left bank. There were also several Kurdish tribes which were a constant cause of trouble in the district. These were the Khalilan,

Khavshdan, Yezdinan and Alan. If one also included the Krav, on the boundaries of Nordouz and Shadakh, whose bandit leaders Shakir and Mirmhe once created mayhem in Shadakh and Nordouz, one understands how tough the Armenians of Shadakh had to be in order to survive in those mountains.

Indeed, the Armenians of those impossible mountains and impassable valleys displayed such bravery and strength that they withstood the combined oppression of the Turkish government and the onslaughts of Kurdish tribes. They remained steadfast in their villages and free mountains, proud like the peaks of Shadakh, even terrifying Kurdish tribes and Turkish officials.

This is why, as we shall see, the authorities in Van first turned on the Shadakh region and tried to destroy it.

As we discussed earlier, during the five years of the constitutional era, the ARF did a lot of organisational work in the provinces. This was possible because members of Armenian political parties were no longer persecuted and started to work freely, setting up schools, defending the people from attacks, intervening in economic affairs and land disputes by raising issues with official bodies. If they did not get results in the provinces, they approached the central authorities to pressure governors to get results. However, the ARF's work took another direction with the outbreak of the European, and later, the Russo-Turkish war, so that the same people now began organising their self-defence for all kinds of scenarios.

All this work was carried out by the committees and sub-committees in the provinces. While it is true that most of the self-defence efforts in the provinces proved to be abortive, the fighting in Shadakh and Van showed how much had been achieved in that direction.

The Shadakh committee was noted by Armenian and government circles for its organisational work. Before the war, and even during mobilisation, it had great influence on the local authorities and the district administrator, making sure that a few important individuals in self-defence work were not conscripted and the military exemption tax was moderate in a few villages. However, this same committee became an object of scorn when the government's stance towards Armenians suddenly changed.

The most prominent activists in the Shadakh committee were:

1. Hovsep Choloian, a young native of Shadakh, who had graduated from the government teachers' academy in Van – the Dar-iul-Muallim. He first became a teacher and then an inspector of parish schools. He was a key activist.

2. Samuel Mesrobian, a young native of Shadakh. He also graduated from the government teachers' academy. He was the treasurer in the district government. A close associate of Hovsep Choloian, he was a link between the committee and the district governor.

3. Baghdig Simonian (Azad) was a peasant from Sivdgin. He had no formal education. He was a committee member and a military leader who became the main leader during the defence of Tagh.

4. Dikran Baghdasarian, also a young native of Tagh. He had graduated from the Catholic school in Van and became a teacher. In 1908 he went to Constantinople and

entered the military academy. When the war broke out, he was sent to the Caucasus as an officer and was wounded in the foot during the fighting at Keopri Keoy. Returning home on March 14, he participated in the defence of Shadakh.

Hovsep Choloian

The Turkish officials involved in the fighting in Shadakh were:

1. District administrator Hamdi Bey, an educated Turk from Constantinople. He had been in Europe and was a drunkard. He came to Shadakh at the beginning of 1913 and was initially a fair man. For example, he solved a problem between Gaghbi, Gorovank, Hinents, Jnoug and Daidzants Armenian villages and the Kurdish village of Sokants by upholding the law in favour of Armenians.

2. Secretary (Tahrirat Kiatibi) Shefket Bey, an Armenian-hating Turk.

3. District Attorney (Mudai Oumoumi) Ahmad Tevfik Bey, orginally from Konia, and an Armenian-hater.

4. Mufti Hasan, a semi-educated Armenian-hater.

Under the command of the district administrator of Shadakh, other than a considerable gendarmerie and militia force, were:

1. The chief of the Krav Lazki, and the bandit Shakir Agha, Gordu Bey and Kyalash.

2. Brahim, the chief of the Khavshdan.

3. The chief of the Khalilan Hasan Bey and Shakir.

4. The chief of the Yezdinan Msdafa and Saydon.

The above list is important because at the beginning of the war, when the massacre of Armenians had not been planned, the kaimakam organised an irregular force composed of these tribes and their leaders and went to war in Persia, returning two months later. It is noteworthy that these forces received their weapons in Bashkale and returned home armed. It is in this context that the fighting

Samuel Mesrobian

in Shadakh broke out.

When Jevdet returned to Van from the front on April 2 and prepared his hellish plans, his first secret instructions were sent to the kaimakam of Shadakh. On April 12 Hovsep Choloian – a well respected young Armenian – and five other young men – Bedros Saroian, Sahag Giulamirian, Boghos Bedrosian, Avedis Melkonian and Bayloz Sapoian – were arrested in broad daylight in Tagh.

Samuel, who was the most important man in the Shadakh organisation after Hovsep, had taken a one week vacation as an official and was in Van. He now had to return to Shadakh because of the arrest of Hovsep and the other five men, as well as the flight of other Armenian young men in Tagh.

Dikran Baghdasarian in an Ottoman officer's uniform

When he saw what was going on, Samuel went to his workplace – the court – and immediately spoke to the kaimakam about Hovsep's arrest. The kaimakam stated that the whole affair was because of a misunderstanding, blamed the police commissioner, and promised to release Hovsep within an hour. Given this promise, Samuel returned home without taking further action. After waiting for two hours, he went to the kaimakam's house and was told that the Ottoman official was asleep. Samuel went to the kaimakam's house a second time and was given the same answer. Previously, Samuel could always approach the kaimakam at will, and the latter did not take any steps without consulting Samuel. The two men spent hours exchanging their thoughts at the kaimakam's house. Now, the same Samuel was not received by the kaimakam. The problem became quite apparent: Hovsep's arrest was arranged by the governor to break relations between the authorities and Armenians.

Samuel gathered his friends and a few elders in Tagh for a meeting. His impressions were shared by Dikran, who had been wounded at the battlefront and had good relations with the kaimakam and other officials. Dikran had also intervened for Hovsep's release and had been treated in a similar manner.

The meeting declared itself a Military Command, designated the whole district a self-defence zone, and sent off a messenger to Van to inform others of what was happening. The relations between the local government and Armenians was now broken.

The task at hand was not simply about the defence of Tagh but the whole district, including the 50 Armenian villages dispersed over a large area of mountains and valleys. They had to cut off enemy access to these villages. Much of the planning had already been done and the men had to finalise them.

Tagh – a well known centre of sheep herding and shawl-making – became a key flash-point where both sides had their main forces.

The Armenians had 70 fighters and the government, which previously had 20–30 gendarmes, now had around 150 men. Their number had been increased over the previous weeks and included militia forces.

Tagh had a population of 220 households, which were divided into Upper, Lower and Watermill quarters. The Upper and Lower quarters lay on the right banks of Sivdgin and Tigris rivers, backing onto Kiureg mountain. The market was between these two quarters. The Watermill quarter was on the left bank of the Sivdgin river to the north-east, on the slopes of Jamlambeg, up to the location where the two rivers joined together. Three government buildings were on the left bank of the Tigris, upstream of the point where the two rivers met each other. These buildings were the offices of the state administration, the telegraph office and the local barracks.

There were three bridges on the Sivdgin river called the Watermill, Stone and Wooden bridges, while two other bridges over the Tigris were called the Government and Telegraph-Office bridges. Watermill Bridge was destroyed by the Armenians for defensive purposes at the beginning of the fighting.

The Watermill quarter had a commanding position over the Upper and Lower quarters. There were over 60 Armenian households there, including a newly-built, spacious, two-storey boy's school. Turkish officials also rented the nicer homes located in this quarter.

When Hovsep and the five men were arrested, the Armenians in the Watermill quarter moved to the Upper and Lower quarters, except for two houses. The Watermill quarter was otherwise left in Turkish hands, while Armenians controlled the Upper and Lower quarters. After this separation, all ties between the two camps were broken and each side took up positions against the other. The best known Armenian positions were:

1. The Der Markarian residence, on the right bank of the Tigris. Opposite this position, on the left bank of the Tigris, was the government building, which was the strongest enemy position.

   This Armenian position was held by 16 men under the command of Hovsep Karounian. He was a native of Tagh and a graduate of Ararots School in Van. During the [Hamidian] dictatorship, he had been arrested and exiled, but had been released and returned home during the Constitutional era.

2. The Karounian residence. This position overlooked the road to Van and Turkish positions. It was held by 14 men under the command of Cholo Der Bedrosian, who was Hovsep Choloian's father, an older fighter.

3. The Haji Mirsik residence, which overlooked Stone Bridge [Kare Gamourch]. It was held by 14 men under the direction of Krikor Haroutiunian. He was a native of Tagh and had seen three years' military service, when he had commanded 25 men. He avoided conscription and supported the self-defence work.

4. The Ayvazian residence, on the western side of Upper quarter. This became an important position after the loss of Sozvants village. The position was entrusted to 15 men under the command Bedros Gelgoian. He was a native of Tagh, had studied at the local school and was involved with the local trades' guild.

5. The Amrgi Hago residence overlooking the Wooden Bridge, the main link between the two quarters. This was called the Wooden Bridge position and was held by 12 men under the command of Shahen Gouzhigian, who was an older trader in the area.

6. The Klgants residence. This position overlooked the government building and other positions on a hill called Pert. Its defence was entrusted to a group of 13 men under the leadership of Milan Mouradkhanian, an Ottoman official.

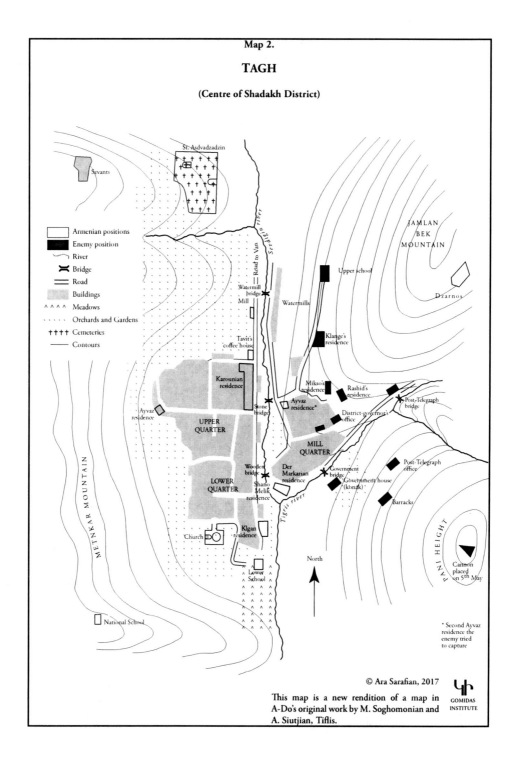

Map 2.

TAGH

(Centre of Shadakh District)

St. Asdvadzadzin

Szvants

JAMLAN
BEK
MOUNTAIN

Dzarnos

Legend:
- Armenian positions
- Enemy position
- River
- Bridge
- Road
- Buildings
- Meadows
- Orchards and Gardens
- Cemeteries
- Contours

Road to Van

Sevdghin river

Watermill
bridge
Mill

Watermills

Upper school

Klange's
residence

Tavit's
coffee house

Karounian
residence

Mikso's
residence

Rashid's
residence

Post-Telegraph
bridge

Ayvaz
residence

Stone
bridge

Ayvaz
residence*

District-governor's
office

UPPER
QUARTER

METNKAR MOUNTAIN

MILL
QUARTER

Post-Telegraph
office

Wooden
bridge

Der
Markarian
residence

Government
bridge

Government house
(konak)

LOWER
QUARTER

Shano
Melik
residence

Barracks

PANI HEIGHT

Klgan
residence

Church

North

Cannon
placed
on 5th May

Lower
School

National School

* Second Ayvaz
residence the
enemy tried
to capture

© Ara Sarafian, 2017

This map is a new rendition of a map in
A-Do's original work by M. Soghomonian and
A. Siutjian, Tiflis.

GOMIDAS
INSTITUTE

7. The National cave. This was behind Lower quarter, on the south-east slopes of Mount Kiureg, 100 metres above Tagh. This proved to be an important position, as it dominated two Turkish positions, as well as the main road running alongside the Tigris. This position was entrusted to two heroic figures, Ziro Mouradian of Dghasbad village, and Mourad Hagopian of Hashgants village. They were both young shepherds. These men terrorised the enemy with their firepower.

The most notable government positions in Tagh were:

1. Government building.
2. Upper Boys' School.
3. The Klange's residence, where the inspector (mustantik) lived.
4. Miko residence, where the population registrar (nufus memouri) lived.
5. The Rashid residence.
6. The Geroz residence, where the mufti lived.
7. Barracks.

The Turkish side was led by the kaimakam, police commissioner (komiser), and the judge Tevfik. Later, as we shall see, they were joined by the kaimakam of Nordouz, Khaled, and the artillery officer named Jelaleddin with two cannons.

While the Armenians prepared their positions, their military leaders ordered the occupation of key points in the district, thus delineating the Armenian-Muslim division of the area.

These key points were:

1. Shahrour Castle, which was a peak in the north of the district, on the southern slopes of Mt. Ardos. Two small rivers joined at this spot to form the Sivdgin river. There were two roads that followed the rivers, one leading to Vosdan over Pesantashd, the other going to Van over Khorzank. These two routes joined along the Sivdgin river and led to Tagh. Pesantashd and Khorzank were two plateaus that produced wheat and formed the northern border of the district. There were four villages on Pesantashd, and all four were Armenian inhabited, while there were some Kurdish villages on Khorzank with a total of 22 Armenian households, 12 of whom were in Georantashd village, and 10 at Mousgaven. Shahrour Castle was located at the intersection of the two rivers and roads. This position guarded the Van-Vosdan route and protected the Sivdgin valley.

    The defence of Shahrour Castle was entrusted to a group of 15 men under the leadership of Pazig Bedrosian. He was an older man from Sivdgin village.

2. Khlkdan Bridge. This bridge, as we saw, was on the Tigris, two hours to the south of Tagh, and was a key communications point to the south of the district. The defence of this point was important because the Khalilan, Khavshdan, Yezdinan and Alan Kurds of the district, as well as others from Parvari were expected to cross and threaten not only the Armenians villages in the south –

Armashd, Kajet, Dzidzants, but also Tagh itself. The defence of this bridge was entrusted to Haroutiun Gchoian from Gorovank and Azo Haroutiunian from Hinents.

Other than Khlkdan Bridge on the Tigris, there were two other bridges further south, the Chalgants and Heshat bridges, which were built of wood and were easily destroyed at the beginning of the fighting.

3. Pols village. This was to the north-west of Tagh, near the border with Mogs, on the slope of Varesar Mountain. This position had two functions. First, it had to guard the road from Mogs, and, second, it had to defend the bridge next to Jvgadan village over the Sivdgin river against several Kurdish villages. The defenders at Pols were made up of 15 men under the command of Set Bozoian, who was a peasant and a teacher from Dzidzants village.

4. Hashgants village. This village was an hour to the north of Tagh, on a hilltop, on the left bank of the Sivdgin. It had to block Dzarnos and the route of Kurdish forces from surrounding villages over the Kasr bridge. This location was defended by Chato and 20 men.

   Chato or Arshag Bedrosian was a brave and dynamic man from Sivdgin. In 1911, the murder of Aghtamar parish inspector Rafael Yeritsian became a major issue around Van. The murder took place in Gargar and was carried out by Hiuseyin Agha of Takhmants with the help of his brother Haji Yaghoub. This murder had to be avenged and one beautiful day Haji Yaghoub was shot dead in the village of Khrordents in Gargar. Chato took part in that revenge killing.

5. Sozvants village. This village was half an hour to the west of Tagh on the slopes of Mount Kiureg. This was a very important location. It defended the rear of Tagh and controlled a busy route. More importantly, it was the only point that linked Tagh to outlying areas. All orders from Tagh were taken to Sozvants at night and then to all points through mountain passes, including to Pesantashd and Van. The same route was used for communications from Van and outlying areas. If Sozvants was lost, it would not have been possible to maintain communications with the outside world, as happened on one occasion. The defence of that important point was entrusted to a group of 20 men under the command of Sahag Choloian.

Other than these important points, there was also a mobile force of 30 men under the command of Azad, who was a member of the military command.

The most notable couriers were:

1. Dikran Sarkisian, a native of Tagh, a teacher by profession, and a sensitive and brave young man.
2. Markar Movsesian, a native of Tagh and a teacher.
3. Mardiros Bedrosian, a peasant from Verin Tarents and a heroic youth.
4. Garabed Kaligian of Sivdgin.

There were also notable women couriers and we will talk about them later.

The government also took precautions, perhaps even a month earlier. For example, it increased the number of sentries at Khan, near Shahrour Castle, to 15 men and placed additional men nearby at Komer. There were also men placed at Sivdgin village and to its south – the latter patrolling villages under the pretext of collecting taxes.

Furthermore, Kurdish tribal leaders received orders to be ready to move against Armenians, as we saw in the case of those returning with their arms from the battlefield.

Armenians and government forces thus came face to face during preparations for an unequal battle. The Armenians, fewer in numbers, were strong in their fighting quality and prepared for an epic struggle.

As we saw earlier, the most respected young man in Tagh, Hovsep Choloian and five others, were unexpectedly arrested. Following these arrests, other Armenian young men disappeared from public view while Samuel, who had just returned from Van, and the military officer Dikran, who had returned from the front, went to the kaimakam and requested Hovsep's release. The kaimakam did not accept their intervention. Indeed, Samuel, who went to the kaimakam's house twice, was turned away on both occasions. This was something Samuel had never experienced before, so a special meeting of the local defence committee was held and it became a military command with a supply committee attached to it. The military command then mobilised the defence of the region and sent messengers to Van, as well as orders to outlying areas.

All of this took place on April 11, Easter Sunday, when there was no activity at the market. The next day, April 12, when normal life was to resume, there was much anxiety in the air and no activity at the market. Young Armenians remained in hiding and there was complete mistrust on both sides. The Armenians in the Watermill quarter quickly moved to the centre of Tagh when news arrived that nine Armenians of Armshad, who had been returning to Tagh through Parvari, had been killed by Kurds. That news made the situation much worse and Armenians began preparing for battle, as did government and militia forces, thereby stopping all movement on the main street.

The women also joined the intense work by fortifying the battle lines. The Stone Bridge position, which had been weak because of its many wooden shops, was turned into a stone fortress in a few hours. It was built with huge rocks brought by the women of Tagh from far away. The women's work made the defensive position impregnable.

This is what the journal of the military command, which neatly noted developments, recorded for that day:

> April 12. We have been to visit Hovsep. The police commissioner has demanded the surrender of all arms, which is impossible to accept. We've sent a messenger to the city [Van] to let them know that our situation is very serious and we will not be able to avoid incidents. There is great activity in the militia force. The enemy has begun to take up positions in the Watermill quarter.

> April 13. Conditions have remained the same. The work continues inside our lines, while outside everything is quiet. Neither side disturbs the silence. The mistrust is getting worse.

On that day, the kaimakam and 15 gendarmes went through the market to the Klgants residence. There were some families from Watermill quarter there, including some young men making military preparations. There was an armed young man stationed at the door. The kaimakam asked the young man why he was armed and standing there. The young man answered that there were people in the house and he had been detailed to guard the premises. Upon hearing this response, the kaimakam pulled back and did not dare to disarm the youngster. Apparently the kaimakam had come to station sentries in that building and realised that there would be a clash if he proceeded. This incident was proof of a government plot and obliged the military command to take some practical steps of its own as recorded in its journal.

> April 13. This is the third day of Hovsep's arrest. We have drawn up our plans for defence. We have arranged the units, positions and weapons accordingly. After midday, the order was given to stop all work in the lower quarter and move. An order was also given to cut the telegraph wires in the upper areas and to block the roads. We are informed that the telegraph wire near Hashgants has been cut in three places and the roads have been blocked at three locations.

April 14 ended with the following incident. The military command decided to occupy the Der Markarian and Rashid houses on the other side of the valley. The residents of these houses had already moved to the centre of Tagh. At 8 p.m., the Der Markarian unit crossed the Wooden Bridge and occupied the Der Markarian house. Immediately afterwards, 10 men proceeded by the same route towards Rashid's house, which was located within Muslim lines. Before getting to their destination, however, the men encountered a night guard who opened fire and others joined in from Muslim positions. The Armenians responded with a few shots and withdrew, some of them entering the Der Markarian premises and others going to the military command to report on developments. The encounter stopped there and the military command gave up on taking over Rashid's house because of the dangers.

Both the military command and its enemy were involved in similar activities when the kaimakam resorted to Jevdet's methods. He sent one of his employees, chief tax collector Mansour, to talk to the Armenians and convince them to open the market and go to work as normal.

The military command responded by saying that Armenians were ready to return to normal work if there was security which could only be assured when:

1. Hovsep Choloian was freed.

2. The gendarmes and the militia forces left the positions they occupied.

3. The militia forces left Tagh.

Naturally, the kaimakam did not accept these conditions, though the negotiations allowed him to gain time and wait for reinforcements.

In order to better understand the developments of the first few days, we can present some official messages between the kaimakam of Shadakh, the governor of Van, and other officials – communications which Armenians found in government offices after the Turks had fled.

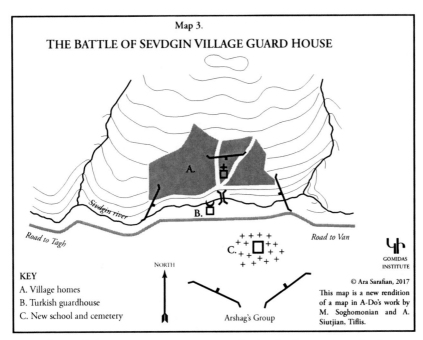

Map 3.

THE BATTLE OF SEVDGIN VILLAGE GUARD HOUSE

KEY

A. Village homes
B. Turkish guardhouse
C. New school and cemetery

NORTH

Arshag's Group

GOMIDAS INSTITUTE

© Ara Sarafian, 2017
This map is a new rendition of a map in A-Do's work by M. Soghomonian and A. Siutjian, Tiflis.

Here is the first of those communications which the kaimakam had written to the governor.

To the governor's office.

Herewith I send you information about conditions in our district.

1. When, in accordance with your orders and the records we hold, we demanded that well known people surrender their weapons, they raised conditions.

2. When they found out that it was impossible to set conditions, the response, on that first day, was to close all the shops. The treasurer Samuel also departed.

The following day, all of the men in the district disappeared and the telegraph wires were cut that same night. Our units which tried to repair the wires were attacked.

3. Today they set up positions at the windows of some houses and other locations in Tagh dominating over government positions in a completely rebellious manner. Since telegraph wires have been cut, we ask your excellency for the necessary force and other means to contain this movement. We will not be able to defend ourselves for long because of a lack of rifles and ammunition.

13 April Kaimakam Hamdi

The situation remained unchanged between 14-16. No one was on the streets and there was no movement between the Watermill and other quarters. There was only movement inside the quarters – the movement of forces – as both sides were strengthening their lines. The Armenians first strengthened the Der Markarian position overlooking both the bridge at the government building and the main road.

The kaimakam could see all this but was not confident enough to forbid it because any such attempt would have been enough for the fighting to start, and he did not want that to happen. He was waiting for reinforcements and orders. Therefore, tax collector Mansour's negotiations were continuing.

The military command also continued with negotiations, though it was convinced that nothing would come of them. It continued because it also had to win time. A messenger had been sent to Van but had not returned. They expected a great deal from him.

While negotiations were continuing in Tagh, the military command issued orders and a number of significant developments took place in surrounding areas pointing to the fighting ahead.

As we saw earlier, there was a group of 20 sentries placed at Sivdgin village under the command of onbashi [corporal] Bahri. This was an important government force.

The village was at a bend in a valley, on the right bank of Sivdgin river, where the slopes ascended to Gadar Mountain. On the left bank of the river was the road between Van and Tagh. A house on the right bank of the river at the edge of the village housed the government sentries. Opposite this position, on the other side of the river, was a cemetery and a new Armenian school that had not yet been completed.

It was important to remove the sentries in Sivdgin. A similar operation had been carried out when other incidents had happened in December. Although Sivdgin had around 20 local armed Armenians, it was decided to simplify the task with the participation of Chato and a few men who were defending Hashgants village in the same valley. By this time the defenders at Sivdgin had blocked the road to Van, the route the gendarmes would have used to escape.

When the gendarmes noticed these movements in the village, they took up their arms and came onto the road as if they were on an exercise. At that time Chato and his men approached the village without being seen, took up positions on the rocks above the cemetery and ordered, "Taslim!" [Surrender!]

This manoeuvre was completely unexpected and the gendarmes immediately rushed into the school building and started firing. A battle began that lasted for one and a half hours. The gendarmes resisted until the Armenians surrounded the school. The first gendarme to be killed was Onbashi Bahri, a brave fighter. Another gendarme was killed with him. These deaths were a great blow to the other gendarmes who put down their arms and surrendered. The Armenians had one wounded.

After capturing the gendarmes at Sivdgin, the daring Chato and his men proceeded to Shahrur castle to remove the sentries at Khan and Komer villages at the bottom of the mountain. However, before getting there, the shooting at Sivdgin had already frightened and dispersed the government troops at those positions. Indeed, they had fled in such haste that they had left a considerable quantity of ammunition for Chato and his men.

While the operations in Sivdgin area were removing government troops, similar incidents were taking place elsewhere in the district.

At the same time, Arif the tax collector was patrolling the region of Gaghbi and Kajet under the pretext of collecting taxes. Usually, tax collectors were accompanied by only one gendarme, but on this occasion Arif was with 20 gendarmes. On April 15, when he was in Gaghbi, he took six gendarmes and went to Tagh, while the remaining 14 went to Namir's house at Sak. When Giulamir Mouradian of Dzidzants village, who was well known for his bravery, heard about these developments, he came to Sak during the night with a few of his men and surrounded Namir's house. He was expected to remove this group of gendarmes. Giulamir first offered the gendarmes surrender terms and, when he was refused, fighting began. As the gendarmes in the house were able to defend themselves for a long time, Giuimar planned to burn the premises down. The gendarmes were thus forced to find a way out, and two of them opened a passage through the rear wall of the

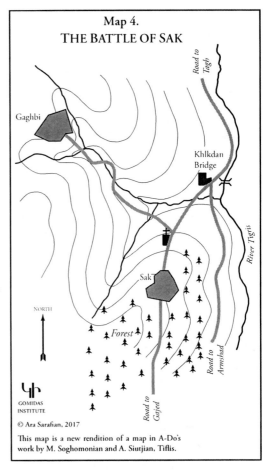

Map 4.
THE BATTLE OF SAK

© Ara Sarafian, 2017

This map is a new rendition of a map in A-Do's work by M. Soghomonian and A. Siutjian, Tiflis.

building and made for Khlkdan Bridge. They were killed during their attempt. A few gendarmes also made for the main road and were shot dead, while some others were able to get into the stable and fought from there. The fighting intensified and the hot-blooded Giulamir and Kajettsi Apro threw caution to the winds and were killed. At that moment Azo and a few men defending Khlkdan Bridge arrived and attacked the stable. All but two of the gendarmes were killed. One Armenian, Hovig, was also killed. The gendarmes lost 12 men, while the Armenians lost three but captured 14 good rifles, which were important spoils in those days.

While armed Armenians were evicting government forces in the north and south of the district, Kurdish forces started attacking in the east.

In the eastern zone – east of Tagh – there were a few small Armenian villages which could not be defended. These were Vakhrov, Arikom, Akrous, Krments, Sheghjants, Arosig, Kvers, Bagh and Babonts, as well as Hashgants, Shino, Shamo and Yeritsou Mzras, a total of 100 households. When the Kurds in this area heard about the deteriorating situation in Tagh, they wanted to attack these Armenians, who were forced to leave for Krmentsou and Babonts Mzre.

The military committee recorded the following concerning these days.

April 14. Chato writes that the cordon at Sivdgin was removed, with two of the 20 [gendarmes] killed, while the rest surrendered.

April 15. Grbo of Babonts Mzre came and related that the Armenians of that region had gathered at Krments and Babonts Mzre. A considerable number of Kurds beyond Arosig had gone on the attack, but they were repelled by the villagers.

April 16. Set writes that Giulamir and his men had surrounded Sak and the fighting started with the policemen. Our people captured 14 rifles – nine Martinis and five Mausers.

These incidents took place before April 16, which marked an important date in the developing situation. As we saw earlier, by now the news of the arrest of Hovsep Choloian and the other five men had reached Van. There was much concern among the young men as Armenian leaders prepared to send a delegation to Shadakh to calm matters down, something that Jevdet also wished for. However, they were convinced that their leaders were wrong to send such a delegation to dampen the successes achieved by the brave Armenians of Shadakh. Eventually Ishkhan and three comrades set off for Shadakh, and when the news of their departure reached Sivdgin, the Armenians armed themselves and released the 18 gendarmes they had captured. Thus, as the Armenians in Sivdgin waited for the peace delegation and released their prisoners, Ishkhan and his three comrades fell victim of treachery.

As April 17 arrived, the Armenians of Tagh had no idea of what had happened in Hirj and became impatient as they had no news from Van. On the other hand, tensions were heightened because of the news that was coming in from surrounding areas. "We have to resolve this tension sapping our morale," the military command decided, as it ordered its men to forbid the movement of gendarmes and militia forces in the streets.

At 10 a.m., a militiaman came out of the government building and tried to cross the bridge to the Waterill quarter. In accordance with that day's orders, Tavit Giulamirian, who was in the Der Markarian position, called out to the militiaman and stated that it was forbidden to cross the bridge. The militiaman ignored the warning and continued to cross it. After a third warning he was shot. The bullet hit the militiaman in the chest and he managed to turn back and collapsed on the doorstep of the government building.

This incident sparked the fighting in Tagh, with both sides exchanging fire. The fighting continued until evening and both sides continued to fire, though not with the same intensity. This was because the military command had ordered its forces to conserve their ammunition so that Armenians responded to five or six shots fired by the enemy with only one.

In order to relate how the fighting in Tagh progressed between April 17 and May 4, let us turn to the daily entries of the military command, as well as the official communications between the kaimakam of Tagh, the governor of Van, and other officials leading the fighting elsewhere.

Here is the record of the military command:

April 17. A policeman was arrested in front of Kelgants position. At 6:30 (11:30) the order was given to stop the enemy's movement. Rifle fire. Chato informs us that the policemen at Khan had escaped, with the village being burnt down by our men, who also captured 240 Mauser pieces [?] and other military supplies. As far as we could ascertain, the enemy only lost five men today, while we lost none.

April 18. Ziro and Mouro were sent to the National Cave before dawn today to stop the movement of the enemy.

April 19. There was little fighting today. All movement between their positions has stopped, but ours have continued through passages between houses. It is possible to move from one side of Tagh to the other without difficulty.

April 20. A great deal of smoke could be seen from the direction of Komer after midday. That means our men have succeeded. During the night they ordered the Watermill bridge to be burnt down because of the possibility of enemy forces crossing it in the darkness. That is no longer possible.

We have lost the eastern region. The enemy has destroyed a great deal and took a significant number of families as prisoners.

April 22. It has been quiet since 2:00 (7:00). We received a letter from Sozvants reporting that the Armenian village of Hashgants has been burnt down. There is fighting at Pols and a strong unit went there to help. During the evening we heard that the Kurds who had gathered around Komer had left their homes and moved to Dzarnos. At 2 (7) a.m. we heard from Bayloz, who had escaped from jail. He stated that Hovsep and his comrades were killed while in jail.

April 23. Today we sent out three scouts to observe the enemy positions. Our men can easily go right up to their lines and open fire, terrorising all their positions.

April 25. We sent master-builder Manoug with a few workers to destroy Khlkdan Bridge. They have been working on the bridge for ten days but the bridge is still standing. All of our anxieties concern that front and we have to admit that our forces there are quite weak.

April 27. Today commemorates the enthronement of Sultan Reshad and the Kurds are celebrating by discharging their rifles. We taxed the rich to meet the needs of the soldiers.

April 29. Sahag exploded a bomb in front of enemy positions that shook all of Mednkar. It was as if there was a wedding, people singing, shouting and cheering everywhere. Spirits are high.

April 30. We decided to cast a cannon under Master Garabed's direction.

May 1. Azad writes that the people of Dzarnos are trying to cross Hashgants Bridge but our guards have not been successful in holding them back. They have lost five men and are withdrawing.

May 3. We started using the cannon we cast and are destroying the enemy positions in an amazing manner. The enemy has been abandoning its positions during the day but rebuilding them at night. They write from Dzidzants that the rabble from Mogs has crossed into our district. We ordered our forces in that area to retrench themselves in suitable defensive positions on the Mogs-Shadakh border.

Time: 3:00 (8:00) Azad and Chatoian came to confer with us. We decided to send Chatoian to the lower region [South] to take care of things there. His task will be to move the villages in the Gaghbi valley to Dzidzants and surrounding areas. We want to consolidate our position because we can not continue to fight on such a long front.

May 6. We built a new half metre long 4 cm calibre cannon today and used it to fire four shells.

Now, let's see what the Turkish officials were writing during those days.

To the governor's office,

Yesterday at 6 (11) o'clock, Chalank, one of the servants of Kravtsi Kourt Bek, was seriously wounded by a bullet fired from Hovan Effendi's position while crossing the government bridge. So far, the fighting continues furiously. The government building is under heavy fire and the Upper quarter, where Muslim officials are sheltering, is in danger. We are defending our positions everywhere, but the situation is grave and we only have 1,200 rounds left for the Mausers. We need a strong military force to dislodge these people. They keep getting reinforcements from the villages. We will soon not have the strength to continue and ask you to send us help as quickly as possible.

17 April, Kaimakam Hamdi

To the Kaimakam,

1. The gendarmes located in the school have been hungry for three days. If there is bread and mutton in Heshat-Shadakh, send as much as necessary. Please send four soldiers to the school from the new forces that will reach you shortly.

2. We have many soldiers between the school and our position and we've not suffered any losses.

3. The soldiers located between our position and the school are almost out of ammunition.

4. Two of the Martini rifles used by our soldiers are not working and we ask for replacements until they are repaired.

5. We have no news from the watermill. Despite our many calls, the workers and policemen there do not respond, nor do they open their door.

6. The gendarmes and the families of officials at our position have not had anything to eat for two days other than dry bread. This situation should be changed.

7. Two soldiers have been guarding the door to Zareh's house since yesterday in accordance with your orders. They are conserving their ammunition as much as possible.

8. Please send us any important news.

Judge Mahmad Tevfik(*)

To the Kaimakam,

At 7:30 p.m. (12:30), 15 soldiers were sent from Vakhrov to Akrous. The courier Yusuf met them on the road. They better not have fled. Other than those soldiers, I have sent five men for supplies, so I now have no reserves. I have stationed my soldiers in different parts of Tag, as far as Hashgants, and unless new forces arrive, I can not send you men from these important positions. I have just been informed that the Dzarnos imam's son, who was arrested at Sivdgin, has been released and will arrive tonight.

April 18 Shefket (*)

To the Kaimakam,

Thank God that we ended the day intact. Send ammunition for 50 Mausers and 50 Martinis, otherwise we will be put to shame. We have no bullets, we can not defend ourselves. Send some flour and mutton for the school and our positions. We did not receive supplies yesterday – neither ammunition, bread, or mutton. If it is impossible to do so, order Toysun Bey to send some grain to Emin Bey's residence to be ground into flour. It seems that this problem is getting prolonged. If you have any news about our cannon, please let us know to console us. We have had to post a permanent and independent force to defend Ayvaz's house as ordered. The four gendarmes detailed to go to the school have not yet arrived. Last night the Karounian and Gamourch positions were strengthened. The enemy fired on our positions continuously this morning. The Mulla can not send forces to Ayvaz's residence from here. If you do not send bullets this evening, it will be impossible to defend that position from here. The men under my command are not regular soldiers and don't know what orders are. They don't know their commanders either and can not withstand hardship. They rush to wherever there is comfort and bread, therefore it is necessary to be strict with them.

19 April Judge Tevfik(*)

Kout Bey and Kyalash Aghas,

The soldiers here at the school have neither bullets nor bread left. As soon as you receive my note, send two sheep, flour and ammunition. If you delay, the forces at these two positions will not be able to withstand any pressure.

Saleh Agha and some men should come immediately in order to hold Ayvaz's residence at the bridge.

19 April, Judge Tevfik

To the Kaimakam,

I hear that the kaimakam of Nordouz, Khaled Bey, and 60 men, have reached Vakhrov but they have been caught in a fight with the rebels at Arikom and Krments. After sorting out the rebels, he should come to Tagh.

19 April, Shevket

Unit Commander Kyamil Bey,

We have been fighting for eight days against well entrenched rebels in Tagh. The resistance at Tagh is weakening the tribes' morale. There are 500 fedayis sheltering in the houses, with others continually arriving from the surrounding destroyed villages. Unless we can occupy the hills surrounding Tagh, we will not be able to do anything. For this reason it is imperative that we receive a cannon under the command of an able officer. Although the long-planned rebellion has been suddenly unleashed and we've not had the opportunity to make the necessary preparations, we are nevertheless defending the honour of the government.

19 April Kaimakam Hamdi

To the Governor's Office,

The Alan, Yezdinan and Khavshdan tribes need rifles. The only men under arms and ready to fight today are 60 of Kourt Bek's men. Our numbers are superior to those of the enemy, and even if we have five rifles to their one, we still ask you to send us 50 good riflemen. Despite all of our precautions, the Armenians dispersed in Hayots Tsor, Vosdan and the mountains are about to come into our region. Please send five cases each of Mauser and Martini cartridges.

19 April, Kaimakam Hamdi

To the Governor's Office,

The fighting at all positions continues day and night. The soldiers and tribes have only 2,000 bullets left. The rebels from the torched villages are joining their central forces. Our own forces are losing men, as the tribal soldiers are deserting to join Kurds in the looting of surrounding villages. We estimate the number of armed Armenians at 600. The mills have been completely taken over. Our supplies can barely last a week. If the current situation continues, there will be famine. The tribes and tribal leaders are also of the same opinion. We request regular forces, ammunition and two mountain cannons as a matter of urgency.

20 April, Kaimakam Hamdi

To the Governor's Office,

The fighting in Tagh is getting more serious and the rebels increasing by the day. The mal miudir of Nordouz was martyred today. We have no news of our forces in Hayots Tsor, Gevash and Mogs. Our greatest problem is the lack of military supples; we haven't received any and those that were sent might have been captured. For that reason it is imperative that you send suppies for our Martini and Mauser rifles and a proper cannon as soon as possible so that I can clear Tagh completely – completely!

Yesterday we liberated the Kurdish village of Komer which had been besieged by Armenians. The nearby Armenian village of Hasghants was destroyed.

23 April, Kaimakam Hamdi

Telegram

To the Kaimakam of Shadakh

I've despatched 10 cases of military supplies to you via Goroban; a detachment of soldiers will also be leaving soon.

24 April Hayots Tsor Miudir Rifat

To Hamdi Bey, Kaimakam of Shadakh and Khaled Bey, Kaimakam of Nordouz.

I received your cipher telegraph of April 21 and, next day, April 22, 10 cases of ammunition for Mausers were despatched to Hayots Tsor for Shadakh. The miudir there has informed us that the supplies were received and are about to be sent on. I am very confident that these supplies will be with you today. Continue working decisively. It is important to pressure and beat these rebels. I wrote to divisional commander Kamil Bey to send a cannon to destroy their positions and hope it is already with you.

Governor Jevdet

To the Kaimakam,

1. At 4:00 (9:00) p.m. they opened sudden and sustained fire but to no avail. Thank God we had no casualties.

2. Today at 12:00 (5:00) Sargeant Osman killed an Armenian near the bridge during their assault.

3. We are all thankful for the good news you sent us yesterday. God willing the cannon will arrive tonight.

4. We have not received the Martini ammunition you sent us yesterday. Please send it this evening.

5. Please send, in addition, four cases of Mauser ammunition for distribution among the soldiers.

27 April, Judge Tevfik

To the Governor's Office,

Enemy forces are becoming greater while our forces are unfortunately diminishing because of looting. Looting has depleted our forces and diminishing numbers have become an obstacle to our occupation of the weaker Armenian villages.

Lazki from Nordouz, after occupying and destroying the villages of Krments and Arikom on his way, incited the Kurdish forces in our central positions to abandon them and take part in the looting. The result was that for the next few days we could hardly defend our positions.

The first blow we were dealt by the revolution was the break-up of our police units and the subsequent loss of our best policemen in Sivdgin-Sak. Thus the government's most disciplined and effective force was destroyed. And, because the revolution suddenly exploded, the policemen were divided into different, disorganised units, so that there has been no force capable to checking Kurdish imprudence. God willing, when the problems are over, we will hand you a list of sergeants and corporals who constantly feigned illness and abandoned their positions. You can be assured that we remain steadfast and thanks to our unwavering and cold-blooded stance, we have been able to oppose Armenian designs and sacrifices and have occupied and held onto the Upper quarter of Tagh for 15 days, despite increasing enemy numbers.

Today our forces number 250 men, barely 100 of whom have Mausers, and 50 Martinis. The rest have pistols and Greek [*sic*] weapons. Other than the Mausers, the remaining weapons have run out of ammunition. The enemy has been amassing the latest weapons and lots of ammunition for their plans over 30 years. These were supposedly to be used against Kurdish raids but are now actually used against the government. In order to give these rebels their just reward as soon as possible, I again dare to ask for the necessary cannon and plenty of ammunition for the useless Martinis and pistols.

29 April, Kaimakam Hamdi

To Kaimakam of Shadakh Hamdi Bey and Kaimakam of Nordouz Khaled Bey,
The cannon is on its way and should be there soon. We are pressing the rebels in Van every day and in a few days it will be over. It is very appropriate that Lazki remains with you. I was very pleased with him and I also expect great services from him there. Please let all the tribal leaders know that I salute them. I wrote to divisional commander Kyamil Bey to immediately send 10 cases of military supplies to Shadakh. The consignment should soon be with you. I expect great dedication and sacrifice from all of you in wiping out these unbelievers [*kaffirs*]. Do not allow Lazki to go anywhere until the work at Tagh is finished.

5 May, Governor Jevdet.

According to the journal of the Armenian military command and the communications between the Turkish officials, we can see that the condition of Armenians in outlying areas was gradually getting worse.

The kaimakam of Nordouz, Khaled Bey, came to the aid of government forces in Shadakh with 60 gendarmes and some officials. He, according to the official communications, was killed in Tagh.

Lazki, the tribal leader of the Krav and the son of Shakir the bandit with his horde have completed the destruction of Hayots Tsor.

Khaled Bey attacked Armenians as he passed through the eastern villages, destroying them as he went. When Lazki and his horde arrived, he ompleted Khaled Bey's work.

It is important to note the following at this point.

As we saw, at the beginning of the unrest, the Armenians in the eastern regions were forced out by the Kurds and came to Krments and Babonts Mrze villages. The Kurds besieged these two villages and were opposed by two brave Armenians: Hago of Krments and Aghegi Manoug who led the defence for three or four days. Hago, who isolated himself in a cave, continued to fight until he was tricked, captured and tortured to death. The population was left defenceless and subjected to the brutalities of the horde. 130 were killed or taken away as prisoner and the rest fled to Tagh and elsewhere.

The Armenians were attacked not only by gendarmes and militiamen but also tribal leaders with Kurdish mobs. As Jevdet wrote, "I was very pleased with Lazki and I also expect great services from him over there. Please let all tribal leaders know that I salute them."

The horde from Mogs crossed into Shadakh and threatened Armenians in the western regions of the district. The southern region was also threatened by Kurds. For that reason the Armenian military command sent master builders to destroy Khlkdan Bridge.

The situation in Tagh also got more serious. Hovsep and his comrades were taken at night to the telegraph office bridge and killed. One of them – Bayloz Sapoian – was miraculously able to throw himself into the river, where the current carried him downstream and flung him against the rocks in the river. He finally washed up in the Armenian quarter, half dead. As the attacks from the boys' school increased, the military command decided to destroy the Watermill Bridge.

Despite these developments, Armenian morale in Tagh was not weakened but actually heightened under the threat of new dangers. The Armenian church was turned into a forge, with people bringing household copper, metal weights and other metal objects for smelting. The work progressed, as men prepared gun-power, repaired damaged weapons, and filled cartridges. As if this was not enough, the people of Shadakh, despite the difficult circumstances, created a unique cannon. It had quite a long barrel made of five layers of white tin, wrapped in two layers of telegraph wire, and then fitted into a wooden casing. It was a primitive, even comical cannon, which nevertheless terrorised the enemy.

"We placed the cannon at Okhnigian's residence and began to bombard the Klange position. It was successful and destroyed all of the window shutters so that the terrorised enemy withdrew to the neighbouring house," the military command recorded.

It should not be surprising that the kaimakam of Shadakh wrote to the divisional commander that "The resistance at Tagh is weakening the tribes' morale. There are 500 fedayis sheltering in the houses."

He also wrote to the governor: "Our numbers are greater than those of the enemy, but even if we have five rifles to their one, we still ask that you despatch 50 good riflemen to us."

The kaimakam did not think five to one superiority in numbers was sufficient to suppress the Shadakh rebels. This was the psychology of Ottoman officials during the fighting.

As for the fighting over 20 days of conflict, the situation grew more complicated for the Armenians, although they fought heroically. The eastern villages were destroyed, the

Kurds of Mogs crossed into Shadakh in the west, Hashgants village was burnt down, and there was a massive movement of Kurds in the south.

The enemy forces pressed forward in the east, west and south, with only the north not providing negative news for the military command.

Indeed, the Armenian fighters in the north blocked the arrival of government forces. The clashes that took place there were on a larger scale. There was a greater number of Armenian refugees there too. We will now look at developments there, as they were closely linked to those in Tagh.

Chapter XIX

The Clashes in Pesantashd

When talking about the northern region during the battle of Shadakh, we mean Pesantashd. This was a small area in the north. There was also another beautiful plateau in this region, Khorzank. However, during the fighting, Pesantashd was of greater strategic significance.

The Pesantashd region was a pretty basin that was 12 versts (7 miles) long and 7 versts (5 miles) wide, surrounded by mountains – the giant peaks of Ardos, Tsmen, Karaplakh and Paradodig. In spring, this basin was covered with water, which evaporated in May, making the soil very fertile. Therefore, despite its small size, Pesantashd was considered the breadbasket of the district. However, the area was often so waterlogged that it took longer to dry and the planting season was missed, leaving the people without a harvest.

There were four Armenian villages in this beautiful basin – Aregh, Gaynemeran, Shidan and Gaghazis. Administratively, Pesantashd was part of Shadakh district, but in terms of its self-defence, it was linked to Gevash and its sub-committee was answerable to the Gevash committee. Consequently, during the fighting, Pesantashd became a sanctuary for the people of Gevash, as well as the major centre for the fighters from that same area.

Levon Shaghoian

It has to be said that among the districts of Van, after Shadakh, Gevash was top in terms of the strength of its committee and the dedication of its youth. A good indication of this fact could be seen in the Atanan incidents, which took place in December, in response to the destruction of Pelou.

Within the Gevash organisation, in terms of military prowess, the most daring fighter was Levon Shaghoian, who was the Armenian commander during the Atanan fighting.

Born in Kharagants on the shores of Lake Van, and having spent his childhood in awe of Aghtamar, Levon was sent to Aghtamar for his schooling but had to leave in his fifth year. This was because the teachers separated into two camps and printed *Dzovag* and *Godosh* news-sheets attacking each other in an unseemly manner. A few mature students, who objected to their teachers' arguments, started to print their own news-sheet *Griv* and attacked the entire teaching body. Thus the exchanges got more complicated, school-life was undermined, the fifth year was closed down, and the students in the top class – including Levon – were sent away. One could see that even at school Levon had the spirit to struggle. Two or three years later, when Levon was watering his family's fields, he had a fight with a Kurd who had cut off the water course to them and killed him. Thereafter, Levon became a fugitive but remained the dynamic leader in charge of organising the defence of that region.

Levon was assisted by:

1. Asbo Krikorian of Untsag village in Gevash. He was the son of a very poor family and semi-literate. He took to the work of defending his people, even to the extent of leaving his family.

2. Mgrdich Manougian of Haght village in Gargar. He was a graduate of the Aghtamar school and was a teacher.

3. Arshag Allahverdian from Yeghekis village in Gargar. He studied at Aghtamar and became a teacher. In the spring of 1913 he and Mgrdich Manougian killed Haso and Kyarim, the sons of Abas Agha of Pergri village in Gargar and became fugitives.

4. Mihran Chatoian.

5. Apraham of Nor Kiugh.

These individuals were the self-defence committee of Gevash.

When Hovsep Choloian was arrested in Tagh and relations between Armenians and the government were severed, the military command in Tagh sent a messenger to Van as well as Vosdan for help. When Levon got this news he immediately took a force of 40 men and went to Tagh through Pesantashd – without realising that there were similar treacherous plans for Gevash as well.

On April 20 Levon left Pesantashd for Tagh and there were incidents in Pesantashd that same day.

The road between Vosdan and Tagh passed through Pesantashd, as did the telegraph wires. There were two routes between Gevash and Pesantashd. One started at Vosdan and passed through the rocky Askan valley, while the other started at Hili village. Both routes were difficult with steep ascents and joined each other at the Paradodig mountain pass, thereafter turning into a sharp descent into Pesantashd. Thus Paradodig, which was on one of the slopes of Mt. Ardos extending westwards, formed the northern edge of Pesantashd, as well as a defensive line that could block the way of government troops.

The first clash took place on April 16 when seven gendarmes set off for Tagh. As these gendarmes approached Paradodig mountain pass, they realised that it was blocked. The pass had been blocked by Armenian forces in Pesantashd, as ordered by Levon when he passed through. When the gendarmes tried to get through, their way remained closed, and there was shooting. The fighting did not last long, as one gendarme was killed and the others fled towards Vosdan.

After a few hours, 50 gendarmes were sent from Vosdan to punish the Armenian rebels. A group of Armenians also blocked their way, so a furious battle took place that lasted until evening. The gendarmes couldn't do anything. Paradodig remained steadfast and the gendarmes withdrew to Hili as soon as it was dark. The fighting continued on April 17 April with the 50 gendarmes who had been reinforced by another 30. The fighting continued until evening, with the Paradodig defenders remaining victorious. The fighting flared up again with the addition of more troops from Vosdan. Enemy numbers had thus reached 100. Yet again, the gendarmes had no success, and the fighting continued in the same manner until April 20, when the gendarmes were recalled. They withdrew in shame and went on to display their bravery elsewhere on weaker, unarmed people.

While the Paradodig fighting continued, the aforementioned incidents took place in Hayots Tsor.

On the eve of April 20, around 50 men and boys were murdered in Hirj. April 19-20 saw the destruction of upper Hayots Tsor, the massacres of Gem and Ankgh, and the fighting at Ishkhani Kom.

We also saw how the government, under the influence of the events in December, sent its troops to Sbidag Vank and Bltents, and how the population of those two villages, as well as those of Atanants, had to flee as their villages were destroyed.

While the massacre and destruction in Hayots Tsor assumed huge proportions, Gevash remained undisturbed, though it was a misleading quiet. Then the kaimakam of Vosdan and Hiusein Agha of Takhmants village pressed notables in Gevash, especially Setrag Effendi of Badgants and Moukhsi Mourad of Nor Kiugh, to collect all arms in the region and present them to the authorities in order to save the district from disaster. These ignorant men were taken in by the deceit and collected around 20 weapons and surrendered them to the government. There was no strong organisation for self-defence or a charismatic like Levon in this district. While the elders were surrendering weapons to the authorities, the youngsters were holding meetings, discussing self-defence, organisation and resistance, but could not agree on a plan for action among themselves. They were divided and dispersed while the government was quietly preparing forces to be used in Gevash.

This process lasted a few days and on April 24 Haji Darvish attacked the village of Paykhner with a large number of Kurds and gendarmes from Karasou. The Armenian forces in Gevash, which could have resisted Haji Darvish had they been united, were divided into two. One part, 40 men under the leadership of Mihran Chatoian, withdrew to the mountain of Paykhner, while the other part under the leadership of Moukhsi Mourad of Nor Kiugh and Bedros of Mokhrapert led the civilian population to the summit of Balakeor mountain. The enemy then dealt with them in a piecemeal manner.

There was a major fight around Paykhner, with the defenders on the mountain resisting the enemy for the whole day. The Armenians lost two youngsters, Khacho and Garo Krikorian of Nareg. The enemy also lost two or three times as many men. However, it was not considered possible to continue resisting, as the enemy forces were getting stronger and the Armenians were running out of ammunition. The defenders therefore moved the civilian population towards Pesantashd when it was dark, while the villages themselves fell into Kurdish hands. A significant number of Armenian women and children remained in the villages.

During the afternoon of the following day, April 25, Haji Darvish went to Nor Kiugh and Mokhrapert, where the Armenians resisted him from their positions on the mountain. When it was dark, the defenders abandoned their positions and made for Pesantashd, while the women and children remained in animal shelters on the mountain plateau of Geodis.

The enemy attacked the mass of women and children and started inflicting cruelties on them, as well as attacking villages, looting, burning down homes, and killing around 100 people. Not only were the villages of Nor Kiugh and Mokhrapert subjected to such treatment, but Kantsag, Varents, Untsag and others were too.

At that point Levon was in Sivdgin village. He had just returned from Tagh, where he had had a meeting with the military command. He was coming to lead the defence of the district's northern region and Gevash. When he heard that the fighting had started in Gevash, he gathered his men and rushed there. However, when he reached Pesantashd, he came across people fleeing from Gevash, including its defenders, so he remained where he was. He had no intention of continuing as Gevash had been destroyed and the enemy had reached the borders of Pesantashd.

Levon remained in Pesantashd, where refugees arrived every day, not only from Gevash but also Hayots Tsor and even Timar, so that by the middle of May there were 6,000 refugees there. It was imperative to defend Pesantashd, not only to safeguard this mass of refugees, but also Tagh – as the government would have used that route to send reinforcements to the kaimakam of Tagh.

Levon thus set to work. He first settled the refugees in the villages of Pesantashd. About four hamlets with 112 houses had to give shelter to 6,000 refugees. This was a complex task on its own, and the organisation was left to Levon.

Then, Levon organised his forces and picked his key defensive positions. He had a total of 150 rifles 70 Mauser pistols at Pesantashd, and naturally, the supply of ammunition was low. The fighters had to be frugal in their use of bullets in order to make an extended defence possible.

The Pesantashd forces were deployed as follows.

1. Paradodig. This was the most important defensive position on the route between Vosdan and Tagh and a key enemy target. 80 riflemen and 40 others with pistols were deployed here under Levon's leadership.

2. Shahrour Castle. As we saw earlier, this position commanded the road between Van and Tagh. Its defence had been entrusted to 15 men from Tagh under the leadership of Pazig Bedrosian. This group was sent back to the military command in Tagh and replaced by 30 riflemen and 15 men with pistols under the command of Areghtsi Mesrob.

3. Karaplakh. This position was allotted 25 riflemen and 10 men with pistols under the leadership of Mourad of Nor Kiugh.

4. Nor Kiugh was given 15 riflemen and 5 men with pistols under the leadership of Hasan Chavoush and Dzgortsi Manoug.

The latter two positions, the first to the west and the second to the south-west, were to defend Pesantashd against hordes coming from Mogs and Gargar. There were no serious incidents at these positions because the abandoned Armenian villages allowed for much looting and the Kurdish mobs were preoccupied with such activities. As for the first two defensive positions, that is Paradodig and Shahrour Castle, they endured many attacks, especially Paradodig.

The most notorious attack on Shahrour Castle took place on April 29. Hiuseyin Agha of Takhmants, who was full of venom towards Armenians because of the murder of his relative Haji Yaghoub, led 70 militiamen and a horde of Kurds from Khorzank and attacked Shahrour Castle from Georantashd village. The fighting lasted for two days. Hiuseyin Agha tried desperately to capture the castle but failed with the loss of 10 men and had to retreat in shame.

The attacks on Paradodig were even fiercer and longer lasting. These attacks were interrupted on April 20 but restarted a week later on April 27. After destroying Paykhner, Nareg, Nor Kiugh, Mokhrapert and other villages, Haji Darvish came to Pesantashd with his gendarmes and a large horde of irregulars and took up positions against Paradodig. On April 28, new forces joined him and they started their grand assault. However, Paradodig did not fall. On April 29, further reinforcements arrived, as well as a mountain cannon, with the enemy numbers reaching 500 men. The rocks of Paradodig were then fortified against the smaller number of Armenian opponents. Despite the bombardment, the fighting continued all day and the attacks failed, leading to 25 dead or wounded.

The fighting restarted again on April 30. As the enemy fought with the Armenian defenders at Paradodig, a group of around 100 gendarmes climbed to the top of Mt. Ardos and descended to the rear of the Armenian defenders. However, their ploy did not work as the Armenians turned their fire on the attackers as some of the gendarmes closed in. The enemy fled under Armenian fire, leaving behind six dead. After this unsuccessful attack, part of the enemy force was recalled and there was no more fighting on the scale of April 29-30. Nevertheless, the attackers left behind enough forces to continue the fighting until the end.

At this point, it is important to present a letter from the kaimakam of Shadakh to divisional commander Kyamil Bey.

> To Unit Commander Kyamil Bey,
>
> The rebels in Tagh have been rebelling for over a month. Despite our occupation of surrounding villages, our failure in Tagh undermines all of our plans. The [Armenian] position in front of our government building can only be destroyed by cannon. Since the entrance to the building is under fire from several positions all day long, we can only enter or leave the building at night – and this is an affront to the government. Nobody dares leave there during daytime. This fact has been reported to the governor many times but nothing has been done so far. For these reasons, our considerable concentration of forces here is still in an

unsettled state against a few Armenians. The governor ordered you on May 8th to send us a significant force with two cannons.

Bearing in mind the above mentioned serious issues, you are requested to move quickly.

May10

Kaimakam Hamdi

While the kaimakam of Shadakh continued to request reinforcements with cannons from Jevdet and the divisional commander, the two roads to Shadakh remained blocked to the government. Therefore, government forces had to use a mountainous route through Mousgaven village and traverse the difficult valleys of the Upper Tigris. The cannons thus reached Tagh only on May 18, as we shall see later.

So, the defenders of Pesantashd at Paradodig and Shahrour Castle were successful in repelling enemy attacks and safeguarding the northern regions while enemy forces got stronger elsewhere and created serious problems.

The [Armenian] villages in the eastern parts of the district were destroyed and there was a Kurdish movement on the border of Mogs. There was similar movement to the south. Tagh was also in an uncomfortable position by May 6-7. Conditions became more serious thereafter, as the military committee recorded.

> May 7. We received news that the enemy has crossed Jalgan Bridge and taken the Armenian village of Armshad. We sent Azad and his men to help and it seems our fate will be decided there. If we are successful there, it will be difficult for the enemy horde to continue.
>
> Today for the first time we lost a man at one of our positions in Tagh – Sahag Aprigian, a brave soldier. We have recently noticed some signs of hopelessness among the population concerning our position, so we released the following circular.
>
> Comrades,
>
> Our first losses in battle were Giulamir and his two comrades. They fell bravely in a heroic battle at Sak, which cost the lives of 12 policemen.
>
> After 25 days of fighting, we have suffered a second loss, with blood spilt on the rocks of our positions. We have to be prepared for the fact that the bloody fight is only beginning. Let us not hope for victory without spilling blood or sacrifice. Each victory has its price, and the price for our success and freedom will be our blood. If we are not willing to spill our own blood, others will not grant us our freedom.
>
> We are now conducting an unbelievable struggle, the battle of a long-tortured and oppressed people. This is the fight of a people who want to live, however fierce and hopeless the battle may seem.
>
> Which nation does not experience upheavals? Which rose doesn't have thorns? Which fight has no blood shed? Which freedom has no sacrifice? We want to be free without spilling blood, but that is impossible, and we'd be committing a crime if that is what we thought.

Our fight today is the same as the beginning and end of the lives of all nations. This is a most hopeless fight for our enemies, who know that they are about to lose the thread of their own lives and want to cut ours before they lose their own.

They have decided to massacre and exterminate us; we have decided to live, and we shall live as we have faith and know that there are two roads in front of us.

We either remain discouraged and allow the enemy to cut off our roots, or we become resolute and firm and sacrifice the blood of some of our people for the salvation of the rest. There is no other way. Let's choose the second of these options and fight with hope.

Military Command

May 8. Umposd writes that the Kurds have repaired and crossed Jvgadan Bridge to the rear of Pols and Tagh. This is not good news.

May 9. There is constant Kurdish movement to Jamlan Beg. Our quarter at Sozvants sent us news [by signalling] with the red flag that the fighting continues at Pols.

Night, 8 p.m. (1 a.m.) A messenger arrived and informed us that there is heavy fighting on the roads to Jvgadan and Hashgants Bridge. The enemy forces number 400 men. We sent Ardziv and Shrchig to Sozvants with 20 men in order to defend the fighting zone. The clashes at Armshad have ended and the village has been sacked, but there have been no casualties. We wrote to Azad to immediately proceed to Sozvants.

May 10. The fighting continues at Pols. The Kurdish movement at Jamlan Beg has continued until the evening.

Night, 8 p.m. (1 a.m.). A messenger arrived. There is no news from Pols. It is surrounded by Kurds. Paylag writes that he has no news from his units but noticed that the fighting had shifted to Tsor and Jvgadoun in the afternoon. A 10 year old girl, Srpig, ascended to Sozvants under enemy fire and brought us news.

Looking beyond the records of the military command, we can examine some of the main developments in the southern zone, especially around Pols.

At the beginning of the fighting, the Armenians destroyed the wooden Jalgani Bridge on the Tigris in the southern zone. The Khalilan, Khavshdan and Yezdinan Kurdish tribes repaired the bridge and crossed onto the right bank of the river and attacked the Armenian village of Sarget. The Kurds committed atrocities and killed over 40 Armenians, and the rest of the Armenian population fled to Gaghbi. The Kurds sacked Sarget and drove off the sheep of Armshad village. The population of Armshad also fled to Gaghbi. Azad, who was sent with 50 men to help the Armenians, halted at Kajet. There he was informed that the Armenians of Sarget and Armshad were fleeing to Gaghbi. He therefore moved to the latter village with his men in order to look after the people and prepare for the defence of Gaghbi.

At this time, that is May 8, a large number of Kurds from Dzarnos and surrounding villages moved overnight and repaired Jvgadan Bridge to cross Sevdgin river above Tagh and attack Pols.

That same night, two Armenian messengers on their way to Sivdgin, Igetsi Malkhas Bedrosian and his comrade Hokhig, fell into Kurdish hands near Jvgadan Bridge and were killed.

The Kurds thus surrounded Pols on three sides. This village was considered the most critical Armenian defensive point in the western zone, and its loss seriously threatened the loss of Sozvants and endangered Tagh. The large Kurdish force was opposed by Set and 15-20 men. Set and a few men ascended to a position above the village while others went to key houses inside the village. The fierce clash that ensued continued until mid-day but the Kurds couldn't occupy the village. The fighting restarted in the afternoon, after the Kurds received reinforcements and surrounded the village. They soon occupied part of the village, with a few defenders fighting and sacrificing their lives heroically. Armshadtsi Shahen, who had fortified himself in a house, killed several Kurds before he was killed himself. In another house, Mousgaventsi Dikran was also killed in a similar manner, after he had killed three Kurds. Soon, all of Verin Tagh passed into enemy hands, while a few men, including Kiurig and Hapet, managed to delay the enemy to allow the village population to escape to Dzidzants. Other fighters ascended and occupied new positions at Varisad. Pols thus fell into enemy hands and was burnt down.

The messenger from Pols reached Gaghbi before Azad had finished the defence of the latter village. The situation around Pols was so serious that Azad had to go to Pols.

After Azad's departure, Armenians in Gaghbi became despondent, the fighters were unable to control the population, and people returned to their villages. At that time Kurds were busy looting Sarget and carrying their plunder to the other side of the Tigris. A few of the armed men from Armshad descended to Sarget, came across Kurdish looters, and killed two of them. Another 10-12 looters fled. However, this area remained without leadership, and Pols attracted outside enemy forces, leading to major incidents.

Azad reached Set when the population of Pols had withdrawn to Dzidzants, and Pols had fallen to into enemy hands and been burnt down. The Armenian defenders had lost three men before ascending to Varisad. At the same time Pols received reinforcements from Mihran Chatoian commanding the Gevash defence forces who were at Dzidzants at that time, as well as Hovsep Karounian from Tagh with 20 men, and Sahag Choloian from Sozvants with his men. The main Armenian forces in that area congregated to save Pols and Sozvants. Only Chato was missing; he was busy defending the bridge at Hashgants village.

Pols was in a valley one and a half hours to the north-west of Tagh. To the west of Pols lay the mountain chain of Varisad, which was horseshoe-shaped and extended to the peak of Kiureg Mountain to the south and the Sivdgin valley just above Jvgadan Bridge. Between these two branches was a small mountain chain called Tsough chain.

Mihran, Azad and their 60 men took the northern branch of the horseshoe chain. While Mihran proceeded to Jvgadan Bridge, Azad remained on the main height. Hovsep Karounian and Set took the southern branch. While Hovsep proceeded on the road to Sozvants, Set remained on the heights above Tsough.

The enemy, numbering over 400 men, had occupied Tsough and surroundings.

All of these movements took place on the night of May 9. The fighting started anew on May 10. The enemy, elated by its successes in the previous day, had not bothered to occupy the principal positions in the region. The fighting was brutal. Despite the superior numbers of Kurds, the Armenians pressured them so much that the Kurds tried to retreat several times, only to be held back with some losses at the hands of Mihran and his men defending the bridge. The enemy fought all day long in a hopeless position.

May 10 ended successfully for the Armenians, but they did not have a resounding victory because of a major mistake. Sure in the knowledge that the demoralised Kurds would make no effort to come out of their positions until the next morning, Hovsep Karounian's men, who were cold and tired, descended to Sozvants to rest, without considering that the desperate Kurds might do anything to break through Armenian lines at night.

Hovsep and a few men, who remained at their positions until 9 p.m., noticed the absence of their comrades and joined them in Sozvants. The freezing mountains of Shadakh played their part, and the undefeated Armenians withdrew from their positions.

The enemy had been surrounded on all sides and it made desperate efforts at night to find a way out. Noticing the absence of their opponents to their left, the Kurds sent some of their forces to the mountain chain to the right of the Armenians, while its larger forces attacked and took over the empty Armenian positions before sunrise. The bad news reached Sozvants while Hovsep and his men were still asleep.

Hovsep awoke like a madman and sent his men to the left and right, while he himself took up the middle to ascent to their lost positions. By now the Kurds had also advanced and even taken up some positions against Sozvants. Hovsep, who was advancing on his own, soon came under fire and took up a position behind some rocks. His fight took on heroic proportions and he fought until his last bullet and was killed. His death atoned for the earlier mistake made by his group.

Not far from the spot where Hovsep fell, to the right, another one of his men fell, the brave Yeprem Margosian. After these deaths, the enemy went forwards towards Sozvants. The Armenians to the left retreated to Dghasbar, and those to the right went to Tagh. The people fled to Dzidzants. The signal-flag at Sozvants was lowered three times, as the military command watched from the roof of the church in Tagh. They could see Sozvants village clearly when the flag went down for a final time; the enemy occupied Sozvants before noon.

At that time Set and his men were still in their positions while Azad and Mihran were busy with their pointless watch of the bridge. They did not know what was happening at the all-important and irreplaceable location of Sozvants.

Meanwhile, let us look at what was happening in Tagh on that day.

It was 7 a.m. The people of Tagh were expecting to see a white flag signalling peace, but the hours passed, and it was not a white flag that was raised but a red one. Furthermore, the flag was tipped once to signal the advance of the enemy and the desperate situation. People in Tagh were in a daze. They had to send a messenger and get detailed information. Sozvants was an hour's ascent and it was impossible to make the trip during daytime because of enemy fire.

So at that difficult moment they called on a young heroine called the mountain-goat of Shadakh mountains, the 12 year old daughter of Koukoyi Avedis, Srpo, a quiet and thin girl who took the letter and dashed off. The shooting continued in Tagh, with bullets flying about, but none bothered the young heroine. She simply started her difficult ascent, jumping from rock to rock and bush to bush like a mountain-goat to complete her mission.

Before the little messenger returned, the military command watched the Sozvants flag nervously. Tagh was living desperate moments, as Armenians were under great pressure, and Muslims forces were moving around them. The moments seemed to be getting longer, seconds seemed like hours, and hours like years, but there was no news and terrible thoughts crossed people's minds. Then, suddenly, the flag moved three times, tipped three times and fell down. Sozvants was no more. Tagh was now surrounded on all sides.

The right wing of Hovsep Karounian's men, eight people, moved towards Tagh. They had no choice, as they were under Kurdish fire from their rear and Turkish fire from the Mill quarter. The bullets were falling around them like hail as they crouched down. The mountain-goat of Shadakh, the courier Srpo, joined the Armenian men in those hellish conditions with her letter. Tagh was still a long way away but the hail of bullets was getting more intense as all the enemy positions fired on them. The fighters were forced to descend and approached Asdvadzadzin Monastery, which was located at the edge of some orchards outside the town's quarters. As they approached the monastery, they came under more

Srpo (Srpouhi)
The messenger girl of Shadakh

intense fire, and one of their number, Zakar Sahakian, was shot dead, while Khachadour Mkhoian, Tovmas Isajanian, Bismark Azizian and Gaghbetsi Mgro were wounded. The men, including those covered in blood, managed to enter the monastery through the entrance. The Turks at Mill quarter crossed the river and surrounded the monastery and a new fight ensued lasting for a few hours. The Turks weren't able to enter the monastery, so they lit a fire at the entrance and pulled back. The dry grass and the monastery entrance door burned together, as a column of fire and smoke rose into the air. It was only then that Azad and Mihran noticed the fire from their positions far away and realised the loss of Sozvants.

Tagh was in confusion and people were congregating in the centre of the town. The military command remained cool-headed but was under a lot of stress, especially as its main forces were elsewhere and Armenians remained encircled. The night was tense and seemed hopeless. It was also very dark. Suddenly, one of Hovsep's men, Tovmas Isajanian, who was wounded in his hand, came into the church yard and informed the people that Asdvadzadzin Monastery was being burnt down and his comrades were in the building.

They had to send people to help, but who would go to the monastery at that hopeless moment, in that dark and dangerous night?

One person stepped forward, a well-educated youngster from Tagh, Sahag Mgrdichian, who was followed by Boghos Tanielian, and then a few more men who soon set off. When Sahag stepped into the smoke-filled monastery, he could feel the darkness and death around him. The Armenian fighters were lying flat on the ground, unconscious, only their grunting noises breaking the silence. The deadly smoke had spread and embraced them and none of them would have remained alive after a few more hours. Courier Srpo was also lying there, unconscious. The entrance to the monastery was still burning and its hazy light lit up the bodies inside. The first to respond to the voices of the rescue team was the little courier Srpo. Then one of the men, Aram Tanielian, was brought back to consciousness. He thought his helpers were Turks and raised his pistol with his weak hands and fired. The bullet lodged into the roof of the monastery. The unconscious and wounded were all carried away and the unusual caravan disappeared into the darkness. Thus a few lives were saved, and only one of them, Khachadour Minasian who had been critically wounded, died.

Azad, Mihran, Set and Pazig with their men tried to attack Sozvants and retake it in order to reach Tagh, but it proved impossible and they moved to Sivdgin.

After the fall of Sozvants, a sens of hopelessness also overtook the people of Kajet and Armshad. While the population of these two villages moved to Gaghbi, some of the people of that village moved to Mogs. Seeing these movements, the people of Armshad returned to their own village, preferring to live or die in their homes. The population of Kajet also returned, but they were attacked on their way by Kurds and suffered significant losses. The Kurds fled when Gorovantsi Abro and a few men intervened.

As to what happened in Tagh after the fall of Sozvants, we turn to the military command's journal entries.

> May 11. During late morning our flag at Sozvants fell down and everything ended. The Kurds occupied it, our Liège fell, and we are surrounded on all sides.
>
> We decided to concentrate people at three points: the church, the Klgants residence and the lower school. We managed to do this. People were remarkably calm and everyone was moved within one and a half hours. The Kurds did not proceed to Tagh from Sozvants and we remained in a state of uncertainty until evening.

April 30. The uncertainty continues. The Kurds have besieged us and we have no news of our forces outside Tagh. Our contact with Sivdgin are severed. We decided to send a messenger and the mission was undertaken by a woman called Asmar.

Tagh was thus besieged on all sides, its Armenian population had moved to three points, and the defenders had left their positions at the National cave which had caused so many problems for the enemy. They also abandoned the Der Markarian and other positions, so that the enemy reached the outskirts of Upper Tagh. As for what was happening in the outside world, the military command had no idea.

"We need a messenger to go to Sivdgin." This was the appeal made by the military committee. The fate of Tagh depended on it.

Sozvants was no more, the mountains were occupied by Kurds, and the road to Sivdgin went through the Khorkhorad valley, which was also in Kurdish hands. Who would volunteer to jump into the jaws of death? Nobody! But the besieged people demanded it. They demanded one more sacrifice, a hero, and Tagh produced such a person. The hero was a woman, a weak person with a broad face, unsettled eyes and missing front teeth. She was around 50 years old. Her name was Asmar, knife-maker Mardo's wife, a mother of four.

This woman had to set off late at night through Sivdgin valley. This valley was extremely difficult to pass during daytime, let alone at night, because of a flooding river and the huge waterfall at Hashgants, as well as the jagged rocks and great barriers at every step.

It was through such a valley that Asmar, that last but not only heroine of Shadakh, set off late at night through terrible enemy lines.

> Dear Azad,
>
> We are surrounded on four sides. You are instructed (1) to send us 10-15 men to fill our unmanned positions in Tagh; (2) gather all the other men and secure Sivdgin-Tagh communication lines as well as occupy Sozvants; (3) inform us about developments outside, and let Pesantashd and Van know of our situation.
>
> Warm regards, Military Command

This was the letter hidden in Asmar's clothes as she got herself together, looked at Asdvadzadzin Monastery and crossed herself before disappearing into the dark night at 8 p.m. (1 a.m.).

This messenger woman returned at 2 (7) a.m. according to the journal of the military command. Asmar had managed to get to Sivdgin, a 15 verst (9 mile) journey, and return with an answer within six hours, thus immortalising the good name of the women of Shadakh.

Asmar's speedy return, as well as the news she conveyed, lifted Armenian spirits. This is how the mood in Tagh was recorded.

> May 14. The defence work at three key locations has not been completed. It is good that the enemy is allowing us time to reinforce our positions.

1 (6) o'clock. The enemy started firing with great intensity at the Der Markarian position. They probably noticed that we had abandoned that position and were now trying to occupy it themselves.

1(6) o'clock. Our positions have once more come under intense fire. What is the enemy trying to achieve? Is it going to launch a real attack or are they trying to keep us busy while they move their forces about?

May 15. At 3 (8) o'clock. The Kurds attacked the Karounian residence from the gardens and managed to enter Tavit's coffee house. All of our fighters concentrated their fire on that front. The shooting continued until evening. Our speedy response resulted in the enemy retreating with seven dead.

May 16. There is an increase in the number of wounded women and children and it is getting difficult to treat them because of a lack of doctors and medicine.

11 p.m. (4 a.m.). A messenger arrived from Sivdgin informing that Azad had tried to break through enemy lines with 40 men and come to Tagh. However, he had failed and retreated.

May 17. The Kurds tried to attack from two points – through the gardens and over the wooden bridge – but had to retreat after losing six men.

10 p.m. (3 a.m.). Pazig entered Tagh with 10 men. Azad is preparing forces to retake Sozvants.

The above journal entries show that Tagh continued to resist under siege, while the Armenians outside managed to break through the siege and come to Tagh's aid.

Perhaps even more noteworthy is the fact that even under these conditions the enemy couldn't organise a final assault, as its own ranks were diminishing through desertions, and it was asking for reinforcements. This is the scenario painted in the communications between the kaimakam and Jevdet, as well as the kaimakam and his commanders.

To the Governor's Office,

1. Today, the commander of a unit coming from Mogs informs us that the miudir of Mogs, Mourtoulla Beg, following an appeal by Armenians, has ordered his men not to touch goods and properties belonging to Armenians. We can see the negative consequences of Mourtoulla Beg's favour in our district. The Armenian villages from Pesantashd to Sivdgin valleys and all the way to the villages of Armshad, Gaghbi, Kajet and others near the borders of Parvari have become the cause of our misfortune. People will compare our district with neighbouring Mogs and one day seek shelter there so that our current repression will remain fruitless.

2. We have a serious lack of military supplies. We have no Mauser cartridges. We can only use Martini and kapakli bullets in the fighting in Tagh. The Kurds, especially the Khavshda tribe, having used cartloads of bullets, are now using Mauser cartridges. We have delayed some important attacks on Armenian villages because of a lack of ammunition. Whatever happens we ask you to send 20 cases of Mauser and 10 cases of other cartridges.

3. Four days ago we captured the Armenian villages of Pols, Ayki and Sozvants. Thus, the rebels of Tagh have been completely surrounded but this decisive blow has been undermined by a tragic development – looting. Now, every Kurd who

has stolen anything is abandoning his position and running away. The distribution of loot is also creating serious strife. We are naturally enduring these shameful developments. In mentioning them, we do not seek to make our dear Effendi uncomfortable, but to remind the authorities to send us regular soldiers if it can.

4. The supplies distributed to the soldiers have been exhausted. We also do not have access to the salt mines in areas controlled by the Khavshda tribe because of the seasonal flooding of streams. Do not stop sending us supplies until we vanquish the enemy in Tagh and are free to move about. Over the past few days, we started to use some of the oil collected in taxes for our lighting, so please send us some candles as well.

5. Our morale is high. Your latest information about the flight of the people of Van has in no way affected us. In accordance with your advice, we have communicated our issues to the [Kurdish] tribes. We remain resolute and will defend the honour and well being of the government.

May 15

Kaimakam Hamdi

To the Kaimakam,

I have been defending the government's honour and well being by undertaking the government defences for 35 days with 24 soldiers. According to your orders, I sent off an additional 10 men to participate in irregular warfare, but the ample supplies and sheep at Sozvants were divided without our people getting anything. Please make appropriate arrangements in this regard.

May 15

Government Official Saleh

To the Kaimakam

The number of soldiers is 38, and the available weapons are 2 Mausers, 9 Martinis, 9 Younanis, 2 Kapaghli and the others sheshkhanas. Each has barely 10 cartridges. I can not come to you as I am unwell, so please send us ammunition immediately. A rock fell on me while we were fortifying our positions and I was hurt.

Saleh

May 18 became an important day in the Shadakh fighting. Tagh, despite being surrounded, was continuing its defence at its final three positions. The Armenian forces outside the siege area were preparing tirelessly to recapture Sozvants. Azad had come to Tsough. Mihran had gone to Gaghbi, gathered forces there, and moved to Pesantashd to gather more men. They were all preparing for a final attack. During these preparations they received news that the Russian army was getting closer, the Turks had fled, and some Armenian volunteers had entered Van. This news created euphoria among the Armenian fighters and bolstered their preparations.

Meanwhile, the Armenians in Tagh remained under siege and had no idea of what was going on elsewhere. Furthermore, the enemy had just received reinforcements, including two mountain cannons.

At 3 p.m. one of the cannons was placed on a hill called Panih and began bombarding the Karounian position. However, the prevailing mood in Tagh was not one of hopelessness but optimism. Pazig's arrival with 10 men had impressed people and given them new energy to resist.

It was a strange scenario: the outside Armenian forces were preparing to recapture Sozvants; the Turks were trying to destroy Tagh and Gaghbi; and the besieged Armenians under bombardment were heartened. This mood was recorded in the journal of the military command, as well as the communications between Turkish officials.

> May 18 3 (8) o'clock. It was peaceful until the first cannon fired its first shell. The enemy brought up two cannons by a secret route. Today 30 shells were fired. Nobody was hurt but our positions have been destroyed. Even so, we'll repair them at night. We sent a messenger to Sivdgin to ask for the speedy recapture of Sozvants.

> May 19. The bombardment continued and 45 shells were fired. There is strange jubilation among the defenders. We released the following announcement.

> "Comrades,

> "The news from all of our positions makes us cheerful. We are confident of your "unity and this gives us great hope.

> The cannon hasn't injured anyone so far. Let it destroy as many houses as it wants. We can repair them at night. There is no reason to despair. We share your belief that the enemy is making last ditch efforts. Let them do what they wish. We have not forgotten that we are, every day, adorning the pages of our historic struggle.

> "So, let's craft a glorious legacy for our generation.

> Military Command."

> May 20. The bombardment continued until 7 (12) o'clock and stopped. Today they fired 25 shells. We suffered no loss of life. We can see signs of desertions among the Kurds. In the evening we sent off two more messengers to Sivdgin and asked them to move on Sozvants at daytime tomorrow.

> At 10 p.m. (3 a.m.) we received news that Armenian volunteers had entered Van.

Now, let's see what the enemy was saying at the same time.

> To the Governor's Office,

> 1. Two cannons arrived today under the command of Lieutenant Jelaleddin Effendi. One of them is inoperable. Jellal Effendi explained the reasons for this and about other matters.

> 2. Like our Effendi we will all remain resolute in our dedication and composure under the command of our leader in carrying out our patriotic duties in our district.

3. The cannons arrived very late but we managed to destroy a few of the rebels' important positions within a few hours of starting the bombardment. We have blocked all of the roads in anticipation of their flight this evening.

4. Our ammunition has completely run out. We only have 100 Mauser and 200 Martini bullets left. In order to proceed with the planned attack on Gaghbi, as I have written previously, we request 20 cases of Mauser and 10 cases of Martini cartridges.

5. Occasional information about the general situation.

6. The quick dispatch of the capsules mentioned in Jelaleddin Effendi's report.

May 18 Kaimakam Hamdi

Our current strategy is to bombard the two-storey Karounian position on the road leading to Van. Infantry units have to be prepared to attack at the right moment in a co-ordinated movement, and a flag must be raised when the house is occupied. When the Armenians turn their attention to this point, our second target should be their position opposite the bridge. As I have written earlier, the soldiers should always be cautious when a position is abandoned, and they should be given clear instruction how those position should be attacked.

May 19 Artilleryman Jelaleddin

This is how preparations were made on the morning of May 21. This was a day of celebration for the people of Shadakh. The enemy was quiet and it was peaceful behind the Armenian lines, while outside, Armenian fighters were preparing behind the mountains to attack Sozvants. The signal was given and the long silence was followed by deafening volleys. One could hear the fugitive soldier Arektsi Mesrob's Turkish bugle on the heights of Sozvants. The church-bells started to resound in Tagh, and the volleys continued. The "hurrahs!" could be heard on the heights above, the exultations in Tagh and, at another point, the roar of a cannon.

"Today's fighting really makes me feel that we are at war. It reminds me of the fighting and the Russian artillery at Pasen" writes Dikran, the Armenian officer.

"A deafening firefight could be heard from the direction of Sozvants. The noise gradually seemed to get closer. Our fighters were getting nearer as we had instructed them. Azad's group signalled with its bugle from Sozvants and Tagh responded with its church bells. There is no doubt at all. Our Liège has been reoccupied. There is no end to our euphoria," recorded the military command.

This is how Sozvants was re-captured after a dogged fight and the flight of the Kurds with 30 losses.

While Tagh was welcoming the capture of Sozvants with celebrations and the toll of church-bells, the kaimakam received the following letter.

We hear that the Governor is due to arrive in Sivdgin through Pesantashd. An official policeman has supposedly reached you with this news. If so, please let us know the good news.

Miudir Shefket of Alan tribe

It seemed somewhat comical and bitterly ironic given that along with the loss of Sozvants, the government official Shevket was complaining to kaimakam Hamdi – that same Hamdi who complained about the peaceful conduct of the miudir of Mogs, Mourtoulla Beg – explaining his own weakness in terms of the anti-government activities of the latter, something he was not able to do convincingly.

The kaimakam of Shadakh, Hamdi Bey, gathered his cannons and soldiers and took an escape route on May 23, bidding farewell to Shefket of the Alan tribe. This was the same escape made by the boastful Jevdet. That same day, March 25, Armenian volunteers under the leadership of Dro reached Sivdgin and Tagh to great cheers. The one-thousand strong force was met with elated celebrations and the uproar of the few dozen worn out and much suffering Armenian fighters of Shadakh. These people of Shadakh with their modest appearance were the pride of their lofty mountains.

By this time, the enemy was leaving Shadakh, with Kurds quickly clearing the mountainsides with their flocks.

After the flight of the Turks and victory in Tagh, Shadakh presented the following scenario. The Armenian villages in the east were destroyed and their population had fled to other areas. The Armenian villages in the west were also destroyed and their population had also taken refuge in different places.

Similarly, most of the Armenian villages in the south were also destroyed. The population of this area had mostly withdrawn to Kajet and Armshad in Gaghbi valley and some had gone to Mogs, Tagh and Sivdgin.

But a large part of the people were in Pesantashd. As we mentioned earlier, there were four Armenian villages in this area with a total of 122 households. People came here for refuge from Gevash, Hayots Tsor, Timar and inner Shadakh, so that there was a total of 7,000 people, including the local population.

Those 7,000 depleted the foodstuffs of Pesantashd. First, bread, then animals ran out, so that nothing remained. No grains, no sheep, no chickens, or cockerels. All had been consumed.

All reserves were about to be finished and there seemed no end to the fighting so that special raiding parties were organised. There were five raids in May against Hili, Padagants, Drshogh and Moushig villages. During these five raids approximately 100 poods [3,600 lbs.] of various grains were brought back. One of these raids against Hili became well-known because the 20 or so soldiers guarding the village showed little resistance and fled, leaving the village to the raiding party.

When the food-stocks ran out and the Turks fled, there was practically no food left in Pesantashd and 7,000 people came out of the siege with stomach aches, but who cared?! They had found freedom and breathed the air of freedom.

Armenian volunteers enter Van (May 18, 1915)

Chapter XX

The Provisional Armenian Government of Van

On May 16, after 27 days of dogged fighting, the Turks withdrew from Van. Jevdet and his forces fled with their cannons and the city passed into the hands of Armenians.

On May 18, a group of Armenian volunteers under the leadership of Khecho, who were among the advance units of the Russian army, entered the city. A day later, on the morning of May 19, the Russian army arrived under the leadership of General Nikolayev.

The arrival of the Russian army and their rapturous reception by Armenians was unprecedented in Van. The entry of the Russian army was marked by an artillery salute from the Turkish cannons in the citadel, the same cannons which had been bombarding Armenian quarters a few days earlier. As the army proceeded, boys and girls sang songs, and flowers were thrown everywhere, covering Khach Poghani square. The procession was eventually met by Armenian clergymen and the heroes who defended Van.

The first words of welcome at Khach Poghani were delivered by Aram, who was chosen by his comrades to represent the Armenian heroes of Van, the city responsible for the most beautiful page in modern Armenian history.

How did the Russian army see the occupation of Van and their reception by Armenians? We can have an idea from the telegram General Nikolayev sent to his commanding officer.

> May 23, 1915, Van
>
> Thanks to the efforts of armed Armenians under the leadership of Aram, a Russian subject, Van defended itself for a month and prevailed three days ago when the Turks began to retreat. The city has been burnt down and only a few Armenian quarters and the Russian consulate remain. As we approached the city, there was an artillery salute from the six cannons in the citadel captured from the Turks. The Armenians handed me the keys to the citadel. The people and the defenders led by their bishop and clergy organised public celebrations and sang "God Save the Emperor." They lined our route and were shouting "hurrah!" and throwing flowers.

This was the atmosphere in Van, where Armenians were now welcoming the victorious Russian army instead of Turkish cannons.

Naturally, the Armenians were recognised by the Russian army as a resolute, capable and constructive people who could be entrusted with the duties of a provisional government. And so it happened.

On May 20, General Nikolayev appointed Aram as the acting governor of Van, entrusting him with the administration of the city and surrounding districts, and requesting him to form a government and a security force.

I

To General Nikolayev, Corps Military Staff

Telegram No. 5452

We endorse your appointment of Aram as the provisional governor of Van and surrounding districts. He should form an entirely Armenian administration and rely on local Armenian territorial forces. In order to appoint a consul, I contacted the head of armed forces and our Tabriz consul to send a temporary representative.

General Oganovski

II

To General Nikolayev, Van

Telegram No 1709

Our commander [Yudenich] has confirmed Aram's appointment in Van on the condition that he is entirely subordinate to Russian military authorities, that is the head of the local forces, who is about to be appointed. Aram should comply with all military arrangements.

General Oganovski

III

Orders to Bayazid Army,

No. 24, 1915, May 31

The Russian army of the Caucasus has appointed Aram as the temporary governor of Van on the condition that he is subject to military authorities, that is, the head of local forces. All arrangements of the military authorities should be made through Aram.

Major General Nikolayev

This was the course of events in Van over a month. The military success was followed by one of government and construction.

It was one thing to say "Go and govern" and another thing to do so.

A people who had endured centuries of bondage and always looked up to be told what to do was to form a provisional government, organise administrative bodies, create the mechanisms of government, and look after a country in ruins and its needy people – while dealing with resentful Kurdish tribes and other forces.

Yes, it was not easy for a people who had never run a state to do all of this, a people who were denied such possibilities for centuries.

And it was here that Armenians showed their natural abilities to rise to challenges and learn. It is true that they had never had a state, but they had the ability to learn and make progress, to deal with other cultured peoples, to administer their communal affairs in terms of religious, educational, and national-administrative life, as they had learnt from the enlightened world.

Because of these national characteristics, the young people of Van, despite the small number of Armenians remaining in the region, began preparing the necessary administrative bodies following General Nikolayev's message of May 20.

We have already seen the various bodies fulfilling social functions during the 27 days of fighting. They were the Military Command, the committees responsible for military supplies, foodstuffs, and distribution, the red cross, the civil and health administrations, the police force, and the judicial body. These bodies were set up to function during the fighting and naturally ceased their activities when the fighting stopped. Now it was necessary to set up an entire government and its bodies in order to undertake peaceful and constructive work. And such a government was set up by copying the government-model that functioned during Ottoman domination. This was a practical solution that the people understood, until a better system could be set up.

Further to Khach Poghani street, at a section called Pokr Kyandarji, was the French Dominican Sisters' orphanage and school. It consisted of a large two-storey building with extensive balconies. It was built in 1910. When the Russo-Turkish war broke out, the Turkish government confiscated the building, which then passed into Armenian hands during the fighting.

The Armenian government was set up in that building. All of the doors opening onto the balconies were covered with signs, such as "Local Administration", "Finance Committee", "Regional Administration", "Municipality", etc.

These signs were made of red square pieces of fabric with white capital letters on them. The Armenian people had sacrificed countless lives, shed rivers of blood, and the signs of its first government were mysteriously expressed in red. That colour had become the symbol of the Armenian people and appeared here for the first time.

The first provisional Armenian government was thus set up, officials were appointed, institutions were formed, and a historic, official appeal was made.

> To the Armenian People
> Citizens!
> The success of the Russian army heralds a new era of stability for the people of our city and surrounding districts. We now see the end of centuries of enslavement and political oppression. We now celebrate the beginning of the constructive and creative spirit of the Armenian people.
> The commander of the Russian forces, General Nikolayev, in recognition of the heroic efforts of the Armenians of Vasbouragan, and in order to neutralise the Turkish Government's genocidal [*azkasban*] policies, as well as seeing the national-cultural disposition of the Armenian people, decided by its special decree No. 16 of May 20, 1915, to appoint me as the governor of the city and surrounding districts and to allow me to organise all aspects of the task ahead.
> We have already organised committees to deal with policing the judiciary, rural economy, refugees, municipal matters and so on.
> I call on all, since a new government has been formed, to deal with the appropriate government committees and contribute to stability in the city and surrounding areas.
> During these momentous days, the Armenian people should have one aim and unify around their government to reorganise the life of the city and surrounding regions in a manner that is worthy of the hopes and memory of the many

martyrs who struggled for a quarter of a century, as well as the dignity and good standing of the Armenian people in this corner of Asia Minor.

The Russian general was fully aware of these hopes when he put his great trust in the Armenian people and me.

Citizens! It is up to you to live up to the trust and expectations of the victorious army and the general. It is up to you to show that you are worthy of more.

May 21, 1915 Governor of Van and surrounding area, Aram

There was only one name at the bottom of this declaration – "Aram" – but this was not the statement of an individual but an entire people. It was a collective call of the Armenian people, a people who had been in a life and death struggle, calling on all to unite around a common task and realise yesterday's dreams.

Consequently, various institutions were set up, new officials took up their positions, and the administrative work began entirely in the Armenian language. The government building's walls were adorned with maps, posters and various notices. The external walls were covered with different announcements and posters. People with requests and grievances milled about both outside and inside the building, and the hustle and bustle began. We have presented this picture of Armenian life in Van in order to highlight the historical significance of this time.

The front of the Armenian government building had a courtyard and a number of rooms opened onto a balcony facing the street. The building stretched eastwards, turning round a corner southwards, and after a considerable distance, once more turning eastwards to the end of the courtyard, forming a neat row. The building, as mentioned, was over two floors, the lower one leading to the upper one by a wide wooden staircase. On the upper floor were the following offices:

1.   Provincial administration
2.   Provincial Secretariat
3.   Regional administrations
4.   Financial Committee
5.   Court
6.   Chief Prosecutor
7.   Court of Arbitration
8.   Prison Administration

The ground floor had the following:

1.   Municipality
2.   Municipal Secretariat
3.   Police Inspectorate
4.   Chief of Police Secretariat
5.   Police quarters
6.   Jail

The city was also divided into police precincts with their own forces.

There were more government departments than the ones mentioned above. The government building was not large enough to accommodate all of them. There were also some departments which could not be formed immediately. The work was new and in its infancy. The Armenian government had not been fully formed, but whatever had been set up over a few weeks was already a great deal.

The Armenian government was composed of the following offices.

1. Provincial Council.

This was the main body of the Armenian government. It oversaw the provincial budget, held officials accountable for their actions, and could appointing or dismissing them. It dealt with land, educational, police and border security issues, as well as taxes. This body was, one could say, both the legislative and main executive authority for the general administration of the province. The members of the provincial council were:

Aram Manougian, Governor
Garabed Ayjian, General Inspector
Siragan Dikranian, Vice-Governor
Aghabeg Hamparian, Judge
Bedros Mozian, Mayor
Mikayel Minasian, Schools' Inspector
Barouyr Levonian, Governor's Assistant
Hrant Kaligian, Chief Prosecutor
Khachadour Zenopian, Agricultural Inspector
Kevork Jidechian, Chief of Financial Committee
Tavit Papazian, Chief of Police
Avedis Terzibashian
Gosdantin Hampartsoumian
Sarkis Araradian

2. Provincial Administration.

This was the main executive body of the province.

Aram Manougian, Governor
Siragan Dikranian, Vice Governor
Barouyr Levonian, Governor's Aide
Ardag Tarpinian, Chief Secretary
Garabed Ajemian, Accountant
Dikran Terlemezian, Treasurer
Hovhannes Mkhitarian, Secretary
Nerses Basian, Executive Officer
Arpiar Safrasdian, Executive Officer
Maghak Shaljian, Executive Officer
Vagharshag Kzartmian, Executive Officer

Nigoghayos Hayrabedian, Executive Officer
Kapriel Shahinian, Executive Officer

3. Financial Committee.

This was the body responsible for all financial affairs of the province, including taking bids for the collection of the tithe. It was the main body managing all income and expenditure issues. Its membership consisted of the following officials.

Kevork Jidechian, President
Armenag Sarkisian, General Inspector
Haroutiun Shalajian, Treasurer
Hagop Der Hagopian, Accountant
Kalousd Torkomian, Chairperson
Garabed Zakarian, Secretary
Vartan Tarpinian, Director
Garabed Jidechian, Administrator

4. Municipal Council.

This body had similar functions to the city dumas and their bodies in Russia.

Bedros Mozian, Mayor
Members:
Armenag Vouvounigian
Vahram S. Boghosian
Mgrdich Hiusian
Vahan Maroutian
Levon Boulgarian, Civil Engineer
Levon Krikorian, Sanitation Inspector
Gharobjan Teghkirian, Treasurer
Kalousd Babajanian, Architect
Dikran Hovhannisian, Secretary

5. Education Inspectorate.

This body oversaw the schools in the province and was composed of the following:

Mikayel Minasian, Education Inspector
Members:
Yeghiazar Rshdouni
Mardiros Nalbandian
Hrachya Der Hovannesian, Secretary

6. Agricultural Committee.

This body was to develop agriculture, provide the latest agricultural implements and organise the communal use of resources among peasants. It was composed of the following members:

Khachig Zenopian, Inspector (graduate of Bursa agricultural school)

Arshavir Avedaghayian, Assistant Inspector, sericulturist

7. Sanitation Committee.

This body looked after the provinces public health and hygiene, as well as the cleanliness of the city. It was composed of:

Dr. Ardashes Babalian, President

Members:

Mampre Mgrian

Hagop Yakoian

Khachig Kalousdian, Surgeon

8. Board of Commerce.

This body had to organise and strengthen provincial trade, improve productivity, and resolve disputes among merchants. It was composed of:

Hamazasb Der Boghosian, President

Members:

Avedis Shahbaghlian

Mgrdich Hiusian

Hovhannes Piroumian

9. Police Inspectorate.

This body focused its work on the city. Its members were:

Tavit Papazian, Chief of Police

Ghevond Khanjian, Assistant Chief of Police

Bedros Krikorian, Assistant in Russian section

Hrant Garinian, Secretary

Hovsep Kardashian, Assistant Secretary

The Police Inspectorate oversaw five sections in the city under the direction of the following authorities:

5 Local chiefs

5 Assistant Local Chiefs

5 Secretaries

60 Policemen (on foot)

12 Mounted policemen

The local police chiefs were:

1. Krikor Jonian, Central Quarter

2. Armenag Teghtsounian, Norashen Quarter

3. Armenag Der Tovmasian, Medz Kyandarji

4. Mgrdich Karaseferian, Arark

5. Roupen Areghtsian, City

The police force included:

1 Jail-keeper

2 Assistants

1 Secretary

2 Porters

10. Judicial Structure.

A. Court of Arbitration

Roupen Shadvorian, Judge

Yenok Bouranian, Secretary

Mihrtad Proudian, Executive

B. Prosecutor

Boghos Chitjian, Examining Judge

C. District Court

Aghapeg Hamparian, Presiding Judge

Yeghishe Kachouni, Judge

Arsen Hatsakordzian, Chairperson

Khachadour Kevorkian, Secretary

Administrators:

Markar Aznavourian

Parounag Tarpinian

D. Prosecutor General

Hrant Kaligian, General Prosecutor

Margos Baldoshian, Secretary

E. Executive Office

Terjan Sinanian, Executive Official

Krikor Kachperouni, Secretary

F. General Inspectorate

This section oversaw all executive bodies.

Garabed Ayjian, Inspector General

Bedros Ashjibashian, Secretary

11. District Administration.

This body was part of the regional administration and worked with district authorities. It was composed of the following members:

Armenag Pokhanian, Chairperson

Mihran Mouradian, Secretary

Sarkis Simonian, Director

12. District Authorities.

Van province was divided into four districts and 12 sub-districts with their own district authorities. The popular title given to district administrators was *kaimakam*, and for sub-districts, *miudir*, as they were called in the days of the Ottoman authorities.

The districts and sub-districts were the following.

1. Shadakh district
District administrator, Samuel Mesrobian
2. Gevash district
District administrator, Levon Shaghoian
3. Arjesh district
District administrator, Nshan Zhamakordzian
4. Alchavaz district
District administrator, Panos Maroutian
5. Hayots Tsor district
District administrator, Nalband Nshan
6. Pergri district
District administrator, Kakig Tokhmakhian
7. Ardamed sub-district
District administrator, Hovhannes Kyamchian
8. Shahbaghi sub-district
District administrator, Apel Aghvanian
9. Aliur sub-district (Timar)
District administrator, Haroutiun Hiusian
10. Janig sub-district (Timar)
District administrator, Apkar Semerjian
11. Arjag sub-district
District administrator, Shirin Hagopian
12. Khoshap sub-district
District administrator, Armenag Der Boghosian
13. Mogs sub-district
District administrator, Krikor Nahabedian
14. Nordouz sub-district
District administrator, Bedros Effendi

The two districts which were to be formed in Garjgan were not formed yet because the people from those regions had not returned due to the ongoing fighting there.

It is noteworthy that the Armenian government was mainly composed of members of the intelligentsia, with a majority of teachers and school inspectors, though there were also Armenians who had served in the former Ottoman administration, as well as a significant number of merchants. This government reflected the intelligent youth of Van.

One should also note that a number of Caucasian Armenian intellectuals were invited to serve in the Armenian government, including people with the highest education. The province was also in the Russian army's zone of operations so that there was a need to deal with Russian forces at each step. It was therefore necessary to have Russian speakers and the Caucasian Armenians played a vital role in this regard. Some district administrators were even appointed with Caucasian Armenian aides.

The district administrations were gradually established, and in some districts the local organisation became quite sophisticated like the central government. We can present an example to give an idea of what was involved.

The Shadakh district administration was formed of the following bodies and administrators.

1. Samuel Mesrobian, District Administrator (*kaimakam*)
Hmayag Baghdasarian, Secretary
Hmayag Choloian, Treasurer

2. Financial Committee
Minas Mouradian, President
Sahag Mardirosian, Secretary
Aram Tanielian, Treasurer

3. Judicial Committee
Mihran Choligian, President
Hagop Tomasian, Secretary
Dikran Sarkisian, Executive

4. Municipality
Shahen Gouzhigian, President
Asbadour Azizian, Member

5. Police Force
Dikran Baghdasarian, Police Chief
Azad Simonian, Aide to Police Chief
Sahag Trshoian, Secretary
Dikran Mgrdichian, Executive
Boghos Tanielian, Regional chief
Markar Movsesian, Secretary

The police forces were organised alongside the different administrations, so that they often included 20, 30, or 40 members, and the total number of policemen was 360 men and 40 officers, half of whom were on foot and half mounted.

The Armenian provisional government in Van and its surrounding districts assumed this complex form within a matter of a few weeks.

Chapter XXI

The Budget of the Provisional Armenian Government

As an elaborate provisional Armenian government was set up, there arose the question of a budget for its expenses. The government had to maintain a number of administrative bodies, a large number of public officials, and a police force. The government had significant expenses.

Where was the vital funding to come from, if not from the Armenians whose interests the government was to serve?

Therefore, from its inception, the Armenian government planned and implemented a taxation system similar to the one implemented by the earlier Ottoman government. This was supposed to be a temporary measure until a new system could be devised. The new system would take time and experience.

The Armenian government's budget, or balance book, painted an interesting picture, which we present here in its entirety. This was an eight-month budget, starting from May 1915, when the government was formed, until the end of that year.

The main sources of income were as follows:

1. Property taxes based on the value of properties.
2. Income tax, mainly levied on merchants.
3. The tithe [ashar], which was set at one eighth of grains and other agricultural produce.
4. Educational tax.
5. Sheep tax [aghnam].
6. Judicial tax.
7. Stamp duty.
8. Municipal taxes.

There was also an expectation of income from empty villages and abandoned properties.

The following is the budget for the Armenian government.

Projected Income of Van Province
May 14, 1915 and January 13, 1916 was as follows.

Property Tax
City and Suburbs

Household	Class	Rubles	Property tax
100	A	16	1,600
300	B	8	2,400
600	C	5	3,000
700	D	3	2,100
1,000	E	2	2,000
Fields and orchards		2.5%	1,200
Total			**12,300**

Province	Villages	Households	Rubles	Kopeks	Property Tax
Timar	34	2,000	2	40	4,800
Hayots Tsor	31	1,488	2	40	3,571.20
Arjag	21	1,055	2	40	2,532
Shadakh	60	1,800	2	40	4,320
Mogs					
Gevash					
Total					15,223.20
TOTAL					27,523.20

Income Tax
City and suburbs

Household	Rubles	Property tax
50	8	400
100	6	600
500	4	2,000
600	2	1,200
Total		4,200

Tithe
Annual levy - 51,200

Educational Tax
One quarter of the tithe - 12,800

Sheep Tax
100,000 animals at 32 k. - 32,000

Judicial Tax
2.5% - 4,000

Stamp Duty

Stamps	Number	Kopek	Tax
Verdicts	400	50	200
Summons	3,000	8	240
Petitions	10,000	8	800
Rents	200	8	16
Contracts	600	40	240
International Identity Papers	500	3	1,500
Internal Identity Papers	600	40	240
Monthly payment stubs	4,000	8	320
Gun permits	200	40	80
Envelopes	4,000	5	200
Total			3,836

Income from Abandoned Villages
Estimate - 16,000

Municipal Taxes

Cleaning	1,665
Income tax (20%)	840
Coffee house permits	240
Irrigation water	320
Sergin (open air markets)	400
Carts	80
Sledges	80
Rentals	320
Building permits	160
Petroleum tax	160
Construction permits	2,400
Animal sales tax	384
Weights and measures tax	288
Fines	400
Shipping taxes	240
Rental validation taxes	80
Total	**8,057**

**Incidental Income According to report
of Financial committee**

Rental validation taxes	16,000

Savings

Due to late appointments of officials	2,723.80

GRAND TOTAL 178,349 rubles

Projected Expenditure of Van Province
14, 1915 to January 13, 1916

Provincial Administration Expenses

Governor's Salary (monthly)	300	
Governor's Aide	200	
Chairperson	100	
Russian Section Secretary	100	
5 Executive Directors	180	
3 Executive Directors (Russian Section)	160	
Provincial Section Secretary	60	
2 Executive Directors	65	
Treasurer	70	
Accountant	70	
Accountant's Aide	30	
4 doorkeepers	80	1,415 rubles per month
Total (8 months)	**11,320 rubles**	

Unforeseen expenses	5,000	
Secret Police	2,000	
Government offices (rent)	1,000	
Government offices (furnishing)	2,000	
Secretariat expenses	1,500	
Fuel (wood) and lightning	350	11,850 rubles per month
Total	**32,170 rubles**	

Financial Committee Expenses

President's Salary (monthly)	100	
Chairperson	70	
5 Executives	300	
Doorkeeper	20	490 rubles per month
Total (8 months)	**3,920 rubles**	

Tithe and Sheep Tax

Collection Expenses	**3,000 rubles**

Police Force

Chief of Police (monthly)	100	
Assistant Chief of Police	80	
Interpreter	80	
Accountant	40	
Secretary	30	
5 Regional Chiefs at 50 rubles	250	
5 Assistants at 40 rubles	200	
5 secretaries at 25 rubles	125	
60 policemen on foot at 20 rubles	1,200	
12 mounted policemen at 30 rubles	360	
Jailkeeper	40	
Assistant Jailkeeper	30	
2 doormen at 20 rubles	40	2,575 rubles per month
Total (for 8 months)	**20,600 rubles**	

Judiciary Expenses

President (monthly)	100
Prosecutor General	100
Court of Arbitration Judge	100
2 Members of the Court	140
Clerk	65
Prosecutor	65
Chief Clerk	60

5 Secretaries	180	
3 Bailiffs	60	
2 Mounted Bailiffs	60	
2 Doormen	40	970 rubles per month
Total (8 months)	**7,760 rubles**	

Municipal Expenses

Mayor (monthly)	100	
Engineer	70	
Aide	40	
Treasurer	50	
2 Secretaries	70	
Foreman	25	
5 Workers	125	
Doorkeeper	20	500 rubles per month
Total (8 months)	**4,000 rubles**	

City Cleaning	800	
Roads and Bridges	400	
Transport for Officials	160	
Food Aid and Burial of Unclaimed Corpses	250	
Public Health	2,000	
Unforeseen expenses	240	3,850 rubles per month
Total	**7,850 rubles**	

General Inspectorate

President (monthly)	100	
Secretary	40	140 rubles per month
Total (8 months)	**1,120 rubles**	

Educational Inspectorate

President (monthly)	100	
Secretary	30	130 rubles per month
Total (8 months)	**1,040 rubles**	

Educational Grants	5,000	
Total	**6,040 rubles**	

Agricultural Committe's Expenses

President (monthly)	70	
Secretary	40	110 rubles per month
Total (8 months)	**880 rubles**	
Seeds and training	1,000	
Total	**1,880 rubles**	

Postal Expenses

Official's salary (monthly)	40	
Distributor	25	65 rubles per month
Total (8 months)	**520 rubles**	

Shadakh District Government's Expenses

District Administrator (monthly)	100	
Interpreter	60	
Secretary	40	
Treasurer	40	
Court of Arbitration Judge	70	
Court Secretary	40	
Crier	20	
Doorkeeper	20	
Administrative expenses	30	420 rubles per month
Total (8 months)	**3,360 rubles**	

Gevash District Government Expenses	3,360
Arjesh District Government Expenses	3,360
Alchavaz District Government Expenses	3,360

4 Districts Expenditure (total)   **13,440 rubles**

Hayots Tsor Sub-District's Expenses

District Administrator (monthly)	70	
Interpreter-Secretary	40	
Administrative expenses	15	125 rubles
Total (8 months)	**1,000 rubles**	

Pergri Sub-District Expenses	1,000
Ardamed Sub-District Expenses	1,000
Shahbaghi Sub-District Expenses	1,000
Aliur Sub-District Expenses	1,000
Janig Sub-District Expenses	1,000
Arjag Sub-District Expenses	1,000
Saray Sub-District Expenses	1,000
Khoshap Sub-Districts Expenses	1,000
Mogs Sub-District Expenses	1,000
Nordouz Sub-District Expenses	1,000
Garjgan Sub-District Expenses	1,000

12 Sub-Districts Expenditure (total) 12,000 rubles

Police Force Expenditure

Police Commander (monthly)	100
Interpreter-Aide	60

8 Sergeants	480	
20 Corporals (on foot)	600	
180 mounted policemen	4,500	
180 policemen (on foot)	6,300	12,840 rubles per month
Total for 6 months[*]	**77,040 rubles**	

TOTAL EXPENDITURE	**178,340 rubles**

Thus, the total eight-month budget of the Armenian provisional government of Van was 178,340 rubles, which would not have been a huge amount had the land not been earlier subjected to destruction, plunder and massacre.

For all of its achievements, it would be wrong to say that the Armenian government was organised in an exemplary fashion and free of faults, if only because it was based on the old Ottoman system with its gross shortcomings. These factors alone compromised the new Armenian government,

For example, the tithe was sold by auction, as in the Ottoman days, so that the actual tax was to be collected by *multezims* visiting the villages. These *multezims* were much hated and the lowest of people, and Armenians especially suffered at their hands.

The existence of a secret police force, which the Armenian government adopted from the Ottoman one, was also unacceptable. Did the fledgling Armenian government need a secret police force? Did such a despised institution in the whole world have any role to play in the new government? Certainly not! But it was adopted alongside other government bodies without serious consideration.

Yes, the Armenian government was not perfect and had its faults, even large faults, leading to complaints against it.

Nevertheless, despite its faults, this young government soon inspired the conviction and demonstrated that the Armenian people were able to take care of themselves and deal with the challenges laying ahead of them.

The government in Van was open to leaving behind objectionable practices that went against the interest of the people and embracing a democratic path towards prosperity and well-being. In order to realise such ideals, they turned to Caucasian Armenian intellectuals. For these reasons, a number of Caucasian Armenians joined the Armenian government and worked day and night to address its shortcomings and introduce modern approaches to government. This was all done despite the difficulties and massive task of reconstruction.

The Armenian government was particularly transparent in its internal and external relations. There were no bureaucratic pretences, and many tasks and discussions took place in a simple, unpretentious and clear manner. The heads of government were ordinary people who fought alongside each other and were friends. The people saw them not as officials but yesterday's Arams, Ardags, and Dickrans, who could be approached

---

[*] The police force was set up in July – A. Do.

District Administrator
Kakig Tokhmakhian, Pergri

Armenian policeman
Levon Khorenian, City

with confidence. They could raise issues with them and even make demands. Needless to say, the Armenian government, like all governments, would have eventually become more bureaucratic, but in those early days it was strictly democratic.

Externally, the government did not have uniforms and probably would never have adopted them. However, its police force was something else, and the question of uniforms was discussed. In all likelihood, the police would have eventually adopted full uniforms, if the Armenian government was not so short lived.

The question of police uniforms was considered a necessity for two reasons. First, the people needed to know with whom they were dealing, and second, the police had to deal with the occupying Russian forces everywhere. The army could only recognise the policemen by their uniforms, especially as Turkish-Armenians could not communicate in Russian.

It was imperative that the police force was recognisable and the Armenian government gave them special arm-bands. The city police wore a white cloth band with the word "VOSDIGAN" [POLICE] written in red letters, a practice that was already in use during the April fighting.

The police force outside the city also wore a white cloth band with the Russian letters "V. D." for "VANSKAYA DROUZHINA" [VAN PEOPLE'S GUARD]. While it is true that they did not wear uniforms, these simple letters served the same purpose, as they stood for the Armenian people, their countless sacrifices, and the blood that brought about that little freedom.

The Armenian government worked incessantly, at incredible speed, focusing on productive work. The government regarded the Armenian people as its precious treasure, its natural constituent, sweet and lovable. The Armenian people, in their turn, looked upon the government as its new-born baby, for which they had suffered and endured so much. They were a family and shared common interests. Like an extended family, they were tied together with love, and looked forward to a happy future.

There was no way to hold back either the government or the people. They were quickly rebuilding the ruins, securing the torched premises, cleaning the streets and public squares, opening shops and markets.

However, as the Armenian government continued in its focused, calm and constructive work, it was thunderstruck and collapsed on the 70th day of its existence. This was because the Russian army announced its preparation to retreat, and Armenians were advised to leave everything behind and take the road to the Caucasus. Such an exodus meant that Armenians would now face famine, thirst, freezing cold, burning sun and even Kurdish attacks. In fact, they would reach the Caucasus leaving hundreds of corpses on the way. They would then be left in the Ararat Plain during the heat of June, resulting in hundreds and thousands of graves that would remain unadorned and forgotten.

The Armenian government ceased to exist after 70 days and the new misery meant that the Armenian government and its sweet memories would soon be forgotten. Life became much more bitter than ever before, and the heroes of April, who were recorded in history in golden letters, were forgotten in the bitterness. The same was also the case with the 70 days of the Armenian government, which had also passed honourably into history, in the aftermath of the heroic struggle of April 1915.

Chapter XXII

The Great Exodus from Vasbouragan

Two-and-a-half months after the April-May fighting, Van was already being rapidly transformed. The Muslim quarters of Aykesdan and the city had been burnt down and in ruins. Centuries of accumulated vengeance of Armenians led to total destruction. All houses and positions on the Armenian front lines during the fighting, in both parts of the city, had also been burnt down and destroyed because of the artillery bombardment they had endured. However, with the Russian occupation and further advances, Armenians started reconstruction everywhere. Everything was rebuilt, quickly.

The construction was particularly extensive on the great street of Aykesdan, between Khach Poghani Square and Pokr Kyandarji.

As previously noted, the main market of Van had been in the old city. Trade was entirely based there. However, the old city had long ceased to be a place of residence. Overcrowded and lacking vegetation, it was not an attractive place to live. Whoever was able to leave the city left for Aykesdan. The old city gradually degenerated as Aykesdan progressed. The city had depended on the market and government institutions. The market, which was chiefly in Armenian hands, was burnt down during the April fighting and most of its goods looted. Very few merchants managed to move their stock to the suburbs and conceal them before the fighting. For these reasons, after the fighting, there were no resources nor willingness to rebuild the market or rehabilitate the area. Aykesdan was deemed the future centre of habitation and trade. The merchant and artisan class in the market always suffered when there was unrest or massacres.

Thus, Armenians decided to move the market to Aykesdan, and the most suitable location was Khach Poghani Square and the wide street leading off it to Medz Kyandarji. This was Aykesdan's busiest part and at the same time it had a wide street and good buildings, including two consulates, hotels, and after the fighting, the seat of the Armenian government.

Consequently, there was fervent activity from Khach Poghani Square to Pokr Kyandarji. There were large doorways erected on both sides of the road, with rapidly built shops rising, as well as new passageways and entrances through existing walls, and new rooms above premises. On both sides of the street, whoever had the space and means, built shops. If one wanted to have an idea of the vigour of Armenians in Van in June–July, one had to observe how that long and broad street changed, how walls were brought down and new shops built, all full of goods. One had to hear the din of the artisans. It was all about work and productive activity reflecting the diligence of the people of Van.

While Van was busy at work, two detachments of the Russian army advanced across the north and south of Lake Van and joined up near Tadvan on their way to Moush and Bitlis. While it is true that Khecho, the leader of one of the Armenian volunteer units, was killed near Tadvan on July 24, 1915 and was buried at the cemetery of Ararouts quarter in Van (honoured by masses of people, armed Armenian fighters, and a full funeral procession), people's morale remained high in the expectation that Bitlis and Moush would soon fall.

Meanwhile, the vibrant life of Van was continuing when on July 27 the atmosphere changed as news arrived that the Russian forces had pulled back to Sorp and Akhlat before they had entered Bitlis and Moush. Rumours also spread that Kurds were active on the borders of Mogs and Shadakh. These developments shook the people of Van. The youngsters in the city held a meeting immediately to discuss the serious developments. 300 men volunteered to go to the aid of Mogs and Shadakh, and already, on July 28, 100 of them set off for Shadakh. The Armenians in Van could not refuse help given their courage and experiences in the April fighting. They went forth firm in the belief that they could contain the Kurds. But circumstances had changed. During the April fighting, Armenians were isolated and had to manage their own affairs. Now they could not act on their own because of the presence of the Russian army with Armenian volunteers and their officers. There was now an Armenian government. Surely, these bodes, collectively, knew what was going on the battlefields, what needed to be done, and where the best interests of Armenians lay. These were the thoughts of the young Armenians in Van, as they gave way to others and did nothing.

It was not possible to get reliable information about what was happening on the battlefields, and the news coming from different quarters did not bode well. The news from Adiljevaz was bad, as Armenian refugees from Moush joined the retreating Russian army. Why were the Armenians at Adiljervaz and Arjesh, who had just been massacred in April 1915, leaving? What were their reasons? There were also reports from different places that the Turks were advancing. The mood in Van wavered and turned into one of despair.

People became more unsettled, especially between July 28–30, when unknown sources spread rumours that the situation in the Caucasus had become dangerous.

"The Turks have entered the Caucasus from Olti!"

"The enemy has reached Ardahan!"

"Turkish forces have occupied Kaghizvan and Koghp and are moving onto Yerevan!"

"The Turks are approaching Tiflis and the Caucasus is in serious danger!"

Such were the rumours spread in Van during two or three days.

What would have happen to the people of Van and Vasbouragan if the Turks had reached Tiflis? Simple! The Russian army would have retreated and Turkish vengeance would have fallen on any Armenians who had remained behind. None would have been spared.

These were the prospects worrying the Armenians of Van when the announcement was made that the Russian army would be retreating.

What were Armenians to do? This issue became a major public concern. The Russian military authorities suggested the immediate departure of people before the army left the region.

"Emigrate? Who? Where to? How?" asked the Armenians of Van. "We will not leave. We will stay and defend our country! We are sure that no Turk or Kurd would dare take a step into our territory."

This was the sentiment of the representatives of the youth in Van. These were the same youngsters who had conducted the April fighting with great honour and saved tens of thousands of lives.

The leaders of the Armenian volunteer units also agreed with this position, as well as the members of the Armenian government. They all had good reasons to be confident. In terms of weapons and ammunition, Van was better prepared now than during the April fighting. Armenians were now two or three times more powerful, and it was not surprising that the locals preferred to stand and fight than face a catastrophic exodus.

Their decision was final and they approached the military commander to ask him to allow the volunteers to remain. This was the situation on the eve of July 30. However, as feared, the commander was against the volunteers remaining behind.

As for the people, he once more suggested that they leave, adding that the army would retreat in two days. If people did not wish to leave, that would be their choice.

Thus the final decision was left to Armenian leaders.

The rumour that the Caucasus was in danger of invasion, as it became apparent, was groundless. It was true that the Turks were quite powerful at that time on the borders with Olti, Sarikamish and Alashgerd, but it was still not that easy for them to invade the Caucasus.

We will one day find out more about the worrying rumours, and why it was seen necessary to remove the people of Van. The key to understanding will be in the politics of "Armenia without Armenians."

The worrying rumours served their purpose, the terror spread, and the leaders who should have been more cool-headed and let the question of emigration be discussed once more by the representatives of the youth, despite their own earlier position that "we will stay and defend our country," made the following announcement on the morning of July 31.

"Prepare five or six days' supplies and take to the road."

This was a difficult moment. The announcement was the first signal to leave and led to the mass exodus that was called the great exodus of Vasbouragan, with its terrible consequences. Many corpses would soon be strewn along the route to exile and later in the sun-soaked Ararat Plain, where countless graves would record a lamentable page in the history of Armenians.

Migration may be a simple word to utter, but it is difficult to imagine what it could entail, if one has not lived through such an event even for an hour. It can be like a beautiful garden destroyed by violent floods or blooming plants pulled by their roots and crushed against rocks, swept away through valleys, sinking, broken and smashed up pieces, thrown about like a mass of drywood. People forced to flee their homes are like such plants, as they submerge and disappear, and leave behind a trail of their dead. This is the way of forced migrations, as was the case of the great exodus of Vasbouragan.

The decision to leave shocked people who accepted their fate as if they had lost their minds with great anguish in their hearts. Alchavaz and Arjesh had already left, the Russian forces there had withdrawn, and the army in Van was soon to leave. The route to Pergri was to close in three days. Such news was coming in rapidly and the situation was becoming more distressing.

There was now no talk of defending the land. The latest news had created even greater consternation and it was not possible to oppose the decision to leave, especially as officials, whose opinions carried weight, had already announced the departure.

Thus, within a day, the city changed, the shops closed, people began leaving, and panic and confusion took over. Women began preparing provisions for the road while men took valuable possessions to hiding places. There were many people who had no time to hide such possessions. The Pergri route was to close in three days and nobody knew what might have happened afterwards. These were the concerns of the people of Van at that time, as homes and possessions lost their meaning and people only thought about their immediate survival.

The fear and hopelessness were universal and people could not rely on each other. Each took their chances alone. The exodus was not organised, there were no provisions made for transportation, and the powerless were abandoned. Nor were any weapons given to guards to secure the roads. Nothing was organised. Those who held public office and had responsibilities panicked like others, as tens of thousands set to the road and shared the same fate like a flock of sheep with no direction.

On July 31, as the sun set on Lake Van, the sun's burning rays gave way to Van's cool evening breeze, and the shadows got longer, the exodus began.

Throughout the day, doors were shut tight, as if not to be opened again, and men, women and children rushed around with their possessions. One could hear the noisy passage of overloaded carts. These were the small number of families which possessed or could rent carts. One sometimes heard the cry of a little child, its mother's soothing voice, or even curses. Here was a small donkey carrying a huge load followed by five or six people. They were hurrying, worried and stern faced. The movement and noise remained constant, and the heavy dust continued to rise. Van, which would normally be quiet at that time as people were at home, was now in turmoil, uncomfortable and tense. Slowly, the moon rose behind the clouds, as if in mourning and pain, and one could see at a short distance, behind some trees, a large building on fire, spewing billowing flames and grey smoke. It seemed that the person who built the house was now setting it alight before going into exile. The fire mocked the owner with its good wishes, as it destroyed the home, its flames consuming the beautiful structure. The death of that building also spelled the death of Van.

It was now August 1, a Sunday. Nobody washed the streets or pavements. No women could be seen outside doorways and most homes were locked. The multitudes were in the streets, where people had been departing all night long. The movement was still continuing.

An Armenian family during the Exodus from Van, July-August 1915

Most people had already left and those who remained behind were mainly those who did not have any means of transportation or helping hands. Their condition was pitiable.

A small family passed by, a woman with three children. They were carrying loads on their backs beyond their strength and were already tired. Another family had a cow with a great load on it. The animal was not used to carrying loads, and the family was not used to loading animals. As the poor cow shook its load, the family possessions fell off, and the straps were entangled around the animal's legs.

Another family passed by with a cart full of their possessions and two children sitting on top. The cart was led by a young boy and an adult male.

Then passed one more family, small and poor, led by a scraggy woman with an anguished face. She was carrying some possessions and clothes, followed by a 12 year old girl carrying her younger sister.

"Where are they going? Varak? To celebrate the feast of Vartavar?" one might have wondered.

They were leaving but did not know where they where going. They were leaving because all others were leaving. They were leaving to adorn the roads with their corpses.

But they too were lucky because they managed to take to the road. There were other families who had sick family members and could not leave. The city was emptying quickly, the streets were becoming deserted, life was coming to an end, and in this emptiness and the expectation of the arrival of the terrible enemy, there still remained some caretakers and their charges.

Two women and an 18 year old youngster stood in front of a door crying and bringing others to tears. The head of their household was bedridden and could not walk. There was no cart to move him. Two women tried to convince the young woman to leave but she would not leave the others behind. The whole scene was distressing and they all hug each other and lamented.

The old city beneath the citadel was entirely empty. The streets were abandoned, the ruins reigned supreme, and a 14 year old girl was crying at a window. The scene inside was particularly distressing, as an old woman, unable to move in a chair, and a young woman, bedridden and barely able to breathe, were surrounded by six children, crying. The eldest was a beautiful 16 year old girl. This was a house of mourning, where all who entered, mourned. The father of the family, Khachadour Nalbandian, was killed outside Van in Autumn, leaving his children to their fate in a heartless world.

Thus many families were left in ruins with no options.

These are all small examples from the terrible episode called the great exodus of Vasbouragan. Such movements are manageable when people can sell their possessions, prepare necessities, arrange transportation and then set off to a new country. However, the exodus from Vasbouragan was not such a process but an escape in panic and confusion. The Armenians of Van could not take anything with them. They left everything behind – homes, lands, orchards, furnished houses. They only took with them provisions for four to five days and then left, only to dot the Ararat Plain with their graves.

These were the conditions over those two days in the city. As for the outlying areas, weren't they also supposed to leave? Those areas near Van and to its north left early, along with the people from the city of Van. However, Hayots Tsor, Gevash, and especially Mogs and Shadakh were left behind. They reached the city of Van three or four days later. Only people who have actually experienced absolute terror can imagine how those far away districts greeted the news of the evacuation of Van and the prospect of Kurdish attacks.

In order to give an idea of what was involved, we present here a description of an eye-witness, one of the heroes of Shadakh, D. Baghdasarian.

> July 30. We have information that the Kurds have entered Mogs and Armenians there have moved to Vosdan. We hear that the Russian army, including the Armenian volunteer groups, are retreating from Bitlis to Vosdan. We do not know what is happening in the outside world. The proud soldiers of Shadakh are standing their ground but the people sense the danger and want to leave.

> July 31, p.m. A letter from Vosdan reveals that Aram has announced a general retreat and that the people of Shadakh should move to Tagh and then continue to Van. It feels as if we have been hit by lightning. Our hair stands on end. We were confused for a while. What should we do? Leave? Where to? Why? We remained in the dark. We wrote down the announcement on news sheets as instructed and within an hour the news was spread throughout the region.

> At 4 p.m. the announcement was plastered to walls and people started to leave. As it got darker, Tagh became deserted. One no longer heard the noise of youngsters, the sweet conversations of women gathered on roof-tops, or the song Kach Zinvor [Brave Soldier]. Only the whistles of the guards could sometimes be heard in the silence. I wander about like a madman and enter the Government House, then the barracks, and talk to some policemen. I go to a room full of

friends and they are all sad and dejected. We try to talk, make sense of the retreat but can not do so.

August 1 was such a long night. As dawn arrived, the sun's rays fell on our positions and then flooded the whole abandoned valley. How awful this valley will be after we leave. At midday, before leaving, we once more ordered a check of the streets and homes in case there were people left behind. We heard that there was a blind person, a sick woman and a sick Assyrian, and we ordered them to be shot immediately. These were the last three shots heard in that historic and deserted valley of Shadakh. The mountain and valley echoed those three shots as our group left. Goodbye mountains, valley and dale. Be well sweet Shadakh. Goodbye martyred friends. You are fortunate not to see this day.

We continued on our way, shooting the elderly, sick and others on the way. Our men shot dead their own people, as they did the enemy two months earlier.

This was the reality of the exodus, as people set off, soon to experience the suffering that awaited them on the road and foreign lands, before seeing worse suffering thereafter.

What was it like on that long road from Van to the Russian border, all the way to Igdir, Echmiadzin and Yerevan?

Van - Avants - Sev Ked - Geolou - Janig - Panz - Pergri - Bayazid Agha - Soough Sou - Gyavreshame Tapariz mountains Karakend Kizildize Karaboulakh Changel Mountains - Orgov and then Igdir. This was the long and arduous, deserted route of over 200 versts [appx. 130 miles], with abandoned villages and barren landscape the poor Armenian refugees had to traverse, hungry and thirsty, in the heat and cold.

There was a flood of people who came in droves over that broad route. It flowed slowly, even in heavy steps, but it moved constantly without rest. It moved like a solid chain through fields and foothills, appearing and disappearing over heights, meandering around mountains and continuing onwards. Some people moved alongside each other, others in line, the rich and the poor, old and young, men and women, boys and girls. Some exhausted, others carrying their children. There were officials, teachers, merchants and craftsmen wearing the same clothes, the same uniform, like ordinary times. They moved slowly and with heavy steps, carrying goods, worrying about the children, all dusty and lost in their own sweat, moving in that heat and under all of that weight. These were the city folk, who did not have carts and animals. The colourful chain moved on, as if it was going on a pilgrimage. That human torrent was going to the Olympic games, perhaps? It was quiet, pensive and worried – and very tired – stopping for a moment here and there, perhaps on a grassy hillside where there was a small fountain. But then, after an hour, the fountain itself got thirsty and dried up.

And now came Sev Ked, broad and full of water, surrounded by grass on both banks, where the human torrent rested side by side, unable to move further. They were in the many thousands. You might have thought the Olympic games would take place here. The tired multitude, men and women, old and young knelt by the river and some got into the water to quench their thirst. It does not matter that the water in July was warm, or that there was a dead dog decomposing and contaminating the water. They continued drinking to quench their thirst.

Next we came to Geolou, the mixed Turkish village in Timar, half of it in ruins. The night had already fallen on the village, its ruined houses and streets coming to life with people everywhere, its ample water spring besieged by women and girls pushing each other. The road was clogged with carts and there was no room to pass. There was nowhere to stop and rest. Only confusion and noise. It soon got dark and one could see the flames of small fires belonging to the lucky ones with carts. Most people were lying on the ground. The commotion and noise did not stop, and in this din one could not miss hearing some unusual calls. Someone had lost their four year old son, someone else had lost their three year old daughter. They shouted names and repeated their calls until midnight, when the noise calmed down a little, though that did not last long, perhaps an hour or so, and then the noise started again, as the flood began to move once more.

The road was congested and there were masses of people on both sides. Many had collapsed under the weight of their loads. They were sleeping and resting longer, while those who were standing were plodding along, surrounded by exhausted, screaming children. It felt as if the road was itself screaming from the pain, as were the mountains and valleys, the whole landscape.

Then there was Pergri with its houses and little market. It was mostly destroyed and surrounded by an army camp, including Antranig and Dro with their volunteers. One could see sick and tired human forms on the streets and the doorless passageways. These people were the remnants of the refugees from Alchavaz and Arjesh in their ragged and torn clothes. That human flood from those two areas had passed this point three days earlier, leaving behind a chain of exhausted and sick people, unable to move. Now, there was a greater flood coming from Van to add to the misery and leave behind its own remnants.

Soon we were in the valley of Pergri, where the bloody Bande Mahou flowed. The same Bande Mahou that saw incredible bloodshed in April and remained silent. In places the rocky and barren road extended to the right edge of the river. Just then the sun was rising, but it was covered by dust clouds, as the wind brought with it dust and sand. The flood was on the road composed of carts, donkeys and a multitude carrying loads. The huge lines of people were tired and moving slowly. Suddenly a noise arose at the rear and the flood gave way to the army rushing by, first the cavalry, then an artillery unit, then a convoy of carts, and then a caravan of camels with supplies.

They all heard the commander shouting "Way!" Way!", as the tortured people with their loads barely managed to pull to the side. Loaded oxen and cows managed to create a small opening, and the heavy carts leaned away and stopped to give way. The noisy heavy and light artillery and carts continued, knocking against other carts. The knocks were significant and the offending drivers tried to move more carefully but it was impossible. The iron-clad cartwheels often smashed whatever was in their way. Some people had to jump out of the way, the loaded oxen and cows veering to the sides, all resulting in a cacophony of incredible noise, cries, confusion and chaos.

And then Davtrish, the Abagha plain, Soough Sou, the ascent and descent of Tapariz, Kizildize and lastly the Changel heights. The same terrible scene could be seen everywhere and it was all heart rending. The usual journey of four or five days took the wearisome flood of people ten days. This flow did not roar but twisted and turned dimly. It was exhausted and worn out. The journey had taken longer than expected, supplies had run out, the hunger was acute and people moved with stomach pains. There was no more strength left, all were emaciated, enfeebled and deformed. The weak had fallen by the roadside, some children left behind, and the orphans, ill and disabled collected at stations. A piece of bread or some water could have saved lives, but both were in short supply. The terrible sight of parched and exhausted people started with the ascent at Changel, where the sun's burning rays were merciless and the road became tortuous. At the crest of that ascent was a former custom's house with a water-spring, but the army controlled it and did not allow the refugees to use it. People passed and fainted on those burning heights.

It is impossible to describe everything that took place on that route taken by refugees. It is beyond the power of the pen to relate everything in its true colours.

The refugees who somehow managed to cross the Pergri valley, Abagha, Tapariz and approached the Russian frontier, for all the difficulties, considered themselves lucky because there were still more refugees in Van who were to reach the Pergri in two or three days, after coming under Kurdish attacks and facing barbarities. These were the refugees from Gevash, Mogs and Shadakh.

On August 6, the Turkish forces moved from Arjesh to Pergri. Although the Russian army was retreating, they did so resisting the enemy onslaught. The refugees who were moving along the coastline of Lake Van were marching towards the sounds of deafening bombardment from Pergri. The surrounding Kurdish tribes took courage from the advance of Turkish forces and occupied the commanding heights of Pergri valley and attacked the refugees a few times.

One of these attacks took place mid-way along the valley on August 6. The Kurdish forces were not many, but even small-scale attacks created disorder and confusion. The refugees fled back to the town of Pergri, leaving behind their carts, belongings and even some children. A few terrified women and children threw themselves into the river out of fear, but a few armed Armenians and volunteers came to their rescue and dispersed the Kurds.

But the main attack on Pergri took place on August 7, when the Russian army and volunteer groups retreated to Abagha while the refugees were still on their way there. A large number of refugees came under fire, when the Kurds took control of the stone bridge on the Bande Mahou river above Pergri and started committing atrocities. According to eye-witnesses, terrible killings took place there, many women and girls were raped and abducted, and those who were able fled back to Pergri in terror. Several women threw themselves into the river on the plain near Bsdig Kiugh, and their example to avoid falling into the hands of wild Kurds proved to be catching. The refugees near Van escaped to Janig, leaving behind their dead to the relentless Kurds pursuing them. The massacre stopped at Janig. The dead were strewn between Pergri and Janig, some falling into the waves of the river, around 1,000 victims according to some.

The Pergri route was closed, and some of the refugees had to be diverted towards Persia and embarked on a new martyrdom. The Kurds were waiting everywhere, even those who had shown submission to the Russians. The Russian retreat led to great excitement among the Kurds and similar attacks took place near Saray. There were more refugees shot or put to the sword, young women and girls abducted, around 600 victims who fell or disappeared.

The Russian army left Van on August 10 and they were away for three or four days. During that period, the great murderer Jevdet entered Van with 400–500 chetes. They committed new atrocities against hundreds of people, including the infirm, who had remained behind in the city and Avants. However, the Turks suffered new defeats at Olti, Sarikamish and Alashgerd so that the Russian army returned to Van. The thunder of Russian arms roared once more under the walls of Van, and Jevdet, the coward that he was, retreated without resistance. The Russians occupied Van, but this time without Armenian help.

Most of Vasbouragan passed into Russian hands once more, but the Armenian people were cast to the wind. Soon the suffering of the refugees in the Ararat Plain, added to the losses suffered earlier in their homeland in the course of a year. And hellish designs took a further toll.

The refugees first concentrated on the Sourmalou flatlands, which was devoid of clean water and air. They then concentrated in a forest near Echmiadzin, as well as the sun-baked squares of the monastery. Then the refugees overran the squares, churchyards and pavements of Yerevan, all burning hot. Over 150,000 refugees came from Khnous, Boulanik, Manazgerd, the Moush plain, Akhlat, Alchavaz, Arjesh and other districts of Vasbouragan, including Mogs and Shadakh. They were exhausted, worn out, sick and helpless, like phantoms. They were like a mass of skeletons, in such need, that all of the associations set up to help them could not provide enough bread. Soon starvation set in, and then infectious diseases and deaths in the public squares and alleys of Echmiadzin, Igdir, and Yerevan. A new terrible catastrophe started, especially in Echmiadzin.

In order to form an opinion about that calamity, we present two descriptions taken from the many reports of newspapers in those days. Here are the two descriptions from *Horizon*.

1. Igdir

Like the dead birds we collect on roads, killed by the cold and freezing wind in Autumn, they are naked and starving, practically dead skeletons.

Look at their faces, there is nothing childlike about them. Their eyes are sad, their foreheads tense. They are thin and pale.

There are thousands of them, young children, the youngest ones only a month old.

2. Igdir

Many have diarrhoea and are lying under the trees, exhausted, in filthy and fetid rags. The merciless summer sun burns them through the leaves. They look at us with their feverish, lifeless eyes and move their skeletal hands.

A middle aged woman makes superhuman efforts to pull her little suckling child towards her and makes a pleading gesture that we should look after her child. We lift the child and take it to the orphanage, which is close to the hospital, again, under some trees. The poor woman falls over on her face. She knows she will not see that child again.

A young girl lies on some rags, practically naked. How rich is her matted hair, how sweet is her face even in such suffering. She has fallen on her own, alone, without anyone. Does she have anyone? Is there nobody to comfort her? Has she ever seen the joy of life? Where are her relatives? She is dying.

Four children are weeping around their mother's motionless corpse. We try to convince them that their mother is sleeping and they should not be crying, but they know what is going on. We carry them to the orphanage but they do not stop crying. And here, in the orphanage, there are so many lost and orphaned children. There are no smiles on their faces. The misery and terror have left their stamp on their sensitive souls.

3. Echmiadzin, August 10

The suffering in Echmiadzin and its surrounding is beyond human imagination. There is nowhere without suffering people.

Many thousands occupy the grounds of the Seminary, the courtyard of the monastery, all sides of Ghazarabad, the lake, even the market and streets. They all cry for bread, but there is no bread. The sick and dying are many. "My child died begging for bread," say weeping and mourning mothers. The need is endless.

4. Echmiadzin, September 10

A Stroll Through "Dante's Inferno."

There are a few women and children at the entrance to the Seminary. They are in the throes of death. Over them are two children, a little boy and a girl, who are weeping with deafening cries.

They enter the Seminary courtyard, which is beyond description, and there are relatives of the children among the dead lying there. I count six corpses of different ages between the entrance and the Seminary building.

I cross the monastery courtyard, and straight in front of the entrance two women are weeping on a corpse and sewing bandages. In front of the printing house and the rooms of the seminarians are old people, women and children in the throes of death, and there are many bodies along the road until the electricity station.

The Nercessian lake has become a source of infectious diseases. On its right bank, groups of human-like creatures are on the damp soil settling their accounts with life, while the entire length of the left bank is covered by corpses of different sizes, some covered and some not.

I go to the forest, and after a few steps, to my left, I see the corpse of an honourable woman who has fallen into a hole full of human waste. She was now lost among the flies and maggots, and it seems she fought with death for a long time.

And here is a heartbreaking sight, a woman who has fallen to the ground with three small children. One of the children has just died, and she, the mother, hearing the cries of her infant, in all of her own agony, is trying to find a way to get the attention of her elder dying child to cover the younger sibling with a piece of cloth. However, her efforts are fruitless.

There are many corpses piled up in front of St. Gayane church and they are piled onto carts which take them onto the forest road. I follow one of them.

On the way through the forest people run from left and right and stop the cart, begging, "Please, brother. I also have a corpse with me, let me bring my child's body... please pick up by husband's body..." and so by the end of the forest road there are 19 corpses on the cart, which the horse pulling the cart can barely move.

At the edge of the forest is a hellish scene. Around 50 peasants are digging graves, and a huge area is already covered by six or seven hundred unburied corpses, all deformed and bloated to such an extent, that the covering of some of them has ripped open. Many are rotting away, lost among the maggots, with their stench spreading everywhere. It is enough to mention that over 100 of these corpses have remained unburied for five days under the hot Echmiadzin sun.

One has to have a strong constitution to watch this terrifying scene, especially to breathe that fetid air, and I rush to leave that shocking death scene as quickly as possible.

Thus death reaps its victims among the poor refugees, left and right, without regard to gender or age.

The Echmiadzin correspondent writes again in *Horizon* two days later, and having no more words to describe what he sees, reverts to plain and simple statistics to state the obvious.

Sept 3	131 dead
Sept 4	168 dead
Sept 5	204 dead
Sept 6	234 dead
Sept 7	280 dead
Sept 8	268 dead
Sept 9	347 dead
Sept 10	357 dead
Sept 11	300 dead
Sept 12	314 dead

The refugees at Echmiadzin have thus lost 2,613 dead over 10 days. This was only in Echmiadzin, as for Igdir, Yerevan and many villages, who knows.

Yes, death took its countless toll among the refugees from Vasbouragan and other districts.

Armenians were shocked and froze, and hopelessness reigned for a while, even in songs of lamentation. Here is an Armenian melody of grief, as sung by Varsenig Aghasian.

Wave after wave they come,
Hunchbacked and trembling,
There is no laughter,
Nor bright smiles.

Young and old, all are tormented,
They cry silently,
Their lips only talk of pain,
To the world passing by.

A bride looks for her lost love,
The mother for her sweet child,
The suns set quietly,
They are unable to let go.

Worn hearts, tortured souls,
The blood stained road of exile,
I no longer know,
Neither song of love, nor yearning.

EPILOGUE

As we end our present work, three years have passed since the start of the European, and now, World War, and it has been two years since the great exodus of Vasbouragan. The Armenian provinces of Turkish Armenia remain mostly empty, desolate and ruined, while more than 200,000 refugees are in exile in the Caucasus, pining after their native land.

The current extraordinary war is coming to its end. It is ending all of its horrors with some consolation: the fall of autocracies, the liberation of the working classes, and granting oppressed people the right to self-determination.

It seems that Armenian exiles will soon be able to return to their ruined homeland and cultivate a new and independent life, allowing a much tortured people a peaceful and civilised existence.

With this hope, we publish this book of horrors as well as acts of heroism, a book that presents a new page in Armenian history, and hopefully the last page of its suffering.

Our work is now being printed in the wake of the Great Russian Revolution [February, 1917], during a time of full press freedoms. However, it was written and submitted for publication a year ago, before the Great Russian Revolution.

Consequently, much of what we had to say had to be masked because of the pressures of the autocracy at that time.

The World War and its consequences also impacted on our work.

Despite the great importance of this publication, we could not secure the superior paper nor the print quality we desired.

Glossary

Administrative divisions and officials in the late Ottoman Empire

Ottoman Turkish	English Equivalent	Armenian Equivalent
Vilayet-Vali	Province-Governor	Nahank-Nahankabed
Sanjak-Mutasarrif	County-Mutasarrif	
Kaza-Kaimakam	District-Kaimakam	Kavar-Kavarabed
Nahiye-Mudur	Sub-district-Miudir	Kavarag-Miudir
Kariye-Mukhtar	Village-Headman	Kiugh-Kiughabed
Mahalle	City quarter	Tagh
Kasaba	Town	Avan
Shehir	City	Kaghak

Distances and Weights

Verst (R) = Distance, 0.663 mile or 1.067 kilometre

Pood (R) = Weight, 36 pounds or 16.3 kilograms

Kile (Ottoman) = A measure of volume that could vary regionally. In Constantinople it was approximately 37 litres of volume. A kile of wheat was around 56lbs or 25 kgs.

Terms

Agha (OT) = Landlord

Amalia (OT) = Worker

Amele Tabouri (OT) = Workers' battalion

ARF = Armenian Revolutionary Federation or Hay Heghapokhagan Tashnagtsoutiun, also simply called Tashnagtsoutiun. Members of the organisation are also known as Tashnags.

Bey (OT) = Mister

Capitulations = A series of concessions by treaty granting special rights to groups of foreigners in the Ottoman Empire

Chete (OT) = An irregular soldier, bandit

CUP or Committee of Union and Progress (Ittihad ve Terakki Jemiyeti). Its members were often called Ittihadists or Unionists.

Chavoush (OT) = Sergeant

Gavur (OT) = Disparaging, offensive and derogatory term to describe non-Muslims in the Ottoman Empire.

Hamidiye = Special Ottoman cavalry force made up of selected Kurdish tribes. Also an individual member of such a forces.

Hunchag *See* SDHP

Irade = Imperial decree of the Sultan

Ittihadist (OT) = Member of the Committee of Union and Progress (CUP) or Ittihad ve Terakki Jemiyeti

Kankan = Underground, sewer workers

Keoshk (OT) = Mansion

Komitaji (OT) = Member of political committee

Khmpabed (A) = Group leader, captain

Kshla (OT) = Military barracks

Mal Mudur (OT) = Head of provincial financial department

Millet (OT) = The Ottoman term for officially recognised religious communities. The Armenian millet was the Armenian Apostolic church community. Armenian Catholics were recognised as a separate, Armenian Catholic millet. Armenian Protestants were part of the Protestant millet.

Milli or Milis Forces = Local paramilitary armed forces

Miudir (OT) = Public official

Pasha (OT) = High ranking military officer

Poghots (A) = Street

Reaya (OT) = Literally flock, used to describe the tax-paying subjects of the Ottoman Empire.

Reis (OT) = Community or village leader,

Salavat (OT) = Muslim prayers, often cited before an attack

SDHP = Social Democratic Hnchakian Party. Membmers of the organisation are also known as Hunchags.

Softa (OT) = Muslim theological student

Sourp (A) = Saint or Holy, as in Sourp Kevork (St. George)

Vank (A) = Monastery

Vartabed = Archimandrite, monk

INDEX

Selective proper nouns of individuals and places

CPSIA information can be obtained
at www.ICGtesting.com
Printed in the USA
FFOW01n2118211017
41405FF